The Perception of Poetry

THE
PERCEPTION
OF
POETRY

Eugene R. Kintgen

INDIANA UNIVERSITY PRESS
Bloomington

Manufactured in the United States of America

Library of Congress Cataloging in Publication Data

Kintgen, Eugene R.
The perception of poetry.

1. Poetry.   2. Reading.   I. Title.
PN1031.K49   1983   801'.3   82-48387
1 2 3 4 5 87 86 85 84 83

ISBN 0-253-34345-3

pd
12-17-83

TO
My Father
AND THE MEMORY OF
My Mother

Contents

Preface

This is a book about what people do when they read poetry, a subject so extensive and various that the boundaries of this treatment of it must be specified a little more precisely at the outset. The most important limitation, and a necessary one, is to a particular variety of reading: what Ingarden calls preaesthetic reading, the kind academics undertake to discover information about a poem in preparation for presenting their knowledge to other academics. It hardly needs remarking that this kind of reading is statistically abnormal and highly specialized, the province of relatively few who have been specifically trained in it, and engaged in even by them only infrequently. It is not the way one reads a newspaper or a periodical or a textbook, and it is not the way most readers read literary works most of the time.

The second important limitation concerns the number and training of my readers. To study their activities in detail it was necessary to limit their number to six, and given the desire to study preaesthetic reading, those six had to be trained in specific ways. There is thus little justification for generalizing conclusions based on these six readers to all readers, or even to all academic readers, though in the last chapter I do speculate on what all readers have in common.

Related to this is a limitation in my research method: in a more important sense than usual, my inquiry created its object, since without my intervention the readers would not have produced tape recordings of their thoughts while reading three poems. For reasons discussed in the sixth chapter, however, it seems clear to me that my readers all had well developed methods of confronting poetry before I enlisted them for this particular study, so while I am responsible for the records of the readings presented here, I am not the cause in any sense of either my readers' general ability to perform such activities or the numerous examples of similar activities they have produced in the past.

The final limitation concerns the mode of analysis of the readings. There are quite obviously many different ways of studying the activities readers perform in their reading, and by focussing on several approaches similar to my own in the first chapter I have tried to explain what I find unsatisfying about them. This is easily summarized: they tend not to deal with the process of reading, preferring instead to treat the complex ways in which knowledge resulting from that process is made public. This is due, I think, not to any particular intellectual intrasigence, but to a basic lack of information: there simply are not many examples of readers reading, and those that are available tend to be anecdotal rather than complete. The protocols provided in the third chapter and in the Appendix, eight in all, should go some small way to supplying this want, and whatever use I make of them, should allow others some modest empirical basis for their own speculations.

The use I have made of them is explained in the second chapter. Building on insights from Artificial Intelligence, I analyzed the processes of the readers into a relatively small group — about two dozen — of elementary operations. There is an obvious danger of circularity here, since one tends to find what he expects to find. But it is not, I hope, a vicious circularity: what is important is that the operations proposed actually describe the activities of readers, not whether there are twenty four or twenty five. Again, since the protocols are included in the Appendix, the reader can test his own favorite schema on them.

Unfortunately, the kind of close analysis required by an information processing account of a reader's activities produces rather tedious reading. In the third chapter, therefore, I begin by exemplifying the elementary operations from one reader's protocol, but then move into a more general discussion of her activities. And in the fourth and fifth chapters I have moved back even further to characterize the idiosyncratic aspects of the other readers' approaches to the poems. These are easier to read because they describe actions at the level we are more accustomed to. But it must be emphasized that such general descriptions are validated only by the closer analysis that lies behind them: as I argue in the last chapter, general discussions of goals must be complemented by precise descriptions of the actions by which one attempts to achieve those goals.

In addition to those from whose scholarship I have profited — the reader may judge from the discussions in the first and last chapters which influences have caused me the greatest anxiety — I owe a special debt of gratitude to David Bleich, whose patient conversations over a decade convinced me that one had to look at readers as well as texts. For the same period of time, Don Gray has provided encouragement and advice. Norman Holland has helped me in many ways, not least by offering insightful suggestions for this book. Bruce Smith was my research assistant for both this book and the research leading to it; his insight and wit made the hours we spent together analyzing the protocols and discussing the method involved if not precisely fun, at least tolerably enjoyable, and his editorial expertise (together with Don Gray's) improved this book. The study would have been impossible without the assistance of the six readers whose names, but not readings, have been altered, and without the help of other colleagues who have over the years provided me with information about their own reading processes. Indiana University and the ACLS generously provided me with Grants-in-Aid of Research to conduct the research for this study, and Patricia O'Callaghan provided the painstaking transcriptions of the protocols.

Nothing I say can acknowledge the support and comfort I derived from my wife and son while working on this book; the time I spent with them was — precisely — fun.

The Perception of Poetry

1 Reader Response and Literary Perception

"Some revolutions occur quietly," the editor of a recent collection of essays on the reader assures us, and goes on to present her view — clearly corroborated by the publication within the past year of two collections of reader-response criticism, each with its own annotated bibliography — that "the words *reader* and *audience* . . . have acceded to a starring role."[1] As so often seems to happen with revolutions, though, issues properly central become obscured in the general hubbub, replaced by those that are easier to grasp. In the reader-response revolution, the feature that defines readers — the act of reading they perform — has become secondary. Without this act, there would be no readers (and no literary work, and no audience, for that matter), and yet those interested in literary response have, for the most part, deflected attention from the act itself to other things associated with it. In so doing, three of the four current approaches to response parallel in a curious way the progress of the major American schools of linguistics and psycholinguistics of the past half century from exclusive attention to the linguistic product to the study of the actual psychological processes involved in language perception and production. My own prejudice is clearly apparent in the choice of *progress* in the previous sentence, and after a brief survey of these four approaches to response I will turn to what they in various ways neglect — the process of perceiving literature.

The earliest tradition, stemming in large part from I. A. Richards's *Practical Criticism*, is strikingly similar to American structuralist descriptions of language based on the seminal work of Leonard Bloomfield. The origin of the modern version of this approach, as Alan C. Purves explains in *Elements of Writing about a Literary Work*, was the desire to analyze and describe the constituents of writing about literature: "We needed some means of describing the process or the constituents of writing about literature, whether that writing be critical or subcritical."[2] Just as the structuralist first segmented a corpus of language and then assigned the segments to a relatively small number of mutually exclusive categories (phonemes, morphemes, etc.), the analyst in Purves's scheme divides the written response into statements, which are the units of analysis, and then assigns each statement to a particular element. The original elements, numbering well over a hundred, were organized into four major categories: *engagement-involvement*, which dealt with the reader's personal relation to the work; *perception*, dealing with the work as an artifact; *interpretation*, in which the work was related to the world the reader knew; and *evaluation*, which is self-explanatory. There were also some half dozen "Miscellaneous Statements."[3] Thus analyzed, the written response could be characterized in terms of its use of the elements or compared to other responses.

Lee Odell and Charles Cooper proposed an extension of this procedure to allow description not only of the statements readers make about literature but also of the intellectual processes that produce these statements. In addition to classifying the units of the written response according to the Purves scheme (as modified by Purves and Beach in *Literature and the Reader*), they suggest an analysis according to the following "intellectual strategies": *focus*, defined operationally as the grammatical subject of the clause; *contrast*, which distinguishes the focussed element from the rest of the universe; *classification*, which suggests the ways in which the focussed item is similar to others; *change*, which describes how the focussed item changes; and *reference to time sequence, logical sequence*, and *physical context*, which all locate the focussed element in some kind of context.[4] Each clause of a written response reflects one Purves element but at least two intellectual strategies, since the grammatical subject defines the focus and the predicate expresses at least one of the other strategies. This enrichment of the Purves scheme allows Odell and Cooper to "identify not only the kinds of responses [the reader] characteristically makes but also some of the processes he habitually uses in formulating these responses,"[5] and thus to extend the kind of research originating with Richards that "has sought to find precise, reliable, and comprehensive ways to describe the expressed responses of readers of fiction."[6]

The parallel between these procedures and those of the American Structuralists, especially the insistence on the segmentation of behavior and the assignment of the segments to a taxonomy of elements, is unmistakable, even if Purves modestly denied that his elements were either exhaustive or taxonomic.[7] Also typical of the structuralist enterprise are the claim that "the elements *describe* subject matter more than they assert"[8] — the orientation is descriptive, not prescriptive — and the reliance on a corpus to analyze. But this last characteristic also distinguishes them, for linguists from Bloomfield on emphasized the priority of speech over written language, and the most elaborate and successful methods of linguistic description were designed to analyze phonology.

By relying on essays written about literature, Purves, Odell, and Cooper necessarily alienate themselves from what Purves in another context claimed was of primary interest: "At the center of the curriculum are *not* works of literature. . . . but rather the mind as it meets the book. The response."[9] An interesting reflection of the equivocation in the term *response* — the mind meeting the book, or the written reaction to that meeting prepared for submission to a teacher or some other audience — occurs at the beginning of Odell and Cooper's article. Not far above the quotation from Purves (which is their epigraph), a reviewer for the journal characterizes their article as "set[ting] forth a technique for analyzing the processes by which a written response is formulated and seek[ing] to combine rhetorical analysis with content analysis."[10] "Rhetorical analysis" — whether or not this is an accurate assessment of what they had proposed — pinpoints the problem: in using written essays as their corpus, these researchers have confounded the elements of response with the elements of rhetoric. The reader's conception of how his knowledge should be presented, however rudimentary it might be, is indistinguishable in the analysis from his knowledge. So when Odell and Cooper claim, for example, that their reader's "descriptive statements . . . almost never focus on *I* and his interpretive statements . . . focus on some aspect of the text twice as often as they focus on *I*,"[11] it is not at all clear whether this reflects the way his mind meets the book or the way his pen meets the paper. The problem of rhetorical interference may not be especially troublesome with secondary school students, but as readers become more sophisticated in both their reading and their expression, it will increasingly compromise the analysis.

Even if there were no rhetorical elaboration, analysis of written responses is unlikely to reveal much about the meeting between mind and book for two reasons. First, since the written response is removed in time from the process of reading, what is produced will be a memorial reconstruction of what occurred, with all the blurring and loss of detail that entails. Second, a five-hundred-word essay about a novel (Odell and Cooper's example is *Of Mice and Men*) is hardly designed to encourage a great deal of specificity about the reading process. The whole task invites (at best) summary re-creations of what happened during the reading, or — worse yet for those interested in the meeting of the mind and the book — later responses to some summary of that act. The result is that instead of abandoning the conception of the literary work as an artifact, those interested in the activity of readers have substituted another, and generally less interesting, artifact as the object of study.

The second tradition, much more recent, avoids these problems by emphasizing competence, the mental ability that underlies and enables the overt behavior — performance — of writing responses. Jonathan Culler has put this view, obviously derived from the linguistic writing of Noam Chomsky, most clearly: "The question is not what actual readers happen to do but what an ideal reader must know implicitly in order to read and interpret works in ways which we consider acceptable, in accordance with the institution of literature."[12] More recently, Culler has rephrased the question slightly, according primacy to the form and meaning of the works themselves, without, however, losing sight of the reader:

> What requires explanation is, above all, facts about form and meaning. . . . To account for the form and meaning of literary works is to make explicit the special conventions and procedures of interpretation that enable readers to move from the linguistic meaning of sentences to the literary meaning of the works. To explain facts about the form and meaning works have for readers is to construct hypotheses about the conditions of meaning, and hypotheses about the conditions of meaning are claims about the conventions and interpretive operations applied in reading.[13]

Since it is an inescapable feature of literary interpretation that readers differ not only in their assessments of works, but more basically, in their underlying understandings of them, these 'facts' do not presuppose any kind of agreement:

> The striking facts that do require explanation are how it is that a work can have a variety of meanings but not just any meaning whatever or how it is that some works give an impression of strangeness, incoherence, incomprehensibility. The model does not imply that there must be unanimity on any particular count. It suggests only that we must designate a set of facts, of whatever kind, which seem to require explanation and then try to construct a model of literary competence which would account for them.[14]

This remarkably latitudinarian approach remains a distinctive feature of Culler's project, for one of his latest formulations asserts that "There are facts aplenty to choose from; those who prize difference of interpretation can take the fact of disagreement about particular works as the fact to be explained."[15]

Though modelled on transformational approaches to the study of language — Culler lauds "the shift from corpus to competence" as providing "a goal and a principle of relevance, leading to new hypotheses and new modes of argument"[16] — these suggestions are curiously naïve in their adaptation of linguistic principles. Most obviously, no linguist would ever attempt to account for "facts, of whatever kind": whether

corpus or competence was to be analyzed, the linguists were quite sure
before they began the analysis what their subject was. And, as Chomsky
has explained, facts may exist outside a theory, but they become rele-
vant and interesting only when they are placed in some relation to a
theory.[17] Culler's facts are thus not "of whatever kind"; they are obser-
vations already related to an unexplicated theory, such as that "*King Lear*
is a tragedy, that Marvell's 'Horation Ode' can be read as praise or
blame, that *The Waste Land* can be unified by thematizing its formal dis-
continuities."[18] The underlying theory is clearly represented by the
words *tragedy, praise, blame, unified, thematizing,* and *formal discontinuities.*

The ability to use such terms meaningfully is the result of education,
and this emphasizes an especially sharp (and frequently discussed) dis-
tinction between linguistic competence and literary competence: every
normal speaker of a language exhibits a linguistic competence, while
literary competence, which is (as Culler admits) the product of educa-
tion, is the possession of only those who have been specifically in-
structed in it. Only a linguistic equivocation allows these two quite dif-
ferent kinds of ability to be equated, and, as Charles Fillmore has re-
cently reminded us, this equivocation is not always avoided even in the
linguistic literature. In the strict linguistic sense, *competence* refers to the
underlying universal human ability to learn a human language or to the
underlying knowledge of a language achieved; but in normal everyday
use it can be "the nominalization of the gradable property 'competent (at
such and such)'."[19] Culler uses the term in this second sense: we may
consider certain critics competent at interpretation (that is, they "read
and interpret works in ways which we consider acceptable, in accordance
with the institution of literature"), while others, we feel, are incompe-
tent, or perhaps less competent, a distinction Culler endorses when he
mentions grading students "on the competence of their reading and on
their progress in learning the art of reading."[20] But that is not a distinc-
tion that it is possible to draw when the term is used technically: there
are no incompetent speakers of a language (except those who are se-
verely brain-damaged). Competent interpreters are thus more like tennis
players or pianists or cooks or mechanics who excel at what they do than
they are like the overwhelming majority of the world's population. This
does not mean that one should not study the mental operations of good
critics, but it does suggest that linguistic methods designed to study and
account for a very different kind of universal ability are unlikely to be
particularly relevant to that enterprise.

This is not the loss it might appear, since early transformational no-
tions about the competence of the "ideal speaker-listener in a com-

pletely homogeneous speech-community"[21] were offered merely as a first approximation to a situation everybody knew to be much more complex, and during the past decade there has been more and more work suggesting how unrealistic (and stifling to linguistic theory) the conception of a monolithic competence shared by all speakers of a language really is.[22] This points up another problem with Culler's program. Both in *Structuralist Poetics* and in the more recent "Prologomena to a Theory of Reading" he allows, even welcomes, variety of interpretation: "a theory of reading is an attempt to come to terms with the single most salient and puzzling fact about literature: that a literary work can have a range of meanings but not just any meaning."[23] This range of meanings exhibited by the literary work corresponds most naturally to the range of pronunciation, vocabulary, and usage that linguistics has long considered the province of dialectology: just as different critics produce various readings of a text, speakers of different dialects disagree in their pronunciation of a given text, and, allowed the freedom to express the same idea, would also differ slightly in vocabulary, morphology, and syntax. This variety was never successfully integrated into the description of languages, and by relegating variation to an adjacent discipline, descriptive linguistics freed itself to concentrate on the analysis of corpus or competence. Transformational theory had a further (if usually implicit) justification for ignoring it: since the aim of linguistic theory was to explain the underlying human capacity for language (rather than the capacity to speak one or another dialect of English), any speaker's intuitions could provide relevant evidence, since any other speaker could have learned the same variety of language (given the proper circumstances) and so could have had the same intuitions. Thus while different intuitions might lead to slightly different analyses of certain (classes of) constructions, they illuminated the underlying language capacity equally. In practice, linguistic variety was present in the data of linguistic inquiry because each linguist presented his own corpus of grammatical, semigrammatical, and ungrammatical sentences as evidence of the intuitions he was trying to account for, but each linguist tried to analyze only his own dialect (or more precisely, idiolect). Only with the pioneering work of William Labov and his notion of the variable rule was there any serious attempt to incorporate linguistic variation into basic linguistic description.[24]

Again, the situation in literary studies is quite different. First, since there is little evidence that interpreters share a competence in the technical sense — and the influence of formal education positively argues against it — there is no reason to expect one theory to explain variation in reading: it may be that each reader requires a distinct theory. Second, even if we assume (somewhat counter to the evidence available) that different readings exhibit a single competence, it is unlikely that methods developed in linguistics specifically to exclude variety will be particularly efficacious in explaining variety in interpretation.

The one bit of evidence suggesting that readers do possess the same competence is "that one can after all often be brought to see the superiority of one interpretation to another. . . . it does happen that one is convinced by arguments, a process which testifies to the existence of a common ground: shared notions of how to read, of what sort of inferences are permitted, of what counts as evidence and what must be explicitly argued for."[25] This claim of mutual intelligibility is similar to the rough-and-ready test to distinguish between dialects and languages: if two linguistic systems are mutually intelligible, they are dialects of the same language. Again, the linguistic analogy suggests the equivocations in the literary formulation. First, there is a shift from seeing literary meaning as the product of literary competence to seeing it as the result of rhetorical efficacy. The whole notion of literary competence is based on justification: the meaning of a poem is not (or not only) what the reader immediately apprehends, or even realizes after much thought (that is, as a result of his literary intuitions), but "the meanings [readers] are willing to accept as plausible and justifiable when they are explained."[26] The "facts, of whatever kind" are no longer the reader's intuitions about literature, but rather his standards for plausibility in critical arguments. This, of course, is similar to transformationalist claims that "tacit knowledge may very well not be immediately available to the user of the language,"[27] and thus sometimes requires stimulation, especially in the cases of ambiguity, paraphrase, and constituent structure. And it is in fact true that speakers can be trained to recognize more ambiguity in everyday speech than they normally do, though this often has the unfortunate side effect of making them inveterate punsters. But it should be remembered that most transformational explanations were based on judgments of grammaticality, which cannot easily be justified or changed, rather than of ambiguity and paraphrase (which can be justified), and that it was the very unchangeability of these judgments about grammaticality that led to the distinction between grammatical and acceptable sentences: recalcitrant constructions that the grammar describes as grammatical but that native speakers reject are "unacceptable."[28] In relying on the kind of judgment that can be argued for, the parallel between literary and linguistic competence depends on the least important kind of evidence used in linguistic argumentation.

The second and more important problem with the notion of plausibility is that it is based on belief. It requires a much more dedicated pluralist than I to assert that he has never read an interpretation he finds implausible, and even judging one interpretation superior to another implies belief in the one over the other. (Consider the strangeness of "Interpretation A is superior to interpretation B, but I believe B.") Again, the difference from linguistics is substantial. Speakers may acknowledge forms from other dialects as valid without committing themselves to believing in or using those forms. Culler's discussion, on the other hand, would seem to limit "plausible" meanings primarily to those the reader would actually use or make his own: the critic "claims that his interpretation is related to the text in ways which he presumes readers will accept once these relations are pointed out: either they will accept his interpretation as an explicit version of what they intuitively felt or they will recognize from their own knowledge of literature the justice of the operations that lead the critic from text to interpretation."[29] But the variety of interpretations and meanings Culler proposes to account for demonstrates that many readers do not agree with the relations the critic discerns between the text and his interpretation, and recurrent arguments about the legitimacy of various approaches to literature indicate that there is no overwhelming agreement about the operations that mediate between text and interpretation either. Thus in linguistics, where all speakers are competent in the technical sense, plausibility does not require adaptation: I can accept a form without using it. But in interpretation, where competence is used in the evaluative sense, plausibility implies acceptance: "that's plausible, but I don't believe it" means that it is really implausible, evidence of incompetence.

In Culler's theory there seem to be two sources of information about literary competence. First, there are readers' "judgments about meaning, well-formedness, deviance, constituent structure, and ambiguity,"[30] complemented by individual introspection: "If one sets out to write an explicit account of one's own literary competence — to explain, step by step, what assumptions, conventions, and interpretive moves make possible one's perceptions and interpretations of various literary works — the act of writing this out, of communicating the grounds of interpretation, stresses everything that is public and explicable in the reading process."[31] This source of information is unmistakably related to the transformational reliance on the intuitions of the native speaker about grammaticality, ambiguity, paraphrase, constituent structure, and so forth. As such it is vulnerable to the same kinds of criticism that have been levelled against that enterprise, the most important being that without an explanation of the relation between the activity of having intuitions about language and other language activities, any theory based on intuitions will remain at most a theory of intuitions about language, not a theory of language.[32] Such a theory might have a certain utility — in linguistics, for example, it might explain what people consider to be the relations between sentences, and in literary theory it might suggest what readers consider some characteristics of well-formedness, deviance, constituent structure, and ambiguity of literary texts — but it will not account for how anybody comprehends a text, or recognizes those characteristics in it, or produces an interpretation from it.

The second source of information is the analysis of published interpretations to determine what plausible operations might lead from the text to the interpretation. Though this flirts with a return to the corpus and thus could possibly result in a taxonomy of characteristics of successful (that is, published) interpretations, Culler is careful to emphasize the mental operations that lead to the readings he discusses, and thus seems similar to the transformationalist citing grammatical sentences to illustrate that they can be produced by applying the rules he proposes. This may be illuminating, but it should not be forgotten that such an undertaking will, at best, produce a formalization of some relations between the text and various published interpretations of it without necessarily showing that any of the readers actually used any of the proposed mechanisms to arrive at his reading. The question here is of psychological reality, and just as psycholinguists have failed to uncover any convincing evidence that hearers use transformations to comprehend sentences,[33] those interested in literature may find that the various strategies and conventions Culler proposes as constituents of literary competence account for certain recurrent features of interpretations without explaining how a critic produces these characteristics. The conventions are thus one way of cataloguing what gets done; they do not necessarily explain the way anybody does it.

A final characteristic of Culler's approach deserves attention: what he claims to be a disinclination to study the behavior of readers. In *Structuralist Poetics* he provided a transformationalist justification for it: "To take surveys of the behaviour of readers would serve little purpose, since one is interested not in performance itself but in the tacit knowledge or competence which underlies it."[34] In "Prolegomena to a Theory of Reading" he urges us to focus on the act of reading rather than on readers, and after criticizing Norman Holland for his interest in the latter, he sets his priorities: "A first priority, then, if one is to study reading rather than readers, is to avoid experimental situations that seek free associations and focus rather on public interpretive processes."[35] This program, for all its appeal to methodological purity, merely disguises a number of troublesome facts. First, the apparent choice offered in the last quotation is *only* apparent, since there are in fact no "public interpretive processes" to study. At best we have inferences about them, and, as I have been trying to demonstrate, the parallels between this approach to literary competence and transformational grammar do not inspire much confidence that these inferences correspond to any real processes, public or private.

Second, "the behaviour of readers" is the only thing that one can study, and while one might prefer to concentrate on some kinds of behavior rather than on others — having intuitions about literature, or producing interpretations rather than free associating, for instance — and on some kinds of readers — one's colleagues, or the authors of published interpretations — it is a delusion to think that some kinds of behavior provide direct access to competence while others are hopelessly entangled in performance. All behavior is performance, and — again the equivocation — though some performances are more competent than others, and thus more apparently deserving of study, they are no less performances, and no less in need of a principled explanation of their relation to the underlying abilities they illustrate.

The analogy with linguistics upon which Culler (explicitly or implicitly) bases his project is thus incorrect in three senses. First, there is an equivocation in the basic terminology. *Competence* was an extremely powerful conception in linguistics in the sense that it enabled a great deal of interesting and revealing research, but it has suffered a semantic sea change in its translation to the field of literary studies that deprives it of much of its interest. Second, Culler's conception of the transformational enterprise seems to derive primarily from the "standard theory" current in 1964 and 1965 and is thus subject to the various criticisms of that formulation that have been made since then by linguists, psycholinguists, and sociolinguists. Third, in his most recent work, he has used a palpably wrong analogy: a linguistic theory designed specifically to account for the ideal speaker-listener in a completely homogeneous speech-community is hardly likely to be useful in explaining the variety of interpretation Culler finds "the single most salient and puzzling fact about literature."

It was probably inevitable that any attempt to explicate interpretation as a rule-governed activity should turn to the model of transformational grammar, since it provided specific and testable formulations, an ambitious program for future research, and philosophical and psychological justifications for its undertakings. But the history of transformational grammar and its associated disciplines during the past two decades is also available as a model, and as a warning against an unthinking adaptation of earlier (and now discarded) formulations. Culler has not, I think, taken Chomsky's warning seriously enough: "For those who wish to apply the achievements of one discipline to the problems of another, it is important to make very clear the exact nature not only of what has been achieved, but equally important, the limitations of what has been achieved."[36]

The third approach, exemplified in the work of Stanley E. Fish, George Dillon, and others who stress the temporal experience of reading, parallels the shift in psycholinguistics away from the formulations of transformational grammar during the past dozen years. Chomsky's *Syntactic Structures* was a boon not only to the linguists but to the psycholinguists as well, who suddenly had something substantive to study: they inquired whether the transformations introduced to account for the competence of the ideal speaker-hearer also governed the behavior of real speaker-hearers in their comprehension and production of language. Were transformations psychologically real? Early experiments suggested that they were, and multidimensional scaling of the "psychological distance" between construction types was even proposed as corroborative evidence for particular syntactic analyses. But negative results began to appear fairly quickly, and soon psycholinguists were introducing "perceptual strategies" by which hearers related what they heard to a psychologically real underlying structure.[37] One major difference between these strategies and transformations is that the strategies operate in real time, accounting for such facts as that at some point a hearer has heard only part of a sentence and yet can predict its possible outcomes, that the completed sentence is understood so soon after it is heard that analysis can hardly occur entirely after hearing, that some sentences which are transformationally more complex than others are perceptually simpler, and so forth. If the hearer used transformations to understand sentences, none of this would be possible, since to "undo" the transformations that had been used to produce the sentence he would have to hear all of it. Perceptual strategies have in turn influenced linguistic theory, and "realistic" grammars that reflect more directly the operations of speakers and hearers are now being proposed even within the traditional transformational camp.[38]

Within the area that he once christened "affective stylistics," Stanley E. Fish has treated strikingly similar topics. His earliest article emphasized reading as a process in real time:

> The concept is simply the rigorous and disinterested asking of the question, what does this word, phrase, sentence, paragraph, chapter, novel, play, poem, *do?* And the execution involves an analysis of the developing responses of the reader in relation to the words as they succeed one another in time. . . . the basis of the method is a consideration of the *temporal* flow of the reading experience, and it is assumed that the reader responds in terms of that flow and not to the whole utterance.[39]

Just as the hearer of an utterance makes certain predictions about possible conclusions after having heard only its beginning, so the reader makes predictions about the conclusions (and significance) of sentences, chapters, stanzas, narratives, and so forth before he has completed them. And just as the mechanisms by which these predictions are made are called perceptual strategies in psycholinguistics, they are called "interpretive strategies" in Fish: "In short, what is noticed is what has been *made* noticeable, not by a clear and undistorting glass, but by an interpretive strategy."[40] Those who share interpretive strategies constitute "interpretive communities,"[41] a notion that has largely displaced the earlier emphasis on the temporal experience of literature in Fish's work.[42]

Unfortunately for those interested in the temporal activities of readers, Fish has been increasingly preoccupied with justifying his position, and has thus all but abandoned, at least in print, his exploration of specific interpretive strategies. And even when he did provide reports of his reading activities, those reports suffered three defects: the activities were *only* his, they weren't only *his*, and they weren't only *reading*. One reader's report of what he thinks he has done, no matter how scrupulous, is always anecdotal, especially when the activities are recollected in tranquility rather than somehow recorded at the time of their occurrence. This is not a matter of willful or even conscious manipulation or falsification, but simply a consequence of our limited perception of our own mental activities and the unreliability of our memorial reconstructions of them. Fish's descriptions, then, are unlikely to be veridical accounts of what actually happened while he was reading the passages in question.

These difficulties are exacerbated in Fish's early examples by his attempt to approximate in his own reading the activities of an ideal, or informed, reader: "I can with some justification project my responses into those of 'the' reader because they have been modified by the constraints placed on me by the assumptions and operations of the method: (1) the conscious attempt to become the informed reader by making my mind the repository of the (potential) responses a given text might call out and (2) the attendant suppressing, in so far as that is possible, of what is personal and idiosyncratic and 1970ish in my response."[43] The difference between this informed reader and an actual one is the basis of Fish's teaching method, which by exposing students to a "series of graduated texts" and asking "what does that _____ do?" teaches them "to recognize and discount what is idiosyncratic in their own response."[44] That is, some kinds of temporal experience while reading are more valuable than others, and the aim of literary education is to encourage the one while discouraging the other. Although it is not clear what method has replaced this one in Fish's classroom, the theoretical distinction between the informed reader and other varieties has been abandoned in favor of interpretive communities. But it remains clear that the temporal experience of the text is always constrained and thus modified by the attempt not to be entirely personal.

And for good reason: Fish's readings are described to make particular points, not as randomly chosen examples of the reading process. There are two consequences of this. First, it is quite probable that Fish's initial temporal experience of a text is never reported. Some of his examples may be serendipitous — the story of Pat Kelly, for instance[45] — but it is unlikely that he had never read the Browne sentence analyzed at length in "Affective Stylistics" or the Milton sonnets in "Interpreting the *Variorum*" before he decided to use them as examples. This means that his reports of temporal experience — in particular his so often incorrect predictions about the final shape of constructions — are contaminated by his knowledge of how those constructions are completed. The reports are thus fictions, exemplary tales of what it might be like to read the sentences or poems from the beginning without knowing how they end. And as fictions, they shift the topic from what readers do to what readers *might* do.

This is directly related to the second consequence: as examples in polemical articles, the descriptions of the reading process are not entirely disinterested; they are presumably chosen as much for their utility in furthering the interpretive claims Fish makes as for their accuracy in reflecting what readers (might) do. So while Fish's descriptions seem plausible, without a great deal more information about how readers actually negotiate the temporal process of reading it is impossible to tell whether they are accurate or merely flattering fictions. And if they are accurate, there is the further question of how typical they are.

But even if Fish's reports of the reading process are not veridical, they may still illustrate without exhausting the typical processes of reading and thus provide evidence about the interpretive strategies or constitutive rules readers use. In Fish's examples, these interpretive strategies deal mainly with either the purely linguistic level or the level of significance (in Hirsch's terms).[46] Thus, in discussing Milton's twentieth sonnet, Fish focusses on the multiple meanings of *spare,* and the discussions of the sentence from Browne, "Avenge O Lord thy slaughtered Saints," "When I consider how my light is spent," and "Lycidas" all illustrate the effect of *closure* — the decision made by the reader that a syntactic unit has been completed.[47] These examples presumably depend on the reader's basic linguistic skills, since choosing the relevant signification of a word or deciding when a construction is complete is required in all linguistic comprehension. The strategies dealing with significance are different, however, in utilizing not linguistic ability but knowledge of the other fields, often but not exclusively literary, that grasping the significance of the text requires. Only somebody who knows who Bacchus is will expect a negative judgment on wine in "Comus" 46–47, and those ignorant of the history of speculation about Iago's evil nature will not feel the tension between the reader and narrator Fish finds at the beginning of *Play It As It Lays.*[48] More obviously, the decision to regard "Lycidas" as a pastoral elegy by Milton, or the Augustinian injunction to see everything in the Bible conducing to charity,[49] are strategies that arrive at "meaning-as-related-to-something-else."[50]

Unfortunately, Fish is more interested in providing examples of the effects of these interpretive strategies than in specifying what they are. This lacuna is partially filled by George L. Dillon in *Language Processing and the Reading of Literature,*[51] who, by considering examples of what is difficult to process, deduces what is easy to process and suggests some relatively precise rules for arriving at phrase or clause boundaries and assigning antecedents. Dillon distinguishes three levels of reading —*perception,* which deals with the propositional structure of individual clauses; *comprehension,* which synthesizes the material from separate clauses into a unified conception; and *interpretation,* which relates "the sense of what is going on to the author's constructive intention."[52] Although these levels interact — Dillon provides many examples of a reader's interpretation guiding either perception or comprehension — it is possible to tease them apart for analysis.

Translating Fish's "interpretive strategies" into Dillon's levels, then, we would expect at least five levels or types of interpretive strategy. The most basic, the strategies of perception, which aim at recovering the propositional structure of clauses, would deal with such matters as lexical meaning, lexical or constructional ambiguity, syntactic closure, and so forth. The next, the strategies of comprehension, would attempt to synthesize the material already perceived "into a world with actors, places, forces, and so on."[53] These two constitute what I have called the basic linguistic level. Strategies of interpretation guide the reader in recovering the author's intention — "why he is saying what he says, or what he is getting at in terms of themes and meaning of the work."[54] These three levels of strategy together constitute Hirsch's "meaning." Next come the strategies of significance, which relate what has been understood of the work to the outside world, to other literary works, the reader's life, etc. Finally, there must be one more level, a governor or control level to decide which strategies to use on particular occasions. Since there is a widespread assumption in recent criticism that *meta* things are better things, I will call these metastrategies, or strategies for using other strategies, corresponding to what Fish calls "interpretive decisions."[55]

The utility of distinguishing these types of strategies is that it allows more specific inquiry into how interpretive communities are actually constituted. Fish's early claim (later abandoned) that "what happens to one informed reader of a work will happen, within a range of nonessential variation, to another"[56] deals primarily with the first three levels, while his reference to Augustinianism relates to the fourth level, and his boast that "in fact" he does not "read *Lycidas* and *The Waste Land* differently,"[57] clearly nonsense on the first three levels, makes sense as a comment about his metastrategies, about how he chooses the interpretive strategies he uses. The burden of Fish's recent work is that metastrategies are dictated by the situation one is in: by force of will, one can choose to apply different strategies at the lower levels and thus perceive, or comprehend, or interpret something differently, but there will always seem to be a normal metastrategy required by the situation. Thus while the metastrategies are referred to as interpretive *decisions* in "Interpreting the *Variorum*," with all the choice *decision* implies — had he not made the decisions about "Lycidas" that he did, he "would have made others"[58] — in a more recent essay these decisions are dictated by the situation: "in any situation there are always assumptions so deeply held that the entities they make available are perceived as part of the world and not as the products of assumptions at all."[59]

I agree fully with this point of view, but for those interested in the process of reading, it has two unfortunate (but not unavoidable) consequences. First, it tends to focus attention on the situation or context itself rather than on the various interpretive strategies the situation requires, and this deemphasizes the real and interesting question of how interpretive communities are constituted. Second, the process of reading has been neglected altogether. Instead of providing examples of the reading process (as he did in his earlier essays), Fish now illustrates that "interpretation is the only game in town"[60] and asks "What Makes an Interpretation Acceptable?" (the title of the second John Crowe Ransom Memorial Lecture at Kenyon College).[61] It seems to me that the earlier questions about the reading process, the use of various interpretive strategies, and the constitution of interpretive communities were abandoned before they were answered, and, as my criticisms of Fish's attempts to answer them suggest, I think that only analysis of what real readers do with texts they are unfamiliar with while they are reading them will provide those answers. At the very least, it will enable us to see whether readers actually do share interpretive strategies at any level, how much variation there is on the various levels, and how much effect the context — reading a particular work in a particular setting — has on the metastrategies used.

A start in this direction has been made, in different ways, by Norman N. Holland and David Bleich. In *5 Readers Reading,* Holland recounts how he chose a group of college English majors to read ten short stories and then discuss each in one-hour recorded interviews. His aim in these interviews was to "get out the free associations to the stories," and to facilitate this he asked questions formulated in advance about each story, questions about how the readers "felt about" the characters or events or situations in the stories, and "impromptu questions to draw out more material on a given point."[62] The readers were also given TAT and Rorschach tests and the COPE questionnaire, but the results of these tests were used only as a check on the analysis of their responses in the interviews.

All of this material was interpreted in two ways. First Holland identified each reader's identity theme — "the constancy that informs everything a human being says or does."[63] Then he analyzed the transcript of each interview to see how an individual reader with his or her identity theme synthesized the story. From these analyses he concluded that *"a reader responds to a literary work by assimilating it to his own psychological process, that is, to his search for successful solutions within his identity theme to the multiple demands, both inner and outer, on his ego,"*[64] or in a more succinct (but still italicized) later formulation, *"we transact literature so as to recreate our identity."*[65] Readers do this by transforming the text to correspond to, or express, their expectations, fantasies, and defenses, four terms conveniently combined in the mnemonic acronym DEFT.[66]

This study is so well known and so frequently commented on and criticized that I need hardly add anything further. But one aspect of it has special relevance for my own study. In discussing the work of Fish and the proposals of Culler I have mentioned the problems caused by analyzing a reader's memorial reconstruction of his reading rather than the original process itself. This is a problem Holland confronts directly:

> I did assume that, by and large, what my readers said about their feelings at the time they read the story was true, but this was not essential. Free associations are like the retelling of a dream—an invented dream will express its teller's mind just as a real dream will. So long as a reader was talking fully and easily, it did not matter whether he was recalling his emotions correctly or even if he was disguising them or making them up to suit [Holland's] professional mien—free associations reveal the act of synthesis and creation behind them.[67]

Two points should be stressed here. First, Holland emphasizes "feelings" ("over and over again, [he] would ask, 'How do you feel about' characters, events, situations, or phrasings"[68]), that is, more or less formulated reactions to something in the mental reconstruction of the text, rather than the process by which the reader arrived at that reconstruction or those reactions. And, as I have been arguing, it is the constructive processes themselves that are difficult to introspect about and remember, not the results of those processes. Second, since Holland is primarily interested in the "teller's mind," accuracy of recall isn't of primary importance in his research because an inaccurate report (or even a falsified one) provides equivalent information about the individual's identity theme: how the reader says something, the words and images chosen, is more important than what he says.[69] In dealing with cognitive processes, however, the situation is reversed; the content is the point of interest, and inaccuracies or falsifications will obviously affect the analysis.

David Bleich has also dealt with real readers reading, but he has deflected interest from the processes by which a reader constructs an internal representation of a text in a slightly different way. For him the topic of primary interest is the reader's response, "the reader's peremptory perceptual identification of the work,"[70] which "aims to record the perception of a reading experience and its natural, spontaneous consequences, among which are feelings, or affects, and peremptory memories and thoughts, or associations."[71] The response is presented as an objectification "to ourselves and then to our community, [of] the affective-perceptual experience, rather than [of] the story,"[72] to serve as the basis for negotiated judgments of value and meaning, which are new knowledge derived by the community through negotiation of these presented experiences.[73]

If the response is not a re-creation of the "story," neither is it the actual experience of reading: "The actual reading experience is as unsusceptible of recording as the actual dream; neither can an actual memory be recorded. . . . it is possible to argue that the recorded perception of the story does not correspond to the experiential perception."[74] The reason for this is that the very production of a response statement alters the experience of reading. First, when these statements are written (as the ones in Bleich's studies are[75]), the very act of writing will fragment the experience of reading. But more importantly, the kind of response Bleich encourages his students to write focusses attention on the reader rather than on the act. For Bleich, perception of symbolic entities is always accompanied by affective evaluation, so the reader's attention to the words, characters, events, and so forth of the text is accompanied by a flow of affective reaction. Writing a response statement encourages identification and articulation of these feelings. Since each reader's feelings are a function of his past experiences, he must allow each feeling named to stimulate "peremptory memories and thoughts" to understand its subjective meaning.[76] Unfortunately, not all these associations "following the recording of an affective response are the subjective definition of that response," and so the reader/responder must engage in a "subjective dialectic," testing "through simple acts of memory to see if the new thoughts do symbolize the named feeling."[77]

Clearly, the fuller the reader's emotional response to the text, the more time will be devoted to expressing feelings, seeking associations for them, and testing whether the memories elicited actually do contribute to the subjective definition of the feeling. Under these conditions, it is reasonable to wonder whether what one normally means by reading has not been replaced by some other activity. The reading is overwhelmed by the flood of associations, with the practical result that only miniscule percentages of the text are actively responded to — one of the fullest response statements in Bleich's book provides responses to twenty-three phrases or scenes in *The Blithedale Romance*,[78] and generally the readers respond to no more than a dozen aspects of the work. The energy devoted to reconstructing the subjective etymology of the feelings encountered tends to obscure questions of why the reader had those particular feelings as a result of reading that particular section of text in the first place, and thus deemphasizes the experience of the text even further. And because the reader responds to so little of the work, and because the quality (in terms of relative negotiability) of the reader's response is emphasized,[79] it is often overlooked that many of these aspects of the work that the reader responds to are the product of private interpretation, constructions such as "Lawrence's descriptions of Connie's relationship with Michaelis," or "the character of Mrs. Bolton."[80] These constructions are never scrutinized as less global examples of "literary meaning" because they are the locus of affective response and thus seem to be provided by the experience of reading. But until they are so scrutinized, it will remain true that much — perhaps most — literary meaning will be the product of individual initiative rather than community negotiation.

Within Bleich's framework, then, the reading experience is not recorded — not only because it is, like the dream and the memory, evanescent, but more importantly, because the kind of response statement he requires effectively destroys it. This is an unfortunate result, for the response statement, as "an articulation of that part of our reading experience we think we can negotiate into knowledge,"[81] authorizes all the later community negotiation based upon it, and if it does not reflect the reading experience, it will frustrate the community's subsequent efforts to produce knowledge about that experience rather than about individual readers.[82] Bleich's solution — "But at this pass the defining authority of the pedagogical relationship will declare that the recorded perception will be communally objectified as 'the story the reader read', with the proviso that the reader may subsequently revise or otherwise alter 'his story' "[83] — may have a certain practical utility, but it hardly confronts the real problem of observing and analyzing the reading experience.

The four approaches I have surveyed thus share the characteristic that, in slightly different ways, each manages to shift attention from the mind meeting the text to something else. Most frequently the new focus of interest is the result of that meeting, some oral or written response produced after the actual meeting. In Culler and Fish, the deflection tends to be in the opposite temporal direction, toward characterizing what the reader must bring to the experience to negotiate it successfully. In either case, the actual experience of reading is neglected. It is this elusive experience that I hope to catch sight of in this book.

2 The Elements of Perception

At the beginning of *The Cognition of the Literary Work of Art*, Roman Ingarden asks his "main question": "How do we cognize the completed literary work?"[1] The question is surely at the center of literary studies, but his answer, provided in dense detail, is unsatisfying, primarily, one suspects, because it is theoretical and stipulative, and the question demands an empirical and verifiable one, an answer based on the observation of what readers actually do instead of on speculation about what they either do or ought to do. This limitation to theory is explained by his identification of the problem as an aesthetic one, even though his initial characterization of "cognition" (it is to be taken "in a rather vague and broad sense, beginning with a primarily passive, receptive 'experience', in which we, as literary consumers, 'become acquainted with' a given work, 'get to know' it somehow, and thereby relate to it in a more or less emotional way, and continuing on to the kind of attitude toward the work which leads to the acquisition of effective knowledge about the work"[2]) places the problem squarely within the purview of perception: "The problem of perception is one of understanding the way in which the organism transforms, organizes, and structures information arising from the world in sense data or memory."[3] If we view the problem of literary cognition as a psychological one, part of the perceptual ecology of the reader, rather than as an aesthetic one, related to questions of value and evaluation, then psychological approaches to other problems of perception may well suggest empirical methods of studying literary perception or cognition.

One of the most detailed attempts to describe the particularity of the mental processes by which one "transforms, organizes, and structures information" to gain "effective knowledge" about a problem is Allen Newell and Herbert A. Simon's *Human Problem Solving*, which focusses on how subjects solve "short (half hour), moderately difficult problems of a symbolic nature."[4] Based on information-processing theory, their analysis tries "to represent in some detail a particular man at work on a particular task."[5] Their explanation is a process model of individual behavior, nonstatistical, oriented toward discrete states of knowledge and the transitions between them. It views man as an information processor with the ability to manipulate only a limited number of symbols at a given time, by means of a limited number of processes, and the model of behavior they derive "is no metaphor, but a precise symbolic model on the basis of which pertinent specific aspects of the man's problem solving behavior can be calculated."[6]

One of the tasks Newell and Simon studied was cryptarithmetic, in which subjects are given an addition problem — two words are added together to produce as their sum a third — and told that each letter represents a digit. Sometimes a hint may be given, as in the second example below:

$$\begin{array}{cc} \text{SEND} & \text{DONALD} \\ +\text{MORE} & +\text{GERALD} \quad \text{D} = 5 \\ \hline \text{MONEY} & \text{ROBERT} \end{array}$$

The subjects verbalize their thoughts while trying to solve the problem, and these are tape recorded and then typed up into protocols that can be analyzed for the elementary processes they contain.

The problem as stated represents the "task environment"; the way the individual internalizes this problem is his own "problem space," which is his understanding of the requirements of the task together with "not only his actual behaviors, but the set of possible behaviors from which these are drawn; and not only his overt behaviors, but also the behaviors he considers in his thinking that don't correspond to possible overt behaviors."[7] This distinction between environment and problem space is necessary because subjects approach what seems to be the same problem quite differently. Most attack cryptarithmetic by considering each digit-letter identification a subproblem to be solved by applying the rules of arithmetic. Thus early conclusions about the second problem above normally include that T = 0, since 5 + 5 = 10, and in sums one writes the zero and "carries" the one. This immediately suggests that R represents an odd number since any number added to itself produces an even number, and adding one to it will make it odd. But other subjects conceived of the problem in quite distinct terms, and one came up with seven different problem spaces for LETS + WAVE = LATER, such as thinking of LETS and WAVE as four-digit numbers and wondering whether he knew any general methods for discovering which two four-digit numbers add up to a five-digit one, and trying to assign digits to the letters on the basis of alphabetical order.[8]

This internal representation of the problem requires some method of symbolization, some set of symbols to be stored in memory and manipulated. In the cryptarithmetic example, there must be some way of representing internally the letters (which are supplied by the environment) and the digits (which are not). And then there must be a set of processes that operate on these symbols, including (for the example given) not only the "substantive" operations of addition, but also such administrative procedures as finding a column to work with, assigning a numerical value to a letter, keeping track of earlier assignments, and so forth. For cryptarithmetic most subjects require nine or ten of these elementary processes; more complex problems demand more.[9]

The obvious question is whether this kind of approach can be adapted to study the perception of poetry. First, of course, there are limitations to the experimental design: asking readers to vocalize their thoughts will undoubtedly interfere with their normal reading activities, perhaps even changing them radically. This is not an important consideration in cryptarithmetic problems because most subjects do not have a 'normal' — i.e., nonexperimental — mode of solving such problems. But readers do have their own ways of reading poems, and interference with them is a real problem. Further, some readers are embarrassed by announcing their thoughts before they have a chance to censor them, and some mental processes are almost certainly either simultaneous or so much faster than vocalization that articulation will overlook or distort them.

To the objection of embarrassment there is a simple practical answer: most people overcome their initial hesitancy after a relatively short time; those who don't should not be used as subjects. To the objection of distortion, there is no completely satisfying answer except that simultaneous verbalization is likely to interfere with mental activities much less than any other method currently available for gathering such information. Writing about those activities, as advocated by David Bleich, is slower than vocalizing and introduces even more distortion and the opportunity for greater censorship; writing or talking after the event, as Norman Holland's subjects did, compounds these problems by introducing the whole process of memorial reconstruction. And introspecting generally about what one does, as suggested by Jonathan Culler and practiced by Stanley Fish and George Dillon, is likely to be both self-confirming and misleading, and in any case will result (as was argued in the first chapter) in a theory about intuitions rather than about the objects of those intuitions. With the third objection — that many of the thought processes involved may be overlooked — I agree; but it should be obvious that we now understand so little about the actual operations involved in literary cognition that the addition of any data will be a tremendous advance in our knowledge, whether or not they are complete. In fact, we will not even know what kinds of information we are lacking until we have systematically gathered and analyzed what is available to us.

Second, it is questionable whether reading poetry is similar enough to solving problems to make such an adaptation worthwhile. Certainly there are some obvious parallels between Newell and Simon's description of problem solving and the process of reading a poem. The Newell-Simon theory, for instance, posits a difference between the problem space and the external environment that corresponds closely to the distinction often drawn in literary studies between the text and the poem, the one an artifact, the other a mental re-creation of it. Similarly, different readers quite clearly have different problem spaces, or different methods of approaching a poem (what Fish would call interpretive strategies). What is more problematical is the notion of "success" in reading, of what would correspond to the solution to the problem: part of problem solving is knowing when you have succeeded in meeting the terms of the problem, of being able to add the triumphant Q.E.D. In reading a poem there seem to be no set criteria of success; indeed, there seems to be no initial problem. And this difference is critical, for without a problem, there is no reason to think that an approach designed to study problem solving will be applicable.

For Newell and Simon, a problem exists when a person "wants something and does not know immediately what series of actions he can perform to get it."[10] More specifically, "To have a problem implies (at least) that certain information is given to the problem solver: information about what is desired, under what conditions, by means of what tools and operations, starting with what initial information, and with access to what resources."[11] By this definition, attempting to understand a poem (as opposed to glancing over it) is always a problem, but it is not the same problem for each reader. Each reader has certain standards for satisfaction — "what is desired" — which may be adapted to the specific circumstances of the reading situation — "the conditions" — including the availability of reference works — "the resources"; and every reader begins with a store of knowledge — the "initial information" — and a way of approaching the poem — the "tools and operations." Some of these aspects of the reading situation will be shared by many readers — some processes of reading and decoding language, for instance — but others will be either idiosyncratic or symptomatic of a particular approach (or interpretive community). The crucial point is that although the poem as artifact is never a problem (except, of course, for the quite distinct problems treated by textual criticism), each reader makes the process of internalizing it a problem. More precisely, since a poem can be internalized in different ways, reading a poem can represent different problems even for the same reader: consider the different aims of reading a poem for an emotional frisson as opposed to discovering the author's political views of deciding whether the poem illustrates a particular point well enough to be included in a class discussion. This study concentrates on the kind of reading Ingarden calls "preaesthetic," which emphasizes the detection of facts about the poem,[12] the kind of interpretive or professional reading trained readers undertake to prepare a poem for discussion in a class or a paper. This type of reading represents a problem trained readers have confronted repeatedly during their literary careers, and they may be expected to have developed stereotyped procedures or strategies for solving it.

This standard or stereotyped behavior is only one example of the large number of stylized situations each of us faces every day. Cognitive science, the intersection of linguistics, psychology, and computer science, has emphasized how large a part these situations play in our lives, and has suggested that we negotiate them by means of *scripts*: "A script is a structure that describes appropriate sequences of events in a particular context. A script is made up of slots and requirements about what can fill those slots. The structure is an interconnected whole, and what is in one slot affects what can be in another. Scripts handle stylized everyday situations. Thus, a script is a predetermined, stereotyped sequence of actions that defines a well-known situation."[13] There is, for instance, a "restaurant script" that structures knowledge and expectations about what typically happens in a restaurant;[14] different "tracks" within the script account for knowledge about different types of restaurants (e.g. it would be strange to encounter a wine steward at a McDonald's; when there is a wine steward you settle — quite handsomely — after dining and include gratuities, while at McDonald's you pay before eating and leave no tip). These scripts allow us to negotiate everyday situations and to understand narratives about them, which typically are highly elliptical: telling a friend about a new restaurant, for instance, one would not generally pause to explain the function of the maitre d' or hostess, waiters and waitresses, menus, and so forth, unless something about them is atypical enough not to be included in a script, as perhaps when the menu is printed on a meat cleaver. Their existence is most obvious when there is some uncertainty about whether a particular script or track applies, as frequently happens the first time one encounters a situation, say in a foreign country (must one tip the usher in a French movie?

Should one wait quietly at the bar in a Soho pub until the publican takes the order?). Once a situation has been encountered several times — often once is enough — it ceases to be novel, which means that a script or a track of some other script has been constructed for it.

In short, a script is a formalization of what one knows about (a part of) the world. Its utility lies in its specification, for by explicating what normally remains tacit, it reveals how much knowledge is required to function in the real world.

Those for whom what I have been calling the "professional" reading of poetry becomes a stylized situation, a structure of expectations guiding the transaction of the text, presumably develop scripts that facilitate their actions. Most such readers have separate tracks within the general poetry-reading script for particular genres, forms, chronological groupings, or authors: certain expectations about sonnets that do not apply to odes, about Keats rather than Wordsworth (or Donne), about tragedy as opposed to comedy or romance. These different tracks guide the reading process by alerting the reader to what is likely to be important, both formally and thematically, and provide a criterion of success by so doing: a reading is successful when the expected elements have been discovered. This suggests, quite rightly I think, that different readers will be satisfied by different types of interpretations, and that the same reader may be satisfied by quite different interpretations of different texts: one does not expect the same kind of work from Shakespeare and Swinburne and therefore does not expect the same kind of interpretation. Finally, these scripts and tracks are the result of education and experience.

An experienced reader reading a poem seriously — reading it in Ingarden's preaesthetic way — thus begins the process of comprehension not merely with the text of the poem (the external environment), but with a rich internal set of expectations about successful comprehension: he will know when the problem of internalizing the poem has been solved. And even though an outside observer may think that there are still serious shortcomings in an interpretation, what is important from the point of view of problem solving is not so much that every problem be solved, but that the solver be able to conceive of a solution and work toward it.

Thus ultimately unsuccessful readings can also provide information, in at least two ways: since for most of the reading the reader does not know that it will ultimately be unsuccessful, he confronts the poem in his habitual manner, and this obviously provides data about the processes he normally uses in reading. Second, readers often indicate, either overtly or by returning frequently to a particular topic, what is unsatisfying about a particular reading and thus suggest indirectly what would be more satisfying.

To discover in more detail what readers actually do while reading, then, I adapted the Newell-Simon procedure to literary study. I hired six advanced graduate students (for seventy-five dollars each) to record all their thoughts while reading three poems and then to take part in taped group discussions of the poems. Three of the students were medievalists, one of whom (Philip) had recently finished his dissertation; the other two (Ann and Carlos) were just beginning theirs. Of the remaining three, Elaine was in the Renaissance, about to begin her dissertation, George was in modern literature, about to begin his, and Joel, less advanced in his graduate program than the others, was in American literature. All of them had taken at least one course from me, though in most cases this occurred years before the experiment, and all had previous experience in verbalizing their processes of interpretation (through pilot studies I had done, in one case with David Bleich, or through taping a reading of a poem not included in the study). These were, then, experienced readers in two senses: experienced in reading into a tape recorder and experienced in interpretation.

The stipend I paid them would serve, I hoped, two purposes: to keep them interested for the five-week period required for the tapings (a poem was distributed every other week), and to compensate them for the time — perhaps ten hours altogehter — that could not be devoted to their other projects: in addition to their own work, all were teaching assistants and were thus teaching at the time. This payment, modest as it was, raises some questions of methodology, for, as David Bleich charges in "Pedagogical Directions in Subjective Criticism," Normal Holland defined a pecuniary situation by paying his readers and thus constrained the process of reading in special ways.[15] This may well be true, but, as Stanley Fish has reminded us, we are never not in some situation,[16] and the only question is whether money exerts more pressure than the other types of reward that might be used. In Bleich's own studies, for instance, the subjects were for the most part not only students, but good students, whose desire to impress the professor may well have affected them more than cash.[17] The only observable effect of the payment on my readers was that they felt bound to keep working on a poem longer than they would normally. With poems they understood, this led to a certain repetitiousness; with those they could not comprehend easily, it encouraged more sustained effort than usual.

This is most obvious in the first poem presented to them, Swinburne's "A Ballad of Dreamland." I chose this particular poem for several rea-

sons. Since none of the readers specialized in nineteenth-century litera-
ture, I expected them all to know vaguely who Swinburne was without
having any very precise idea what he had done, and to have a generally
negative reaction toward him. This reaction was confirmed by the re-
sponses to a typographical error in the dittoed copy of the poem that was
distributed: instead of "what bids the lids of thy sleep dispart," what
appeared was "what bids the lids of thy sleep depart," producing a
rather striking image that several readers commented on. Second, I as-
sumed that they would all be most comfortable with poetry that posed
intellectual or logical difficulties of interpretation, and the Swinburne
poem relies heavily on sensuous effects and seems to be an alogical re-
flection of dreamland. Third, the poem has a very definite form — it is a
medieval ballade — but that form is less familiar than, say, a sonnet
would have been. Finally, I didn't expect anybody to have read it be-
fore: it is not in the Norton *Anthology*, and it is not even routinely in-
cluded in anthologies of nineteenth-century poetry. In general, then, I
expected it to be something of a shock, a new poem not entirely ame-
nable to the kind of close reading the students were used to practicing.

The second poem, Shakespeare's sonnet 94, was chosen for different
reasons. All the students, I thought, would be well acquainted with
Shakespeare in general, and would probably have read the sonnets
through several times. They would thus have a richer fund of back-
ground information about the author and the form than they had for
Swinburne. Sonnet 94, however, is extremely puzzling, as the available
criticism indicates;[18] both the tone and the structure are problematical,
and though they appear to be amenable to logical and intellectual
analysis (an appearance buttressed by general expectations about Shake-
speare's sonnets), few readers have been able to interpret them satisfac-
torily. The dittoed version of this poem also contained a typo (the first
line read "they that have power to do hurt and will do none") which
seemed at first to be merely another example of incompetent typing but
proved eventually to be an extremely interesting occasion to observe the
readers' approaches to textual criticism.

Gerard Manley Hopkins's "Carrion Comfort" was the third poem,
chosen because of the syntactic and structural difficulties it presented. I
wanted some information about how the readers would unravel the
compressed syntax, and whether they would notice the strong formal
structure obscured to some extent by the long lines. I was also curious
about the effects on reading of the concepts *inscape, instress,* and *sprung
rhythm*, which I assumed (incorrectly, as it turned out) all the readers
would have encountered when they studied Hopkins.

The readers were given the poems (the first two dittoed, the last one reproduced) and two hours' worth of tape cassettes on a Monday, and had to return the cassettes just before they took part in the group discussions on Friday afternoon. The following instructions were included with the first poem:

> Please try to verbalize everything you do in coming to a complete understanding of this poem, complete enough so you will be prepared to discuss any and all aspects of it on Friday. Try not to censor anything — if you read through the poem several times, if you start in on one train of thought and then switch to another, if stray thoughts occur to you, if you use any reference works or other books — whatever, please do it verbally rather than silently so it will be included. Feel free to return to the poem as often as you wish; each time you return, please indicate the time and date, and whatever thoughts about the poem may have occurred to you since the last taping.

In an attempt to re-create, as much as possible, the "normal" situation of reading a poem, I left the readers free to choose when and where to read the poem, to return to it as frequently as they wanted, and to use any resources they felt necessary. The group discussion at the end of the week gave them a context for the reading: the aim would be to prepare the poem to discuss it with a group of peers, all of whom would also be reading and preparing for the meeting. This seemed a relatively natural situation for "professional" readers, one that would stimulate them without being bizarre, as a laboratory setting would have been. Undoubtedly it affected their reading behavior in some ways — all experiments, indeed all situations, have demand characteristics[19] — but I hoped it would affect them as little as possible.

The tapes were then typed verbatim into eight protocols, one of which appears in the next chapter and the others, in the appendix. These are unedited except for punctuation. By contrast, I have lightly edited the excerpts I quote in the following chapters; the reader may see how much by comparing the quotations with the protocol.

The next stage was the analysis of the protocols. First they were divided into segments that seemed to express one elementary operation or process (the protocol in chapter 3 is so divided). This initial division was largely impressionistic, attempting to separate different mental operations; since these don't necessarily correspond with linguistic units, no formal method is readily available. And, in fact, the initial segmentation does not matter greatly, since errors will be detected and corrected during the analysis phase, which follows.

The elementary operations are combined into episodes in the reading that I call *Moves*. Typically consisting of between half a dozen and two dozen elementary operations, each move treats a single topic. Early in the process of reading, a move may be defined by a textual unit, as when a reader reads a quatrain (or a line) and then proceeds to figure it out. Later in the process, moves tend to be determined by what the reader has already done: they may be devoted to discussing typical Shakespearean imagery, or the relation between the given poem and the rest of the sonnet sequence, or the relevance of the author's biography. These moves are an analytical convenience as much as anything else; they represent in a general way the organization of the reader's experience and provide the units I have used for referring to the protocols.

Analysis of the elementary operations is more complex, since the aim here is to state precisely what mental operation is being performed, and, naturally, the operations one finds are a reflection of what one expects to find. For that purpose there are a number of inventories of processes available, most notably those proposed by Alan Purves in *Elements of Writing about a Literary Work* and by Lee Odell and Charles Cooper in "Describing Responses to Works of Fiction."[20] As I argued in the first chapter, these are unsatisfactory because they were developed to analyze writing about literature rather than the perception of literature. They thus work with units much larger than the elementary processes I was interested in, and with statements *about* literature rather than with the processes that are used *to constitute* literature. As an alternative to them, I derived a set of about two dozen elementary processes that recur in the protocols I studied. These are primarily descriptive insofar as they reflect what a reader is doing rather than why or how he is doing it. A short characterization of each follows. The examples are taken from Ann's protocol in the appendix.

The first process is the most basic, in terms of reading and understanding a poem, if not in itself. READ occurs when a reader reads either the entire poem or some portion of it: Ann begins both her second and third moves by READing the entire poem and READs the octave at the beginning of the fifth. This operation indicates the level of analysis used in this study: READ is hardly an elementary process, psychologically speaking, since it consists of many different acts of attending, identifying, matching, predicting, and so forth. But it would shed very little light on the process of understanding a poem to specify all these constituent actions (even if that were possible, which of course it isn't) because they are too atomic, too distant from what the reader is conscious of trying to do. Readers typically READ a section of the poem at the beginning of a Move, especially early in the reading process, since this is one way of setting a topic.

READ is often followed by SELECT, in which the reader chooses some relatively small section of the poem to work with, often a word or a line. In the fifth move, Ann READs the first eight lines, and then SELECTs the first line to concentrate on; similarly the next two moves begin with SELECTs. Sometimes READ and SELECT coincide, as when Ann READs a line and then proceeds to say something about all of it; and frequently the actual SELECT is hidden in whatever the reader does with the line. I might point out in passing that SELECT corresponds more or less to the psychological process of attending, in which the subject chooses part of the environment for specific consideration and relegates the rest of it to background or context.

The third operation, similar to READ and SELECT, is ILLUSTRATE, which occurs when a reader reads part of the poem to corroborate or provide an example of what has been said. In justifying her use of the *Norton Anthology* text of the sonnet, Ann says, "I'm using the *Norton Anthology of English Literature, Volume One*, and the first line is different in this. I think on the paper it's 'They that have power to do hurt and will do none'" (Move 1), the final sentence ILLUSTRATing how the Norton text and the one distributed differ. Her reading of lines seven through ten in the fourth move ILLUSTRATEs her previous statement that the poem has some great lines.

Final among the relatively simple operations is LOCATE, which occurs when a reader either searches for something in the text or specifies where it is to be found. In the third move, Ann LOCATEs the major units of punctuation in the poem: "and beyond that, major units of punctuation occur at the end of line four, line six, the period at line eight, nine ten eleven, and then line twelve and thirteen," and in the tenth move she LOCATEs the last line and the next-to-last line before READing them.

These four operations emphasize the relation between the reader and the text, and at the same time function as simple signposts to the process of reading. Especially in the early phases of comprehension, that process is text-driven, with the topics being determined primarily by sections of the text; for that reason, many moves begin with a READ followed by a SELECT. Later in the interpretation, moves tend to be determined more by what the reader has already done than by textual units.

In the next group there are two operations, NARRATE and COMMENT. NARRATE refers to the reader's narration of what he is doing. Ann begins her protocol by NARRATing, "Ok, I'm going to start now," and soon continues her narration: "First I should read the poem." Since a NARRATE is a report of what the reader is doing (or about to do) rather than the record of actually doing it, it reflects a conscious monitoring of the reading process similar to what one might expect from a reader's introspection. COMMENT refers to the reader's own situation, likes and dislikes, emotional reactions and so forth. Ann's setting of the stage in the first move ("It's Friday morning quite early and I've devoted a stretch of time to see if I can do this all at once") is a COMMENT, as are her reactions that "it's a strange poem," "It really is hard to figure out," and "Has some great lines" (all Move 4). COMMENT and NARRATE frequently seem to overlap, for instance in her explanation of why she is not using the distributed copy of the text, but NARRATE is used specifically to report the reader's mental activities, and so that explanation is considered a COMMENT. It should be noted that COMMENT is another severely underdifferentiated category, since I have made no attempt to distinguish cognitive COMMENTs ("It really is hard to figure out") from affective ("Has some great lines") and purely temporal ones ("It's Friday morning . . .").

The third group consists of the simplest processes, linguistically defined, that can be performed on the text. PHONOLOGY refers to any comment about the phonology of the poem, including such matters as stress, rhyme, alliteration, assonance, etc. Ann's third move consists primarily of a quick formal analysis of the poem, including some comments on PHONOLOGY: "The rhyme scheme . . . A-B-A-B-C-D-C-D-E-F-E-die and dignity . . . F, G-G." As is apparent from this example, PHONOLOGY often occurs in concert with the next operation, FORM, which refers to any observation about the poetic form or structure of the poem, such as Ann's observation at the beginning of the third move that "it's a sonnet." FORM is really a kind of abstraction, since the form that is perceived must be embodied somehow, usually in either phonology or syntax: "The syntactic division is into an octave . . . and a sestet"; "the thing would be divided up according to the rhyme scheme into an octave . . . and a sestet, the last two lines of which form a kind of couplet" (Move 3). The concept of a rhyme belongs to PHONOLOGY, as in the *die-dignity* example; that of a rhyme scheme, to FORM.

WORD refers to any process that concerns the meaning (in a broad sense) of the words of the poem, lexical choice, or diction. This includes using a dictionary to ascertain the possible meanings of a word, identifying puns (i.e., words that have two or more meanings operative simultaneously), and testing the connotations that words may have. Ann consults reference works less than the other readers, but her habit of supplying a series of synonyms for words illustrates this operation, as in the seventeenth move: " 'others but stewards', ok, others but caretakers, protectors, cultivators, guardians. . . ."

More complex linguistically is SYNTAX, which occurs when the reader tries to unravel any aspect of the syntax, including the identification of antecedents. Ann's references to the syntactic division of the poem into an octave and a sestet and the identification of the punctuation marks in the third move are examples of SYNTAX. Unfortunately, she does not devote much time to consideration of the syntax of the poem, but other readers spent some of their time wondering whether *their* in 1. 8 was anaphoric to *others*, or to *they* in the previous line. Closely related to SYNTAX is TONE, which occurs when a reader either refers to the tone of the poem or tries to decipher it. Ann is intrigued by the tone: "The thing that interests me most about it is the tone. . . . the tone of the thing really is intriguing" (Move 12). TONE refers not only to the comments people make when they mention tone explicitly, but also to such assessments of tone as sarcasm, irony, and so forth: "the irony in those four lines it seems, or potential irony, whatever, is much more biting" (Move 33) illustrates TONE mixed with a LOCATE and a QUALIFY (for which see below).

The processes in this group — PHONOLOGY, FORM, WORD, SYNTAX, and TONE — all deal with the linguistic strata of the text in one way or another. PHONOLOGY, WORD, and FORM seem to be the result of specific literary training, since speakers don't normally notice such aspects of every day speech. SYNTAX and TONE are different insofar as they represent conscious, problem-solving counterparts of operations normally performed unconsciously: one only comments on, or tries to disentangle, syntax when the already-developed mechanisms for processing it break down. Since tone depends to a large extent on syntactic variables (at least on what are today considered syntactic variables — e.g., the relation between semantics and presupposition), the same is presumably true of TONE: the operation only appears when there is some question about its outcome. SYNTAX and TONE thus provide no information about how readers normally process syntax; they occur only when such normal processing is unsuccessful. Most of the normal syntactic processing of the text of the poem occurs at an unconscious level as the reader is reading the text, and so is included in READ.

These 'linguistic' operations are, like the first group, underdifferentiated from a psychological point of view. Some could presumably be analyzed into more elementary processes now: PHONOLOGY, for instance, relies on relatively simple operations of matching the phonological features of two segments, and it would be easy enough to set up a flow chart describing the process. The others, however, require greater information about the structure of the mind and mental processes than is

currently available. WORD is obviously related to the structure of the
mental lexicon, but there are several conflicting views of its organization.
Similarly, SYNTAX relies on conscious versions of the unconscious pro-
cesses used in language comprehension, and while it is possible to guess
at what these are like — especially in comparatively straightforward cases
like deciding anaphoric relations or determining the basic structure of a
simple clause — there are again several competing theories, and it is un-
clear which is to be preferred.[21]

The next group consists of the operations usually thought of as con-
stituting the heart of interpretation. The simplest of these is PARA-
PHRASE, a close restatement of what the poem says, either by a linguistic
transformation or by the substitution of synonyms. While many readers
prefer to paraphrase the poem early in the reading, Ann offers such re-
statements only sporadically. After READing the octave at the beginning
of the fifth move, she PARAPHRASEs the first line and then the second:
"All right, those people who have power to hurt others, . . . that do not
act in the way they would seem to act. . . ." PARAPHRASE often shades
off into DEDUCE, in which the reader tries to ascertain what the poem
means rather than what it says, either by filling in the text or by drawing
logical deductions from it. The examples of PARAPHRASE given above
surround the following example of PARAPHRASE followed by a DEDUCE:
"they that have the power to hurt others but disdain to do so presum-
ably"; what is DEDUCEd from the text here is the idea that they disdain
to do so. Ann continues with a PARAPHRASE of the beginning of the third
line — "who move others" — and then returns to DEDUCE what the
others are moved to: "To passion, or to rage, to hurt, whatever." Fre-
quently it is not altogether clear whether a particular operation should be
labeled PARAPHRASE or DEDUCE: which is Ann's rendering of *are them-
selves as stone* as "but themselves remain impassive"? It would, of course,
be possible to collapse these two operations into one, but the fact re-
mains that there is some point at which the reader can clearly be seen
drawing deductions from what is said, as in the reference to disdain
above, or in the suggestion that *nature's riches* refers to "something to do
with appearance, fortune, disposition, personal qualities" later in the
same move.

The difficulty in distinguishing between these two operations is in-
creased by the difficulty in distinguishing between deductions based on
linguistic knowledge and those based on knowledge of the world. The
line I would like to draw here is between knowledge that should be
represented in a dictionary and that found in an encyclopedia. The
practical problem is that almost all world knowledge is encoded linguisti-

cally and thus becomes part of the linguistic repertoire of the reader. Still, there are some cases where the knowledge seems to be securely based on knowledge of the world, as when Ann DEDUCEs from the ninth line that the flower "presages the coming of another season, or the arrival of a season, or whatever" (Move 8), and these I call DEDUCE:WORLD. These two different kinds of deduction are juxtaposed in the ninth move: after READing the eleventh line, Ann continues, "OK, presumably if it rots, whatever, gets some kind of blight." Here the rotting seems to be a linguistic deduction from *infection,* but the idea of a blight as the kind of rotting applicable to flowers seems to be based on world knowledge. And, of course, either kind of DEDUCE can be incorrect, based on misinformation about the world or the language.

The next operation in this group is CONNECT, which is actually four related operations that might have been given individual names except that different names would obscure the fact that very similar mental processes are involved in all. The first type, CONNECT:POEM, occurs when a reader relates one poetic element to another. At the simplest level this involves two words, as when Ann links *base infection* with *deeds* — "OK, a base infection is certainly not a deed" (Move 10); more complexly, it can involve entire sections of the poem, as her reaction to the penultimate line illustrates: "all right, that links the octave to the sestet, in an odd kind of way" (Move 10). The second, CONNECT:WORLD, links a poetic element to something in the real world (an alternative name for this would be REFER). After linking *base infection* with *deeds,* Ann CONNECTs it to the world: "OK, a base infection is certainly not a deed, not necessarily unless flowers get gonorrhea, something that they bring on themselves" (Move 10). While it is fairly easy to distinguish CONNECT:POEM from CONNECT:WORLD — the one requires two poetic elements, and the other forbids them — it should be noted that many CONNECT:WORLDs may, as this one, be strings of DEDUCEs. Here the fact that *base infection* is not a *deed* (already a deduction in addition to a CONNECT:POEM) presumably leads to speculation about what kind of base infection could be a deed, and this leads, via a DEDUCE:WORLD, to gonorrhea. On the other hand, there are some CONNECT:WORLDs that don't seem to be the result of series of deductions, but rather of immediately perceived similarity. Much of Ann's protocol depends on an encounter with a friend that the tone of the poem reminds her of: "I had a discussion recently with a very disturbed person who was very upset about something, and the tone of the discussion or of the things that the person said to me were very much like this, the sonnet" (Move 12).

The third kind of connection the reader may make is CONNECT: LITERATURE, which relates something in the poem to its author, another literary work, or to literary history in general. Ann refers only infrequently to other literary works, but she does link the poem to a commentary on the sonnets she has read (in the eleventh move). In a sense, any reference to FORM is also a CONNECT:LITERATURE, since to recognize that a poem is a sonnet is to place it within a literary tradition. A slightly broader classification here would be CONNECT:HISTORY, which would refer to any connection a reader made between the poem and anything he had read about. This would include, in addition to literature, philosophy, religion, social and economic history, politics, and so forth. I have limited the field to literature because the readers in this study referred only to literary works (if the Bible is considered literature, which for most of the present readers it is), but it could easily be expanded, simply because the sources of our knowledge about Henry VIII, for instance, are very similar to our sources for Hamlet (and quite different from those for flowers, gonorrhea, etc.).

The fourth category of connection could easily be subsumed under the third, except that it seems to function differently within the process of reading. A CONNECT:FIGURE occurs when a reader indentifies a textual element as a trope, such as a metaphor, symbol, or aphorism: "it's a perfect aphoristic, very concise, illustration of what's being talked about in the first four lines of the sestet" (CONNECT:FIGURE followed by COMMENT and CONNECT:POEM; Move 10); "The summer's flower is to the summer sweet: the summer's flower is beautiful, it's an emblem of something" (READ, DEDUCE, CONNECT:FIGURE, Move 8). CONNECT:FIGURE is obviously dependent on literary knowledge, just as CONNECT:LITERATURE is, but it differs in that it is often related to the operations in the previous group: to identify something as a metaphor is to suggest how to understand it, what the possibilities for paraphrase and deduction are.

The final operation in this group is GENERALIZE, which analyzes two or more elements in the poem, identifies what they have in common, and then reifies that commonality. Sometimes this is presented as a kind of summary: "The point in the first eight lines though is that the people don't do anything" (Move 19) is a GENERALIZE, followed in the protocol by a listing of the evidence for it. GENERALIZE differs from CONNECT: POEM by not merely suggesting that two elements are similar, but specifying what that similarity is. Unfortunately, GENERALIZE is often incomplete; what appears is the assertion that a section of the poem treats a certain topic or theme without any detailed explanation of what the topic or theme is: after noting that the thirteenth line "links the octave to the sestet, in an odd kind of way," Ann GENERALIZEs about the topic: "It's clear that something very different is being talked about" (Move 10), and later, introducing a summary of the octave, she refers twice to "the thrust of the octet" (Move 13). It might be noted that other readers supply better examples of this operation than Ann.

The next group of operations contain two that concern validity, TEST and JUSTIFY: after making a connection or drawing a deduction, readers often either test its validity or offer some justification for it. After Ann has recounted what she remembers of the story behind the sonnets, she TESTs its utility: "I don't know enough about the sonnets to know whether that makes any sense at all, and I simply don't know enough about Shakespeare's proclivities or love life or anything else to know whether that makes any sense at all" (Move 11). From this example it is clear that a TEST does not necessarily arrive at a final assessment of correctness; it merely has to seek it. JUSTIFY, as the name indicates, adduces information to support a conclusion that has been drawn. Ann JUSTIFies her connection between flowers and beauty by pointing out that "certain kinds of physical beauty are transient" (Move 23), and later JUSTIFies her feeling that the *they* in the poem become "a false object of respect" by listing the phrases involved and then saying, "those words make me read the poem in that light, and make me read those lines in that light" (Move 26). Just as a TEST may be inconclusive, a JUSTIFY may be logically invalid: what matters in identifying the reader's operations is not whether he correctly tests or justifies his conclusions, but rather that he makes the attempt to.

In a final group are a number of operations that deal more with the style of the protocol than with its content, with the way in which the reader presents his processes. First, the reader may choose to RESTATE something he has already said, either saying roughly the same thing in different words or providing a more specific version of it. Ann frequently does this, sometimes repeating herself ("refuse to become tempted to do anything, refuse to be tempted," Move 5), sometimes supplying a more precise word ("OK, after this series of statements, this series of reflections . . . ," Move 8) or definition ("The syntactic division is into an octave, or an eight-line unit . . . ," Move 3), sometimes a different example of the same thing ("If you mutilate a tulip, or if you mutilate a jonquil or whatever . . . ," Move 9). One of the characteristic features of her protocol is the series of synonyms or near synonyms, which hovers between a series of RESTATEs and DEDUCEs: "who move others, to passion, or to rage, to hurt, whatever" (Move 5); "Others but stewards: ok, others but caretakers, protectors, cultivators, guardians" (Move 17). I have considered the first of these a series of DEDUCEs, since it seems that the aim was not to restate the immediately preceding word or phrase, but rather to get a better view of the textual phrase by specifying the range of meanings possible; the second is a series of WORDs, each supplying a definition of *stewards*.

QUALIFY mitigates or reduces the scope of the previous statement, usually parenthetically ("or else to a series of inadequate responses, I suppose," Move 21; "in fact can't help, it would seem, but move others," Move 28). RECALL refers to a reader's repeating a previous operation, as occurs quite frequently after the first several readings. Sometimes this repetition occurs after a brief interruption, reestablishing the reader's place in the reading, as when Ann's reading is interrupted by noisemakers in the hall outside the room where she is recording: "Again, they're lords, they're owners, and all that implies: haughty, in a position to dispense crumbs or not dispense crumbs, or not dispense anything — More crazies in the hall — OK, they're in a position to be haughty, and to dispense, you know, deign to dispense disdainfully, or not to dispense at all" (Move 17). More frequently, insights from early in the reading keep recurring, defining major themes of the interpretation. One of these themes in Ann's reading is that the poem is an expression of pique; this is introduced in the fourth move ("it's the kind of poem one would show to someone having written it in a fit of pique"), continued in the eleventh ("and this was a kind of sustained, the sonnet was a kind of sustained expression of pique at this person"), the twentieth ("the whole thing comes out as much more, as an instance of pique, as pique"), and finally, with the addition of the idea of psychological escalation, itself first suggested in the twentieth move, in the thirty-third ("If it is an expression of pique and has the same kind of psychological escalation that expressions of that kind . . . tend to have") and thirty-fourth ("it's getting back to the escalation of pique"). By following these RECALLS, one can trace the process by which a hypothesis becomes accepted as a fact, equal in influence on the succeeding reading to the words of the text.

As the reading progresses, operations tend to become nested within each other: a series of DEDUCTions may be offered as a JUSTIFY, and CONNECTions may be made between deductions or generalizations that have previously been drawn. In this way, what seems to be a relatively sophisticated interpretation is constructed from simple elementary operations, a process illustrated in the detailed discussion of Elaine's protocol in the next chapter.

The inventory of elementary operations necessary to account for the readers' processes is thus the following:

I.   READ, SELECT, LOCATE
II.   COMMENT, NARRATE
III. PHONOLOGY, FORM, WORD, SYNTAX, TONE
IV.   PARAPHRASE, DEDUCE, DEDUCE:WORLD, CONNECT:
      POEM, CONNECT:WORLD, CONNECT:LITERATURE, CON-
      NECT:FIGURE, GENERALIZE
V.   TEST, JUSTIFY
VI.   RESTATE, ILLUSTRATE, QUALIFY, RECALL

As I have already suggested, this listing is tentative, since several of the operations — for instance, READ and SYNTAX — require further analysis, and others, notably those in group IV, might be segmented differently.

In addition, it should be clear that these processes are not completely determinate or predictive. Once a reader has made a CONNECT:LITERA-TURE we can recognize it, but we can never be sure in advance what particular literary work will be chosen as an example, since we do not know the extent of a reader's previous reading, or what particular aspect of the present text will remind him of another text. And as the examples in Elaine's protocol in the next chapter suggest, the connections made by a reader are not necessarily valid in the sense that the text referred to is remembered correctly or that it actually illustrates the point the reader is making. Similarly, it is apparent when a reader has made a deduction, but so many different deductions could be drawn from a given line that it is impossible to predict its content. And the same is true of the other types of CONNECT and GENERALIZE.

The situation is quite different when the external environment and problem space are more severely constrained. In cryptarithmetic, the operations most useful are arithmetical, and so when a set of numbers has been selected for attention it is easier to predict just what will be done with them. Given the second cryptarithmetic problem above (D O N A L D + G E R A L D = R O B E R T, D = 5), we can be relatively confident that a subject who SELECTs the final column will apply the rules of arithmetic and DEDUCE that T = 0, since 5 + 5 = 10 and in sums the zero is written and the one carried. In the reading of poetry there is nothing corresponding to the rules of arithmetic, and so it is possible to predict the form of the operations the reader will use, but not all the details of their content.

Naturally, the more we know about the reader, the more precisely we will be able to predict the content of his operations as well as their form. This can be seen most clearly in the fifth chapter, where the comparison of Carlos's readings of three quite different poems reveals not only the typical structure of his reading but also its typical contents, the kinds of connections and deductions he habitually seeks. What this suggests is that the problem space a reader uses to understand a poem may be just as deterministic as the one used in solving cryptarithmetic problems, but that much more information about the reader and his reading experiences is necessary to specify it. Over the years, each reader develops a particular method for reading poems, partially through specific training in the methods of literary interpretation, partially through the reinforcement of the institutional rewards successful readings receive. In experienced readers these methods have become systematic enough to be considered scripts (in the sense discussed earlier) that define the problem space for understanding a poem.

Analysis of the protocols thus has two aims. The preliminary one is to understand and characterize what the reader is doing at each moment of the perception process. In Newell and Simon's terms, this requires the specification of a series of knowledge states and the operations that provide the transition from each to the succeeding one.[22] The next chapter provides this kind of step-by-step analysis of Elaine's reading of sonnet 94. At each stage it would be possible to specify what she knows about the poem, and each elementary operation she performs changes her knowledge, however slightly. Providing a running inventory of her knowledge would be extremely unwieldy, however, and so in my discussion I have emphasized the operations she performs and the ways in which they modify her knowledge. (In this discussion it should be remembered that her knowledge and operations are concepts derived from her protocol; she may well have known things about the poem that she did not express, but they are not available for analysis.)

The second goal of analysis is to specify the problem space the reader uses. The fourth chapter explores the variation possible in these internal representations by comparing the spaces used by four other readers of sonnet 94. These problem spaces share certain obvious features, presumably because of the demand characteristics of the situation and the similarity in the training all the readers have received, but even within these generally similar approaches great variations in organization and content are apparent. The fifth chapter compares Carlos's readings of all three poems in an attempt to isolate the components of his script for reading poems. This provides more detail about his background and typical behavior, and it becomes possible to suggest what a typical reading would be like for him. Much more detail is necessary, of course, and if we had his readings of another half dozen poems it would be possible to be more specific still. But the first approximation presented there does suggest the possibilities for the future.

3 One Reader Reading Sonnet 94

In this chapter the reading process of one reader will be examined in detail. For ease of reference, moves from Elaine's protocol are presented and followed by discussions of them; operations within the moves are separated by diagonal lines. To illustrate how detailed a discussion could be, I have named many of the elementary operations Elaine performs in the early moves; these are printed in small capital letters and used as both nouns and verbs. Later on, however, I have emphasized how the operations modify earlier conclusions and work toward specific interpretive goals rather than labelling them.

I. Oh . . . I'm not good at Shakespeare sonnets, / so I already feel hostile towards this poem / and uh, when we did this when I was in college every time someone tried, well the teacher started out saying that nobody had ever understood this poem and that nobody ever would / and any time anybody tried to give an interpretation of it the teacher said that the poem was incomprehensible. / But this is a very famous poem — / that I've never understood.

MOVE 1

This is an introduction. Perhaps because of the situation of taping comments, all the readers provided some sort of introduction, ranging from a simple announcement of the time and day to this rather more elaborate one.

Within the reading process it serves a number of functions. It establishes that Elaine has seen the poem before, and has even studied it, but does not feel that she understands it. (Indeed, this sonnet was chosen for exactly that reason: everybody has read it, but few have lingered to unravel its various difficulties.) This becomes in Elaine's recollection an admonition that the poem is impenetrable; her college teacher assured the class that nobody had ever understood this poem and that nobody ever would and then apparently did his best to discourage any comprehension. It also provides a framework for Elaine's reading: since the poem is known to be incomprehensible, whatever shortcomings exist in her attempt will not reflect badly on her own abilities, a point especially important after her unsatisfying confrontation with Swinburne's "A Ballad of Dreamland." (Elaine's final comment is about how "much happier about this poem than about that last one" she is.) But she is willing to admit that she is "not good at Shakespeare sonnets," and this feeling of inadequacy leads to a certain hostility. Again, this seems to be more preparation based on the previous poem than anything else: little in the rest of this protocol suggests hostility or even annoyance.

The function of the introduction is to set the reading within some kind of a framework by enunciating three major themes: first, that the poem is famous and that Elaine is at least vaguely familiar with it; second, that she is not good with Shakespeare sonnets in general and in particular with this one, since it is well known to be incomprehensible; and third, that these two facts lead to a certain amount of anxiety and hostility.

II. //read poem with l. 4: Unmovéd, Unmovéd, cold and to temptation slow.// / I really like that, / I think that's a nice poem. / Haven't got the faintest notion of what this means. / This is I think a 'young man' sonnet— / but I don't like that kind of interp-, / though this is to the young man. / I don't think that works all that well.

MOVE 2

After the introduction comes the first reading of the poem. Like Elaine, most readers read through the entire text; fewer read until they become confused or want to think about something and then begin to work on the poem right away. Also typical is the evaluative reaction (a COMMENT) and the claim that nothing has been understood from the first reading. But as is clear from the connection drawn between line 1 and line 7 in Move 3 below, this claim is at least partially a rhetorical flourish.

Elaine's familiarity with the Renaissance period allows her to make an immediate CONNECT:LITERATURE: this poem may be one of the "young man" sonnets. The connection is quickly TESTed. This theme reemerges below (Move 14), and although the specific identification never proves very important for the reading, it does suggest part of Elaine's problem space, which must be defined in terms of the typical concerns and intended audiences of Shakespeare's sonnets. This will be developed more fully in Moves 23, 50, and 54.

III. //read ll. 1 – 4// / OK the people that have "pow'r to
hurt," / hurt people in love? / a-, as in a kind of love, sexual-
ly? / or even sexually, and don't do it, / "do not do the . . . they
most do show." / Does that have to do with the "owners of their
faces"? / "Who, moving others, are themselves as
stone, | Unmoved, cold, and to temptation slow." / Now what I
don't understand is why do they "inherit heaven's graces"? / Be-
cause it, in the first quatrain / i-, it sounds like that's bad.

MOVE 3

After the first full reading and initial reaction, readers usually progress
through the poem more or less systematically a number of times, READ-
ing a section, SELECTing something within it to deal with, and then
performing a number of different operations on the selected portion.
Elaine chooses the first quatrain to READ, and then immediately
SELECTs the first full line, PARAPHRASing it slightly. Her first operation
is a DEDUCE to specify further the kind of hurting involved — love, as
opposed to a physical, political, economic, or any other kind of hurt —
and she then calls on her world knowledge (a DEDUCE:WORLD) to
further narrow the kind of hurt in love to a sexual hurt. The basis for this
initial DEDUCE, upon which so much of the rest of her reading depends,
seems to be her knowledge of Shakespearean sonnets. She has already
identified the poem as a "young man" sonnet (Move 2) and thus as one
concerned with personal relationships. This then forms the basis for un-
derstanding the second half of the first line and the second line: *they*
could hurt others sexually but "don't do it." She then ILLUSTRATEs the
correctness of her paraphrase by reading the second line. This ILLUS-
TRATE, as is often the case, shades off into another SELECT, since the
final few words — *they most do show* — form the basis for the next opera-
tion, a CONNECT:POEM between *show* and *owners of their faces* in line 7.
The connection is only tentative — it is developed more fully in Move
9 — but it suggests that the reference to *faces* is retained in some form
from the first reading.

Next, she SELECTs the following two lines and again CONNECTs them
with something later in the poem. Here, however, the focus is not on
the connection itself but rather on the justification for it: why would
action (or lack of action) that sounds "bad" lead to inheriting heaven's
graces? This is the first hint of the polarities that characterize Elaine's
problem space for this poem: actions and characteristics are either good
or bad, internal or external, with no middle ground, and to assign some-

thing to one category it is sufficient to show that it doesn't belong in the other.

IV. "They rightly do inherit heaven's graces | And husband nature's riches from expense." / And husband- / to farm, / "from expense"? / Oh from holding, / they're holding in those graces, / they're husban-, husbanding, / they're taking care of, / of "nature's riches from expense," / expenditure. / All I can think of is "The expense of spirit in a waste of shame."

MOVE 4

Elaine READS the next two lines and SELECTs the word *husbands* for attention. She tries to think of a meaning (a WORD) — "to farm?" — and then reconstructs the syntax: while *husband* by itself could mean 'to farm', *husband . . . from expense* could not; it must mean something like "holding in" or "taking care of." She then provides a meaning for *expense*: "expenditure." Having arrived at a paraphrase of line 4, she uses "expense" as the basis of a CONNECT:LITERATURE to the famous sonnet about the expense of spirit. Notice that Elaine performs very few operations on what she selects: she is concerned with the basic meaning of *husbands*, not its overtones (which will be treated in Move 45), and with the basic meaning of *expense* and then with a line it reminds her of. At this point neither operation is pursued any further, though both will be developed later in the reading. This is typical of one type of reader, who goes through the poem and performs one or two operations on what he selects; another type of reader selects a passage and then performs all the operations he can, providing meanings, connecting it with other sections in the poem or with other works, drawing deductions and so forth. The important point is that Elaine is utilizing only a very small subgroup of the possible operations: she could have worried more about why the "bad" people in the first quatrain *inherit heaven's graces*, or she could have wondered what *nature's riches* are.

We can also see here the beginning of another polarity: that between owning or holding and spending, a topic that will occupy much of her time later.

V. OK. "They are the lords and owners of their faces, | Others but stewards of their excellence," / What is, what is "stewards"? / I don't know, exactly.

MOVE 5

A very short move illustrating again the lack of any attempt to be complete or exhaustive in this first progress through the poem. It consists of a READ followed by a question about a WORD and a COMMENT.

VI. "The summer's flow'r is to the summer sweet, | Though to itself it only live and die." / That's so nice. / "Though to itself it only live and die." / Oh, so "The summer's flow'r" has beauty, / gives beauty to the summer, / what's outside of it, / "Though to itself it only live and die." / It's not a rare event. / The flower has, has no awareness. . . .

MOVE 6

This move considers the first two lines of the sestet: they are first READ and then each is SELECTed for attention. After COMMENTing briefly on the second, Elaine returns to the first to try to DEDUCE its implications. The fact that the summer's flower has beauty seems to be only tangentially connected to its sweetness; in fact Elaine seems to have substituted the one for the other because in nature flowers are beautiful as well as sweet (a DEDUCE:WORLD). And although the connection is not made explicitly, this substitution is probably facilitated by the concern with appearance Elaine found in the octave in the relation between *show* and *face*. The internal/external polarity begins to develop here: certainly characterizing the summer as "what's outside of" the flower is strange on the face of it, since everything is outside the flower: only within a schema that expects to find polarities and especially a play between the internal (the flower) and the external (the summer) would such a connection be drawn.

When she returns to the second line, it is to CONNECT it with the WORLD: what is said in the poem about the flower is CONNECTed to what happens in the outside world. Thus the flower's solitary life and death are not rare events in nature (or in literature either, for that matter, though Elaine does not seem to be referring to literature here). Returning to the world of the poem, she DEDUCEs that the flower has no awareness from the fact that it only lives and dies "to itself." In this early stage of comprehension the DEDUCtions are often quite vague — "The flower has no awareness" is as much in need of explication as the line it is supposed to explain.

VII. "To itself it only live and die; | But if that flow'r with base infection meet, | The basest weed outbraves his dignity." / So the flower is fragile. / Probably some sexual, venereal disease / is "meet with base infection." / "The basest weed outbraves his digni- ty." / "Outbraves." / That's nice too.

MOVE 7

The next move considers the following two lines. First Elaine DE- DUCEs from both, apparently, that since the flower is liable to meet with infection and be outbraved by the weed, it is fragile. Then she SELECTs "base infection" and CONNECTs it to the WORLD as a venereal disease. This illustrates again the influence of previous choices and the schemata or frames they implicate: the *base infection* a flower is likely to meet could hardly be venereal, but the context Elaine is constructing (and partly assumes from her knowledge of literature and more particularly, of Shakespearean sonnets) deals with love and sex, and so the kind of dis- ease is specified within that framework.

The obverse side of such a framework becomes apparent in the rest of this move when Elaine SELECTs *outbraves*, a word no longer current, which her knowledge of Renaissance literature should allow her to interpret fairly precisely. But she doesn't; instead she merely COM- MENTs on it, and the same is true when she returns to it (see Moves 14 and 22). Presumably one reason for this is that she cannot fit it into her developing sexual interpretation. As a strange word it has a kind of sa- lience, but it remains essentially outside her interpretation no matter how many times she returns to it.

VIII. "For sweetest things turn sourest by their deeds; | Lilies that fester smell far worse than weeds." / What's strange is that it, / until that, the last couplet, / there's no talk about "deeds." / First quatrain, / the sweetest thing, / it moves others / just as this, as the flower, / in some ways moves the summer, / is sweet to the summer. / They're not doing it, / the person's not doing anything, / so is this a compli- ment? / Terrible language for a compliment, / "base infection," "basest weed." / So it's, is it a compliment saying that he's not doing a-, that, that he's not doing anything, / and his unmoving- ness, / so he's not turning sour. / "Lilies that fester smell far worse than weeds." / "Lilies," / purity, / beauty, / and then that, that image / of festering, / of rotting. / So, you, you rot even if, if you don't move though, that's the thing. / It doesn't matter what you do, you will rot. / "It only live and die," / the flower and, and people too, "only live and die."

MOVE 8

This move completes the first detailed pass through the poem. She READS the couplet and focuses on *deeds*, CONNECTing the mention of *deeds* at the end with each of the specific actions that could be called deeds earlier in the poem. She CONNECTs the *sweetest thing* of the couplet with the *they* of the first quatrain; since *they* move others, the sweetest thing, now identified with the summer's flower, must also move others, and since the only other mentioned with the flower is the summer, it must be the summer that the flower moves. This provides an elaboration for the reading of line 9: in Move 5 *to the summer sweet* was interpreted as giving beauty to the summer; now (in this new framework) it seems to mean "moves the summer." But *they*, the flower, and the sweetest thing are unconscious agents, evoking reactions in others not by their own actions but simply by the way they are. And this becomes a problem in two senses: first, within the poem, the *deeds* in the couplet don't seem to relate back to anything else in the poem, even though the sweetest thing that performs the deeds does seem to relate to other (non) actors.

Second, Elaine isn't sure whether not doing anything can deserve a compliment. This derives from the good-bad polarity first apparent in Move 3: acts and beings are good or bad; good ones deserve compliments, bad ones don't. *They rightly do inherit heaven's graces* suggests the compliment, which is then TESTed and found wanting; the language in the couplet is not what one would expect of a compliment, especially as ILLUSTRATed by *base infection* and *basest weed*. But the possibility remains that by not acting, by not performing anything that could be considered *deeds* in the sense of line 12, *they* avoid meeting with base infection and so festering.

Interestingly, both *sweetest things* and *they* are singularized, perhaps because of their identification with the singular *summer's flower*. But that can hardly be the major reason, since if it were, the plurals in the poem would be expected to make the flower multiple, not vice versa. Instead (as Moves 2 and 59 indicate) the reason for the specificity of reference is that Elaine has already identified this as a "young man" sonnet, and that suggests a particular addressee as both topic and implied audience.

There is also at least a hint (tested in Move 30) of another polarity, this one between movement and stasis. The textual basis of this is *moving others*, but here the sweetness of the summer's flower is redefined as something that moves the summer, and the restraint of the *they* in the octave is defined as unmovingness, the absence of deeds.

After a general discussion of the relation between the couplet and the rest of the poem, Elaine returns to a consideration of the last line, first recalling the standard literary associations of *lilies* (a CONNECT: LITERATURE) — "purity, beauty" — and then defining *festering* as "rotting." Next she DEDUCEs from the final line that festering is a natural and inescapable condition, though whether she deduces this solely from the last line (reading it as "all lilies fester eventually and thus smell worse than weeds") or from her knowledge of the world is not entirely clear. This provides her with a general truth upon which to base most of her following interpretation — "It doesn't matter what you do, you will rot" — and immediately allows her to invest the summer's flower with greater significance. In Move 6 she had expressed her admiration of line 10, but could only interpret it as "the flower has no awareness"; now, however, the flower becomes emblematic of life in general: if everything rots eventually, then "the flower, and people too, only live and die."

In her first detailed reading of the poem, then, Elaine has decided that it is a poem about sexual love, a compliment problematical in its apparently negative language, strangely structured because the first twelve lines describe the avoidance of action and the last two condemn *deeds*. She identifies the world as one in which everything dies (or more forcefully, "rots") whatever it does, and sees this world, perhaps unconsciously, as organized by a series of polarities: good-bad, action-stasis, compliment-insult.

IX.   "They that have pow'r to hurt and will do none," they "do not do the thing they most do show." / So the hurt lies within their faces, / they don't do it?

MOVE 9

In Move 9 she begins through the poem again, seeking further evidence of the action-stasis and good-bad polarities. After READing the first two lines, she proposes two DEDUCEs based on the CONNECT between *faces* and *show* she had made in Move 3: the power to hurt is what *they most do show*, particularly in their faces, but this power is *only* show; they refrain from action, and can thus be located on the stasis side of the action-stasis polarity.

X. "Who, moving others, are themselves as stone." / That doesn't seem to be so great, / "as stone."

MOVE 10

The next move considers only the third line, and in a COMMENT assigns the quality of being *as stone* to the good-bad polarity. She is now supplying specific evidence for her initial impression, expressed in Move 3, that "in the first quatrain, it sounds like that's bad."

XI. "Unmoved, cold, and to temptation slow." / So he does move, / he's just slow. / There's some i-, "Unmoved, cold," "stone," and then in that "temptation s-," "to temptation slow" / there's some kind of um hint at movement.

MOVE 11

The fourth line is read and immediately related to the action-stasis polarity, as Elaine DEDUCEs from *to temptation slow* that he (again the assumption of singularity) "does move, he's just slow," even though this directly contradicts *unmoved* at the beginning of the line. She has already decided (in Move 8) that everybody and everything festers and thus dies, but the couplet seems to relate that festering or souring to specific deeds, so she is eager to find evidence of deeds in the octave that would justify a connection between *they* and *sweetest things*. Here she groups together the terms suggesting stasis — *unmoved, cold, stone* — and opposes to them the one connoting some kind of action — *to temptation slow*. There may be a hint of a progression here: since *to temptation slow* is the final description, it is perhaps the most accurate or comprehensive.

XII. "They," / interesting that he keeps saying 'they,' 'they,' 'they,' / never 'you.' / He's making some kind of generalization; / in many of the other ones he talks about 'you,' or 'thou,' / like "that time of year thou mayest in me," / the "thou" that, "in me" / some kind of interiority um.

MOVE 12

In this move, Elaine seems to READ only the first word of line 5 before she stops to offer the GENERALIZation that the subjects in the octave are third person and plural rather than second person singular, and to DEDUCE from that that Shakespeare is generalizing in the poem. This is contrasted (a CONNECT:LITERATURE) with his practice in other sonnets, in which the singulars and the first and second person pronouns suggest to her "some kind of interiority"; that is, some discussion of the emotions of the participants in a specific situation rather than a general characterization of a set of people. This "interiority" could be contrasted to the "exteriority" of *faces* and *show*, but Elaine doesn't make the connection explicit. However, it is related to her frequent substitution of *he* for *they*: in Move 50, she will suggest that the poem is really addressed to a single person, and thus presumably could be in the second person singular instead of the third plural.

XIII.   The only things in here I, I know are typical   /   are the, the imagery   /   of commerce and business and money,   /   "lords," "owners," um "expense."   /   I always felt stupid about Shakespeare sonnets though.   /   "None," "stone," "show," "slow," "graces," "faces," "expense," "excellence," "sweet," "meet," "die," "dignity," "deeds," "weeds."

MOVE 13

The reference to Shakespeare's other sonnets, and especially to what they have in common, leads her to CONNECT this sonnet with what she knows of Shakespeare. First typical imagery is noted (in a CONNECT: FIGURE, a DEDUCE, and an ILLUSTRATE), and then the rhyme scheme is checked (PHONOLOGY); sandwiched between is a repetition of her initial COMMENT that she is no good at Shakespeare sonnets, perhaps suggesting that this sonnet does in fact have more in common with the others than she can see.

XIV.   Well that "deeds," "weeds," that rhyme,   /   that's weird   /   because it ends with "weeds,"   /   "weeds" proliferate.   /   This is too, this isn't one of the, the marriage, the, the urging the young man to marry, poems   /   I don't think.   /   It's too late,   /   I think;   /   those are the earlier poems, beginning of the sequence.   /   But it's the weeds that proliferate and grow,   /   not the lilies.   /   Lilies fester and the weeds live.   /   Ah, maybe it's not a compliment,   /   maybe this is a tremendous insult.   /   Huh. . . . Because the person lives and dies,   /   why would "base infection" come in,   /   if, if you take "base infection" as some kind of sexual contact,   /   "But if that flow'r with base infection meet, | The basest weed outbraves his dignity." / "Outbraves," / well that's, that's a complimentary verb, / "his dignity," / um. So that the, the flower can't, it's a pure thing, / I guess, / can't sustain any contact with the "base infection."

MOVE 14

In this move the utility of formal analysis of the poem becomes apparent. Checking the rhyme scheme (in Move 13) revealed that the final rhyme is *deeds-weeds*, and this rhyme is SELECTed for extended treatment in this move. *Weeds* is the last word in the poem, a position of possible importance, and Elaine CONNECTs this conclusion to the real-world fact that "weeds proliferate." "Proliferate," especially in the context of sexual relationships she has constructed for the poem, leads obviously to the idea of reproduction and thus to a reconsideration of whether this poem is one of the group "urging the young man to marry" and reproduce. Again this idea is TESTed (as it was in Move 2) and rejected on the basis of her knowledge of the sonnet sequence.

She then returns to the main theme: weeds proliferate (in the world if not in the poem) while lilies fester: relating this to her earlier (Move 8) scheme that the lilies rot and die, she expresses this contrast between the lilies and the weeds as the lilies festering while the weeds live. And this newly found contrast between what lives — the weeds — and what festers and dies — *they, the summer's flower, sweetest things*, and *lilies* — suggests that the poem is not a compliment at all (see Move 8) but rather an insult.

Two observations are important here. First, notice how much of this is not actually "in" the poem, but is rather contributed by Elaine; in particular the poem says nothing about whether *all* lilies fester and die, or whether weeds proliferate and thus live. Second, the reliance on binary classes, which I have been calling polarities, pressures the translation from differences (lilies are different from weeds) to oppositions (lilies fester and die; weeds live.) This is most obvious, of course, in the opposition between compliment and insult: once Elaine has hit upon the idea that the poem could be a compliment, the only other possibility is defined — it could also be an insult. But it could not be neither.

Having suggested the possibility of an insult, she returns to the poem to TEST it, first recalling the action/stasis polarity: if the person (a singular again) only "lives and dies" — i.e., stays to himself like the flower, performing no deeds — how could he meet base infection? In Move 7, the *base infection* was interpreted as venereal disease; here, in a modification that will resonate throughout the rest of her reading, the cause is substituted for the result, and attention is shifted from a specific disease to sexuality in general. Further evidence against the possibility of an insult is provided by two words that are "complimentary" — *outbraves* and *dignity*. Elaine seems not to notice that it is the *weed* that *outbraves* the flower's *dignity*, so the poem could still be an insult to the flower.

Finally, the flower (like the lily in Move 8) is "a pure thing" (which sounds complimentary rather than insulting), unable to sustain contact with the base infection of sexuality.

XV. "They that have pow'r to," "to *do* hurt," / I always thought it was "They that have pow'r to hurt." / "They that have pow'r" — / God, I've been reading it wrong all this time. / "They that have pow'r to do hurt and will do none." / That's a mistake. / Where's my Shakespeare? / I think this is a, I'm going to look this up in the Norton and see if that first line is right or if I can [sound of pages turning] / well, I think this is in the Norton, maybe not. . . . Can't find. / I think they have sonnets in here. Rome, oh sixteenth-century lyrics, I wonder if Shakespeare comes in that . . . Sidney. Ok Shakespeare, s-, ninety-four, yup. / No it's different in ninety-four. / I knew, oh I wasn't, / well maybe that's the edition. Yeah / They give the first line as "They that have pow'r to hurt." / Let me see if anything else if diff-. / "They that have pow'r to hurt and will do none, | That do not do the thing they most do show." / That's the same. / "Who, moving others, are themselves as stone, | Unmoved, cold, and to temptation slow." / Punctuation's the same. / //read ll. 5–14 with "uhuh" after l. 12// / . . . Huh. I, I don't think it makes much difference, / I mean the meaning. / It sounds, it just didn't sound right. / But maybe, I don't know, maybe this is taken from a different, I don't know, I wonder what the manuscripts of this are. / It's beside the point.

MOVE 15

Elaine begins a third pass through the poem but is quickly sidetracked when she notices that the first line in the text she has been given reads "They that have power to do hurt and will do none." It is a minor illustration of the effect of the expectations one brings to the poem that she has read this line three times ignoring the errant *do* before she actually notices it on the fourth. She checks the version she's been given with the printed version in *The Norton Anthology*, and then compares the two texts of the entire poem. Then she in a sense TESTs and QUALIFies her entire procedure, concluding that the extra *do* doesn't make much difference to the meaning, and that perhaps another manuscript is involved. She cuts short this line of inquiry by deciding that it is "beside the point" and returns to the poem, omitting the extra *do* from now on. In Move 43, however, she returns to this textual problem and tries to relate it to her interpretation.

XVI. //read ll. 1–5 omitting "do" in 1. 1 and with 1. 2: They do not do the thing they most do show.// / In a way that's sarcastic.

MOVE 16

She now resumes her third pass through the poem, READing the first five lines. By this time she has developed the idea of the insult and linked that with sexual contact and venereal disease, and these themes will become increasingly apparent. In this move, she attempts to mitigate the apparently positive (or complimentary) content of the first five lines by calling them sarcastic, a label for which she provides no justification. But the reason is relatively clear: if the poem is basically an insult, the object of the insult — the people the poem discusses — must somehow deserve it, and so what initially seem to be laudable qualities must be revealed as somehow blameworthy. The precise reasons why they are blameworthy are less important (in an interpretation) than asserting that they are.

XVII. "And husband nature's riches from expense." / Well "expense" / also has some sexual meaning / as in "The expense of spirit in a waste of shame." / So he's hol–, oh, y–, n–, that's, that's what that Wallace Stevens poem, / "so retentive," which one oh, "The One of Fictive Music" — "so retentive of themselves" / and then the holding, holding himself in, / that maybe that is sarcastic, I,

MOVE 17

The next line is the subject of the next move. *Expense* is SELECTed and its sexual connotations illuminated by comparison with sonnet 129. Once the sexual connotation of *expense* has been established, Elaine apparently equates the *expense of spirit* with the *expense of nature's riches,* and the earlier reading of husbanding as "taking care of" (Move 4) is replaced by "holding himself in" (here the textual plural has become not only singular but also masculine, as in sonnet 129). This translation, bolstered by reference to Stevens's "To the One of Fictive Music," (another CONNECT:LITERATURE) provides additional evidence for seeing the octave as sarcastic: husbanding nature's riches may be unnatural and thus blameworthy.

XVIII. "They rightly," / if it's ri−, there's that "rightly" there, / "do inherit heaven's graces / And" husbands, "And husband nature's riches from expense." / He's holding himself back, / holding himself in, / both sexually / and um, I don't know, metaphorically, um. / He's not giving of himself. / "Husband nature's riches from expense." / But you can't do that, / I, to, to holding yourself in, that's that's unnatural, / it's not right, / but then compared to a flower which is natural, um.

MOVE 18

This move overlaps the preceding one: in Move 16 Elaine had READ the first five lines; in Move 17 she SELECTed line six; here she SELECTs lines five and six for more extended consideration. The suggestion in the previous move of retentiveness is developed into two polarities: retention vs. spending and what is natural vs. what is unnatural. She elaborates "the holding himself in" to "He's holding himself back, holding himself in, both sexually and — I don't know — metaphorically. He's not giving of himself." With the possibility of further development apparent in "metaphorically," this retention is clearly unnatural, in terms of both Elaine's view of the world and her knowledge of the "young man" sonnets.

The opposite extreme of this polarity presents itself in the flower, which, since she had already linked it with the *they* in Move 8, prevents any simple application of the natural/unnatural polarity to the poem. Similarly, *rightly,* which she notices at the beginning of this Move, prevents her from seeing the octave as completely sarcastic.

XIX. "They are the lords and owners of their faces, | Others but stewards of their excellence." / "Stewards," / what does a steward on a ship do, / that, someone, oh I guess steward like a

stewardess, / a helper? / Huh, oh yeah I can't keep, I can't be-
lieve I can't think of exactly what "steward" means, / But a−, uh, it
seems to mean that um they're in possession of themselves, / self-
possession, / that, that that's oh, p−, possession, / the idea of
owning, / that has to do with "expense." / "Stewards of their ex-
cellence." / They're outside, the "stewards" / obviously.

MOVE 19

The last two lines of the octave are READ and "stewards" is again
SELECTed for consideration (cf. Move 5). Elaine still can't remember
what it means, which she finds embarrassing, and tries to deduce a
meaning from the stewards active today — stewards on ships, stew-
ardesses on airplaines. The most specific she can get is "helper." She
then returns to line 7, and again the precise meaning of the line is unim-
portant since the stewards/owners can be fitted into the scheme she is
constructing: the *lords and owners of their faces* are those who are in "pos-
session of themselves," in however vague a sense; they are *owners*, those
who *own*. And since owning is CONNECTed to *expense* by being antony-
mous, the self-possession associated with it can presumably be related to
retention. The stewards still aren't explicitly linked to this; they are
vaguely relegated to an external position on the internal/external polarity
(see Move 6) and abandoned, though there may be a hint (undeveloped)
that since the lords and owners are the possessors, the retainers, and
thus the unnatural ones, the stewards are in some sense spenders, natu-
ral like the flower.

XX. "The summer's flow'r is to the summer sweet, | Though to
itself it only live and die." / Oh so there, there, that might, there
might be some kind of implicit or even explicit reproach in that /
because he's retaining himself, / he's only living and dying
/ within himself. / This is *like* those, those early poems,
/ sort of, / the one where he, the ones where he urges the young
man to marry so that he will be perpetuated. / There's no talk of
perpetuation in this poem, / not in the poetry, at all, / they, how
he lives in his lines / that you have in some of the other poems.

MOVE 20

This move considers the first two lines of the sestet. The *summer's
flower,* which previously had "no awareness" (Move 6) and so gave its

beauty unselfconsciously to the summer, is now related to the natural/ unnatural scheme. As a natural object to which the *they* of the octave are compared (see Move 18), it seems to prevent full identification of *they* as both unnatural and retentive. But if the flower can be shown to be retentive and thus unnatural the comparison will fit nicely. Thus Elaine no longer sees line ten as expressing an event that is not rare (Move 6); instead it becomes a condemnation — implicit or explicit — of retentiveness because the flower only lives and dies "within himself." The fact that the flower gives its sweetness and beauty to the summer (Move 6) is no longer relevant, superseded by the implications of identifying the flower as "he" instead of "it."

Elaine then CONNECTs this poem again to the earlier sonnets urging the young man to marry. The flower, living and dying to itself, is like the young man in those sonnets, but this poem differs from those because there is no overt discussion of perpetuation, especially through the vivifying power of poetry. This does not diminish the utility of the comparison, however, for its main function is to provide further evidence for the natural/unnatural, spending/retaining schema by reasserting that Shakespeare does treat such concerns in other poems.

XXI.   What you're left with in the poem is "weeds." /   I mean you could think of, of the weeds outlasting everything el−, outlasting all cultivation, /   the "base" things, /   the "weeds," /   but the "weeds" are also natural, /   I mean they're part of nature too. /   They're not as beautiful, um. /   I wonder if "Lilies," were mainly cultiva−, /   well no, lilies grow wild, /   tiger lilies. /   But I wonder if lilies were cultivated flowers then also. /   But in any event the lily is, is fragile.

MOVE 21

The next move skips over the eleventh line to reconsider the ramifications of ending the poem with *weeds* (first noticed in Move 14). The textual position of the word *weeds* becomes first a fact of reading — "what you're left with in the poem is weeds" — and then a physical characteristic: weeds endure, "outlasting all cultivation" even though they are base. To mitigate the criticism inherent in *base* and *basest*, Elaine tries to identify the weeds as natural, while the lilies become cultivated hothouse plants and thus unnatural. If this identification worked it would strengthen the natural/unnatural reading immensely, since the flower and lily would only seem to be natural; actually, their retentiveness and cultivation would contrast with the natural, uncultivated — but perpetuated — weeds. Unfortunately, it doesn't: Elaine calls upon her world knowledge for an example of a lily (the tiger lily) that grows wild and so cannot be unnatural. Still the point can be partially maintained if *some* lilies were cultivated, and Elaine settles for that possibility.

Her final comment is both a DEDUCE and a CONNECT with the flower, which had been identified as fragile in Move 7. In her attempt to relate all aspects of the poem to the natural/unnatural scheme, Elaine abandons her earlier associations with lilies — "purity, beauty" (Move 8) — and instead concentrates on how they differ from the natural weeds.

XXII. "The basest weed outbraves," / see, that, I mean the, the weed is the one who's winning in this, / I mean winning both physically / in that it outlasts the flower / but also "outbraves," / the lil — , the weed takes over whatever the, the flower had / because uh h — , he's outbraving it, "his dignity."

MOVE 22

This expands upon the preceding move to consider line twelve. Again the weed is seen to be superior to the lily and the flower, not only physically, "in that it outlasts the flower," but also more abstractly, because the weed *outbraves* the lily. Elaine never finds a very good meaning for this word — strange in view of her Renaissance background — and so settles for "the weed takes over whatever the flower had." Had she looked the word up, she could have related it to the concern with appearance she found earlier in the poem. But at this point, such a precise definition is not necessary: as earlier with *stewards* (Move 19), a rough-and-ready characterization of the word that locates it within the basic polarities she has set up is all that's required.

Here also is the first hint of one consequence of her tendency to see polarities: contrasts becomes conflicts. In Move 14, the weeds and lilies were merely juxtaposed ("lilies fester and the weeds live"), but here they are in open conflict, and the weed is "winning." Although the first line suggests some sort of potential confrontation, Elaine does not discuss this until after the lily and weed become antagonists; only then does she create two clearly opposing parties in the first lines (Move 25). This suggests that the conflicts she sees in the poem are determined at least as much by her own predispositions as by the words on the page.

XXIII. "For sweetest things turn sourest by their deeds." / Well, a deed / can be a not doing something, also. / "Sweetest things turn sourest by their deeds." / I wonder if, if the deed lies in, in not doing it.   /   I guess I can't believe that, that Shakespeare in the son-nets would talk about how holding oneself in is a good thing,   /   that, that this poem is a compliment,   /   'cause it goes against my whole sense of what, of the poet's attitudes in the poems.   /   I mean he just, th−, a−, a little, as poorly as I know them,   /   it just seems as though he would never um counsel holding yourself in like that,   /   the, the "rightly do inherit heaven's graces."   /   I can't see, I guess I jumped immediately to thinking,   /   or readily concluded by thinking   /   that was sarcastic,   /   because my whole sense of the Shake-speare,   /   I−E−he−I came up with, the famous one "The ex-pense of spirit,"   /   he recoils against his own lust   /   and yet he in the end seems to say well uh it's natural,   /   I will do it again.   /   "Shun the heaven that leads men to this hell,"   /   it's not that he's not going to do it again.   /   He recognizes it   /   but he rec-ognizes it as a fact of human experience.   /   O−, maybe I'm twisting this thing around   /   but I wonder if there's any kind of allusion in "inherit heaven's graces,"   /   I mean if there's some kind of allusion to something else.   /   Kind of has that sound.

MOVE 23

The next move, considering the thirteenth line, returns to confront at greater length the problem (originally raised in Move 8) that the refer-ence to *deeds* in the final couplet seems to conflict with the lack of action earlier in the sonnet. By now, however, not doing anything has been redefined as doing something, as being retentive: holding oneself in is an action that "you can't [or shouldn't] *do*" (Move 18). This implicit redefinition becomes explicit here: "a deed can be a not doing some-thing also," and if this is true, the deed that leads to souring could be a refraining from action.

This line of reasoning is bolstered by Elaine's sense of Shakespeare's attitudes in the other sonnets, presumably in the early sonnets she has already mentioned (Move 20) and in 129. "Holding oneself in" is no longer a hypothesis about what the poem suggests; it is by now part of the poem she has internalized, and so the question she confronts now is not whether the poem is in fact about retentiveness, but whether Shake-speare could be complimenting such an activity. This question is ex-plicitly related to the natural/unnatural and good/bad polarities in her interpretation of sonnet 129, where lust can be seen as both bad — something to recoil from — and natural — something that will be re-peated. What is natural is not necessarily what is good. A curious sidelight here, of course, is that by making Shakespeare himself the speaker in 129, Elaine has him expressing an attitude directly opposed to the unnatural retentiveness she finds in this poem. Somebody who read 129 as a condemnation of lust rather than as an apology for a kind of natural and uncontrollable human licentiousness would obviously relate the two poems quite differently.

This conception of Shakespeare's attitudes forms the basis for interpreting line five. Elaine now sees the line as sarcastic, forgetting that earlier (Moves 3, 7, 18) *rightly*, not taken sarcastically, had counted as evidence against her interpretation. If it is sarcastic, then Shakespeare's viewpoint in this poem accords with his views elsewhere. But there is an alternative hinted at in her final comments: since *heaven* in sonnet 129 is used metaphorically, perhaps *inherit heaven's graces* in this poem is similarly metaphorical or allusive. If, for instance, *heaven's graces* referred to the physical characteristics that lead to sexual attraction (as *heaven* in 129 refers to sexual pleasure), then *rightly* would not have to be sarcastic, since the line wouldn't be so clearly a compliment.

XXIV. Every word is loaded, / typically. / "Husband," / I mean uh he's holding in "nature's riches from expense," / from being let out. / The thing about "nature's riches" / is that as you spend them you don't, as you let them out you don't use them up, / they're not used up, / they're, well maybe, maybe the, but he's saying that you can't just to yourself "live and die." / I mean he's saying you can / but if you do, you rot, / "fester." / The lily that festers, / I don't think is festering because it meets, *only* because it meets with "base infection" / but also because of nature, / it only lives and dies, / it, it dies at the end of the summer, / the weeds outlast the summer. / Summer can also be a time of life, / a time in one's life.

MOVE 24

Move 23 leads directly into Move 24, as the final topic mentioned in it—the possibility of an allusion in *inherit heaven's graces*—is generalized to the topic of 24—the fact that every word is loaded, or alludes to more than it seems to say. (*Typically* again relates this reading to Elaine's experience with Shakespeare's other sonnets). *Husband* has already been redefined—at first it was "holding in" in the laudable sense of "taking care of" (Move 4), but then the negative implications of "holding himself in, both sexually and metaphorically" (Move 18) in an unnatural way became more important. Here "he" is holding not only himself in, but also *nature's riches,* almost as if he is a jailer: *from expense* is translated "from being let out." *Nature's riches,* which before seemed to refer to the good qualities of *they* (Move 4, 18) are now more generally interpreted to suggest nature in general, so "he" becomes doubly unnatural in remaining aloof from his own natural functions and in holding nature's riches hostage. And this is especially unnatural because it serves no purpose: in Elaine's view, *nature's riches* are not used up, so there is no reason to try to save or preserve them.

She would like to elaborate on this insight but is unable to specify further what happens to *nature's riches,* so she returns to the question of personal retentiveness. (By now *they, the summer's flower, sweetest things,* and *lilies* are all seen as different ways of referring to the particular subject of the poem, "he.") The *summer's flower* was earlier applauded for giving beauty to the summer (Move 6) and was seen as part of the natural world where flowers and people die whatever they do (Move 8); then it became the object of implicit or explicit reproach because it is "retaining" itself (Move 10). But here this kind of self-retention leads specifically to festering and rotting: as retention is perceived as more clearly unnatural, so are its results. The connection between death and rotting had been suggested before (Move 8); the difference here is that Elaine begins to apply this lesson to the lily as well as to the "he" and the flower. But then she realizes that *deeds* and *base infection* are too closely associated with the lily's festering to ignore, and she revises her statement: the lily doesn't fester "*only* because it meets with 'base infection,' but also because of nature."

At this point, Elaine begins to push her interpretation too far, not beyond the bounds of credibility (which are notoriously hard to define in the realm of interpretation anyway), but beyond what is useful to her. If everything dies because of nature, then what anything does before death presumably doesn't matter very much. She tries to avoid this conclusion by bringing in the factitious bit of world knowledge that weeds outlast summer while flowers don't, but that leads nowhere. She tries to associate the seasons of the year with the stages of human life (a typical comparison, derived perhaps from sonnet 73 or Keats's "To Autumn"; see Move 47), but that also leads nowhere, and so she abandons this particular line of inquiry.

By this time, her basic reading of the poem is in place. She will proceed to elaborate on it, and on the second day even to provide an altogether different interpretation to compare with it, but she will not modify it greatly.

XXV. I can't remember at all what we did in class when we did this poem when I was in college, / but that was, uh I mean I probably wasn't listening. / But I can, I can see why it's difficult, / I don't see why it's so, oh I guess maybe the, the, the critical problem of this poem that, that the, the teacher talked about was, was that in that first quatrain it sounds bad / and then the "They rightly," and then he talks about "excellence" — / although in that there does seem to be something negative, / the husbanding "nature's riches from expense." / So the first quatrain is negative towards that um / — well first that sounds nice, / you know, that you have the "pow'r to hurt and will do none," / who "do not do the thing," "That do not do the thing they most do show." / But then the "stone," "moving others are the —," / there's one who's moved and the other one who inspires the person's being moved. / Who's unyielding, / that's not good, / "Unmoved, cold, and to temptation," / all right "temptation" / usually is a bad word, / not a bad, a bir—, a word with negative connotations, / especially in literature, of the, of this period, / but, but temptation is also natural.

Move 25

By the end of the twenty-fourth move, the reading based on the natural/unnatural polarity had been pushed as far as it could be, at least for the time being. In this move, Elaine returns to the good/bad or positive/negative polarity she abandoned in Move 7. But first, as a kind of break, she tries to recall what she had done with the poem in college. As explained in Move 1, the poem was presented then as incomprehensible; now it seems to her merely difficult and she wishes she could remember what made it supposedly impossible to understand.

Her guess about the basic critical problem is based on the positive/negative polarity: positive and negative elements seems to be mingled so intimately that it is difficult to derive a simple single position for the entire poem. The first quatrain still sounds negative (see Move 9), but that seems to be contradicted in the second quatrain by *rightly*, which she has already noticed (Move 18) and *excellence*, which she has been prevented from treating by questions about the meaning of *stewards* (see Moves 5, 19). Upon close inspection, however, both quatrains prove to be ambivalent: the second because of the unnatural aspects of husbanding nature's riches discussed in Moves 17 and 24, the first because the negative qualities seem to be offset by the laudable restraint in the first two lines.

Being *as stone* has already been commented on (Move 10); now *moving others* while being *unmoved* oneself is translated into "unyielding," a clearly negative characteristic, and a new character—the one who is moved—is introduced. This is presumably in preparation for the discussion of control below (see Moves 28 and 30): just as the *they* has been particularized into a *he* in her reading, the *others* become singular and specific.

Temptation has—curiously enough—escaped attention until now, even in the discussion of the relation between this poem and sonnet 129. When it is treated here it is immediately located on the positive/negative scale, and then located also on the natural/unnatural scale. Her treatment of *temptation* is similar to the earlier discussion of "lust" (Move 23): both are clearly negative, and yet both are in some sense natural. This, of course, is the crux of her problem, since what seems to her negative in the poem also seems somehow natural, and what seems good is unnatural. And it is a sign of how much this central problem constrains her developing interpretation that she stops reading here before reaching *slow*, which qualifies within the poem whatever negative overtones *temptation* by itself might have.

XXVI. "They rightly do inherit heaven's graces, | And husbands nas–, husband nature's riches from expense." / It's selfishness, / it's, it's holding yourself in, / there's, oh, there's that person in *The Faerie Queene* / Marinell, / hoards things, who hoards, / Book Three, Four, the Book maybe, / he hoards, / he lives in the sea and he hoards all the treasures from the ships, / but he also holds himself in / and he won't love either, / and he's hurt because of that, / of course he, later does, he does yield, / but he, he's compared to a stone also, / his rocky heart. / And "temptation" / is an ambiguous word in there, / a–, because it's, "temptation" is, is bad, / I mean you think of Adam and Eve, / but it's natural, / it's human to be tempted.

MOVE 26

Move 26 begins to consider the second quatrain, but gets no further than the second line before the retentiveness which had previously been "something negative" (Move 25), unnecessary in nature and thus unnatural (Move 24), is redefined as selfishness, making it both more personal and more culpable. This immediately reminds her of Marinell in Book III of *The Faerie Queene*, though the relation—in fact, not in her memory — is rather tenuous. Marinell does hoard things; but they are the gift of Nereus, his grandfather, who makes all the sea's treasures available to him. And the hurt he encounters had been foretold years before by Proteus, who warned that "A virgin strange and stout him should dismay, or kill" (III, iv. 25). Marinell's mother, Cymoent, assumes this means in love, and so keeps him from woman, but Britomart fells him in battle. This misremembering is precisely what we should expect: just as elements in the poem are being fitted into a schema that Elaine is constructing, so the works she cites will be modified to support the same schema. The purpose of this literary reference is to increase the probability of her reading by showing that other poems treat the same problem she finds in this poem in roughly the way she sees it being treated here, and accuracy of recall is less important than the fact of it.

After the brief excursus on Marinell, she returns to the consideration of *temptation* to stress its ambiguity: now there is a specific literary example of its negative connotations — Adam and Eve — but its naturalness is also reasserted. This reference, which prepares for the distinction in Move 29 between what is theoretically good and what is natural or human, again illustrates how particularizing abstract qualities in human characters seems to help Elaine draw her conclusions.

XXVII. "They rightly do inherit heaven's graces." / That's the problem, / because they, th-, eh, it can't really be, I mean he can't say outright, / well that's sarcastic. / "They rightly do inherit heaven's graces | And husband nature's riches from expense."

MOVE 27

This brief move returns to the first two lines of the second quatrain and basically repeats what has been said before: *rightly* must be sarcastic (see Move 23), because to take it otherwise would go against her whole conception of Shakespeare.

XXVIII. The "lords," / in that they control it, / the "owners," / well that's control too, to own. / So there again, the "lords," "owners," / that, that's control / like the control of n-, not doing "the thing they most do show." / But the thing you show is external, / so, and it's an internal problem, / being moved i-, is an internal thing.

MOVE 28

This moves on to the seventh and eighth lines and introduces overtly the idea of control. Earlier (Move 19) she had discussed these lines in terms of possession, contrasting that to *expense*. Now the *lords* and *owners* both control "it," apparently whatever *their faces* refers to, though "it" is perhaps related to her mind to *heaven's graces* and *nature's riches*, especially the latter, since if they *husband*—i.e., hoard—*nature's riches* they control them. The idea of control (a GENERALIZE) is extended to the first quatrain: not doing the thing they most do show is another kind of control, and presumably so is moving others, especially if *others* is particularized to a single exemplar (see Move 26).

The interior/exterior polarity returns (see Moves 6, 12, and 19), even though its relevance is not very apparent here. She suggests that while external qualities can be controlled, interior emotions cannot be. Thus the one who controls his exterior is again unnatural, though in a slightly different sense, while the *others* who are *moved* are more natural.

XXIX. "The summer's flow'r is to the summer sweet." / I can't help see it, but see this as a kind of reproach, / and at the end / it's almost like a k-, terrible curse. / "For sweetest things turn sourest by their deeds." / First, it's, well "deeds," / "deeds" can be the meeting with "base infection" / that, that, that kills the flower, / but then even the word "base" / is turned into something um positive / or at least natural. / Oh so maybe this is, the b-, "The basest weed," / but maybe this is a um poem abou-, ho-, the difference between what's theoretically good, / "rightly do inherit heaven's graces" / and what is natural, / what is human, / and how it's sort of unnatural and inhuman not to be moved. /

MOVE 29

This move seems to consider the entire sestet: only the first line is READ at the beginning, but the DEDUCE immediately following refers more to the rest of the sestet than to its first line, and the thirteenth line is read as an ILLUSTRATion of the curse. The earlier DEDUCtions that the poem is an insult rather than a compliment (Move 14) and that these lines are a reproach are here sharpened: the sestet as a whole is a kind of reproach, which develops into a curse in the couplet. *Deeds* remains a problem (see Moves 23 and 8); here it is identified more specifically with the meeting with *base infection* rather than with actions or their absence in the octave. But since Elaine sees the poem in terms of polarities, that confers a kind of naturalness or goodness on the *base in-fection*: if the flower dies, it must be bad or at least unnatural (the paragon of nature is what lives forever — the weeds); therefore what opposes it must be good or natural.

But this positive interpretation of *base* is a strange one even to Elaine, and she tries to avoid it by disassociating the positive/negative and natural/unnatural scales. Until now, what was natural was good, and what was unnatural was bad. But if something can be good but unnatural — only *theoretically* good — then the weed can be both natural and *base* (or *theoretically* bad). Projected back into the rest of the poem, this allows *rightly*, which had to be seen as sarcastic (because it referred to unnatural acts but was itself positive), to be redefined as *theoretically* good and still unnatural.

This is a brilliant solution to the problem that has been plaguing her interpretation, and it opens a wide range of possibilities because it replaces the earlier single polarity (good and natural vs. bad and unnatural) with four possibilities: something can be good and natural, good and unnatural, bad and natural, or bad and unnatural. Thus such words or ideas as *temptation* and *base*, which were difficult to locate on a single scale, can be accommodated: they are bad but natural. And by adding *theoretically*, she can avoid calling anything overtly bad: what seems to be good (e.g., inheriting *heaven's riches*) becomes *theoretically good*, while what seems bad (temptation, baseness) becomes natural. In this way she can harmonize her own ideas, her conception of Shakespeare's general attitudes, and what the poem seems to be saying.

XXX. What's, interior, / i-, it seems as though the person being acted upon, the person who's moved, the person, that's an interior kind of movement / and a-, uh, of feelings, / emotions, / and o-, of the f-, of the one who has the power to do the hurt, / does he, does he have any interior, / except for the "Unmoved," / is there anything about his interior mo-, feelings or movements. / "Husband nature's riches," "owners of their faces," / again external. / "Stewards of their excellence,"

MOVE 30

This new insight is immediately related to the interior/exterior polarity, though it seems that Elaine still identifies the interior/exterior scale with the natural/unnatural one. The person who is theoretically good — good but unnatural — seems to be described primarily in terms of external characteristics, while the one who is moved is described internally. Since the movement is of feelings and emotions, it is natural and human (i.e., "good" as opposed to "theoretically good"). She immediately TESTs this, for her neat scheme would be ruined if the unmoved mover had any "interior feelings or movements." Fortunately, the direct descriptions of him are all external.

XXXI. "summer's flow'r is to the s-," / "Though to itself" — / well that can mean, "Though to itself," I mean as far as it knows, / not that it knows, / but also, O-, oh, "to itself," / holding itself in, / "to itself," / um, left to itself, / and so when it left, when it's left to itself it only lives and dies, / and when it's not left to itself, / when it meets "base infection," / it dies too.

MOVE 31

This move is a continuation of the previous one: as Elaine looks for evidence of internal characteristics of the character described, she comes to the phrase *though to itself*, which had intrigued her before (Move 6) and now seems to be related to the question of interiority. But the question is sidestepped: where the phrase was previously thought to mean "the flower has no awareness," referring to an internal characteristic, it now becomes "as far as it knows" and then the idea of unnatural retentiveness returns. A third possibility is introduced here for the first time, though it had been hinted at before (Move 24, discussing the lily): *to itself* could mean "left to itself." This corroborates her feeling that the lily is doomed by nature even if it avoids contamination; the flower dies "when it's left to itself" just as surely as when it meets *base infection*. It is interesting to note in passing that a polarity suggested by the poem — *live and die* — provides her with a way of organizing *fester* and *outbrave*: whatever their precise meanings, they can be generally associated with death and thus opposed to life. The flower dies — is outbraved — if it meets *base infection*; the lily dies — *festers* — by its deeds.

XXXII. "Weeds" just, the word "weeds" / sort of reminds me of graves unkept, / uncared for, / anything uncared for, full of "weeds," / not outside, / I mean i-, any kind of cultivated place, / anyway, not, not necessarily unkept if it's, / if it's natural that the weeds win in nature. / Weeds win even in cultivated gardens, / O-, or if they don't win it's by a lot of human effort.

MOVE 32

The last word, *weeds*, is SELECTed for treatment in this move. Elaine had previously noted the importance of the final word — "It's the weeds that proliferate and grow, not the lilies" (Move 14) — and it had prompted her to consider the poem an insult rather than a compliment. Now she returns to it to consider her associations with it, just as she had earlier elicited her associations to *lilies* (Move 8). All of her associations (a series of CONNECT:WORLDs) could be related to her reading, but she never overtly does this. "Graves unkept" recalls the life/death polarity and the flower and lily that die no matter what they do. The distinction between cultivation and the unkept, uncared-for appearance of the weeds could be related specifically to *husbanding nature's riches* and more generally to the idea of control (Move 28) and the external/internal polarity. Toward the end of the move these general connections become more specific: weeds naturally win in nature and even in gardens unless "a lot of human effort" defeats them. This suggests that even though aloofness and retentiveness may prevent meeting *base infection*, such inaction will not guarantee final victory over the weeds: they must be actively combatted. Elaine never draws these conclusions, probably because she is beginning to feel frustrated by the poem.

XXXIII.   //read ll. 1 – 4// / What is the sentence here, / the first sentence ends with "excellence," / well punctuation, / you know, this is really conjectural, / I mean this is probably not the punctuation of the printed edition of the sonnets, / but even that, I mean, it's probably not Shakespeare's punctuation. / Ok, so the first full stop / comes in the eighth line, / and then, if that colon there is right, / then the next full stop / is at the end, / so it's after six lines. / There is a break between the first quatrain and the second, / but jus-, it's just a semicolon. / So the first unit is those first four lines / and the second unit next two lines, / and the next unit — hum, there's not really there that the semicolon after "die" — / next four lines / then the couplet. / //read ll. 1 – 4// / I feel stuck on this.

MOVE 33

In this move Elaine begins through the poem again — her sixth time — but quickly turns to form rather than content. Judging from the practice of other readers (see next chapter), this is a sign that she is stuck: readers usually look at the form either immediately or only when they can think of nothing else to do, when they hope that some formal element or some relation between form and meaning will provide new material. Indeed, Elaine noticed just such a relation in Move 14, where the fact that the final word of the poem (and thus the last rhyme) was *weeds* was given special emphasis. This time through she examines the relation between syntax and the formal sonnet structure, qualifying in advance whatever untoward results might occur by pointing out that the punctuation is probably not authorial. The fact that the syntax and formal structure seem to be consonant — one sentence for the octave, one for the sestet — suggests nothing new, nor does breaking the sentences down into units separated by colons and semicolons. She starts to read the poem again, admits she is stuck, and gives up.

By the time she stops at the end of Move 33, Elaine has been working on the poem for almost half an hour. She has read through it half a dozen times, related it to other poems by Shakespeare, Stevens, and Spenser, and considered both its form and its content. The form is what she expects from a Shakespearean sonnet; the content is organized in terms of a number of polarities, so that the poem becomes a discussion of what is good or bad, natural or unnatural, internal or external, controlling or controlled, and alive or dead. She assumes that the poem expresses an attitude toward a situation that can be located among these polarities, and that since it is a sonnet it is probably fairly personal; whatever the syntax, individuals rather than groups are being discussed. While it would be possible to find literary exemplars for most of the distinctions she makes (Malvolio and Sir Toby adumbrate the theoretically good/ natural distinction, for instance), she tends not to cite them. Also, as will become clear in what she says when she returns to the poem, her initial assumption — that the *hurt* referred to is sexual — leads more or less directly the rest of her reading, for if the *hurt* were simply physical injury, the first stanza would seem much less negative, there would be no problem with the people inheriting *heaven's graces*, and so forth. In fact, this is the realization she comes to during the day she takes off before taping again.

Throughout her reading there is an alternation between close attention to the language of the poem and recollection of information from outside the poem — whether about the author, other literature, "world knowledge" — which illustrates very clearly the use and utility of frames in perception. She has a well-elaborated method of reading a poem, and a set of expectations about it: poems are understood in relation to other poems; the moral stance in one poem can be illuminated by the moral stance in other poems (since Stevens and Spenser are against retentiveness, it makes sense that Shakespeare would be too); a poet's concern in one poem can illuminate his concerns in other poems. The reading she has developed so far seems to have three sources, not always articulated: first, that the sonnets often deal with love, especially sexual love (apparent from the reference to "young man" sonnets, Move 2); second, the Shakespearean sonnets tend to be either compliments or insults (hinted at in Moves 8 and 14); and third, that retentiveness is bad (apparent from the reference to Stevens, Move 17, and Spenser, Move 26, but especially from her conclusion that this poem is like the early poems that urge reproduction and perpetuation, Move 20).

The framework a reader brings to a poem also determines which aspects of the poem are problematical. At the simplest level this has to do with the text itself: while Elaine was bothered by the extra *do* in the first line and devoted some time to testing whether it was correct, other readers — as we will see in the next chapters — either didn't notice it or incorporated it into their readings. More complexly, the ultimate position of *weeds* emphasizes the word for her, and she is at pains to account for it. Like most readers, she needs to connect the *deeds* of the sestet with the inaction of the octave, but this is complicated for her because her belief that the poem is an insult requires her to find negative aspects of that stasis and to mitigate the praise that *rightly* and *excellence* normally carry.

The influence of the previous frame is clearest when she returns to the poem the next day.

XXXIV.   Looked up "steward" in the O, in the OED,   /   means um officer of a royal household,   /   which is sort of neat um.

MOVE 34

This move deals with the single word *steward*. Elaine now knows the meaning, but since the meaning did not really matter one way or the other to her reading — though her inability to recall it was annoying — there is not much she can do with it. The new information doesn't relate to any of her problems with the poem, so she drops it.

XXXV.   What I was thinking was that, I think that when I did this yesterday I jumped to the conclusion that the hurt was a sexual hurt   /   and that the um, that that was a bad thing   /   in some ways,   /   at the beginning,   /   because a person who doesn't do the hurt is a -"stone,"   /   which i-, which is weird   /   because one would

think that when you read this for the first time, "They that have pow'r
to hurt and will do none, | That do not do the thing they most do
show . . . to temptation slow," / that the temptation wa-, was temp-
tation to something bad / and that it's a good thing not to do
hurt— / but for some reason I seem to have jumped to the less obvi-
ous meaning of that, / I don't know why I did that, / I'm not *that*
familiar with th-, with this poem, / nor am I that familiar with uh
Shakespeare's other poems. / But if you read it that way i-, is, / if
the first response was that oh that's great that they're not doing the
hurt / and then when you go to line five, / "They rightly do in-
herit heaven's graces," / well then that makes a load of
sense, / "husbands nature's riches from expense," / um, well
that's good too / 'cause "husband" is a, is a, to husband isn't to
farm / but is to be a good caretaker, / and you're not spend-
ing, / you're saving up. / "They are the lords and owners of their
faces, / Others but stewards of their excellence." / Only with that
"faces" / do you really know what that "do not do the thing they
most do show" means, / well it doesn't, that's not exactly what they
don't "most do show," / what uh, do, do "most do show," / but
the externality of "faces" goes with that. / And if you read it that
way, with the, with the first uh um eight lines as being very
positive, / that they're not doing the hurt that they could do / and
isn't that wonderful that they're controlling themselves, / then the
last six lines *are* very puzzling. / "Sweetest things," / But then
when you got to / the "sweetest things turn sourest by their
deeds," / that would mean, if you, if you read it this other way that
I'm, I'm doing now, / um, that since, that i-, well so many of Shake-
speare's couplets / at the end are like little epigrams / um, little
mottoes you know, / "sweetest things can turn sourest by their
deeds" / —that the sweet thing, the one who has the "pow'r to" do
"hurt and will be none," / is good / because he's not doing any-
thing / and therefore um isn't turning sour. / "Lilies that fester
smell far worse than weeds" —that, that the deeds is what makes you
fester.

MOVE 35

In this long move Elaine offers an alternative reading of the poem,
one that even she admits is more obvious. The key to her earlier reading
was the assumption that it was bad to refrain from hurting. Reject that
and the poem falls into place: it is good to withstand temptation (which
is to something bad); those who do withstand temptation deserve

heaven's graces because of their moral fortitude and because they preserve *nature's riches*; and even the sestet, initially puzzling, makes sense, because those who withstand temptation don't *do* anything, perform no defaming deeds, and so never turn sour.

This new reading changes the problems in the poem. The relation between the octave and sestet is still initially puzzling, but now the puzzle can be solved by seeing in the poem characterizations of two mutually exclusive classes: those who do no hurt in the octave, and those who do in the sestet. Shakespeare's typical practice supports this interpretation: since other final couplets are "like little epigrams, little mottoes" — i.e., warnings or general statements about behavior or situations, not reports of specific actions — this couplet might refer to a hypothetical situation: the sweetest thing would turn sourest if it performed deeds, but since it doesn't, it remains sweet. The couplet is subjunctive, not indicative. It is no longer necessary to see "not doing anything" as a kind of deed, and *husband* can be given its normal positive sense of being a good caretaker or saving up. Other problems can be bypassed: from the very beginning she has CONNECTed *the thing they most do show* with *faces* (Move 3), but earlier this seemed to be negative: "so the hurt lies within their faces; they don't do it?" (Move 9). Here the two are still linked, but although she cannot say how, precisely — the faces are "not exactly what they don't *most do show*" — it doesn't matter, since both are now positive.

An especially striking aspect of this new reading is that she returns to the plurals of the text. The association between the singular and the first reading is most obvious in the contrast between the singular in her reconstruction of the earlier reading — "because a person who doesn't do the hurt is a stone" — and the general use of plurals in developing the new one. The singular only appears in this second reading in the discussion of the couplet, perhaps influenced by the single (if generic) *summer's flower*.

XXXVI.   But what seems weird to me is that I seem to have jumped to a second reading,   /   I mean looked to all the problems   /   before I looked at the more obvious connotations of all the lines.   /   I don't know if that's seeing through the ambiguity before the real,   /   not the real but the uh apparent meaning.   /   I do tend to do that though.

MOVE 36

In this commentary on the reading she has just offered, she characterizes her initial reading (called here the "second reading") as dealing with all the problems rather than with the obvious connotations of the lines. Focussing on the difficulties rather than on the simpler and more obvious meanings is what she normally does; it is her standard method of interpreting a poem, apparent already to one of her professors in college (Move 52). It should be remembered, however, that what seem now to be "the more obvious connotations" did not seem that way at the time of the initial reading, since if they had, they would have constituted that reading.

XXXVII.   But even with that reading then there are problems   /   'cause, because "The basest weed" is outbraving "his dignity."   /   Oh no no — well see with that reading the person who withstands everything,   /   then that flower won't meet with "base infection."   /   Oh, hum. So the one reading is, ok, that does cohere pretty well,   /   i-, it is much more obvious than what I was doing yesterday   /   I think.   /   The peri-. Those that have, that "have pow'r to hurt" and don't do it,   /   that's good,   /   they "inherit heaven's graces,"   /   they're good farmers with "nature's riches,"   /   "nature's riches"   /   are perhaps themselves,   /   well no that wouldn't work with that reading,   /   um — well yeah, "nature's riches" are themselves   /   but they're not hurting.   /   "They are the lords and owners of their faces."   /   And then that, that kind of person is compared to a flower who is sweet to others,   /   to, to the outside,   /   to, to the summer,   /   "Though to itself it only live and die; | But if that flow'r with base infection meet" —   /   so with this reading that's like a warning,   /   if, if that flower meets baseness   /   and does a base deed,   /   a hurting deed,   /   "The basest weed outbraves his dignity."   /   That that person when he goes to "base infection" can't withstand it   /   whereas the lower people by comparison with the weed,   /   who do go around hurting everybody,   /   um, survives the dignity of the flower,   /   and then a little moral.

MOVE 37

Move 37 returns to the poem to TEST the new reading, and everything is found to fit very nicely. The *basest weed* will not outbrave the dignity of the *sweetest flower*, because the flower will never do anything bad and so will never meet *base infection*. Forgotten now is the consideration, so important in the initial reading, that "it doesn't matter what you do, you will rot" (Move 8); mortality has ceased to be a problem. Or more precisely, has ceased to be part of the poem for her. *Nature's riches* still refers to the people (cf. Moves 17 and 18) but now the meaning of *husband* is positive: "they're good farmers," and husbanding themselves complements not hurting others. The kind of person discussed is still compared to a flower, but now the entire sestet is seen as a warning against particular kinds of actions rather than a report of them.

This new reading also resolves one hidden problem of the original reading: while the *summer's flower* and *lilies* were associated with people, the human characters of the octave, the weeds remained only weeds; there was never any hint that the weeds represented a class of people the way the flowers did. Instead, they were flora whose physical characteristics provided the basis for much of the reading: they proliferate (Move 14), outlast "all cultivation" (Move 21), outlast "the summer (Move 24), and finally "win even in cultivated gardens or if they don't win it's by a lot of human effort" (Move 32). But in this second reading the weeds represent the "lower people . . . who do go around hurting everybody." While it would not be impossible to identify the weeds with these people in the first reading, it would require special pleading to explain why the good people — the higher people — rot no matter what they do while the lower people last forever. This neat opposition is possible now only because Elaine has forgotten the problem of mortality; the single hint of it in this second reading is the gloss for *outbraves* — still not very precise — "survives."

XXXVIII.   But I think actually that um the reading I did yesterday which was very much stranger, / is truer to my sense of Shakespeare, / this is a sense mostly from the plays, / I don't know which play exactly, / 'cause I think that "They that have pow'r to hurt and will do none," "Who, moving others, are themselves as stone," / it doesn't matter whether they *will* to "do none," / that they, that they consciously do, do no hurt / because they hurt anyway, / they hurt the other person anyway, / "Who, moving others," / so that even in passivity they're hurting . . . / So that I think that, that somehow though this poem, even though the, that my first, my second, the one I just did, that reading is um sort of more obvious / and more apparent, / that there is, that there is that reproach in there, / and the "husband nature's riches from expense," / they're holding themselves / and they're hoarding themselves / —I think this is what I did yesterday. / "Though to itself," / there's another image of hoarding, / "to it-self," / held into itself.

MOVE 38

Like Move 36, this move is a kind of TEST of the two readings Elaine has now proposed, and again illustrates the power of the scheme one brings to the reading situation. The original reading, which she agrees is "very much stranger," is nevertheless preferred because it is "truer to [her] sense of Shakespeare," derived mainly from the plays rather than from the sonnets. This sense presumably has to do with the typical ending of the comedies in marriage, with the promise of reproduction and regeneration, the exiling of the malcontent characters like Jacques and Malvolio (the retentive ones), and the ever-expanding implications of action and power of any kind in the tragedies and the histories. This last theme is identified in the poem: whether or not *they* consciously intend to hurt, they do it anyway because they can't help *moving others;* even their passivity affects others. More precisely, even their passivity *hurts* others, and they become doubly unnatural and deserving of reproach because they both hurt others and hoard themselves. To strengthen this reading, Elaine searches for further evidence of hoarding, and ends the move considering "to itself," something she has already treated several times (see Move 31).

By this point, the reading process has taken an interesting turn, since Elaine is no longer simply trying to understand the poem; she is now trying to choose between two alternative readings and to justify her choice.

XXXIX.   "it only live and die; | But if that flow'r with base infection meet, | The basest weed outbraves his dignity." / Uh what's "base infection"? / Um, oh, "The basest weed" / —could be that, / I mean there is some kind of connection there. / In a way this poem is very dislocating—

MOVE 39

This move is a continuation of the previous one, as Elaine begins by READing the beginning of the sestet and SELECTing *base infection*. Earlier (Move 7) she had decided almost immediately that this must be "some sexual, venereal disease," but in Move 37 she had redefined it to be a "base deed, a hurting deed" in line with the second, nonsexual, reading. By now, it is no longer clear just what *base infection* refers to, and she attempts to pin it down by CONNECTing it to the *basest weed*. This represents a quite different strategy, since she is now trying to understand the phrase by specifying its connections within the poem instead of by guessing immediately what it might refer to in the outside world.

The COMMENT about the poem being disconcerting reflects again the importance of the preexisting frameworks one brings to the reading process. What is disconcerting is not that the poem is difficult to understand — indeed, with two quite different interpretations to choose between, one a compliment, the other an insult, Elaine has an *embarras de richesse* — but that it is difficult to relate to her conception of Shakespeare and his attitudes, difficult to reconcile with her schemata. The reading she prefers leads to two kinds of problems. The first is specifying the referents of several words and phrases (CONNECT:NATUREs) such as *base infection, stewards, outbraves*, and so forth. The second is maintaining some kind of internal consistency within the poem (CON-NECT:POEMs). Some things sound as if they should belong together — *base infection* and *basest weed*, for instance, share the idea of baseness — but precisely how they are related is not clear. Other things sound distinct, even antithetical — the people who do no hurt *rightly inherit heaven's graces* and are linked with excellence, yet they are also *as stone, unmoved*, and excessively retentive — but her preferred reading assigns them to the same category. The poem is dislocating because it is difficult for her to make all its parts fit together and fit her expectations about Shakespeare at the same time.

XL. "For sweetest things turn sourest by their deeds; | Lilies that fester smell far worse than weeds." / On one level he's saying, when you know that lily meets with "base infection," / as it festers, / its falling from grace, / is much greater, / i-, the sweetness that it has within it can't w-, stand up against the baseness. / But in a way also, those last two lines are not necessarily connected / — "sweetest things turn sourest by their deeds." / It seems to me that um even as the people in the first line will to do nothing, / they are doing something anyway, / "moving others," / they are doing that, / whether they will it or not, / and so that "Lilies that fester smell far worse than weeds," / that looks back to the "Though to itself it only live and die" / — it's going to die anyway, / it's going to fester anyway. / You can fester either by your deeds or you can fester as you die, / because "The summer's flow'r," / that's the flower *in* summer —

MOVE 40

This move, concentrating on the couplet, completes the pass through the poem. The basic ideas have been suggested before, especially the connection between living only to oneself and dying, dying and fester-

ing, and the inevitability of death (Move 24). The CONNECTion be-
tween those who *will do no hurt* and *deeds* is reinforced by the realization
(see Move 38) that whether they intend to or not, they do move other
people, and so do in some sense perform deeds. This is more satisfactory
than the earlier indentification of *deeds* with doing nothing ("well, a deed
can be a not doing something also," Move 23) because it manages to im-
plicate the *they* in actions without compromising their aloof retentiveness.

What is new here — and perhaps another reason for the poem's dis-
locating effect — is the suggestion that the couplet can be seen either as
a cause and effect unit (a warning or a curse; see Moves 29 and 35) or as
two separate statements. In the first case, the *deeds* are the same as the
meeting with *base infection* (Move 29), and the festering (see Move 35)
seems to refer to this general process of debasement, which is "its falling
from grace." This fall is greater — presumably than the fall of "the lower
people" would be (Move 37) — because of the lily's initial sweetness:
the highest fall the furthest. In the second case, the *deeds* are associated
with *moving others* rather than with the *base infection*, while the lilies'
festering relates to the *summer's flower* that lives and dies *to itself*, which
Elaine continues to see as a reference to inevitable death. So the last two
lines suggest two different routes to death — a deserved one, based on
past deeds, and an underserved albeit natural one unconnected with
what has been done during the previous life. And since she has consis-
tently read *fester* as "rot" and associated it simply with death and not
specifically with disease (see Moves 8 and 24), she can relate it either to
base infection or to the inevitability of *the summer's flower* living only during
the summer, as she seems to be doing when she breaks off at the end of
this move.

XLI.   oh it's odd,   /   it's first it's "They,"   /   generalized,   /
"They," "They,"   /   flower,   /   then it moves even more specific to
lily,   /   which is just about as specific as it gets, um.

MOVE 41

This move repeats the observation (in Move 12) that third person
plural pronouns are used (rather than first and second person), and adds
to it the notion of a progression toward specificity. *They* is plural and
"generalized," while the *flower* and the *lily* (*not* plural, as in the text) are
singular and more specific. Nothing is done with this progression here,
but it will be treated again in Moves 49 and 50.

XLII. This does seem to me that underlying all this a-, the apparent praise for not doing it, there's some kind of bitterness, / the "fester," / that's a bitter word / — that's the most, I was going to say visual, / but not visual, / I mean it's just strong image, / the smelling and the festering of the lilly, / a souring. / I mean if this was a poem of praise / as it seems to be at the beginning, / where it, at its most obvious level, / very strange to end with the sour, / smelling and festering, / I mean "weeds," / the last word is "weeds." / In a way you fester when you stay to yourself, / you rot when you stay to yourself. / So you don't just fester by meeting "base infection."

Move 42

Again this move recapitulates what had been done the day before, where one of her earliest reactions had been that this is "terrible language for a compliment" (Move 8; see also Moves 20, 25, and 36). This reflects the fact that as one continues to read and interpret a poem, what is actually being processed becomes the text plus one's earlier interpretations rather than simply the text itself (or more precisely, the text and the schemata or preconceptions one brings to it). In a sense, much of what is done the second day is a kind of TEST of what had been done the first day. This is especially true in Elaine's case, since she wants to justify her preference for her earlier, stranger reading. The initial tension between compliment and terrible language is recast: the bitterness obvious at the end of the poem underlies the apparent praise throughout. This is a refinement of the good-bad polarity discussed in Move 25, where she tried to show that there is something negative about even what seems to be most positive in the octave, for here the suggestion — only hinted at — is that the tone is strange. This is another and more sophisticated attempt to bridge the gap between what is theoretically good and what is natural (Move 29): the speaker of the poem can be seen as bitter about behavior that seems to be good (or perhaps seems to be *too* good), a possibility that will be developed more fully later (Move 48).

The basis of this reading is that the strength of the lilies' festering overpowers, as it were, the rest of the poem; that image, the last word, and Elaine's own feeling that "you fester when you stay to yourself" dictate the tone of the entire poem. Clearly, much of her difficulty with the poem stems from her belief that keeping to oneself is a bad thing, and much of her time is spent trying to reconcile that belief with her understanding of the poem.

XLIII. "They that have pow'r to hurt" / — I am sticking to this other reading, / although the "do hurt" is kind of interesting, / I don't, I don't know if that's from another edition. / I did call Ann and ask her to check in her book / an-, and hers is, is also as it was in the, in my Norton, / the "They that," "that have pow'r to hurt," / but I don't know if that "do" is in some other edition. / The "do" actually is kind of interesting / because i-, it's repeated then in the first line, / "do hurt," "will do none" / e-, the emphasis on action, / and then twice in the next line, / "That do not do the thing they most do sh-" / or three times in the next line. / Hum, this is five — / either four or five, / depending on whether the first one was a mistake. / Wonder if there are any others, / "do." . . . "To," oh, "They rightly *do* inherit heaven's graces." / Well, that's a passive thing if you inherit. / First is active, / oh the first four are, all right, are active, / although the, "they most do show," / that's not active, / you're just showing it, / so that's in a way passive, / they can't help showing it. / "Do inherit," and there, "though to," / no more, / but that's — one two three four five six — six or, five or six times.

MOVE 43

This move begins another reading through the poem, but she immediately gets sidetracked to comment again on the discrepancy in the texts of the poem (see Move 15). In the meantime she has called up another student in the project to check texts. *Do* is then SELECTed for attention because it is repeated, and presumably also because it is the least specific action verb and thus could potentially be connected with *deeds*. She notes that there are four or five *do*'s in the first two lines, and that the consequent emphasis on action suggests a contrast between the signification of the words — that *they* don't *do* anything — and the actual words used. In view of her theory that bitterness underlies the apparent praise in the octave, she might suggest that underlying the apparent statement that *they will do none* is the implication, enforced by the repeated emphasis on action, that they do. But she never does this overtly.

Elaine next investigates whether this emphasis on action expressed by the verb *do* is sustained throughout the poem. She identifies another action but realizes (by a DEDUCE) that inheriting is essentially passive, and this suggests another polarity: active/passive. In proposing the polarity she notices that *they most do show* is not really active either. But nothing more can be made of this polarity, and it is dropped.

Even though it is not incorporated into her interpretation, this move illustrates very clearly Elaine's typical strategies and operations. When she notices something—and there is no way to predict exactly what she will notice—she usually searches within the poem for other examples of the same thing or of something related to it. She then tries to relate what she has found to something already present in her interpretation or to a polarity, not always successfully. In this process minor distinctions may be overlooked, as is the case here: in her group of active examples, she has one full verb (*do the thing*) one auxiliary (*do not*) and one pro-verb (*do none*); the "passives" are an emphatic marker (*do inherit*) and a redundant *do* added for the verse (*do show*). And since all of the "active" examples are negated, the overall effect is as likely to be the denial of potential action as the suggestion of it.

XLIV. Interesting / interlocking of words anyway. / Um, Why are there only two, "moving," "Unmoved," "slow," "inherit," "base," "basest" / — maybe there's not much interlocking. / "They rightly do inherit heaven's graces," "riches from expense," "the lords and owners of their faces," "sweetest things," and then weed is repeated, / that's no big deal, um.

MOVE 44

This grows directly out of the previous one. In fact, "Interesting interlocking of words anyway" almost seems to be a COMMENT followed by a GENERALIZE closing the discussion of the repeated *do*. In the rest of the move she TESTs whether there is much interesting interlocking of words by seeking examples, first specifically of single words—*moving* and *unmoved, base* and *baseness*—but then more generally of ideas, so *slow* belongs with *moving* and *unmoved* and the various lines referring to owing or inheriting are linked. Again she cannot relate this GENERALIZation to her interpretation, and she drops the topic abruptly.

XLV. No the, i-, no, this, I think my, the, the reading I did yesterday / was truer to the spirit of this poem / in some ways, / though this other's more obvious now. / //read ll. 1–4// / All sorts of loaded words here, / "temptation" / which, "temptation" to something bad   /   or to, t-, "temptation" which, as a human conti-, condition.   /   "They rightly do inherit heaven's graces | And husband nature's riches from expense" —   /   that's also dual.   /   In a way that's good,   /   nice and thrifty,   /   in a way too it's bad   /   because it's thwarting   /   — I mean you don't have to, and how can somebody "husband nature's riches from expense"?   /   Well I guess there's some kind of, I don't know,   /   a s-, in-, uh, allusion uh in a sort of slanted way   /   to the gardening,   /   which would go with the flower and the weeds,   /   and their confrontation,   /   but um, "husband nature's riches from expense"   /   — but in a way, nature takes care of itself,   /   human beings don't,   /   it's not that, it's not your job to hoard up nature   /   — well hoard   /   is, is a terribly loaded word   /   and I'm sticking it in there.   /   The "husband"   /   — and with "husband" there is some kind of sexual implication underlying   /   or within or something,   /   underlying that word.   /   "ex-," and "expense"   /   has that, the sexual implication,   /   as in "The expense of spirit in a waste of shame" uh.   /   I mean are " nature's riches" his own riches,   /   is the, th-, th-, the "nature's riches" are the riches of that person,   /   of those people "that have pow'r to" do "hurt and will do none."

MOVE 45

This move returns to the beginning of the poem to illustrate again how the original reading is "truer to the spirit of this poem in some ways" than the second, more obvious, reading. The major evidence presented here consists of the "loaded" words (see Moves 24, 25, and 31), which presumably suggest the kind of double vision discussed in Move 17. Both this double vision and the "loaded words" — which turn out to be "dual" — continue covertly the overt polarities so apparent in the first day's reading. After repeating essentially what she had already said about *temptation* in Moves 24 and 25, she considers lines 5 and 6, lines that are central to her interpretation and have been frequently dealt with before. Here she combines the negative implications from Moves 24 and 26 with the positive ones from the second reading in Move 35. But several new ideas are added. First, husbanding *nature's riches* is "thwarting," apparently because it is unnecessary and impossible. Although it is not clear who is thwarted, this seems to be an extension of the claim (in Move 24) "that living and dying only to oneself leads to festering." Since "nature takes care of itself," humans are not supposed to "hoard up nature";

those who do so perhaps interfere with the course of nature, and certainly inhibit their own fullest development, as Marinell did (see Move 26). Interestingly, she qualifies her use of "hoard" here even though she was perfectly happy with it during her last extended discussion of these lines (she repeated it four times in Move 26), and she does not object to "thwart."

Second, the initial suggestion that *husband* means *farm* (Move 4) is revived and CONNECTed briefly with the flower and the weed, though since the reference to gardening is made only "in a sort of slanted way" (i.e., obliquely), nothing much is done with it.

Third, the sexual implications of *husband* are identified for the first time and CONNECTed to the similar implications of *expense*. But again not much can be done with this new insight because it is still not clear what *nature's riches* are: another loaded phrase, it could refer specifically to the people themselves, as she has been assuming, or, more generally, to the riches that these people own. Had she developed this last possibility, it would have solved at least one of her problems, since if *they* are the *owners of nature's riches*, then husbanding them would not be hoarding, and would be both natural and possible.

XLVI.   "They are the lords and owners of their faces" /   — that's the imagery / of business and commerce / and, well not really, "lords," / royal, / "stewards of their excellence." /   Stewardship I suppose is, is temporary,   /   lordship and ownership is not.

MOVE 46

This short move is devoted to the final two lines of the octave, perhaps in an attempt to develop the notion of ownership just introduced. Again (see Move 13) these lines are CONNECTed to typical Shakespearean imagery of commerce and business, as is obvious from the definite article in "*the* imagery." But two new DEDUCEs are made. Apparently building on the definition of steward as "an officer of a royal household" (Move 34), *lords* is now recognized as royal. Secondly, stewardship is a temporary state while lordship and ownership are permanent. Although this distinction could presumably be related to the earlier polarity between interior and exterior (see Move 30) — what is permanent is somehow interior or inherent; what is temporary is exterior — it is not, in spite of the fact that these lines were previously (in Move 28) discussed in terms of control and explicitly linked with the interior/exterior scale.

XLVII.   "The summer's flow'r is to the summer sweet." / Oh,
"The summer's flo-" / it's the flower of summer, / so there again
there's some kind of, a slant implied, / seasonal thing. / But
"The summer's flow'r" is *only* sweet in the summer. / And so many
of Shakespeare's poems are about growing old, / like um oh
seventy-three, / "That time of year thou mayest in me be-
hold / When yellow leaves," / a-, and he's talking about the
autumn of his own life / a-, as a time of year / and a time of
day / and a time of life in that poem. / Stephen Booth in that
terrific book on Shakespeare's sonnets talks about how you can only, or
not only, but one way of looking at these poems is as they allude to
other poems, to other s-, well not, other poems and other of Sh-, the
Shakespeare sonnets, that i-, it doesn't really matter about the strict
order but that um words and phrases will be picked up even in sonnets
that i-, in number a-, are very far away from each other. / So maybe
that image / of summer, / not necessarily to that one poem about
autumn, / but I think in a lot of the poems he talks about
dying, / and so many of the poems are about time, / and so in the
summer, / like, in its, this cou-, this is sort of like the um, well not
really, but I, I, I was just thinking of the "To Autumn" poem by
Keats, / about i-, i-, it's a time of culmination / but it's also a
time, / but that's a fall poem, / implying the death / and the,
and the winter that will come.

MOVE 47

Continuing to justify her first reading, Elaine SELECTs the first line of
the sestet. Although she has treated this section several times, the em-
phasis has generally been on the next line — *though to itself it only live and
die.* Here the implications of summer are considered. The *summer's
flower* is only seasonal (as opposed to the weeds that outlast the summer,
Move 24), and so is another example of the "loaded words" she finds
throughout the poem: the flower may be sweet in the summer (Move
40), but we know it is going to die at the end of the summer. This leads
back to the theme of mortality (first suggested in Move 24: "summer can
also be a time of life, a time in one's life"), and is CONNECTed to Shake-
speare's concern throughout the sonnets with growing old. Specifically,
she thinks of sonnet 73, but aside from the fact that it is about growing
old it seems to have little in common with this poem. Stephen Booth's
An Essay on Shakespeare's Sonnets is brought in to validate the CON-
NECTion by suggesting that sonnets far apart in the sequence allude to

each other, both verbally and thematically. Thus the slender relation —
this sonnet and #73 both refer to seasons, though here it is the summer
and there it is late autumn — is perhaps potentially meaningful.

To support further the suggestion that *summer* refers to a time of life,
she recalls Keats's "To Autumn." What she wants from that poem is not
its magnificent rendering of completeness and "culmination," but the
simple fact that since it is about fall, it implies winter and thus death.
Elaine has by now CONNECTed this poem specifically to five others:
Stevens's "To the One of Fictive Music" (Move 17), Shakespeare's son-
nets 129 (Moves 4, 17, 23, and 45) and 73 (here), Spenser's *Faerie Queene*
(Move 26), and "To Autumn." What is characteristic of her literary ref-
erences in how little they seem (to another reader) to have in common
with this poem. With the exception of sonnet 129, where *expense* may or
may not be used in the same sense as here, these other poems share
nothing with this poem; instead they are recalled because they express
themes she finds in this poem. Stevens and Spenser are brought in to
illustrate the effects of retentiveness and hoarding; sonnet 73 and "To
Autumn" because they discuss aging in the terms of seasons. The func-
tion of these literary allusions, as I have suggested in the discussion of
Move 26, is to support her interpretation by showing that the concerns
she finds in this poem are "literary" and thus inherently plausible. And
the treatment of these themes in other poems can also suggest possible
approaches to this poem, as the sarcasm in Stevens makes the sarcasm
here more apparent (Move 17), and sonnet 129 supports the suggestion
of unnatural retentiveness (Move 23).

XLVIII.   Well which are the negative words,   /   that are specifically
negative?   /   Die: /   I don't think there's a sexual thing in
that   /   — "die," "base infection," "weed," "basest," "sour," "fester,"
"weeds," "smell."   /   Earlier   /   it's, well the only st−, pretty bad
words, negative connotations,   /   are "cold," "stone," "tempta-
tion,"   /   There are a lot of good words there,   /   "graces,"
"Heaven's," "riches," "nature," "lords," "owners," "excel-
lence."   /   It seems that most of the negative words, specifically nega-
tive words are clustered at, at the end.   /   It's as if in trying to make a
poem of praise,   /   I mean it's like he's gritting his teeth   /   and then
suddenly all these bad things come out   /   even as he's um — seeming
to talk about something sweet.   /   But, you know, the negativeness
does seem to all cluster at the end.   /   So it's as if while, yeah that's a
kind of, I can't exactly articulate this yet,   /   but as he's writing it
looks like a p−, a poem of praise   /   at the beginning,   /   which is

full of, when you look, in, in the light of the end,   /   of all these am-
biguities,   /   "Who, moving others, are themselves as
stone, | Unmoved, cold, and to temptation slow."   /   I mean in the
light of the fact that the person is revealed later as a hoarder of
himself,   /   and as a, somebody who, who holds himself in,   /   who
won't yield,   /   but even in not yielding, even not meaning, even
meaning to do nothing,   /   to do no hurt,   /   does it any-
way.   /   That the beginning of the poem,   /   retrospectively,   /   is
much more negative,   /   I, i−, i−, double, everything is double-
edged.   /   And maybe that "They rightly do inherit" − s heaven,
heaven, "inherit heaven's graces"   /   is, is sarcastic,   /   maybe
"They *rightly* do inherit heaven's graces"   /   — but that's heaven and
that's not earth.   /   Oh heaven,   /   hum, heaven can be opposed to,
to nature and "nature's riches"   /   or maybe heaven includes those
things.

MOVE 48

This move grows out of several previous ones. Primarily a develop-
ment of the observation from Move 40 that there are "all sorts of loaded
words here," it also seeks evidence for the idea of imminent winter and
death from the previous move, and of course, returns to the good/bad or
positive/negative polarity from Moves 7, 25, and 38. After discounting
the possibility of a sexual connotation in *die,* which would CONNECT it
with *husband* and *expense* (see Move 40), Elaine lists the negative words
in the poem. Set against these are the overtly positive ones, though
curiously she omits *flower* and especially *lilies,* which had originally been
considered in terms of "purity, beauty" (Move 8), certainly good char-
acteristics. In fact, both lists are selective: from the list of negatives she
omits *hurt,* the negatives *not* and *none,* and the negative prefix *un-* from
the beginning of the poem and *worse* from the end; from the positive,
sweet, sweetest, outbraves (Move 14) and *dignity* (see Move 22). This selec-
tive listing leads to a GENERALIZation that the specifically negative
words are clustered at the end. This observation, together with the im-
plication that since the negative words appear at the end, the positive
words must be at the beginning, and with the second, positive reading of
the poem, which saw the octave as clearly complimentary (Move 35),
leads to the reassertion (see Moves 8, 14, 23, and 42) that what seems at
the beginning to be a poem of praise turns out in the end to be an insult.
This early suggestion is reinforced here in two ways. First, she

suggests that the poet has developed a more inclusive view during the course of writing the poem, that only in trying to write a poem of praise does he come to recognize the negative implications of what he had originally (and naïvely) thought laudable. Second, she suggests that the reader's experience in some way parallels the writer's: having confronted the explicit negatives at the end, the reader becomes more aware of the ambiguities, the negative implications, the "loaded," "double-edged" quality (Move 40) of what had originally been taken as simple praise. To bolster this view, she elevates to the status of facts what had previously been only interpretations: "The fact that the person is revealed later as a hoarder of himself, . . . [who] even meaning to do nothing, to do no hurt, does it anyway." And since so many apparently positive things have negative characteristics or undertones, it makes sense to see line five as somehow negative, either as sarcastic (see Moves 16 and 23) or as an opposition between what is theoretically good but unnat- ural — *heaven's graces* — and what is natural and is understandable (see Move 29). The frequency with which she returns to this line to find some negative implication in it indicates how strongly she feels it to be positive and complimentary.

What this move adds to her reading (and what will be added more specifically in the next) is the idea of progression. Until now, her in- terpretation has been relatively static: good characteristics are juxtaposed with bad ones, the lesson to be learned deriving from that juxtaposition. Here, however, there is a suggestion that the poem actually progresses, both in the poet's mind and in the reader's, so that what is learned is the result of re-cognition, of seeing progressively subtler implications in what is said. The poem is thus an experience that has to be lived through, not something that can be merely abstracted. This is, of course, a view that has been the burden of a good deal of criticism, and by relating the poem to a progression, Elaine is allying herself with a well- known critical tradition. I don't mean that she does this intentionally, but rather that any graduate student today knows that it is both reason- able and laudable to see a poem as a kind of progressive uncovering of implications, even if one stops short of the ultimate *mise en abyme*.

XLIX. Hum, heaven, nature, "lords and owners," / so it's going from heaven to the world of nature to the world of human activity then to "nature's riches," / then more specifically to the human world / w — , with the flower, / and even more specifically with the lily. / Th — , there's a much, it's a, this poem never gets particu- larly specific / in a way, / I mean it's not zeroing in on one

time / or even one person, / it's, it's "They" and "The summer's
flow'r is to the summer sweet." / That's more specific than what's
gone before / but still generalized, um.

MOVE 49

This move complements the idea of the poem as a progressive unfold-
ing of implications with an actual progression within the poem. Elaine
ended the previous move by opposing heaven and earth, but then
realized that their relation was more complex. Within the poem, this
relation is seen as a progression both spatial and abstract: spatial in the
sense that the movement is from the heavens to the earth, "the world of
human activity," then to the ground—*heaven's riches* seem to be things,
perhaps crops or goods here—and finally to the flower and lily.
Abstractly the movement is one of increasing specificity, from the very
general heaven to the specific lily (she continues to see the lily as a
singular rather than a plural).

But even though the poem becomes more specific, she admits that it
never becomes as specific as, say, a proper noun would be, or the time
of life described in the three images of sonnet 73. The *summer's flower* is
more specific than *heaven*, but it is still generic rather than par-
ticularized—it could be *any* flower in summer. Similarly, the plural *they*
refers to a generic class rather than to a specific individual, as *you* or *thou*
would.

L. This poem i–, in fact never does quite make it into human
reality, / for instance in that seven, in sonnet seventy-three, /
that "in me," "The time of year thou mayst in me behold." / It's
more and more interior, / and it that poem is addressed t–, to a
'you,' / this is about a "They." / Hum, I wonder if that's typical
in Shakespeare, / I mean which is more typical, the "They" or the
'you,' / the singular or the plural. / The plural is much more
generalized, / it's almost as if he starts out trying to make some kind
of a s–, general statement, / never does get specific enough /
and yet, I don't know why / but you feel that, that this is addressed
to one person, / to the one person that the poet himself, maybe as,
well, maybe, you know, whether really / or fictionally / or as a
persona or whatever, / is responding to, / he's trying to distance it
by talking about "They" "moving others," / and in fact it's moving
himself. / And the end t–, I think he says, it essentially is like a
curse, / "Lilies that fester," / that, that he's festering by not do-

ing, / by, by not acting / and that he acts even as he thinks he's not acting / or a−, as he wills not to act.

Move 50

This move, although it develops directly out of the progression from general to specific suggested in the previous one, recalls the discussion of the pronouns in Moves 12 and 41. In Move 12, Elaine had identified first- and second-person pronouns with "some kind of interiority," especially as they are found in sonnet 73; here she returns to the same insight, emphasizing again the *in me* in sonnet 73 and the fact that it is addressed to a *you* (actually a *thou*). But now she projects the idea of progression onto sonnet 73, so that "it's more and more interior," perhaps referring to the progression of images.

After a brief query about Shakespeare's typical practice, she returns to the poem to confront a problem in her reading: throughout most of her earlier discussion of the poem she translated the plurals in the text into singulars in an apparently unconscious expression of her insight, overtly expressed here, that "this is addressed to one person." But now she would like to strengthen her conception of the poem as a progression by complementing the movement from *heaven* to human activity to *nature's riches* with a similar one from the generalized plurals at the beginning to more specific singulars at the end. Two versions of this sequence are suggested: one in which the poet tries to make a generalized statement at the beginning and then to particularize it during the course of the poem, and one in which the poet is from the beginning addressing and discussing a specific person, the one who has moved him and to whom he is — in fact or fiction — responding. The first version implies a poetic failure, since the poet "never does get specific enough," and so she adopts the second, in which the plurals at the beginning are a consciously exploited part of the psychological structure of the poem.

This perspective reinforces the earlier view that the end of the poem is a curse (Move 29) rather than a warning (Move 37). If the poem is a personal reaction intentionally disguised as a third-person meditation, then the ending probably is a curse, because the whole poem is real rather than hypothetical. *They that have power to hurt* no longer delimits a hypothetical class; now it refers to a specific individual who had the power to hurt the narrator and did hurt him, perhaps not intending to, and the poem is in a sense the narrator's (and the poet's) revenge.

Seeing the poem in this way makes it more typical for her, since it now "make[s] it into human reality" like Shakespeare's other sonnets.

In fact, this sonnet *is* atypical in its pronouns and Elaine has found a way to rationalize that difference.

LI. I'm looking uh it over again now. / "They that have pow'r to hurt and will do none," they "do not do the thing they most do show." / In this sense showing, / which is being, / the, the, the fact is just what you are, / what you appear to be, / this do no moving / //read ll. 3 – 14 with l. ll: But if that flow'r with, with base infection meet.// / Yeah, should read that in a n – , nasty tone, maybe. / But that nastiness is there, / there's real hostili-ty / and nastiness / and anger / it seems, underneath that, / and that's why everything at the beginning is so loaded.

MOVE 51

This move is a quick reading through the poem, TESTing the conclu-sion in the previous move that the poem is a personal reproach that becomes a kind of curse even though it seems to be distanced and gen-eralized by the plural pronouns. A minor problem — the relation of *show* to *faces* (see Moves 3 and 35) is resolved neoplatonically: the fact is the reality; what you show — your face — is what you are; the external should be a faithful expression of the internal. She does not make the connec-tion explicit, but this seems to be to the justification for the nastiness and hostility: *They* are hypocritical, promising something they do not de-liver, not acting the way they seem to promise to. It isn't clear whether she finds the hostility, nastiness, and anger underneath the entire poem or only the final couplet; in either case this conclusion is a development of the idea of the bitter tone in Move 42, and provides another justifica-tion for the ambiguity she has found in the poem: the poet is angry throughout, and the less savory implications of the apparent compli-ments are the expression of that anger.

LII. I don't know why I got the first means. / One of my teachers told me that I noted all the subtleties and missed everything obvious and maybe that's what I'm doing here.

MOVE 52

This recapitulates the remarks in Move 36, referring again to the fact that she saw the less obvious but finally more satisfying meaning of the poem first. It is a kind of a TEST and a compliment: by calling what she has found "subtleties," she confers a validity on them and suggests how much they are to be preferred to "everything obvious."

LIII.   Maybe there is a contrast between the "heaven's graces," / so he's getting the "graces" from heaven, / in heaven, whatever, / but he's not behaving as a human being behaves while on earth as a part of nature.

MOVE 53

This short move, continued in Move 55, returns to line 5, which remains the most problematic line for her. She repeats the contrast (first suggested in Move 29) between *heaven's graces* as what is theoretically correct but unnatural and what is human and natural — the way one should behave "as a human being behaves while on earth as a part of nature." Here the contrast is still presented as a hypothesis: "Maybe there is a contrast . . ."; in Move 55 it will be a conclusion.

LIV.   It's all "They," "They," "They" — and then a flower. / It's as though he, the poet himself i — , in describing this person, / because I don't know why / but I just get the feeling / it is addressed to one person / and it's not just a little generalized statement, / there's too much underlying anger in it, / it's, I mean that's just a very natural human thing to do / is to, is to distance that way, / the "They," / and then talking about "Others," / when you're talking about yourself, / t — , t — , to try to make it into some kind of generalization about human nature / when it's really your own pain / and your own anger.

MOVE 54

This move interrupts the consideration of *heaven's riches* to return to the topic of Move 50, this time to supply further evidence for the poet's distancing his own feelings by presenting them in the third person: since people today normally talk about themselves and their enemies as *others* and *they*, it is conceivable that Shakespeare would also. Move 50 established that this sonnet treats the same kind of specific personal experience as the other sonnets, even though it is more generalized in expression; this move provides a psychological explanation for that form of expression. Just as the references to Stevens, Keats, Spenser, and Shakespeare's other works demonstrate the literary plausibility of her interpretation, this allusion to "a very natural human thing to do" indicates its psychological plausibility.

LV. No, / I think this a poem about not being human, / and that in the eyes of conventional whatever, / in the eyes of heaven, / this is the right thing to do, / to be "cold" and "Unmoved" to these things, / and yet maybe even in the eyes of heaven that's not so good / because you're moving others / and, and you're hurting others. / So you're doing it even when you think you're not doing it. / "They are the lords and owners of their faces." / I'm again looking, just sort of skimming over this, not reading it, just looking at things, trying to see something to light upon, but I feel stuck so I'm going to stop now.

MOVE 55

This continues Move 53: Elaine has decided definitely that there is a contrast in the poem between what is human and what is heavenly, between naturally good and theoretically good conduct. The characteristics that were previously seen as negative (see Moves 3 and 10), are now positive from heaven's point of view and negative from a human point of view. But she is still uneasy about this position, understandably, because her view that the poem is about a personal experience that caused hostility and anger in the poet implies that *they do* hurt people, and she cannot see how this can be good in any framework, particularly "in the eyes of heaven." This is a problem she never resolves.

LVI. Well I feel much better about what I did with this poem, better than I did about the other one, the last one, um. / I wish I could remember what the great critical problem with this poem was, / what I um, well because then I could work on figuring it out, / but um, I think what it probably was judging from the two readings that I've come up with / is that it does seem to be praise at the beginning / and that um, but then why end with that awful image / of rotting lilies at the end, / except that the reading that I did the first time, and that I did a little more of yesterday um, I think, does deal with, does deal with that problem / and I feel like it's got a, um, I don't know, that it's not a phony / or an imposed reading, / that um that is what's going on / I mean it's not just to say that the bird is the poet's soul or something / but that um trying to, sort of for self-consolation / but that that really is one of the problems. / I don't know if I can think of anything else about this poem, but I'll see.

Move 56

This move, an introduction to her activities on the third day of reading, reviews briefly what has been accomplished so far. She is still satisfied with her basic reading, primarily because it explains what she can reconstruct of "the great critical problem with this poem" she heard about in college. Further, the reading seems natural — "not a phony or an imposed reading" — because she has found both literary and psychological precedents for it. (In this it contrasts with her reading of the first poem in the project, Swinburne's "A Ballad of Dreamland," in which bird images abound and the refrain is "Only the song of a secret bird." For most of the readers, the key to understanding the poem was the identification of this "secret bird.")

The one new suggestion here is that the poem is a kind of self-consolation as well as retaliation. Although this view is never developed, its relevance is clear: the poet both consoles himself and insults the addressee by arguing that he will fester and become worse than a weed, and thus, presumably, worse than the poet.

LVII. //read ll. 1 – 4// / Hum, I wonder if he maybe with that "Unmoved, cold," / those words set off from each other, / isolated, / as though they've been slowed down, / they're single, / they're just there by themselves.

Move 57

She begins to read through the poem again. She SELECTs *unmoved* and *cold* as words "set off from each other, isolated," presumably because the two stressed syllables are separated only by a comma, reinforcing the normal intonational pause between them. She may be hinting that the isolation of the words in reading reflects the isolation and aloofness of those who are *unmoved* and *cold*, but she never states that connection explicitly.

LVIII. //read ll. 5 – 14// / No, I do, do think that what I came up with the first day and a little more of yesterday, does account for this, / does take into account everything that's in this, / that there's, at the beginning even though it sounds like a compli-

ment   /   there's what is the submerged reproach or insult   /   that be-
comes more and more apparent at the end.   /   There is a problem in
this poem,   /   it's as if the poet is trying to write one way and
can't.   /   He's trying to write about one thing and he can't do
it   /   and that the problems come out more and more at the
end,   /   towards the end of, in the, in the latter part of the
poem.   /   But it's as if he's still trying to stick to it,   /   "The basest
weed outbraves his dignity: /   For sweetest things turn sourest by
their deeds,"   /   as if to just be as you are, willing to do no
hurt,   /   is all right   /   but then with all the other things about the,
"The basest weed" outbraving,   /   because the weed is what, is, in
some sense is more natural,   /   well not more natural than the
lily,   /   well yeah, tiger-lilies or weeds also,   /   the weed is more
common,   /   the weed is what in some ways can't be controlled by
man,   /   I mean weeds always invade the garden,   /   they can but it's
a constant battle,   /   you can't kill them out.   /   Huh, that's what's
interesting because then, saying that to be a weed i—, *is* more natural
than to be the lily.

MOVE 58

In this move she finishes her reading and again expresses satisfaction
with the interpretation she has developed. The explanation of the poem
follows that given in Move 48 quite closely. What is new in the sugges-
tion that the poet tries to "stick to it" until the end of the poem, writing
a poem of praise throughout. Developing the split between the last two
lines suggested in Move 45, she takes the sestet both as a warning and as
a curse: insofar as the *they* will to do no hurt, perform no deeds, they will
not turn sour, and the sestet merely warns them of the consequences of
abandoning this behavior. On the other hand, since the weed—and this
is again a real weed (see Move 32)—is more common, more difficult to
eradicate, and so in a sense more natural than the lily, the weed will win
whatever the rest of us do, even if we try to be good gardeners. There-
fore whether *they* will to hurt or not, the weed will outbrave the *flower's
dignity,* and *they* (the flower, the lilies) will fester.

LIX.   I think, well I maybe said this yesterday but I think that the fact,
the "They," "They," "They,"   /   who, it's a, in, in that "expense of
spirit" poem,   /   the poet—which is also about a very painful topic for
the poet,   /   ab—, it's about revulsion   /   a—, and about
lust   /   —the poet never says 'I' in that poem either,   /   you know,

he doesn't um, so there is some kind of attempt at distancing. / I mean the sonnet is usually, or at least it usually pretends to be, / a much more intimate form / and it's being written *to* somebody, / well not really, / I mean sonnets are usually more about the poet than about the beloved, / but even here there's nothing really specific about the beloved, / I mean you don't even know that it is about a beloved / but I make that assumption partly because it's part of the sequence / and partly because that's what sonnets usually are / or pretend to be / in this period.

Move 59

The next move returns to the topic of the third-person plural pronouns and the distancing they effect (see Moves 40 and 54). That distancing is related to sonnet 129, "also about a very painful topic for the poet," and also totally lacking in first- or second-person pronouns. The formal similarity between the two poems reinforces the thematic one: if that poem explicitly treats lust and revulsion, painful topics that lead the poet to distance them by avoiding "I" and "me," it makes sense to suggest that this one at least implicitly concerns something similar, though here the question is more what is natural and unnatural. This formal similarity is more striking when displayed against the background of the normal practice in sonnets of the period, which usually either are or pretend to be written to somebody, addressed to a specific audience, usually a beloved. This knowledge of typical sonnet practice validates a good bit of Elaine's reading: the facts that the poet is expressing his own feelings rather than meditating generally on human nature, that behind the plural references there is a specific audience intended, a beloved, and that the poem finally reveals more about the poet than about the beloved, all support her view of the poem as a reaction to a specific kind of behavior.

LX. And yet the husbanding "nature's riches," / that has something to do with nature / but it's really only when it gets into the flower / that the poet starts talking about natural process, / but I think the whole poem works sort of in a, a skewed / or, or slanted way. I mean the reproach is very slanted / and it's, I don't know if that's the right word but it's the only one I can think of / — to say that somebody's not being natural, / somebody's not living according to, to natural processes / but it holds "to itself," / it's, it's held, holding itself into itself.

MOVE 60

This returns to the topic of Move 58: what is and isn't natural. Line 6 remains problematical (see Move 45), since husbanding *nature's riches* is presumably CONNECTed to the *flower* and *weeds* and is in any case clearly related to nature and thus to what is natural, but she would prefer to see it as a suggestion of unnatural and unnecessary hoarding. She attempts to solve this problem by claiming that "natural processes" are not discussed until the sestet; if this is true, line 6 only apparently refers to them, and must really be about something else, perhaps unnatural retentiveness.

She then returns to what she calls the slanted (or oblique) approach of the poem (Moves 45 and 47). That is, the message she sees as central to the poem is carried more by the implications of what is said than by what is said itself. The poem never comes out and says "that somebody's not being natural, somebody's not living according to natural processes"; instead it hints at this by referring to the flower "holding itself to itself" (notice the substitution for *live* and *die*: see Moves 20 and 31) or by referring to the unnecessary and unnatural husbanding of nature's riches.

LXI.   And I think I'm going to again, just sort of skimming the whole thing, not reading it but just looking at things. / (cough) "They that have" (clear throat) //read poem// / No, I do think I got it, / because um i-, i-, the poem is just absolutely about one thing, / that there's something, that things keep coming up that, that the poet can't quite control, / can't quite s-, uh, make all these, the, the, the festering, / submit to this, / to, to the original praise. . . .

MOVE 61

The final reading: Elaine again decides that the poem is "just absolutely about one thing," that is, the contrast or contest between what is natural and what is unnatural, and that the poet tries but fails to write a poem praising a kind of restraint that seems appealing at first but is eventually revealed to be unnatural and thwarting.

LXII.   I really can't think of anything else to say. / Or maybe you could look at the poem instead of that a-, as a thing sort of coming out, / th-, that the poet can't control, / the poem is a process of discovery, / that he starts out thinking that it, that it's good / but that, I mean and this is just really another way of looking at the same thing, / but that as he writes, the negative aspects of that kind of behavior, / that kind of way of living, / that kind of being, / um, emerge / . . . oh, I'm so much happier about this poem than about that last one.

MOVE 62

The final move develops the suggestion of Move 48 that the poem is a process of education for the author. He begins with a relatively naïve view, but in writing about it comes to realize its shortcomings. She claims that this is "just really another way of looking at the same thing," which in a sense it is, but in a sense it is quite different: in the second view, the author learns something and the poem intentionally reflects his new knowledge, while in the first view the author writes better than he knows, revealing for the astute reader insights he himself is not aware of and cannot control.

Elaine's procedures in reading this sonnet quite clearly illustrate the five levels or types of interpretive strategies (derived from Fish and Dillon) discussed in the first chapter. The strategies of perception, which decode the propositional structure of the clauses and register phonological properties, are among the most difficult to observe, simply because they operate almost automatically. Of the elementary operations that constitute perception (SYNTAX, PHONOLOGY, WORD, PARAPHRASE, and DEDUCE), SYNTAX is infrequent, and, as was discussed in the second chapter, even when observed, sheds little light on the normal processes of syntactic comprehension. WORD, however, is more frequent: throughout the first day Elaine is annoyed by her inability to recall a precise meaning for *stewards* (see Moves 5 and 19), and she begins taping on the second day by supplying one meaning from the OED. Similarly, she offers paraphrases for *husband* and *expense*, which, since they deal with the meaning of one word, are considered WORD; when she offers paraphrases of phrases or clauses, as she does throughout the first day, they are PARAPHRASE. DEDUCE is used to ascertain the basic propositional structure of clauses when she tries to determine not merely what a word means, but what it suggests, as when *hurt* is immediately linked to a sexual hurt (Move 3) and *base infection* is glossed as venereal disease (Move 7). PHONOLOGY is not particularly evident in Elaine's protocol, though she does check the rhyme scheme fairly early (Move 13).
  Much easier to observe are the strategies of comprehension, which attempt to construct a unified conception of the world or situation dis-

cussed in the poem. The most important elementary processes at this
level are CONNECT:POEM and DEDUCE. CONNECT:POEM is useful here
because by linking two different poetic elements it allows them to be
considered different aspects of one entity. So *they* in the first quatrain are
like the flower in the third (Move 8), and more complexly, the relation
between the *deeds* of the couplet and the apparent inaction discussed in
the octave remains a recurrent problem for her interpretation. DEDUCE
operates on this level insofar as it supplies something beyond the literal
meanings of words and phrases to facilitate this process of seeing con-
nections, as when she decides that "a deed can be a not doing some-
thing also" (Move 23) to relate the couplet to the beginning of the
poem.

On these two levels — perception and comprehension — my readers
agree for the most part, since they have all been trained to comprehend
the individual clauses, to entertain multiple meanings for the words in-
volved, to check the phonology of the poem for possible clues to mean-
ing, and to expect and seek some kind of unity. But the differences of
detail even at these levels — other readers cultivate multiple meanings
more assiduously than Elaine, spend more time on paraphrase, and try to
make more of the phonology, as the next chapter will illustrate — suggest
how idiosyncratically even shared strategies are used.

It is at the next level, with strategies of interpretation, that readers
begin to differ strikingly, for the attempt to relate the poem to the
author's constructive intention activates a wide variety of conceptions
about plausibility and intention, and relies, more than perception and
comprehension, on the idiosyncratic elements of the reader's memory.
Three elementary processes are important here: CONNECT:LITERATURE,
CONNECT: WORLD, and DEDUCE:WORLD. CONNECT:LITERATURE is
used to refer to the reader's conception of the author's typical practices
or intentions. The influence of this operation on Elaine's reading is im-
mense: throughout she reiterates her view that Shakespeare could not
possibly advocate what she sees as unnatural and inhuman
retentiveness — "I guess I can't believe that Shakespeare in the sonnets
would talk about how holding oneself in is a good thing . . . 'cause it
goes against my whole sense of the poet's attitudes in the poems" (Move
23) — and it is this sense of Shakespeare that makes her prefer her initial
reading to the second, more straightforward one she offers on the second
day (Move 38). Her reference to Stephen Booth's "terrific book on
Shakespeare's sonnets" (Move 47) suggests the influence of secondary
materials on this private sense of typical authorial intention.

But no one derives his conception of authorial intention solely from reading; personal conceptions of psychological and poetic plausibility also enter in, and here the operations of CONNECT:WORLD and DE-DUCE:WORLD may be used to certify the correctness of the reader's view of some aspect of the poem. This is particularly clear in Elaine's reading when she relies on her view that excessive aloofness is unnatural — "to hold yourself in, that's unnatural, it's not right" (Move 18) — not to relate the poem to her own concerns, but to determine what Shakespeare could be getting at: if holding oneself in is unnatural, then nobody, certainly not Shakespeare, could advocate it, and so (whatever the poem seems to say) such a position could not have been Shakespeare's intention. Similarly, the fact that "that's just a very natural human thing to do . . . to distance that way — the they, and then talking about others — when you're talking about yourself" (Move 39) allows her to relate the plurals in the poem to Shakespeare's more specific intention. Since readers differ widely in their assessment of plausible psychological positions and in the extent to which they consider contemporary plausibility when reconstructing authorial intention, this level of interpretation is the first one at which they can be seen to differ strikingly.

At the levels of perception and comprehension, readers differ in how frequently they use specific elementary processes: one will worry the meanings of words more than another or will pay more attention to the phonology of the poem. But since these operations all deal with the text, their content is fairly uniform, being to a large extent dictated by the text itself. On the level of interpretation, however, it is the content that differs from reader to reader, since each reader has his own conceptions of psychological plausibility, Shakespeare's typical intentions, and the relation between them. Two readers trying to recover Shakespeare's intention, then, will be likely to disagree, not because they are trying to do different things, but because their different attempts to do the same thing must necessarily work with different materials.

Whatever the theoretical advantages of distinguishing between meaning and significance, they are very difficult to disentangle during the process of reading. One would expect the strategies of significance — of the work as related to something else — to include the elementary operations of CONNECT:LITERATURE, CONNECT:WORLD, and DE-DUCE:WORLD. But in many cases, the real-world knowledge adduced by the latter two operations is called upon, not to reveal the filiations between the work and the world, but to establish what Shakespeare could have meant by referring to objects in the natural world. Elaine's discussion of whether all lilies are cultivated (Move 21) and her misconception — so important for her reading — that weeds live forever (Move

21) are thus not attempts to relate the meaning of the poem to a contemporary situation, but are rather part of the project of constructing that meaning, similar to attempts to settle the meaning of words or to specify plausible psychological processes. And since world knowledge must be represented in memory somehow, it is difficult to distinguish between the kind of linguistic knowledge operating on the first two levels and the world knowledge that would be expected at this level: when she decides of the lily that it festers not "only because it meets with base infection, but also because of nature — it only lives and dies; it dies at the end of the summer" (Move 24), is she relying on some private meaning of "fester" or on some conception of the world? In either case, she is not trying to relate to the lily in the poem to something outside itself; she is trying to assess the import within the poem of the lily's festering. (As we shall see in the next chapter, other readers provide better and clearer examples of this kind of significance.)

The other elementary operation at this level is CONNECT:LITERATURE, and here the distinction between meaning and significance is at least a little clearer. Some types of CONNECT:LITERATURE belong to "the public tradition" that is taught in schools, consisting of received knowledge about Elizabethan conventions, Shakespeare's interests, the typical forms and uses of sonnets, and so forth. This is public in the sense that it is publicly transmitted and tested, so there is a criterion of accuracy: Elaine could be wrong about Elizabethan conventions just as she could be wrong about weeds' longevity. Public knowledge about literature provides many of the expectations readers bring to literary works, and as such functions as part of the attempt to determine the work's meaning. But complementing this is a private tradition based on the reader's interests, conceptions of authors, recent reading, and chance recollections. CONNECT:LITERATUREs of this type, revealing as they do the reader's own (perhaps momentary) mental structure, are not testable in any public sense. Elaine's references to Spenser, Keats, and Stevens, and to her own ideas about Shakespeare, fall into this category: they illustrate how she locates the sonnet within her mind, the kind of poem it is for her.

Connections to the private tradition seem much more like attempts at assessing a poem's significance, but even here the distinction is not as crisp as one would like: Elaine's protocol shows her making these connections, not randomly, but in the attempt to convince herself that certain topics and ways of discussing them are properly literary. She is thus using these other works to validate her conception of the meaning of the sonnet, rather than for the sake of applying what she has learned from the sonnet to some other situation.

Unlike the other strategies, which can be directly observed in the elementary operations, metastrategies — rules for using the other strategies — must be deduced from what the reader does. Evidence of two different types of metastrategy can be found in Elaine's reading. First there is a script (in the sense described in the second chapter) for reading poetry that embodies her general expectations about unity, the importance of individual words and phrases, and the coherence and significance (in the nontechnical sense) of the attitudes the poem expresses. (These may not seem to be operative assumptions among the readers in this study because they are universally accepted and so seem to be natural rather than conventional. But experience with those who have not yet developed such expectations — e.g., beginning students — reveals just how conventional they are.) This general script is refined in two more precisely defined tracks. The first track, designed to treat Elizabethan poetry, and more specifically sonnets, enables the discussion of the overtones of *temptation* in the period (Move 25) and the typical topics and audiences of Elizabethan sonnets (Move 59). More specific still, the track for Shakespearean sonnets activates her knowledge of the sonnet sequence and its concerns (apparent in the references to the "young man" sonnets and to Shakespeare's typical attitudes, and in the immediate assumption of the centrality of sexuality) as well as the information about textual matters elicited by the typographical error in the first line.

The second kind of metastrategy, too vague to be called a script, deals with the reader's general approach to the world. In this category are Elaine's expectation that the world can be organized into polar classes, her assumptions about what is psychologically plausible and right, and her further assumption that Shakespeare shared these conceptions. These metastrategies enable the operations that find specific examples of polarities and of what Shakespeare could or could not have believed in. Again, these assumptions are so much part of the fabric of her reading that it is difficult to see them as assumptions that might not have been made. But consider the effect of changing them: how different her reading would have been had she not assumed that Shakespeare shared her abhorrence of aloof retentiveness, for instance, or (to refer back to the Shakespearean sonnet script) that the attitudes in one sonnet provide evidence about the meaning of another.

As these examples suggest, the script, and more generally, the metastrategies, are not the strategies with which one actually confronts a text. They are rather instructions about what to look for and thus about what elementary operations to use: the expectation of poetic unity leads to the use of CONNECT:POEM but is not itself a CONNECT:POEM. Similarly,

Elaine's assumption that typical attitudes in other Shakespearean sonnets will illuminate sonnet 94 leads to CONNECT:LITERATUREs, and her belief that characteristics of the entities in the poem may be important in determining the poem's meaning leads to CONNECT:WORLDs. The metastrategies are thus beliefs that predispose a reader to act in particular ways when confronted with a literary text. They are usually associated with scripts that guide the act of reading or combined with more loosely structured systems of belief (about typical motives, desires, actions, consequences, and so forth) that allow one to negotiate both literary texts and the world.

Strictly speaking, the individual strategies used, particularly at the first four levels, are operations, and what they operate on are the substantive contents of the problem space. These contents include the work as internalized, as opposed to the text, which is part of the external task environment, a distinction especially clear in this example because the text of sonnet 94 distributed to the readers had an additional *do* in the first line. Half the readers noticed the mistake, checked another text to confirm that it was a mistake, and internalized the standard version of the text, but three others (Joel, George, and Carlos) internalized the error, and Carlos even discussed its scansion at length. The problem space also includes the various reference works the readers consult to establish the text or provide information about it. Elaine used *The Norton Anthology*, the OED, and Stephen Booth's *An Essay on Shakespeare's Sonnets*; other readers referred to various collegiate dictionaries, the Penguin edition of the sonnets, and introductions by Douglas Bush and Hardin Craig. The range of literary works available for allusion is also part of the problem space, and similarly varies from reader to reader. For Elaine this included the sonnet sequence, Shakespeare's other works, the Elizabethan sonnet traditions, and the private tradition represented by Spenser, Keats, and Stevens; others mentioned the Bible, Marlowe, Jane Austen, Verdi, Ingmar Bergman, and various other literary traditions.

Since scripts consist of operations and information about expectations, and problem spaces include these operations, expectations, and substantive information (derived from memory and provided by the task environment) it is impossible for a problem space to coincide with a script. The problem space is the more inclusive concept, and also more variable, since it deals with how a reader approaches a particular poem on a particular occasion. The same reader might use different problem spaces in reading the same poem at different times, just as he might choose to use different scripts. But the assumption I am making is that each reader performs the same kind of reading on each of the poems in this study. By examining the reading of one poem, then, we can characterize the problem space in which it is understood; by comparing the problem spaces used for three poems and abstracting what they have in common, we can begin to define a reader's script.

4 Four Readers Reading Sonnet 94

In the previous chapter we examined in some detail the processes of one reader trying to comprehend Shakespeare's sonnet 94. As might be expected, all competent readers share some characteristics of the reading process: nobody who has not considered the relation between the octave and sestet, for instance, can be said to have understood the poem. And, more minutely, each reader must unravel the syntax, derive the meanings of the words (especially of the problematical ones like *husband* and *expense*), relate different parts of the poem to each other, and so forth. Further, most graduate students will locate the poem in its historical and literary context and will call upon their encyclopedic knowledge for information about lilies, weeds, and psychology.

That is, each reader must use all (or almost all) of the elementary processes in understanding a poem. But readers differ greatly both in the organization of their activities and in the types of elementary processes emphasized: where one reader will stress the relation of the poem to other poems (and thus make frequent CONNECT:LITERATUREs), another will try to understand the poem in terms of Elizabethan society or modern psychology (and thus prefer CONNECT:WORLDs and DEDUCT:WORLDs). Lexical and syntactic ambiguities may occupy much of one reader's time, while another will hardly consider them, concentrating instead on images and their relation to one another.

In this chapter we will examine the practice of four different readers. For each I will discuss the salient characteristics of the reading first and then summarize the development of the interpretation. The protocols are provided in the appendix, and I urge the reader to compare my characterizations and summaries with them closely.

JOEL

If Elaine's general approach to a poem consists primarily of constructing a series of polarities against which various aspects of the poem can be graphed, Joel explores the possibilities of matching the poem or aspects of it with constructs that already exist. In this approach he exemplifies best of all the readers the view of perception as a filling out or modification of frames or scripts explained in the second chapter. At a purely formal level, such schema matching involves checking the structure of the poem to verify that it has the proper formal characteristics. With a Shakespearean sonnet this is relatively straightforward, and Joel here turns to the rhyme scheme and punctuation only when his progress with the poem has stopped (Moves 28 and 29) and he is searching for new clues. With Swinburne's "A Ballad of Dreamland," however, he looked up *Envoi* in a literary handbook to be sure he knew precisely what it meant, and that led him to a definition of the ballade form that he proceeded to check, point by point, against the poem. As this example suggests, emphasis on external exemplars leads to reliance on reference works of all sorts — dictionaries, encyclopedias, handbooks, critical works — to discover just what these exemplars may be.

At the thematic level, Joel seeks a central organizing principle that exists outside the poem and independent of it. While the other readers base their practice on the assumption that a poem presents or constructs a unique situation, emotion, or person, and try to re-present or reconstruct for themselves what it is, he assumes that the situation, emotion, or person can be best understood by finding the most similar preexisting example of it, and then modifying that example as necessary. For sonnet 94, this preexistent exemplar is a literary character — Iago — but Joel makes it clear that the device is strictly hermeneutic:

> I'm continuing with this casting of Iago in the role of the person that's described in the sonnet simply because I have a feeling, a hunch, that it may help me visualize the poem as I go through it. And when I get to words and phrases that do not jive with my understanding of Iago, then I can make corrections at that point and go back through the poem and try to get a clear idea of precisely the sort of character that Shakespeare is talking about in the poem. So it's a lucky guess as to what the character may be that's being portrayed, but I don't put much stock in this guess; I'm also using it sort of as a device for interpreting what is meant, I guess sort of hermeneutical device. (Move 5)

As is evident from the metaphor of the first sentence, he sees this process in theatrical terms, with the poem presenting a character for which the reader as director and producer tries to find the perfect actor, though of course the situation is complicated by the fact that many of the candidates themselves are characters whose potential is thoroughly known. That is, they can't grow into the role; they must match it. This theatrical metaphor continues throughout his reading:

> I would be able to see Iago in this role only with all the soliloquies he has cut out (Move 4); . . . I have really cast the wrong person from the

beginning of this poem (Move 7); The little allegory of the flower and
summer and the weed, those three actors (Move 14); now all of a sudden
the character that comes to mind is (Move 34); so I'm getting now the
picture of a sort of an ideal ruler, the virtuous ruler (Move 35).

Just which character is chosen as the exemplar seems to be partially a
matter of chance. As Joel explains in the second move, he is reminded of
Iago because he has recently seen the Verdi opera; the fact that he calls
this "a lucky guess" suggests that under different circumstances — say
soon after seeing *Measure for Measure* — another character would suggest
itself. But since he proceeds with a rigorous course of TESTing his iden-
tification, the accuracy of the proposed exemplar is less important than
its utility in organizing his reading, in giving him, as he suggests, an
initial conceptualization to modify as he progresses.

Several characteristics of his reading stem directly from this strategy.
First, since the exemplars he calls upon are for the most part literary
characters — Iago, the Duke, and Angelo (whom he calls Antonio) in
Measure for Measure — there are frequent CONNECT:LITERATUREs in his
reading. This is true even when the character is not specifically named:
"The virtuous ruler" (Move 35) and "a mistress who is slow to respond
to sexual temptation with the suitor" (Move 6) are stock characters from
literature rather than people one might meet on the street, as the defi-
nite article in the first description and the stilted language of the second
suggest. This type of CONNECT:LITERATURE is quite different in pur-
pose from Elaine's or even from Joel's own reference to Richard II
(Move 35), which are used to support a particular understanding of a
word or phrase by adducing literary precedents. Here the aim is not to
see whether Iago or the Duke or Angelo resembles the character de-
scribed in the poem but to gauge the extent to which this poem and the
play in which the characters appear are really alternative descriptions of
the *same* character. Identity is at stake, not similarity.

Second, this is obviously a dialectical process, and so requires a good
deal of TESTing. Once he has proposed Iago, or the Duke, as the char-
acter described, Joel goes through the poem (or at least begins to) to
TEST whether each trait mentioned in the poem matches his proposed
exemplar. What is being TESTed is not so much any understanding of
the poem itself as the relation between the poem and this central char-
acter. It is only when he moves away (and even then, not very far away)
from testing the identification that he worries about the poem itself;
while he is discussing his identification, much of his time is spent ex-
plaining the sense in which enumerated characteristics in the poem
could apply to his suggested character.

Third, since the process of TESTing his identification presupposes a clear understanding of what the poem says, he relies heavily on PARA-PHRASE to restate and DEDUCE to expand the descriptions in the poem. Thus *as stone* becomes "emotionally as stone" (Move 4), and *lords and owners of their faces* is successively reinterpreted, from "someone . . . who can completely control the outward expression, what he reveals to the public" (Move 4), to "so the *lords* are *owners* of their outward appear-ance, simply the façade" (Move 9), to "*faces* maybe in the sense of repu-tation, to save face" (Move 33), to "they're in complete command in other words of their semblance, what they show and what they don't show" (Move 37).

Given his general strategy of matching characteristics in the poem to an external character, it is not surprising that Joel's PARAPHRASEs often shade off into CONNECT:LITERATUREs, a kind of paraphrase by exam-ple. *That do not do the thing they most do show* is thus understood not by providing a linguistic restatement but by seeing it as "a kind of Machiavellian virtue of not showing your hand" that Shakespeare com-mends in *Measure for Measure* and *Richard II* (Move 35); and *others but stewards of their excellence* is exemplified and thus explained by all the other characters in *Measure for Measure,* since the Duke "has power over their excellence because he can put them in situations which will cause them to make decisions about staying firm or giving in" (Move 38). How close this kind of illustration is to paraphrase is suggested by the way he approaches the phrase *moving others* on successive days. At first he pro-vides an example: Iago having "his henchmen, unwitting henchmen, help him do his dirty deed" (Move 4); on the second day he offers first a PARAPHRASE and then an example: "*Who, moving others:* that is, through others? Or does that mean — *who moving others* — some sort of, someone indifferent to love?" (Move 20).

To paraphrase something, it is often necessary to unravel its SYNTAX, especially to specify anaphoric relations, and we find Joel worrying the syntactic relations in the poem more frequently than the other readers. The best example of this occurs in his discussion of lines 7 and 8 in Move 33. Earlier he had assumed that *their* in both lines referred back to *they* in line 7: "so the lords are owners of their outward appearance, simply the façade, while the stewards are the owners of their riches or their virtue, their power" (Move 9). But now he suggests that *their* in line 7 refers to *they*, while *their* in line 8 refers to *others:* "But it could be that *their* refers to stewards, that is of their own excellence: other people are but stewards of their own excellence." And then after checking the definition of *steward* again, he offers a paraphrase "other people are not owners of their own excellence but only stewards. They manage their own virtue, their own excellence." This is the reading he retains to the end, where the Duke is a lord and owner of his face, while the others in the play are merely stewards of their own excellence: "They're not in complete control" (Move 38).

Another example, not so successfully resolved, concerns the antecedent of *their* in line 13. At first he suggests *sweetest things* as the anaphor, but then realizes that *they* may be related to the other occurrences of *they* in the poem: "*Their:* does that refer to sweetest things? Or does it refer to the they that have power to do hurt, the lords and owners of their faces. The summer—is that who *their* refers to?" (Move 12). I'm not sure why *summer* is included in the list, except that, like the other *they's* mentioned, it is something outside the flower (see Move 8). When he returns to this line, it is to paraphrase *turn* by "*can* turn" (Move 18). This doesn't solve the original problem, but in a sense the original problem has disappeared. At the end of the first day's taping, Joel declared that one of his problems was relating "the little allegory of the flower and summer and the weed" to "the human characters in the first two quatrains" (Move 14), suggesting that the syntactic link he had initially sought can be replaced by a thematic one. *Their* refers syntactically to *sweetest things*, but since these *sweetest things* are compared in the poem to *they that have power to hurt*, it recalls them thematically. This connection becomes clearer when he returns to consider the possible *deeds* in Move 30. He proceeds through the poem, identifying the deeds that are mentioned in the octave, TESTing whether any of them could cause a sweet thing to sour, and concluding "well, none of the deeds in the first part of the poem really make sense to me in this little apothegm in the couplet." So the link cannot be syntactic, and although the possibility of a thematic link is left open, his TESTing renders it unlikely.

The fourth characteristic of Joel's reading occasioned by his reliance on an external exemplar is his use of CONNECT:POEMs. Sometimes these connections are mediated through the external character, as the connection between the summer's flower and the faces discussed in Move 39. In the thirty-third move, he had remarked the similarity between the appearance of people suggested by *faces* and "the appearance of the poor sick flower in the third quatrain," but did nothing more with it. After the suggestion of the Duke and Angelo as exemplars, however, the equation is much firmer—the flower is like "the lord's face, the steward's excellence, that is reputation, outward semblance and reputation, outward reputation" (Move 39)—and meeting with *base infection* consists of not being "firm in your semblance, in your reputation, in your face, your excellence, meet[ing] with some kind of sullying influence." Similarly, *as stone* is related to lords and owners of their faces, both referring to someone who "can completely control the outward expression, what he reveals to the public" (Move 4) during the discussion of Iago, though it forms a bit of evidence against the identification of Iago with the character discussed in the poem.

More often, however, the CONNECT:POEMs are straightforward. Joel — like all the other readers I studied — expects some kind of organic unity in a poem, as his remarks at the end of the first day of reading indicate: "Ok, now my problem at this point is trying to relate the little allegory of the flower and summer and weed, those three actors, together with the concluding couplet . . . trying to relate that to the characters, the human characters, in the first two quatrains" (Move 14). On the first day, he devotes most of his time to paraphrasing the poem and testing the extent to which Iago is the character described; when he returns to it on the next day he progresses from paraphrase and word definitions to a detailed consideration of the connections between various parts of the poem. In the twenty-sixth move, he relates the imagery in the various quatrains, and after checking the rhyme scheme and punctuation to see whether they suggest new connections, he embarks on a long and systematic attempt to identify some action in the octave with the *deeds* of line 13 (Move 30). He then considers the various pairs in the poem — weeds and lilies, weed and flower, stewards and lord, others and movers — for parallels (Moves 31 – 34). At that point he hits upon Angelo in *Measure for Measure* as another pattern for the character in the poem, and his attention shifts back to testing the connection between the character and the poem.

The fifth characteristic of Joel's reading related to his use of external exemplars has already been mentioned: his frequent recourse to outside sources. Other readers suggested that if they were preparing a poem to teach, they would research it a bit; Joel actually does this. A substantial part of his reading of Swinburne's "A Ballad of Dreamland" was devoted to matching the definition of ballade in Hugh Holman's *Guide to Literature* against the poem, and he stopped at the library and looked through several critical studies of Hopkins while working with "Carrion Comfort." Here he relies on two dictionaries to provide possible meanings for *husband* and *expense* — words from the line he consistently finds problematical — and *stewards*. In Move 24, he returns to the sixth line and turns to the dictionary for more precise definitions of the important words, a lexical analogue of looking outside the poem for an organizing character or principle. With meanings, however, he prefers to retain as many as possible, so he considers all four definitions in *Webster's New World Dictionary* for *husband,* accepting the first two and the last as possibly relevant. The first two — "to marry" and "to conserve" — are the two he had suggested in the twenty-second move, and his comment ("well, there's a possibility there of still a pun,") is a TEST of the earlier hypothesis that a pun was involved. The archaic definition is passed over, but since "obsolete doesn't mean Shakespeare couldn't have used it, obviously, or that it wasn't current in his day," the obsolete meaning is apparently accepted. And in fact it is this meaning that he tries, not altogether successfully, to explicate in the thirty-sixth move.

For *expense* he turns to the OED, supplying the meaning of the Latin etymon himself, and reads through the definitions looking for one that fits the poem. None of them seems particularly apt, and he tries a different and interesting strategy of looking for citations to Shakespeare instead of definitions. Again the strategies Joel and Elaine use differ sharply: when Elaine needed a definition or exemplification for *expense,* she retrieved one from memory; when Joel needs one he looks it up in a reference. Neither approach is entirely successful, of course, because both are selective; consider how different Elaine's reading would have been had she remembered the use of *expense* in sonnet 30 ("And moan the expense of many a vanished sight") instead of 129. And Joel's strategy would have been more successful had he had access to a Shakespeare concordance rather than the OED, but it probably would not have affected his reading greatly, since line 6 merely remains unexplained for him at the end, something that seems to fit, but precisely how is unclear.

The use of the dictionary is the most obvious example of Joel's practice throughout his reading of supplying meanings, often multiple, for the words he considers problematical. This is presumably linked to his emphasis on paraphrase, for meanings are essential to paraphrase. Thus he progresses through the poem, glossing *stewards* as "keepers, owners" (Move 9) before he looks it up to find his hypothesis confirmed (Move 33); *outbraves* is "will outshine . . . as far as being larger and looking healthier" and "look dignified" (Move 11); *rightly* is "by right" (Move 22), and *husband* is "as in husbandry, but also as in to mate" (Move 22).

What characterizes Joel's practice is its extremely systematic nature. Unlike Elaine, he never just abandons topics or problems; instead, they are shelved (Move 6) or specifically put aside for later ("I'll have to come back to that," Move 8). And when he puts something aside, he returns to it. His taping on the first day ends with a brief catalogue of his two basic problems in understanding the poem: relating the allegory of the sestet to the human characters in the octave, and establishing Shake-speare's tone. When he resumes taping over thirty hours later, the "big problem" he immediately takes up is "whether to take Shakespeare at his word or to attribute to him an irony that may be in reality more characteristic of later centuries, or at least of other poets" (Move 15). And even long after he has stopped overtly considering Iago, the figure is still present: he surfaces briefly in the twenty-first move, and when Angelo springs to his mind it is *instead of* Iago, as is indicated by the initial adverbials: "Now all of a sudden the character that comes to mind is, I believe his name is Antonio" (Move 34).

Similarly systematic are his several progressions through the poem, first building up paraphrases and then seeking connections, his consid-eration of different definitions of problematical words, his attempts to discover what actions in the octave could qualify as *deeds* in the sestet, and his attempts to match the description in the sonnet with a character he already knows. Curiously, what is unsystematic about his readings is their conclusion. He often just breaks off, promising to return to clear up a few minor difficulties, but he never does, so the sixth and tenth lines remain unexplained,

As we turn to his reading of the poem we can see how the initial postulation of an external figure immediately affects comprehension: *rightly* in line 5 strikes him as ironic, presumably because a character like Iago does not deserve *heaven's graces*. Elaine also decided that *rightly* was sarcastic or ironic, but only after worrying about it for almost half of her reading. If the character described is Iago, however, the case is clear. The plurals in the poem — *they, themselves, lords and owners, faces,* etc. are immediately and unconsciously translated into singulars: "Shakespeare . . . is speaking about someone who . . . is the true lord and owner of his face" (Move 4); "I'm continuing with this casting Iago in the role of the person that's described in the sonnet" (Move 5). When he moves away from the identification with Iago to consider the "image of a castle-keep or a medieval or Renaissance courtly life" (Move 9), he returns to the plurals in the poem, since it is possible to visualize several lords and stewards around a castle, and after using the plurals consistently in the long middle section, continues them even when he casts the Duke in the central role. Part of the reason for this, I think, is that in the four-teenth move he had identified the sestet as "the little allegory of the flower and summer and the weed, those three actors" and suggested that they should relate to "the human characters in the first two quatrains": the plurality of actors in the sestet reinforces the plurality in the octave. So he returns to the poem a day later (Move 15) with the concept of a group, and he maintains the plural, even when talking of Iago, with only one exception: *who, worrying others* might mean "someone indifferent to love" (198). In fact, what happens now is that he realizes that the poem describes a class, and Iago, the reluctant mistress, the Duke, and Angelo all become possible exemplars of the class.

The process of arriving at an external exemplar occurs again late in the reading. The first identification with Iago is not altogether satisfactory, because Iago is not *as stone, unmoved*, or *to temptation slow*. Similarly, the reluctant mistress suggested by the fourth line (Moves 5 and 6) conflicts with the masculine gender of *lords and owners* in the seventh (Move 23). In the thirty-third move, Joel is considering the unmoved movers who have the *power to hurt*, two characteristics that nicely describe Angelo in *Measure for Measure*. Once he has suggested this interpretation, he proceeds to TEST it by seeing whether "he is an example of a character who, one of these flowers who meets base infection." As he proceeds with his TEST, it seems that though Angelo fits the initial description, he is actually thinking of the Duke; he tests the characteristics in the poem against what he knows of the Duke until he is stopped by line 6 ("The tough line for [him]," Move 36). But he resumes and finishes the octave, completing his matching.

When he turns to the sestet (Move 39), his identification is less clear: he never mentions either the Duke or Angelo, and although Angelo seems to be a much better example than the Duke of a flower meeting with base infection, the discussion of the last line, linking it specifically with a kind of Machiavellian virtue, recalls the discussion of the Duke in Move 33. By this stage in the reading, however, the precise identification is less important because it has served its function as a hermeneutic device allowing Joel to visualize the kind of character described in the poem.

By the time he reaches the thirty-seventh move, he feels that he understands the poem — thanks to the combined figure of the Duke and Angelo — as a discussion about the nurture of one's reputation, or "face." The successful people described in the octave are in control of themselves and the situations in which they find themselves, and thus most importantly, of how they face the world; others are only stewards of their excellence in the sense that they can be manipulated by the lords and owners. The sestet is a warning that reputation and virtue can be compromised. Joel still cannot fit two lines into this reading: line 6 is problematical because his settling on 'cultivate' as the operative meaning of *husband* makes it difficult to find a definition of *expense* that allows paraphrase (see Moves 24 and 36), and line 10 because reputation — the flower—doesn't seem to be something that can remain entirely private (Move 40). But he has solved the two problems he mentioned at the end of the first day: the "little allegory" in the sestet has been related to the human characters of the octave, and any question about Shakespeare's tone has been resolved by the discovery of laudable characters in the plays who exhibit the traits mentioned in the poem.

To characterize Joel's problem space, then, a poem has a central unifying element that may be an image or character, to which everything in the poem relates. One way to discover this central element is to turn to external means, either by consulting critical works or by guessing at literary characters, and then progressing through the poem, first ascertaining what the poem says and testing that against the postulated unifying element, and then relating parts of the poem to each other in an attempt to refine the initial hypothesis. As many different possibilities as reasonable should be considered for word meanings, syntactic constructions, and relations within the poem, but all must be rigorously tested for relevance and either accepted, rejected, or put aside for later consideration.

PHILIP

Similarly systematic is Philip, who in an almost textbook manner proceeds through the poem several times providing PARAPHRASEs and suggesting CONNECTIONs. His problem space is characterized by two central concerns: supplying what he calls paraphrase, and locating the work within its literary and historical setting.

In his introduction—which follows the initial reading of the poem instead of preceding it—Philip explains the procedure he will follow: "So what I'm going to try and do is just what I usually wind up doing with Shakespeare sonnets it seems, is spend a lot of time just trying to paraphrase it, and in the process sort of unravelling the word plays" (Move 3). Though he states it as though this were an approach he reserves for Shakespeare sonnets, perhaps to avoid "the tendency [with Shakespeare sonnets] . . . to just let the flow of the verse carry you without understanding" (Move 12), it is in fact the same approach he uses on all three poems. But to understand what he means by this we must see it in action, for he intends a rather broad definition of paraphrase.

The first component is naturally supplying the meanings of words, which he usually does without referring to the dictionary, as *husband* is glossed "do not expend them," and "they keep them, say if they nurture them" (Move 6). When he does look up a meaning, he tests its completeness and applicability: the Pelican edition of the sonnets, which he consults for glosses (another indication of the premium he puts on paraphrase), suggests "dispensers" as the intended meaning of *stewards*, a meaning he retains as only secondary to his own favored one of "executors" (Move 30).

Generally, though, he has little trouble with the meanings of words or with the next level, that of offering a paraphrase of the syntactic constructions within the poem. Some do give him momentary pause, as when he translates line 5, "I take it husband their own resources and do not expend them; *from expense* they don't use them up, they keep them say if they nurture them, they husband them" (Move 6). But more frequently he unravels the syntax as effortlessly as he decides on the antecedent for *they* in line 3: *"they rightly do inherit heaven's graces* — the people who show these characteristics . . ." (Move 6).

Perception at these lower linguistic levels is almost automatic for Philip, and apparently not what he means by paraphrase. What occupies the bulk of his time is comprehension: relating different lines and clauses to each other in the attempt to build up a unified conception of what is being described. The relation between the first two lines, for example, is not obvious: "The two lines are in apposition, but they don't seem right away to say the same thing, since the first line suggests some kind of restraint, while the second suggests not restraint but a misleading if not false appearance" (Move 4). Alternatively, he suggests, the first three lines may list three unrelated characteristics of the people described rather than being three different expressions of the same characteristic. He leaves the matter open, but continues to find the relation between these lines problematical.

In the thirteenth move he suggests a more specific connection — "Well what they *do not do* is *hurt*, and what they *most do show* is perhaps that they have the *power"* — but in the twenty-seventh move he admits that the second line is still difficult. It is not until he decides that the *power to hurt* refers specifically to arousing love in others that the relation between the two lines becomes clear, for then the second line means "they don't fall in love even though they look as if that's what they're made for" (Move 28).

An extension of the attempt to relate successive clauses or lines to each other is to CONNECT words and phrases from different parts of the poem, a strategy Philip consciously acknowledges in the eleventh move: "somehow we've got to make a connection between the *they*, the first word, and these flowers." Most simply this happens with repeated words: "and of course the *others* of line eight have presumably got to be the same others as the *other* of line three" (Move 30). More complexly, he attempts to CONNECT different phrases discussing the same topic, constructing what might be called semantic nets except that often a certain amount of interpretation is necessary before the putative semantic relation becomes clear. *Owners of their faces,* for instance, "seems not to jibe completely with *do not do the thing they most do show;* that is, if at line two their appearance is somehow deceptive, how are they *owners of their faces?*" (Move 7). The particular solution ("Perhaps in the sense that they've got perfect control of their faces, perfect control of the appearance they present, even though it may be in some sense a false appearance or a deceptive one") is less important for our purposes than the fact that Philip sees the necessity and difficulty of relating the two phrases.

Frequently these larger connections are mediated by relating the poem to a relatively specific external situation. At the most obvious level this involves relating the characters described to some general group of real people. Philip's initial response after reading the first line during the first detailed progress through is "no guesses yet as to who *they* are" (Move 3), but it is not long before he's "wondering if maybe these are, maybe some, maybe the nobility or certain nobles" (Move 5), a guess strengthened by the metaphor of the lord in the manor in the second quatrain.

More complex in terms of literary strategies is his realization (between the first and second day of taping) that the Shakespearean sonnets, and Elizabethan sonnets generally, are usually quite personal, written (or ostensibly written) to a single person rather than about a group of people. This leads naturally to speculation about the young man and the Dark Lady, possible objects of the sonnets, and to locate 94 within the sequence, he reads the sonnets around it. He finds that 93 treats both love and deceptive appearance, and this suggests that *power to hurt* refers to hurting in a personal relationship, perhaps with specific reference to the young man, a hypothesis later refined to "*hurt* with some suggestion of the old courtly poetic convention of love itself as a wound." The first line would then be paraphrased "they that arouse love without intending to," and the problem with the second line is simultaneously solved—"they don't fall in love even though they look as if that's what they're made for" (Move 28). *Unmoved* and *cold* refer to "unpassionate and uninvolved," the temptation they are *slow* to becomes sexual temptation rather than indulging the *power to hurt,* and the first quatrain falls into place.

Joel and Philip thus both use external situations or characters to crystallize their readings, but they use them in quite different ways. From the very beginning of his reading, Joel postulated an external character for the poem to describe, and his reading became in large part a dialectical process of testing poem and character against each other to see whether the postulated character was the right one. For Philip, the external situation is referred to only after his initial attempts at paraphrase (the reading of the first day) leave him unsatisfied, and then that situation is re-created on the basis of the poem. Further, his postulated situation is much more general than a specific character, consisting mainly of some kind of vague disappointment in love combined with deceptive appearances. In his reading there is thus no dialectical process; he reconstructs the experience the poem refers to from what the poem says and hints from sonnet 93.

These hints are evidence of the other important characteristic of his problem space, the fact that from the very beginning of his reading he locates the poem within a fairly precise literary context. For Philip a poem exists within the institution of literature and literary study, and, especially with so institutional an author as Shakespeare, he takes pains to check his own hypotheses and interpretations against the others available. He is unique among the six readers in noticing the misprint in the first line immediately, which gives his protocol a strange appearance, since instead of an introduction describing the setting or his expectations or even an initial reading of the poem, he begins with a bit of textual sleuthing. He recognizes immediately that the line with the errant *do* doesn't scan, but it is characteristic that he checks another text anyway. Similarly characteristic is his referring to the Pelican edition of the sonnets for glosses even though he retains his own reading when he disagrees with a proposed definition and concludes (of the glosses in general), "ok, really not much help there, which is fairly common" (Move 23).

Knowing that the poem is a Shakespeare sonnet activates several different kinds of expectations for him. Formal or structural considerations are not emphasized, but he does "pause for structure" (Move 8) to ascertain that the poem breaks down syntactically into three quatrains and a couplet, and that "as so often the strongest stop is after the eighth line, so that in a sense there's an octave and a sestet too." Experience has taught him that "the problem is obviously going to be, once we figure out what the octave is talking about, to see what the connection is bridging that period at the end of line eight" (Move 8), a strategy that is later specified as "somehow we've got to make a connection between the *they*, the first word, and these flowers" (Move 11).

More importantly, it places the poem in a number of literary contexts. There is the general literary context, consisting of examples from the whole literary tradition of concerns similar to those in the poem. Thus the final couplet is interpreted "a great man brought low descends into worse villainies than a man of less stature" and is immediately related to Macbeth, Othello, Lear, Richard III, and Faustus (Move 10). This is the kind of CONNECT:LITERATURE predominant in Elaine's reading; its function is to certify a topic or sentiment as properly literary by adducing other examples of it. More specifically, the poem is an Elizabethan sonnet, and Philip realizes on the second day that this suggests strongly that it is personal rather than general, discussing "a class of people with a very specific application to the person, whoever it is, that the poet is addressing" (Move 27). As a Shakespearean sonnet the poem has a still more specific literary background, provided by "the sort of shadowy narrative behind" the sonnets (Move 42), peopled by the young man, the rival poet, and the Dark Lady. This narrative is even more shadowy in his recollection, and it is to illuminate this aspect of the literary context that he reads the poems preceding 94 (Moves 22 and 26) and the introductions by Douglas Bush (Move 42) and Hardin Craig (Move 44).

This sonnet narrative shades off into the real or concrete context (he uses both terms in Move 44), which consists of the real historical actions that are referred to by the poem. The difference between the narrative context within the sonnet sequence and the real or concrete background is that the former is a fictionalized version of the latter; it is thus possible to place the poem within the sequence without understanding its historical origin. He has throughout characterized the poem's relation to its historical context as tenous ("it's pretty vague, at least it seems to be that it's pretty vague, really what he's getting at," Move 36; "obviously the line is much too vague to be able to pin down to that," Move 36; "in paraphrasing you want to keep trying to substitute something more specific for Shakespeare's metaphor, and it's very hard to know what to substitute," Move 37). This is typical (in his view) of the sonnets: "you have the feeling of a story behind it that you can never uncover, that what the poet is saying and what perhaps the person addressed, if this was in fact a single person, what the poet understands or what the poet intends and what the person addressed understands, is something very concrete, but to everyone else, it remains simply elusive and mysterious, and more in the realm of suggestion than any sort of real narration" (Move 40). Without knowledge of this concrete occurrence the poem can be paraphrased, but not interpreted, which involves relating it to its historical impetus: "certainly I think 94 alone . . . can be paraphrased, but it can't really be interpreted; that is it's deliberately esoteric, concealing essential information you need to be able to understand it in concrete terms" (Move 40).

And so, for Philip, the two basic characteristics of his problem space are intimately related. Paraphrase—by which he means a complete explication of the poem—is necessary for interpretation but not in itself sufficient; for an interpretation the poem must be not only understood but related to the historical context from which it originated. He thus feels that his reading is satisfactory but not, finally, as complete as he would like, since the concrete situation behind all the sonnets remains shadowy.

The course of his reading is fairly straightforward, though it is frequently interrupted by commentary. After setting the text in Move 1, he reads the poem in Move 2 and explains his initial expectations in Move 3. The next four moves are devoted to paraphrasing (in Philip's sense) the octave, not altogether satisfactorily. After the eighth move, devoted to form and the expectations deriving from it, he returns to the poem to paraphrase the sestet and relate the couplet to literary examples.

The twelfth move seems to begin a second detailed reading of the poem (the third altogether) but becomes instead a short disquisition on the distractions a Shakespearean sonnet offers to the task of paraphrase. Moves 13–15 progress through the octave once more, detailing the manorial image in the second quatrain. By the end of the first day's reading, he has read the poem several times, offered paraphrases of the individual lines, and tried unsuccessfully to combine the different lines of the octave into a unified conception. The major problem he faces is relating the other lines to the first: the *power to hurt* sounds like temptation avoided, but if that is so, how can *they* move *others?* He tries to resolve this by elaborating the hints in the text about a manor in lines 7 and 8: *they* become *lords* and *owners unmoved* in the manor house, while the *others* are *stewards* either influenced or commanded by the lords. But this does not work very well: not only is it difficult to see how the others "turn the lord's *excellence* into some sort of profitable action" (Move 15), it is difficult to know even what that might mean. And this solution tends to ignore the first two lines and the reference to temptation. So he is not entirely pleased when he stops after about twenty minutes.

He begins again the next morning with a long introduction explaining what he finds atypical about his reading behavior the previous day and how he intends to change it. This time through he is going to refer to the Pelican edition of the sonnets for glosses of the lines, assume that the sonnet is personal rather than general, and perhaps try to place it

within the general narrative of the sonnet sequence. Seven moves de-
voted to reading the sonnet with the Pelican glosses add little new, a not
unexpected outcome, but the next three moves, in which he reads the
sonnets preceding 94 in the sequence, provide the turning point for his
interpretation. Sonnets 91 and 93 both treat love, and 93 combines with
that a concern about deceptive appearance, which he immediately links
to *owners of their faces* (Move 26). The line from 93 he repeats is *"like a
deceived husband, so shall I live, supposing thou art true like a deceived hus-
band"* (Move 26), and the idea of deceit or disappointment in love,
coupled with the suggestion that in spite of the plural pronouns, the
poem is actually about a specific person, leads to the new and apparently
satisfying reading that he gives in Moves 27 to 34 and reiterates, adding
speculation about the concrete situation behind the sonnet (does it refer
primarily to the young nobleman or to the Dark Lady?) in 35 through 40.
The octave describes a class of people who arouse strong feelings in
others without themselves being moved; instead they "are in perfect
control, they're in complete possession of their faculties" (Move 38)
while others somehow work for them. The sestet is a warning to these
people, specific in the quatrain and then general again in the final cou-
plet, to avoid going wrong, since, having as much power as they do,
"they can turn into monsters" (Move 40).

This reading is coherent and satisfying except in two respects. First,
there is a more or less constant fluctuation between his feeling that the
poem is actually about Shakespeare's (perhaps a persona rather than the
poet) relationship with either the young man or the Dark Lady and the
attempt to remain true to the plurals in the poem. This fluctuation sur-
faces in the comment that "the octave then suggests real approval for
people like this, with the suggestion that, not explicitly in the poem but
the suggestion in context [i.e., of the sonnet sequence] that this — well I
think for the whole poem that all these *they's* and *them's* are really being
held up as an example to a particular person . . ." (Move 31). This leads
to difficulty with his interpretation of the stewards. If the references are
actually singular, then the poet is a *steward* of the lord's excellence in the
sense that he both preserves and dispenses to others the lord's excel-
lence through his verse (Move 31). But when *stewards* is taken to refer to
a class, it is less clear how they in general preserve or dispense "the
resources of the estate, in this case standing for the personal resources of
people of this sort" (Move 31). This problem is never resolved, and in
his last reading, Philip merely sidesteps it: "others are simply the people
who execute their orders or who in some sense or other work for them"
(Move 38).

Second, he never comes up with a satisfactory justification of lines
nine and ten. He explains them—"contributes to the total effect and a
long-lasting effect though its lifespan is brief and in itself it's perhaps—
this goes a little beyond the line—but perhaps unaware of its contribu-
tion to a greater whole"—but immediately adds that "It's a little hard to
see how those two lines really fit into the poem" (Move 32), and leaves
them as a problem to return to. His only justification for the lines is as a
means of introducing the flower "because it's the metaphor for people of
this sort throughout the sestet" (Move 32), and when he does return to
it, it is only to reiterate that "that still seems like almost a gratuitous
sentiment tossed in there, to establish the flower and fill lines nine and
ten because the short life of the flower really doesn't seem relevant to
what the poet is doing with it" (Move 34).

Other problems disappear in the course of the reading. *Temptation* was
originally related to *power to hurt* (Move 5), but is finally seen to be
"sexual temptation perhaps" (Move 29), connected with *husband*[ing]
nature's riches from expense (Move 37) and *base infection* (Move 40). The
fifth line is initially surprising—"that firm judgment comes as maybe
something of a surprise" because "the picture you get of this type in the
first quatrain is a mixed one" (Move 29)—but by the final reading the
judgment provides a guide for the reader—"they move others but
they're unmoved themselves—*cold, and to temptation slow*—and lest you
think that this is undesirable, we go right on to *they rightly do inherit
heaven's graces*" (Move 37). And *nature's riches*, first explained as "their
own resources" (Move 6), then confusingly as "the riches of the estate"
(Move 15), become more closely identified with attributes related to
love: "perhaps their beauty, perhaps their capacity for love, affection,
whatever" (Move 30), and finally chastity or virtue: "it's possible that he
really does mean that line six to be sexual, but of course it could also be
the resources of personality, of personal strength or courage or almost
anything, a general sort of noble character" (Move 37).

The concluding five moves treat what Philip sees as "the real problem
with this poem"—"in isolation you simply don't have enough evidence
to know what the poet is talking about" (Move 41). He's satisfied with
his paraphrase—"I think I have pretty well worked out what he's saying
about this situation"—but not with his interpretation—"but without
knowing what the situation is, what occasion gives rise to the poem—
and it's obviously an occasional poem—it's almost impossible to pin
down its meaning" (Move 41). He refers to Douglas Bush and Hardin
Craig in search of an explanation of the concrete situation behind the
poem, and while he finds hints, especially the reference to "the expense

of spirit" (Move 43) that influenced Elaine's reading so greatly, there is no mention of any situation specific enough to satisfy him, and he ends advocating the general kind of reading he has derived as the only one possible in the circumstances.

The most significant aspect of Philip's problem space, then, is his reliance on literary history. Alone among the readers he checks the other sonnets close in the sequence for hints about the topic of the poem, and although other readers refer to dictionaries and other texts (usually in *The Norton Anthology*), he is the only one to consult critical discussions of the sonnets. He is also the only one to use an edition of the sonnets systematically to provide glosses, something related to the other basic characteristic of his problem space, his attempt to "paraphrase" the poem, to arrive at a unified conception of its meaning. He believes that a full interpretation requires relating the work to the real-world context it refers to, however fictionally, and is slightly frustrated that he cannot make this final step, but is generally satisfied with his paraphrase, which relies on hints from other poems and critics as well as close attention to the language and suggestions of the text.

ANN

A fitting title for Ann's reading of the poem would be "Shakespeare Our Contemporary," since the salient characteristic of her problem space is the tendency to refer the general circumstances and all the details in the poem to a contemporary situation. This is a strategy she explains in her reading of Swinburne's "A Ballad of Dreamland": "I like to have a way into a poem that has to do with my own preoccupations or with something that I can hook on to, something that appeals to me or intrigues me." Swinburne's poem was difficult for her to come to grips with because she could relate it to no immediate concern; sonnet 94, on the other hand, is related to her preoccupations in several important ways.

First there is an encounter with a friend, "a very disturbed person":

> I had a discussion recently with a very disturbed person who was very upset about something, and the tone of the discussion or of the things that the person said to me were very much like this, the sonnet, very bitter, kind of ironic, expressing intense frustration with the way things were, yet at the same time hoping that something terrible would happen to the person that had upset her and at the same time trying to indicate that this of course, this terrible thing, would happen to the person who had upset her. (Move 12)

This encounter is initially recounted to explicate the tone of the sonnet, but later the first quatrain is linked to this contemporary situation (Move 21), and then the sestet (Move 33).

The reliance on this situation is merely the most overt example of a strategy that informs Ann's reading. While other readers try to relate the poem to some kind of an external state of affairs — Elaine and Philip constructing one from the poem, Joel trying to match the one in the poem against some literary prototype — Ann sees the poem in terms of contemporary conditions, of events that could occur today. One of her first reactions to the poem is that "it seems inaccessible," but that inaccessibility is immediately explained in terms of a familiar situation — "it's the kind of poem one would show to someone having written it in a fit of pique" (Move 3). Since "it seems to have a very personalized kind of meaning . . . it seems very personal" (Move 3), it makes a certain kind of sense to explicate it in terms of a personal situation, and that is, naturally, a contemporary personal situation. This leads to seeing the *they* in the poem as contemporaries, a group refusing to respond in a normal human way to those that love them (Move 13): "they don't squander nature's gifts, but presumably they should, or at least allow others, those who care about them, or care for them, or who react strongly to them, to participate in nature's gifts" (Move 14). The octave in general treats a person (or people) who "is inhuman . . . refusing to be human, refusing to participate in the natural cycle of things" (Move 26). The second line suggests deceit, overt or implied: "it will seem as though he or she will respond to me but he or she really won't respond to me. He or she is a tease, promises to respond yet doesn't respond" (Move 27). In refusing to respond, *they* misuse their potential — "it's like yeah, yeah, all right, you know, do it to me but don't expect to get anything back" (Move 28). They are so immovable that they "can't even be provoked into doing something nasty or crummy" (Move 29). Ultimately, the expression of pique that is the poem stems from the lack of reciprocity or mutuality in the relationship: "I mean if you posit a relationship and conduct yourself as though there's a relationship and the other person refuses to nod ot turn his or her head, you know, that's pretty demeaning; you do become the steward of someone else's excellence in that case" (Move 33).

Throughout, both the language used — "pique," "caring about or for others," the choice between "he" and "she," "tease," "respond to," "do it to me," "something nasty or crummy," "relationship" — and the situations suggested indicate how contemporary is the personal situation to which the poem is being related. The obvious consequence of reading about an Elizabethan personal experience in terms of a similar contemporary experience is that the sense of perspective is lost: there is no suggestion that Elizabethan morals or expectations might have been different; Shakespeare (or the narrator of the poem) becomes one of us. And in fact this identification is facilitated rather than hindered by what Ann remembers of the posited situation behind the sonnets. She knows the story of the young nobleman and the Dark Lady, but she doesn't know enough about the sonnets or about "Shakespeare's proclivities or love life or anything else to know whether that makes any sense at all" (Move 11), and this ignorance sanctions the possibility of understanding what seem to be personal dynamics in the poem in terms of current personal dynamics, as when she tries to justify the flower as an illustration of what could happen to the *they*. Flowers often express beauty "because certain kinds of physical beauty are transient. And if this is written to a young male, I mean certainly that kind of appeal is transient." But this suggested homosexuality is very quickly converted into a more familiar heterosexual relationship: "I mean, Shakespeare is older and everything, and women's, you know, one has one's bloom and then it goes very quickly," in Jane Austen if not in the twentieth century (Move 23). The effect of this conversion is to retain the expression of pique that seems to be contained in the poem, but to substitute for whatever originally caused it something that could cause it today and perhaps did in the case of her friend, the "very disturbed person."

The psychology of the characters is likewise modernized, with what was originally seen as an expression of pique becoming an "escalation" of pique: "If it is an expression of pique and has the same kind of psychological escalation that expressions of that kind, if you try to sustain them in some kind of protracted utterance, tend to have" (Move 33), then the structure becomes explicable. Alternatively, "the thirteenth line contains maybe more than the poet wanted to say about (or to bring up about) what is really upsetting him or is upsetting her" (Move 36). In either case, the contemporary translation is clear: a sonnet hardly seems "a protracted utterance," and "upset" and — again — the choice between "him" and "her" suggest characters and a situation more modern than Shakespearean.

There are two other indications of this collapsing of the Elizabethan and contemporary world pictures. First, discussing *they* on the second day, Ann suggests that "*They* also become in an odd way a sort of a false object of respect, an object of esteem, much like the despised aristocrat or the hated property owner, or the landlord whom you respect because you, seem to respect, because you have to, but is a real piece of shit"

(Move 26). The aristocrat and property owner seem to be literary characters, as indicated by their generic definite articles and single defining adjectives, but the landlord, vivified by his relative clause, is a contemporary person, somebody Ann might actually know. That these characters from quite different realms can be so casually included on the same list suggests that there is, in her mind, little distinction between them.

The second is her especially vivid contemporary way of relating references in the poem to actual occurrences. Elaine immediately identified *base infection* as venereal disease; when Ann makes the same identification it is more specifically in terms of gonorrhea (Move 10), and the link between *deeds* and *inherit* elicits "that's a passive thing: someone gives you a bunch of clap and that's it" (Move 19). Similarly, Elaine emphasized the difference between the weeds that endure and the flowers that do not, but not in the striking detail that Ann does: "if you mutilate a tulip or if you mutilate a jonquil or whatever, it's very clear that it has been mutilated, there's no way to disguise that, where I suppose a weed just grows back in about a day" (Move 9), and "stuff happens to plants: people do things to plants, animals do things to plants, ultimately other plants even do things to plants, I mean weeds can fuck up I suppose certain kinds of flowering plants simply by crowding them out of their area, you know, taking up the nutrients and taking up the sunlight and taking up the space and so on and so forth" (Move 37). Elaine wonders whether Elizabethan cultivation differed from ours, whether lilies were *only* cultivated (as opposed to the wild weeds); Ann never does, and relates the flowers directly to varieties — jonquils and tulips — that are well known today. And her whole vocabulary for discussing the situation, from "positing a relationship" (Move 33) to "pissing somebody off" (passim), is vividly contemporary.

Related to this vividness is her habit, evident in the example of the flower, of constructing a series of descriptions as a kind of triangulation to gloss something from the poem. Sometimes, as in the previous example, the members of the series are different; more often they are similar expressions of the same basic idea, a progression of near synonyms that tends to drift away from the original textual stimulus. Her protocol is studded with these series — "who move others, to passion, or to rage, to hurt, whatever" (Move 5); *lords and owners* suggests "haughty, in a position to dispense crumbs, or not dispense crumbs or not dispense anything . . . to dispense disdainfully or not to dispense at all" (Move 17); *others but stewards* is glossed "others but caretakers, protectors, cultivators, guardians of the excellence of these people; at their beck and call" (Move 17). While these series perform a number of func-

tions in her reading—sometimes she uses them to refine her concep-
tions, sometimes to suggest the openness of the text, sometimes, appar-
ently, just out of habit—the overall effect of their frequency is to
suggest that the text can be understood against a wide background of
contemporary concerns and examples.

This collapsing of the contemporary and the Elizabethan is reflected
in the very few CONNECT:LITERATUREs Ann makes: they are unneces-
sary if the basic situation discussed in the poem can be as easily and
faithfully exemplified today as in Shakespeare's time. We have already
seen how information about Shakespeare's life and the narrative behind
the sonnets is naturalized in contemporary terms. The only other refer-
ences to literature or literary characters are to Jane Austen (Move 23),
Ingmar Bergman (Moves 23 and 31), and the oblique references to stock
literary characters ("the despised aristocrat" and "the hated property
owner," Move 26), sayings ("how the mighty have fallen, if you're high,
you know you fall a greater distance than most people," Move 33), and
situations ("I mean if something is written on the death of the lover,
then the motivation for it is very straightforward. Something is written
on the departure of the lover, the marriage of the lover to another, the
direct cessation of affections that the lover has for the other lover, you
know, those kind of things make for I think a much more accessible
sonnet than this does," Move 35). Instead of literary references, Ann has
many more connections to the real world and deductions from it; where
the other readers tend to read the poem against the background of litera-
ture, she reads it against her life.

What prevents this general approach from degenerating into the kind
of anecdotal commentary one often finds among neophytes is her well-
developed method of confronting a poem. After the initial reading in
both sessions of taping, she turns immediately to questions of form. Dur-
ing the first taping she ascertains the rhyme scheme, the syntactic and
poetic structures, and the relation between them (Move 3). During the
second, she explains why formal considerations have not occupied more
of her time: "the form is fairly straightforward, and the uses to which
this form can be put are almost a commonplace; they're something that
it would seem dumb to talk about at great length" (Move 25). For Ann,
form is important because it embodies certain expectations: since there
are standard uses for standard forms, especially such common ones as the
sonnet (see her representative list quoted above), considering the struc-
ture of the poem is a necessary prelude or complement to understanding
it. As she said of a poem in a pilot study: "Look at the shape of it—the
physical and the verbal shape."

One reason why form is so important is that it suggests what the separate parts of the poem are, parts that must be unified in a satisfying reading. She expects the sestet and the octave to be thematically linked, and after a first attempt to relate line 14 to the third quatrain and line 13 to the octave (Move 10), the fact that the explicit mention of *deeds* does not relate in any obvious way to the passivity in the rest of the poem becomes the central concern of her reading. As late as the thirty-second move, she is still complaining "I don't know that [line 13 is] a true line or a legitimate line . . . simply cause it doesn't, although it does kind of get you thinking back to the first eight lines, doesn't make any kind of clear, explicated or legitimate connection, and it certainly doesn't connect in any kind of legitimate or clear way with the *base infection*." The emphasis on the "clear, explicated, or legitimate connection" indicates what she expects. The only way she can finally account for the line is to set it in contemporary terms, either as the culmination of the expression of pique in the poem (Move 34) or as a psychologically real overstatement by the poet (Move 36). Given her general approach, the conclusions are not unexpected. But more revealing of her expectations are the fact that she recognizes the connection as problematical in the first place, the frequency with which she returns to it, and her unwillingness to settle for unexamined or specious justifications of it.

Although her references to contemporary situations are the most noticeable feature of her problem space, she only introduces them after she has provided a close textual analysis of the poem and recalled what she knows about Shakespeare and this sonnet. The analysis is devoted to paraphrase in Philip's sense: a reading through the poem making deductions and connections, supplying justifications, and drawing conclusions. In this process, her frequent series of synonyms or deductions create a penumbra of suggestion around the basic meaning of the poem. But she remains committed to the specific language of the text, a commitment well illustrated by her return to the plurals in the poem immediately after recounting the story of her disturbed friend and noting as an interesting aspect of the poem the disparity between these plurals and the fact that "the sonnet seems to have a very clear focus and seems to be directed sort of toward some particular act, some particular incident of behavior that has upset the author very, very much" (Move 13). Such fidelity is especially striking in contrast to the other readers (most notably Elaine and Joel) who converted the plurals to singulars even without the influence of a contemporary situation.

This close attention to the text is reflected in her habit of progressing through the poem several times slowly, treating a particular topic each time through. Her introduction surrounds the first reading of the poem; at the very beginning of the tape she announces that she is about to start, and then after the reading explains why she is using the text in the *Norton Anthology* instead of the dittoed copy that was distributed. The second reading of the poem is followed by a brief formal analysis that establishes primarily that the poem is in the standard sonnet form, and so, presumably, the standard assumptions about sonnets apply to it, a point that is made more clearly in the introduction to the second session of taping (Move 25).

The fourth move introduces the main themes of the reading: the poem is very personal and thus inaccessible apart from the private experience that occasioned it; it seems to be an expression of pique; and it "doesn't seem to hang together particularly well." The next five moves constitute the first detailed progression through the poem. Ann proceeds line by line, making deductions, relating the hints in the poem to real-world actions, and justifying her reading by means of CONNECT:POEMs and CONNECT:WORLDs. She immediately assumes that the *they* "disdain" to hurt others, and that what the *others* are moved to is some kind of emotion — "to passion, or to rage, to hurt, whatever"; from the beginning the situation she postulates for the poem is one dealing primarily with emotional responses: disdain, passion, rage, hurt. The fifth line is seen as the result of the sixth — "presumably they inherit these things because they don't squander *nature's riches*, they don't spend themselves on anybody else or for anybody else." *Husbanding nature's riches* is located within a world of interpersonal relationships ("they don't spend themselves on anyone else or for anything else"), an identification reinforced by the seventh and eighth lines — the *others* are those who either respond to the lords and owners or try to elicit some response from them (she never considers the possibility that *their* in line 8 is anaphoric to *others*). The whole octave is summed up as a "series of statements, this series of reflections on a type in human nature or a person," the conversion from the plurals in the poem to the singular "type" and then "person" again reflecting the specific personal nature of the situation behind the poem.

Although she doesn't say so explicitly, she seems to be following her expectations about how sonnets work when she explains that after the "reflections on a type" in the octave, "we get into kind of an illustration." The ninth line is again naturalized: instead of explaining how the flower can be "to the summer sweet," Ann concentrates on how it can be generally significant to something (i.e., people) outside itself. Similarly, though she here mentions "blight" and later "gonorrhea" (Move 10) in relation to the *base infection*, that concept of real disease (even real venereal disease) does not sort well with her emphasis on emotions in the octave, and she explicates the phrase in terms of physical mutilation that are easier to translate into psychological injury. Curiously similar to Elaine's is her assumption that *the basest weed* would survive the same misfortune better than the flower — the flower carries the signs of its mutilation, while the weed "just grows back in about a day." Again, it is not difficult to see how this reading could be related to a discussion of interpersonal relationships.

The final couplet raises the problem that becomes the crux of the poem for Ann: while it is easy enough to relate the final line to the third quatrain ("it's a perfect aphoristic, very concise illustration of what's being talked about in the first four lines of the sestet"), the thirteenth line cannot be related to the sestet (since the flowers just *meet with base infection*; they do not bring it on themselves as a result of any deeds they perform) and so must "link the octave to the sestet, in an odd kind of way." Much of the rest of her reading is an attempt to understand that "odd kind of way."

After her first detailed pass through the poem, Ann pauses in the eleventh move to recount the history of her knowledge of the poem. As is typical of the readers, she has read the poem before, has even read some commentary on it; also typically, she doesn't recall very precisely what she has read, except that the poem was linked to a personal situation that elicited the sonnet as "a kind of sustained expression of pique at this person." "Pique" is, I think, Ann's own word rather than one she recalls from her reading several years before; it is her initial reaction to the poem (Move 4) and leads directly into the subject of the next move — the encounter with the "very disturbed person." What interests her about the poem is "the tone, the audience," and that concern, combined with her initial assumption that the poem is about interpersonal relationships and her identification of what the *others* are moved to as emotions, naturally suggests a real person in emotional distress. The tone of the poem is explicated by the tone of her friend's story, and this provides important (if unstated) evidence that a personal situation similar to her friend's lies behind the poem. She reads the poem through again, imposing on it this time the tone she has derived from her friend's story, in which frustration and disappointment figure largely.

In this second pass, the personal nature of the poem, its origin in personal action, becomes clearer. "The sonnet seems to have a very clear focus and seems to be directed sort of toward some particular act, some particular incident of behavior that has upset the author very, very much and has particularly colored his regard to a certain person" (Move

13). Though she talks about "they" and "them," she apparently continues to think in terms of "the person being described here, the person being talked about or addressed directly by the writer" (Move 16). The *others*, who before were merely *moved* emotionally, now become disappointed lovers or friends; the *they* refrain not only from hurting but from giving any response whatever; and the octave, instead of being a "series of reflections on a type in human nature" (Move 8) becomes "a railing against people who don't deign to respond to others who either care for them or care about them, even to the extent of hurting them . . . they can't be inveigled to react or respond at all" (Move 13). In this new reading, which clearly derives as much from Ann's remembered conversation as it does from the poem, *rightly* becomes a problem, since it conflicts with her understanding that "they don't squander nature's gifts, but presumably they should, or at least allow others, those who care about them or care for them, or who react strongly to them, to participate in nature's gifts" (Move 14). But the contemporary situation expressed in "those who care about them, or care for them, or who react strongly to them" is compelling enough to allow her to skip over this momentary difficulty. As she continues to read, the *they* become worse and worse, "deceitful," "frozen, and in a way sort of dead" (Move 16).

Without explicating in any detail the image of a manor that other readers found in the second quatrain, Ann naturalizes it to her reading: *they* "become aristocratic, become property owners, become those in control," who not only don't squander the riches they have inherited (cf. Move 9) but "presumably . . . don't give them out to people when they should, or when the gifts are deserved" (Move 17). As *lords and owners*, they are haughty and disdainful, while the others, the stewards, become the true protectors of their excellence — "others but caretakers, protectors, cultivators, guardians or the excellence of these people" (Move 17). By following her series, Ann has arrived at a position where the *excellence* of the *lords and owners* is preserved primarily through the care of a devoted band of retainers ill rewarded for their service.

When she turns to the sestet, it is to refine what she has said before: the third quatrain, instead of being "kind of an illustration" (Move 8), is now seen as an implied commentary on the *they* of the octave (Move 18). The thirteenth line "jumps right back to the first eight lines," implying that *they* will come to grief "through this deception, through this coldness, through this refusing to react to other people, . . . as a result of the way they act" (Move 19). Though this is apparently the intended connection, it is still not satisfying, since the thirteenth line links souring with deeds, and "The point in the first eight lines though is that the people don't do anything" (Move 19), something she goes on to illustrate.

This lack of logical connection leads back to her original reaction that the poem is an expression of pique, as if these are the only two alternatives: "instead of any kind of reasoned meditation or reasoned series of accusations, the while thing comes out as, much more as an instance of, as pique, the kind of thing that one would write to a lover who had really pissed one off" (Move 20). As such, it is inaccessible except insofar as one knows the original circumstances.

Moves 21–23 constitute another quick progression through the poem, reasserting the basic points she has already made: that the poem is addressed to one person ("all that is a reaction to one particular person," Move 21; "well it's *they* and *others*, but it's really thee and me," Move 22); that it is a reaction to an actual incident ("presumably either to one incident, some kind of sexual disappointment, or else to a series of inadequate responses, I suppose," Move 21); and that in these characteristics (and in its tone) the poem is similar to the conversation she has recently had. The third quatrain is reconsidered, and the aptness of the flower is questioned: it is a standard comparison, but it doesn't really illustrate what Shakespeare wants it to, since flowers all die "in the nature of things," while the *they* are going to "lose their *riches*, their *excellence*, as a result of particular things that they do, as a result of the way they conduct themselves." Interestingly, Elaine and Ann noticed the same thing about the flowers — that they die — but drew quite different conclusions.

Ann's introduction to her second attempt at taping is longer than the introduction to the first. She has met Elaine, and they have exchanged views about the poem. After a justification of why her tape will be shorter than the first one (Move 25), she turns to test Elaine's hypothesis that the poem begins as a poem of praise but becomes a condemnation or an insult. She reads the octave as ironic rather than laudatory, and progresses through it, marshalling the evidence for her point of view: "the *they* becomes an unnatural thing, an artifact"; "They also become in an odd way a sort of a false object of respect or object of esteem"; the person discussed "is inhuman, and is husbanding his or her gifts, charms, attributes by refusing to be human, refusing to participate in the natural cycle of things," "a constant source of pain to anyone who is attracted to him or her," putting those attracted to him "in a demeaning position, as a steward is to a lord." The next move details the ways in which the person described is deceitful; the ones after that treat wasted potential and unnaturalness. Notable in these moves are, first, how systematically Ann offers the evidence: she picks a topic and then goes through finding evidence for her view on it; and second, how much her view depends on her previous readings and on the contemporary situation that lies behind them.

By this stage in her reading, it is fair to say that the external scene Ann has built up has all but replaced the text for her. There is no dialectical process, as there was with Joel, to test the extent to which the text and the scene correspond; instead, the text is translated directly into a commentary on the scene. Several aspects of the text have been identified as problematic and they remain so, but those that have not been so identified tend to disappear. So, for instance, *and will do none* in the first line is glossed over quickly ("even though this person refuses to hurt, the person is a constant source of pain," Move 26), and the apparently positive statements in the second quatrain are dismissed with "those next four lines really do seem to be heavily ironic" (Move 30). The sestet is not only an illustration of or a warning about what will happen when the persons described in the octave "meet with some kind of adversity, meet with a situation that they can't control" (Move 18); it also suggests that *they* "are ultimately subject to the natural order of things" no matter how much they try to pervert that natural order during their lives (Move 31). At least, this would be the expected response; "the problem with the poem" is that it doesn't exactly say that—"the analogy isn't really right" (Move 32), and the thirteenth line remains the one that doesn't fit. The problem for Ann is that she is equally committed to her constructed situation and to her notion of close reading and organic unity, and here she cannot reconcile them.

Unwilling to relinquish either of them, she finally hits on a way "to try to explain the thing" (Move 32). Typically this involves another external contemporary scene: if the poem is seen as an expression of pique, with "the same kind of psychological escalation that expressions of that kind, if you try to sustain them in some kind of protracted utterance, tend to have," then the thirteenth line is explicable as a "direct jab," the pique getting out of hand, so to speak (Move 33). As such it need not relate back to the octave logically; the poem is a reflection of a state of mind rather than a logical argument. Even this explanation is not altogether satisfying: the third quatrain "has to do with some kind of an attempt to construct an analogy . . . on the person who piques or pisses off the author's behavior," but it is "not really a clear analogy" (Move 33). The thirteenth line is a way of connecting that analogy with the more straightforward railing of the octave, but "that connection is made in an odd way" (Move 34).

An alternative justification for the thirteenth line is offered in Move 35. Since there seems to be a real action or situation — "some kind of rejection, spurning of affections" — there is at least the possibility that *deeds* refers to some specific behavior. Unfortunately, any record of this behavior has been lost, and this leads to a sonnet less accessible than one based on the stock situations Ann enumerates.

The thirty-sixth move combines these two explanations: the octave describes what annoys the poet, the third quatrain is an analogy based on it, and "the thirteenth line contains maybe more than the poet had wanted to say about . . . what is really upsetting him . . . that's ultimately the motivation, you know, whatever is behind that thirteenth line is the motivation of the sonnet and what's behind the sense of frustration." In Elaine's view, the poet learned as he wrote; in Ann's he lost control: the one is a typical literary situation; the other, something that can be observed every day.

No matter how often she explains the thirteenth line, she is dissatisfied with it, and she devotes a long move to a final "problem" or "kind of a point of issue" — the fact that most of the poem deals with passivity, while the thirteenth line refers to *deeds*. She catalogues the passivity throughout the poem, from the *they* doing *no hurt* to the passive flowers, and suggests a vague resemblance to sins of omission, but the problem still remains: both line thirteen and psychological reality suggest that "clearly something has been done that piqued the poet very much" (Move 37), but whatever it is isn't mentioned in the poem. Thus the poem is "about passivity" in the sense that it discusses or expresses many kinds of passivity, "but it isn't about passivity" in the sense that the ending reflects the real actions that drove the poet to write it in the first place.

The salient characteristic of Ann's reading, then, is her attempt to naturalize the poem to a real-life situation. When she happens to know the biographical context of a work (as she did with Hopkins's "Carrion Comfort"), she happily uses it to illuminate the poem. When she doesn't, as with sonnet 94, she constructs a contemporary situation, relying on what is going on in her life at the time. In this instance, a disturbed friend suggested both the tone of the sonnet and a set of circumstances that could give rise to such a tone. This situation was so compelling that Ann overlooked the possibility that the poem was not about something similar; even Elaine's suggestion that the octave sounds like praise did not suggest a rereading or the kind of shift we have seen in all the other readers — Elaine with her two contradictory readings, Joel replacing Iago with an amalgam of the Duke and Angelo as the main character, Philip realizing the ways in which his first contact with the poem was unnatural for him and modifying them. Ann consistently strengthens the resemblance between her reading of the poem and the external situation on each of half a dozen detailed pauses through the poem.

Balancing this contemporary reference is a devotion to form and logic. The poem is unsatisfying or confusing to her because it has the formal characteristics of a sonnet but lacks the logical ones: there is no logical way to relate the couplet as a whole to the octave or third quatrain. And in fact, these two characteristics reinforce each other in her reading: her disturbed friend's story elucidates the tone of the poem, and the difficulty of relating line 13 to the rest of the poem logically suggests that the principle of organization is psychological, explicable only in emotional terms, which naturally reemphasizes the relevance of her friend's story.

GEORGE

The characteristics of George's problem space depend, to a large extent, on the fact that (alone among the readers) he is a serious and prize-winning poet. He thus tends to interpret poems in terms of his own practice. Most important, this means that for him each poem grows out of a definite situation, often but not necessarily biographical. As he explains while discussing the poem with two other readers, "What I usually do is come up with a little story that explicates the poem." Hopkins's "Carrion Comfort," for instance, he thought to be based on the stories of Prometheus and Jacob, and he read long passages from the Bible onto the tape in support of his contention. He understands this sonnet in terms of "what circumstances would have occasioned [him] to write a poem like this," and these circumstances are projected back onto Shakespeare, leading to frequent CONNECT:WORLDs in his protocol. Although "the key to [his] entire reading is the biographical details," the situation he constructs is hypothetical: he "would never know whether the nobleman ever told, whether the quarrel actually happened" (Move 28): plausibility, not fact, is at stake. And despite its very real utility to his reading, George finds the fantasy slightly embarrassing: "see how that goes, now [laugh] that I've made up my own little story of what really happened behind the poem" (Move 22). So the external situation he constructs for the poem is a compromise, not entirely contemporary like Ann's, but modern enough to ring true psychologically; at the same time, not entirely factual and historically accurate like Philip's unrecoverable occasion for the poem, but a more or less plausible Elizabethan re-creation. George's occasion is an amalgam of what he knows about Elizabethan society and thought, Shakespeare, and contemporary psychology. And he proposes this setting, and understands the poem in terms of it, in spite (or perhaps in defiance) of his training: "I can't help, even though my New Critical tendency is to say shame on you, poem has no existence except on a page, but I keep thinking of Shakespeare smarting from some rebuff, Shakespeare the commoner being hurt" (Move 10).

This external situation is constructed very quickly. By the third move, George sees the *they* as manipulative people; by the fourth, he suggests that the flowers of the sestet might refer to the nobility. The implications of these identifications are worked out, and in the tenth move — roughly a quarter of the way through his protocol — he suggests the situation and immediately tries to relate it to what he knows of Shakespeare's life. For the rest of his reading, he assumes that this is in fact the occasion for the poem (even though he admits several times that he'll never know whether his conjectured quarrel actually occurred), refines it to fit the opening lines better, and toward the end explains it fully: "This is after a quarrel, during which, rather than responding as he would have done naturally, the nobleman refused to argue with the commoner Shakespeare and withdrew into a typical class role of a kind of disdain and haughtiness . . ." (Move 28).

A second characteristic of his problem space presumably related to his own writing is his cultivation of multiple meanings. As he says in his reconsideration of lines 9 and 10, "if I were writing the line, I would leave that secondary meaning in there, I mean, put as much meaning as I possibly could in the line" (Move 24), and earlier he had consulted a dictionary for *expense* "to see if he was slipping something in here that I wasn't going to catch" (Move 7). Just as he attributes to Shakespeare circumstances similar to those that would have caused him to write the poem, he assumes that Shakespeare cultivated ambiguity: "but I think Shakespeare is, loving [apparently something like "double meanings"] sneaked another reading in here" (Move 10). He is thus only being fair to Shakespeare when he retains as many meanings as possible. ("Why should I cripple Shakespeare and make an either-or situation?" Move 20). *Excellence* can be either the title of a nobleman or a quality reflected by faces, and the *stewards* are thus both servants of their lords (i.e., "of their Excellence") and keepers of the excellence their own faces express (Move 9). *Summer* refers both to the nobility in general (so the young man is the flower of the nobility) and to the actual season, so the flower being sweet to the summer alludes to a life unconcerned with title and inheritance (Move 24); and since *outbraves* contains a play on "bravos," the poem contrasts the natural dignity of the flower with the inherited dignity of the titled classes (Move 28). George thus devotes more time to the elementary process WORD than the other readers.

A third characteristic related to his own writing is his attention to form. Like the other readers, he expects some relation between form and content; unlike them, he tends to find it. The fact that *rightly* is stressed ("Even the stress comes down almost as a pointer: pay attention to this word," Move 13) provides evidence for his early (Move 3) hypothesis that it is ironic: "the stress coming down on *rightly* really I think is the key to my seeing any kind of sarcasm" (Move 28). Initially disappointed that he can find so little relation between the rhyme scheme and meaning of the poem, he later decides that the *faces-graces* rhyme is more prominent than the others. At first he "can't do anything with the rhyme being a little stronger thematically," but then he suggests tentatively that Shakespeare may be "trying to relate the nobleman's face as one of heaven's graces," justifying it as "a fairly typical compliment" before abandoning it as "no real help to [his] reading of the poem" (Move 26). There are thus more frequent connections between FORM and CONTENT than usual.

A fourth characteristic of his reading practice is his habit of relating poems to mythology, the Bible, and to other poems by the same author, but not to poetry in general. Here this tendency is apparent in his references to the parable of the lilies of the field, first mentioned in the fourth move and used throughout the reading as a yardstick for the young nobleman's behavior, and to Hamlet ("it sounds like 'to thine own self be true'," Move 3). The closest he comes to referring to other poems is to mention clichés ("is that a possible change on the cliché, the flower of the nobility?" Move 18), "the poetic tradition" (Move 18), and "fairly typical" compliments (Move 27). But only the relation to the Bible (and Christian tradition) seems to affect his reading very much. This is perhaps also due to the fact that he is a poet: the other readers referred to other literature either to certify that what they understood in this poem was in fact properly poetic, or to provide examples to guide comprehension. George finds both of these in his own poetic practice: when he imagines a situation that would lead him to write a poem similar to the one he is reading, he both certifies the poeticality of the subject and provides an example — his own — to help interpretation. Implicit in his reading is the question: what would *I* mean (or intend, etc.) if I wrote this? The other readers, lacking this personal certification, must rely on more traditional kinds.

The protocol itself is longer than the others. George spent nearly two hours on the poem, talking slowly and deliberately. His speaking is slow, but his thought is not, and often he has tested and rejected an idea before he has fully expressed it, a trait that can make the protocol a little difficult to follow. Like the other readers, he begins with a brief introduction and follows his first reading of the poem with what almost seems a ritual disclaimer of understanding. In the third move he comments on the octave, noting his initial reaction that it seems generally ironic, and changing his mind about the manipulative people counterfeiting emotion as soon as he expresses it. At the end he raises a problem that will return throughout the reading — the referent of *their* in line 8.

The fourth move treats the sestet, linking it generally to *Hamlet* and then, more specifically, to the parable of the lilies of the field. The concrete situation behind the poem, only hinted at in the "manipulative people" of the third move, gains definition: the flowers represent the nobility, who should live "true to their own nature," like the lilies of the field; when they don't, when they meet with the infection of ambition, they become worse than the basest weed — "the commonest of commoners." The poem is thus not about the nobility in general, but only about "powerful men who go bad in some sense."

He announces the topic of the next several moves as the tone, but he doesn't seem to treat that per se. In the fifth move he establishes the historical context, suggesting that any insult against the powerful would have to be oblique. Move six then begins a second detailed progress through the poem, initially to establish tone, but by the seventh move the exclusive concern with tone is dropped. The sixth move establishes the terms in the first quatrain that are overtly positive or negative, and then introduces the idea — apparently stemming from the lilies of the field parable — of unnatural restraint founded on a hypocritical appearance of Christian virtue: "These people have the same quote-unquote virtue as Christians but with them it's been twisted from its natural purpose or original purpose . . . being slow to temptation comes not from any kind of natural goodness . . . but from an unnatural kind of self-control and a willingness to manipulate."

The seventh move begins to consider the second quatrain, but becomes instead a check on the definition of *expense;* the eighth actually considers lines 5 and 6. The manipulative powerful men from the first quatrain are found to be even more unnatural, since they "manipulate others into doing the work and making them rich" instead of doing it themselves, "the way say a farmer would gather a harvest." *Expense* is a pun: the others harvest *nature's riches* for the *lords and owners,* but it is also at the *expense* or cost of the lords and owners because they lose "something essential in their own nature by paying for having nature's riches husbanded for them, for twisting the natural order again."

The ninth move considers lines 7 and 8. The *lords* are the "manipulative nobles" who "have absolute control over their facial expressions." *Their excellence* first appears to be a title (similar to *"Your Excellency"*), a reading finally justified by Shakespeare's love of multiple meanings, so "other people are their servants and their excellence is a title by which these powerful men are known." On the other hand, *their faces* could refer to "their own faces," so the *others* would be "people who show the emotion on their faces," and *excellence* suggests "a judgment saying that that's a better condition, that the faces that show emotion are excellent; the faces therefore that don't show emotion because of an unnatural kind of self-control aren't excellent."

In the tenth move George begins to consider the sestet as a parable clarifying the topic of the octave, when he is suddenly struck by what seems to be a more personal tone in the couplet, and he suggests that the poem is the result of an actual insult to Shakespeare by a nobleman. This naturally leads to the biographical details (similar to the way the first pass through the poem in Moves 3–5 led to the historical context in Move 6). The explanation of the insight follows: "the emotion in [the final line] seems personal and singular in spite of the fact that he's written more than one lily into the poem." The justification for the private story is thus based on three assumptions: that poems stem from particular occasions '"why would Shakespeare write this poem?"'); that some insult from a member of the nobility — reflected in the couplet — "is the most plausible [occasion] for the poem against the nobility"; and that there was a young nobleman "who was not only his patron but with whom Shakespeare was supposed to be in love." From these assumptions it is easy enough to draw the conclusions George does, and from these conclusions the rest of the reading develops.

Interestingly, George arrives at the same conclusion the other readers do about the poem having a single intended audience or subject even though it discusses a group of people, but he does it quite differently. Joel from the beginning posited a single figure — Iago — and so there was never a problem for him; Philip relied on his knowledge of Elizabethan and Shakespearean sonnets to decide that they typically are addressed to, or discuss, individuals rather than groups; his earlier, more literal reading preserving the plurals was thus a false start. Ann related the singular-plural problem to psychological realism: upset people often discuss classes when they are actually talking about an individual. Elaine immediately identified the poem as a "young-man" sonnet, and this encouraged her to understand both a singular subject and a single audience. George, however, relies entirely on the *feeling* he finds in the poem: "The emotion in it seems personal, and therefore singular" (Move 10), something related to his view of the origin of poetry in personal experience and presumably also to his own experiences as a poet.

As he returns to the poem to check his hypothesis in the eleventh move, the constructed situation immediately suggests new meaning in the opening lines. Lines 2 and 3 can be seen as referring directly to Shakespeare and his patron/lover, the one being moved by the other's false show of affection. After a brief interlude to consider the proper pronunciation of *Unmoved*, he returns to the second quatrain to provide more evidence for seeing *rightly* as ironic: it bears metrical ictus. But more importantly, if this refers to "Shakespeare's patron who's hurt him," it can hardly be other than ironic, and this allows George to sneak in another justification that is more contemporary than Elizabethan: "Well Shakespeare knows as well as anyone that that's a simple accident of birth."

The fourteenth move is devoted to deciding whether the punctuation at the end of line 6 is a semicolon; the content of lines 5 and 6 is the subject of the fifteenth. As is becoming clearer, George's postulation of a specific incident behind the poem allows him to see the poem as both personal and general: the patron/lover becomes the exemplar of a privileged class that "inherit[s] all the beauty and intelligence that heaven can bestow. . . . They're talented, beautiful, rich," and Shakespeare becomes "the commoner rebuffed." In this way he can reconcile the personal emotion behind the couplet with the plurals throughout the poem. The conflict suggests a preferred reading for the eighth line, which he now sees as "saying very directly, others are their go-fers. Shakespeare as the commoner rebuffed writes in bitterness, *they are the lords and owners of their faces,* yeah of their faces as well. They own everything else, all the land" (Move 16). This preferred reading does not, however, completely replace the old ones, which are not rejected as incorrect; they simply don't "seem in line with the reading that [he's] giving now."

The next three moves try to assimilate the sestet to his new reading. *Base infection* now seems to refer to the coldness of the patron/lover rather than to ambition, and this throws the lilies of the field parallel into jeopardy. Seeing *outbraves* as a play on 'outbravos' makes the couplet even more of an insult to the patron/lover, who appears to be a superficial bravo, and even less successful at it than "the lowest commoner." But the problem lies in lines 9 and 10, not in the couplet; and George tries several possibilities before arriving at one that is satisfying (in the twenty-fourth move). Perhaps summer is an emblem for the nobility and the patron/lover the flower of the nobility; this is buttressed by some casuistry about the Great Chain of Being. That solves the problem of the ninth line, at least for the time being, but the tenth line is still difficult, and he devotes the long nineteenth move to explicating it. He keeps trying to relate it to the lilies of the field, finally deciding that it represents "an extension of the lilies of the field parable": that the young nobleman would be better relying on his natural beauty (with perhaps a glance back to the discussion of "bravos") than becoming infected with "a kind of class conceit."

Move 20 TESTs and extends this interpretation. At first he attempts to suggest a new, less symbolic meaning for summer: since flowers grow in the summer, the line could simply be a statement of when the nobleman lives. But this reading does not account for why the flower is sweet to the summer, and he finally decides to retain both possibilities. Between them, they do seem to account for the line: insofar as the flower is a figure for the nobleman, its lifetime—the summer—is his lifetime; if the summer represents the nobility, then the nobleman as a paragon is sweet to the nobility in general. But then the next line causes trouble because the earlier reading—that the nobleman lived *for* himself—conflicts with the double meaning of line 9. George's solution is ingenious—the nobleman is the flower of the nobility, and would be better off living "in its own natural sweetness, the sweetness of the nobleman's own personality without, that is, adding any defects of the noble class which is a kind of condescension, uppityness, and a tendency to hurt commoners"—except that it ignores the first word of the line.

The twenty-first move returns to the beginning of the poem to TEST again his understanding of the poem, to see whether the situation he has suggested fits all the particulars mentioned. And he finds a problem in the first line: if the nobleman will do no hurt, why is Shakespeare insulting him? The second line suggests a modified scenario in which the nobleman refuses to argue on a personal level with the commoner Shakespeare, instead retreating "into his class dignity." This also accounts for the third and fourth lines, and ratifies the earlier guess that the people referred to are twisting Christian virtues.

Building on the reference to *smelling far worse than weeds* in the final line, George in Move 22 considers what he later refers to as his "open-ended speculation" (Move 28) and modifies: that the specific occasion of the argument might have been the nobleman's insulting Shakespeare for smelling. This seems a little far-fetched, even in view of the frequent references in the plays to bad breath and body odor, but it stems from precisely the same assumptions that led to the postulation of the quasi-historical scene in the first place. If a real event lies behind the poem, something in that event must account for the reference to odor (just as "bravos" explains the reference to *outbraving*), and George is merely suggesting as an initial hypothesis, suitably hedged ("My imagination is getting away from me today"), what first comes to mind.

The twenty-third move concludes the reading for the first day by going through the poem once more and relating it to his reading. By the time he stops after roughly an hour and twenty minutes of taping, he has read through the poem half a dozen times and has constructed a possible external situation that explains both the poem and its origin. The readings attempt to coordinate poem and situation at the same time they allow the greatest possible latitude for multiple meanings.

When he returns to the poem it is to explicate the first two lines of the sestet; significantly the explanation is more concerned with the story behind the poem than with the text. Typically he retains his earlier readings, but claims that they are secondary to what he now sees as the basic reading, that the flower lives for only one summer, while the essence of the nobility is inheritance and duty to the hereditary title. The young nobleman would be better living as a flower, forgetting "about his class as nobleman whose duty it is to pass on his title," because if he doesn't, he may meet with *base infection*, "a real tendency to ignore and to condescend and to hurt commoners." This reading nicely combines the lilies of the field and the implicit warning against ambition with the class consciousness and condescension in the occasion George has postulated for the poem.

Two days later he returns to the poem to pick up some loose ends. There is detailed treatment of form in Move 25 and a closer consideration of the *graces-faces* rhyme in 26, but in neither case can he relate formal features to the content, and he returns to reading the poem. Move 27 restates the irony he has found in line 5 (Move 28 provides some formal evidence for it) and then reconsiders and rejects the earlier suggestion (Move 8) that *from expense* refers to the cost to the nobility of unnaturally employing others to *husband nature's riches* for them.

Move 28 reiterates the entire situation, adding more specifically that "the natural dignity of the flower is much better than the supposed inherited dignity of the titled classes," and toning down the speculation about Shakespeare's odor being the origin of the quarrel. A curious implication of this final reading is that if "the insult there that Shakespeare smells bad is inherent is the reason that the nobleman didn't quarrel with Shakespeare" and *only* inherent, then Shakespeare is the one who self-consciously brings it up.

Move 29 concludes by placing the reading in a context similar to the one supplied by most of the other readers. He has had some experience with the poem before but only vaguely remembers what it was.

George's problem space for the poem, then, consists mainly of locating it within a quasi-historical context. He tries to provide a specific occasion for the poem, and this allows him to see the poem as directed primarily at Shakespeare's patron/lover and more generally at other members of the nobility who behave like him. There is no attempt to place the poem within the context of the other sonnets, or even of Shakespeare's typical concerns and attitudes in his other works, and in this George differs markedly from Elaine, Philip, and Joel. He shares with Ann an interest in psychological realism, but, unlike her, tries to reconstruct a situation in which Shakespeare would plausibly have written the sonnet. This situation is primarily a projection back into Elizabethan times of his own reactions: he first asks what would make him (as a poet) write such a poem and then adapts his answer to what he knows of Shakespeare's life.

5 One Reader Reading Three Poems

The last chapter demonstrated the different problem spaces readers use to approach poems. These spaces are not altogether dissimilar, because close reading is largely a learned activity in which all of the readers have been specifically trained. By the time they are finishing Ph.D. programs in English, students have well-defined notions of what constitutes serious (or professional) reading and what does not: simple expression of personal likes and dislikes, for instance, is not serious, but if such an expression is supported by sufficient evidence, it can constitute part of a reading. Some expectation that the poem is unified, that each facet of it can be related to one central concern, is part of serious reading, and all the readers express some interest in incorporating as much of the poem into their reading as possible. Within their general consensus, however, there is still quite a bit of latitude for individual approaches. Some idea of the variety of them was given in the last chapter.

In this chapter, we turn to consider one reader reading the three poems, to see how his typical approach manifests itself with quite different materials. The four readers discussed in the previous chapter tend to see the Shakespeare sonnet in relatively static terms: in their different ways, they all see it as the damning description of one person or of a class of people written in response to a real or imagined or probable situation. Elaine is the only one to add to this conception the suggestion of a progression within the poem or the reader's experience of it: either the poem begins as a poem of praise and ends as an insult, or Shakespeare began to compose a poem of praise but then realized that censure was more apposite. For Carlos, however, the idea of a progression is the *sine qua non* of interpretation; in all three poems he seeks progressions of various kinds, and is satisfied with a reading only when it centers on some kind of progression.

Concern with progressions manifests itself in the second phase of his reading (the first will be discussed below), after the spadework has been done. In the reading of sonnet 94, he spends about fifteen minutes going through the poem, reading it, identifying images, isolating themes, attempting to relate them to each other, and scanning the poem "just because, for Shakespeare it is always a good idea" (Move 10).

When he returns to the poem the second day, he quickly identifies his first progression, based on the natural images and the way the poem moves from one to the next.

> They're all natural images in this. You move from stone, . . . *unmoved, cold, and to temptation slow,* to someone who rightly husbands—*And husbands natures riches from expense:* Ok, and then in the last quatrain—Ok that first quatrain, stone; second quatrain, there are the husbanders of nature. In the third quatrain we talk about the *summer's flower,* so we go from stone to husbandman to [the sestet]. (Move 13)

This progression is immediately regularized by recognizing in the second quatrain "a gardener image" (Move 14), which relates it in an obvious way to the flower imagery in the sestet, a link that is strengthened by the reinterpretation of the eleventh line: "in other words, if that flower is not well tended . . ." (Move 15). But even so, "it's a strange movement because there's something, it seems very ironic or sarcastic or something about the opening quatrain" (Move 16), and he interrupts his consideration of the progression to work out the tone in more detail.

When he returns to the notion of progression, it is in terms of some "Tillyardesque idea of the hierarchy" (Move 18) derived from *The Elizabethan World Picture.* The tone he finds in the first quatrain is reflected in "the irony" of the aristocracy's being compared to a stone, "and a stone is the lowest of inanimate objects on that sort of a scale" (Move 18). Before he can develop this movement, however, another catches his eye: "Ok, *But if that flower,* and then suddenly we've moved away, we're moving into a question of . . . some sort of infection, and we've moved several steps away from the question of aristocracy, and moved it to some much more universal image" (Move 20). But it is not long before the original progression is reasserted: "And then suddenly we're back into the terms, aristocratic terms, when before we're talking about flower as some sort of a, I mean a flower is a flower. . . . Ok, so suddenly [in line 12] we have a real class consciousness arrive out of this otherwise perfectly natural image, and suddenly nature is set up hierarchically" (Move 21).

One interesting aspect of this hierarchy is how little evidence from the poem Carlos bases it on. Once he hits upon the idea, he mentions two items—the stone and the aristocracy—and later adds two more—the flower and the weed. The flower and the weed do seem to be hierarchically ordered, since the weed is base, but the stone and the aristocracy are not, except in the ironic terms he has already suggested. What makes the notion of hierarchy so attractive to Carlos is that it is Elizabethan and that it describes a progression, and so he is willing — even eager — to see it in the poem on the slightest provocation.

To make it work a certain amount of special pleading is needed: at first the comparison between the aristocrat and the stone seems "ironic" because they should theoretically be at opposite ends of the hierarchy; later, the flower and the weed are an imperfect example of a hierarchical relationship because "*the basest weed* in some sense is pure to itself, more pure than a flower, than an aristocrat who falls further and harder, I suppose" (Move 21). This suggests a special artificial kind of hierarchy rather than a natural one, and perhaps developing the implications of his characterization of the weed as "pure to itself," Carlos suggests "a sense of a moral hierarchy, a moral aristocracy is I think, actually that probably is it, it's a moral aristocracy that we're talking about. He's using the language of . . . power, natural power but it suddenly is turned into a moral question" (Move 21).

In testing this progression Carlos is disturbed by the disparity between the first quatrain — "a very worldly description somewhat, a real, a very realistic factor" (Move 21) — and the metaphor of the flower in the ninth and tenth lines. To relate them to each other he reverts to his earlier progression of images, converting *as stone* into the stone walls surrounding a garden: "But nonetheless they [lines 4 and 9] hook up, ok, because unmoved, cold, and to temptation slow — it's like the walls of the garden, I think: they are themselves as stone, keeping up the garden image" (Move 25). This identification is a little difficult to follow since he justifies different aspects of it in different places. What is "as stone" is "their external feature, their face, their façade" (Move 27), and this stone becomes the stone walls of a garden. The wall itself — which Carlos calls "forbidding" — suggests "the power of . . . an old medieval castle or something, all the associations you have with walls and the person who built them, that being a sign of power perhaps, a wall being a sign of possession of power" (Move 27). Within these forbidding walls, the aristocrats of the first line are *husbanding nature's riches from expense,* which he sees as an agricultural image expressing the conservation of their spirits from useless expenditure, a reading bolstered by a reference to sonnet 129. The seventh line suggests that "they are the lords of this whole situation" (Move 29), while the eighth moves "beyond just the moral question of power to some sort of spiritual question . . . a moral excellence or some sort of excellence is communicated to others" (Move 29). The flower in the sestet is a flower in the garden surrounded by the walls, and now seems to be a figure not for the aristocrat but for the aristocrat's spirit: "ok, so we've moved from stone to the gardener, to the element of the garden itself, which is now I think — we're not talking about the whole person but we're talking about the spirit, the spirit inside this wall of stone and so forth" (Move 31).

The importance of this progression for Carlos can be gauged by the paucity of the evidence in the poem for it. Other readers identified an image of gardening or of a manor in the second quatrain, and Philip even suggested, very hesitantly, that "the single flower could be a single flower in one of these fields" (Move 32) on the manor, but nobody else moved from the phrase "as stone" to stone walls and the associations readers have with them. Carlos has adopted a visual, almost cinematic approach, a progressive narrowing of focus, and proceeded to make the poem fit the progression as closely as possible. In this process, the comparison *as stone* is reified into stone and then refashioned into walls having their own associations of power and control, within which the aristocrats cultivate their moral excellence or spirit, expressed by the flower.

By the time he has established this progression, Carlos feels that he understands the poem, though he is suspicious that "it seems more accessible now to me than it probably should" (Move 33). In his subsequent readings he identifies several more progressions or movements and restates the two he has discovered in slightly different terms. The idea of a spiritual hierarchy combined with the flower as an emblem of the spirit gives rise to a progression based more or less on the idea that "the wielding of power is in itself the corruption of the spirit" (Move 39). In this view,

> the poem is a very clear discussion of power . . . and actually the three quatrains are, we move from power to the relationship between power and spirit . . . in the second quatrain, and then the discussion of the spirit itself in the third quatrain. And then the issue of power and spirit are summarized in *For sweetest things turn sourest by their deeds . . . Lilies that fester smell far worse than weeds* — the spiritual consequence. (Move 41)

Further, the movement from the plurals of the octave to the singular in the sestet matches a growing abstractness in the metaphors. In the first quatrain, the real world is concretely discussed; *they* presumably refer to specific people. In the second, "we move to a larger metaphor for this real world . . . they suddenly become gardeners of their virtues. And then in the third quatrain it suddenly, we have the spirit, and it's almost as if it's a single immutable thing, it's almost a metaphor for a metaphor" (Move 43). The two progressions discussed earlier are here combined: the metaphors become more concrete, but since they represent more abstract things, the distance between vehicle and tenor increases:

so there is a real movement through these three quatrains, and the discussion, it evolves from the purely mundane discussion of power . . . moving to the garden idea and a middle-level abstraction . . . and then we get all the way to a pastoral image or to a elysian, a Platonic image. It's sort of like you go from real world to pastoral to Platonic in the three quatrains. (Move 43)

Carlos admits that the progression requires a certain amount of qualification — the flower really isn't Platonic, and the garden (let alone the wall) is never explicitly mentioned in the poem; instead it is constructed out of elements that "interconnect by an upper-level association, I mean, in a more abstract level association of ideas" (Move 44). But he defends the progression he has suggested: "those three opening lines of the quatrains all really delineate the schema, I mean the schema of the kinds of images that get used, and, it changes significantly from one quatrain to the next, I think, and progresses in a way that I've been talking" (Move 45).

This approach to the sonnet, constructing so much from so modest a textual stimulus, seems highly idiosyncratic. And it is, in the fullest sense, for it is the way Carlos confronts all three poems. In Hopkins's "Carrion Comfort" he finds a circular progression closely related to the theme of the poem. By the end of that poem, a conclusion of sorts (expressed in *now done darkness*) is reached, "but the conclusion is that the fighting is over, the questioning is not, or the understanding of it is not sort of captured actually" (Move 29). The questions at the end of the poem suggest that "despair was not engendered during the struggle with God, the struggle with God was something separate. Despair seems to be engendered afterwards, something that comes to him after he's gone through all this process of fighting with God" (Move 30). Even after the purification referred to in the first tercet, there are still questions — Carlos is not clear about what precisely, except that they have to do with the speaker's relationship with God (Move 30) — and they are related to the despair at the beginning of the poem because despair is one possible response to "man's perennial state in relationship to God" (Move 30).

This linkage of the end and beginning of the poem suggests a circle, and further evidence for it is soon discovered. The present tense with a future signification appears in the octave, but the sestet is in the past and "the last line actually seals the past for you" (Move 32); to return to the present you have to return to the first stanza with its discussion of despair and suicide. He struggles to develop this idea ("well I'm having trouble articulating this," Move 34), but it seems to be based on two considerations: first, that the discussion in the octave, since it is in the present tense, reflects either a present or an ongoing situation ("in the first stanza we're talking about sort of a perennial situation," Move 33), while the sestet, being in the preterite, reflects a situation the narrator has passed through. Thus there is, in real terms, the implication that the despair and questioning continue after the dark night of wrestling with God: "in other words, even though the second stanza tells us that he's already gone through it, now he's done and he's received his improvement'. . . he's still in the first stanza clearly in the process of questioning, even though the second stanza tells us that he's gotten past it to some extent, and he still is thinking of the possibilities of an ongoing battle with God" (Move 33).

Second, the progression of tenses from future to past leaves the reader in the past; to bring himself back to the present he must return to the beginning of the poem and the present tenses there:

> the way he sets it up — starts with the future, goes to the present, and then some of subjunctive or optative or whatever and then to the past, in the second stanza that does not return to the present, means you to return to the present, means you to recall the first stanza by the time the second stanza is over because there is no return in the sense of recalling you to the present of the voice. (Move 34)

A second formal structure reinforces this cyclical motion. The octave initiates a pattern of statement (first quatrain) followed by question (second quatrain); the answers to the questions come in the immediately following statement section of the sestet (first tercet). But the questions in the second tercet are followed by no statements to answer them, and so "the answer to the questioning is in going back to the opening line" (Move 35). The poem thus draws the reader "into a circle, into an eternal circle of conflict, partial resolution and the facing up to the question of despair and suicide, as if that's a permanent cycle of man's life in the world" (Move 35).

In addition to this major cyclic progression, Carlos finds two minor progressions within the poem. There is one between lines three and four: "The idea of being able to take it is embodied in [line 3], but then it's brought to the next step from mere passive suffering to an active choosing not to die . . . so the struggle, it moves the passivity of being willing to accept the struggle of God to a certain active statement that you're going to actively engage God" (Move 38). He is not sure that his terms are right, but about the progression itself he has no doubts. Finally, at the very end of the tape, he begins to discuss another progression, again a formal one, from small units defined by alliteration at the beginning of the poem to (apparently — the tape runs out before he finishes) larger units with more frequent enjambing in the sestet, especially in the second tercet.

Clearly, Carlos prefers to express whatever he finds dynamically, and it must be stressed that he *chooses* to state things this way: other readers might notice the same patterns that he does — for instance, the tenses in the poem, or the alternation of statement and anguished question. But they would not necessarily see these patterns as progressions. For them — and this would depend on their individual problem spaces — these patterns would be static, perhaps oppositions or polarities. Even Carlos often notices patterns first and only later translates them into progressions. For instance, the alternation between questioning and affirmation or statement which he sees as one of the strongest pieces of evidence for the cyclic progression of "Carrion Comfort" is first perceived as simply an alternation between statement and question (Moves 14–15), then as an alternation reinforced by the rhyme scheme (Move 23). The third time the topic comes up, he is developing the idea of a progression, and there are hints in his choice of verbs that he is beginning to see the alternation dynamically ("then again we go back to the questioning," Move 28; "so when we return to the questioning," Move 29), but this is balanced by a purely static opposition: "*heaven-handling flung me* doesn't refer specifically to anything in the first stanza, though *foot trod Me* does of course" (Move 28); "Again it's connected, there are two three-line segments to that" (Move 29). On the one hand there are connections, on the other, becomings. Only by the next time through — the fourth time he has treated this alternation — is it finally perceived as a progression from statement to question with implications for the meaning of the poem.

This same progressive refining of patterns into progressions is evident in his reading of Swinburne's "A Ballad of Dreamland." In this poem he finds two important progressions, one formal, the other thematic. The latter is summarized about two-thirds of the way through the reading:

> The interesting thing I guess is that it starts with the nest of roses, moves out to the wind and the sun and the sea in the second stanza. In the third stanza we get the garden delimited specifically for us, and then in the fourth stanza we connect to the real world, I mean, its relationship to the real world is defined specifically for us. So there is sort of a progression there. (Move 37)

The concluding statement is almost a test to see whether he has achieved a satisfactory reading of the poem; since there is at least some kind of progression, he has.

Before he defines this progression, however, he keeps trying to identify small movements within the poem that might add up to an all-inclusive one. At first he tries, unsuccessfully, to see some development between the first two stanzas: "ok so we move from, all right, move, start with the description of the heart and where it [is] . . . the second half it's clear, I mean the second stanza, it's clear that the heart is affected . . . by love, unrequited love" (Move 11). What he would like to see as a movement between the two stanzas, he can't, and so must simply describe what they discuss. Similarly with the next stanzaic break: in the third stanza "we move away from that question [what is it that prevents the heart's sleeping] back into the garden, much more specifically defined there" (Move 12). The problem he has is that he is trying to collapse two topics into one; when he finally realizes that the descriptions of the setting in each stanza relate to each other independently of the discussions of the heart, he is able to define satisfying progressions.

The first piece he is able to fit into his larger progression is the relation of the third stanza to the previous ones. This attempt is successful, unlike the earlier one, because he does separate the heart from the landscape ("and we get more description, description entirely actually separate from the heart: there's no discussion of the heart in this stanza," Move 24): "in the third stanza we expand to start considering this whole thing within . . . the world . . . I mean you start setting the landscape, setting up the landscape in terms of the world, somehow defining it in terms of the world" (Move 24). This general description picks up and modifies several details from earlier stanzas (notice that there is no contrast, there is a "change," a "transfiguration"): "and also we have a transfiguration, I don't know, a change in the use of the word *dart* . . . and actually this seems to me to start moving into more of a sleepy quality . . . we aren't talking about the keen sun anymore, or the wind, we're talking about "*swallows*" and *sleep's are the tunes in its dim fields heard*" (Move 25). And the *heart-hart* echo is more than simply a pun; it too represents a kind of movement: "we come full circle from a natural creature back to a final personification really of the heart of the poet" (Move 26).

The full progression is, as I have suggested, the result of splitting the heart and the external description. This begins on the second day of taping when he realizes that each of the first two stanzas is split into a description of the setting and a discussion of the heart (Move 34). Earlier he had noticed a division within the stanzas, in rhyme scheme and distribution of feminine rhymes (Move 21). But once he sees the first half of each stanza as descriptive, he is able to link that with the movement to the description of the external world he has already discerned in the third stanza. And once he has done that, the descriptive progression is obvious.

He immediately tries, much less successfully, to define a complementary progression in the descriptions of the heart: "And in the second half of each one of these stanzas, addressing the issues of the heart itself, we start from the question of why wouldn't it sleep, to stanza two when . . . we're told that it's the song of a secret bird . . ." (Move 38). But the bird is so distracting a topic that he gets sidetracked, and the only conclusion he can come to is that "the heart is awake and perceiving and somehow functional within its imaginative context" (Move 38) throughout the poem. Since this contrasts strangely with the reference to sleep in the Envoi, Carlos postulates a split between the persona and the heart: "And so I, the persona, the social persona, is probably sleeping and it's this inner spirit, this heart that's being hidden within the nest of roses that is . . . present, functional. . . . And the movement is towards that, is towards understanding that the heart is alive and aware in this garden, separate from the world, per se, and the persona, the I of the poem is asleep" (Move 39). This progression is not nearly as convincing as the one about the descriptions, but it is a progression nonetheless, and that is what Carlos strives for.

The formal progression he finds is expressed in terms of a climax. After he has defined the basic thematic progression of the poem, he returns to consider the language. Apparently picking up his earlier observation that though the poem is based on "a slight conceit," the language is highly ornamented, highly poetical, and pretty (Move 14), he admits that he's "tempted to be judgmental with this poem" (Move 43), repeats that "the language is very pretty, I mean, overall" (Move 44), and begins to study alliteration, assonance, rhyme, and meter (Move 46). He discovers that *wind's wing closes* contains three consecutive stresses, and devotes some time to searching for similar constructions. The distribution of these triple-stress groupings is soon seen as a movement or progression: "Ok, so it does build to a real climax, a language climax there in the Envoi, in terms of the way the stresses sit; it goes one-four-one, in terms of the number of triple-stress lines in the ballad [in the stanzas], or one-four-two maybe, and then in the Envoi there's that very strong build-up to *true love's truth or light love's art*" (Moves 50–51). Precisely how he develops this progression will be discussed in more detail below.

In his reading of all three poems, then, Carlos seeks progressions rather than patterns, and this attempt to convert stasis into movement is apparent even in his language. The frequent use of "suddenly," "we move," and "movement" and verbs expressing movement reflects his belief that the poem is itself a temporal process, not simply a static pattern that can be apprehended at one time. Discussing the split between the octave and the sestet in Shakespeare's sonnet, he says "Ok, *But if that flower* and then suddenly we've moved away, we're moving into a question of a, which has not come up before anywhere, of the question of some sort of infection, and we've moved several steps away from the question of aristocracy and moved it to some much more universal image in the summer's flower" (Move 20). With the eleventh and twelfth lines, "suddenly we're back into aristocratic terms . . . suddenly we have a real class consciousness arrive out of this otherwise perfectly natural image, and suddenly nature is set up hierarchically" (Move 21). But the class is more moral or ethical than economic: "he's using the language of an aristocrat, of power, natural power but it suddenly is turned into a moral question" (Move 21).

Carlos's protocols are studded with similar descriptions of the reading process: after his first detailed pass through "Carrion Comfort," he sees as "fairly crucial" the fact that "somehow we've moved from despair to God" (Move 12); considering the break between the octave and sestet, he decides of *fan . . . in turns of tempest,* "then that becomes the image when you go into the second strophe, second stanza rather, it gets taken up in the opening line" (Move 27). And before he is able to define the basic progression he finds in "A Ballad of Dreamland," he sees the poem in terms of several unconnected movements, for instance, at the opening of the third stanza, "again we get the, we go, we move to the external world again, and we finally, in this paragraph, move out further to, to the garden per se" (Move 35).

These characteristic expressions testify to a habitual emphasis on movement—of the reader's consciousness if not of the poem—rather than on static pattern. And this naturally leads to the desire to find progressions, for that is the way to describe purposeful (rather than random) movement. So what other readers may see in terms of patterns of contrast, juxtaposition, etc., he converts into progressions. This gives him a relatively well-defined criterion of success for interpretation, and, having discerned several progressions in each poem, he can announce that he is satisfied with his comprehension.

The second characteristic of Carlos's problem space is his attention to form. All of the readers at least glance at the form of the poem in passing, and sometimes devote sustained attention to it. Joel, for instance, found a description of the ballade form in a secondary book and then went through it phrase by phrase, testing whether "A Ballad of Dreamland" fit the definition. But the more typical attitude is reflected by what Ann said about her lack of attention to form in sonnet 94: "it would seem dumb to spend a great deal of time talking about things like the rhyme scheme, the fact that it's set up in units of eight and six lines, that it ends with a couplet, to scan the poem" (Move 24). And as we have seen, they tend to consider form when they get stuck in the hopes that it will reveal something new about the poem to them. To a certain extent this is also true of Carlos, but he turns to form much more frequently, and always with the expectation that it will be informative: "What exactly the roses refer to, I really am not sure, so I"m going to leave that for the moment, take a look at it structurally and see if that gives me any help" ("A Ballad of Dreamland," Moves 20–21); later he returns to the form: "let me see if I can find any structural things that open it up any more" (Move 40).

Not surprisingly, he usually discovers a connection between some aspect of form and the overall meaning he finds in the poem. The most spectacular example occurs in "A Ballad of Dreamland," in the discovery of the triple-stress groupings discussed briefly above. While scanning, he notices the three contiguous stresses in *wind's wing closes*, and then almost immediately sees similar constructions in *keen sun's dart* and *warm sea closes*. A search for others reveals several more examples: *soft white snow's, thorn's wound smart, dim fields dart, true love's truth,* and *light love's art,* with *wildwood hart* and *hear no word* more questionable (Moves 46–48).

Since he prefers to see patterns as progressions, this pattern — if it is well enough defined to be that — is immediately converted into two progressions, one internal and one external. Internally, these groups tend to consist of an adjective, a noun, and a verb, in that order; that construction is translated into movement: "it's . . . almost always a verb and a . . . noun; adjective-noun-verb" (Move 48) becomes "these triple-stresses with that sort of effect leading up to a verb" (Move 48). And this movement is immediately contrasted with the general lack of action in the poem: "the poem doesn't seem to express much in the way of action whatsoever, but the emphasis does tend to lead up to these verbs" (Move 48).

The external progression deals with the distribution of these triple-stresses throughout the poem. At first he thinks they merely "build up to the point in the final lines . . . it does build to a real climax, a language climax there in the Envoi" (Move 50), since the penultimate line is the only one to contain two triple-stresses (in addition to being the only enjambed line). But this is unsatisfying, and he prods himself to push further: "I don't know how much it, else it tells me about the meaning offhand" (Move 51). A reconsideration stressing the lack of enjambing earlier in the poem gets him no further — "as far as the meaning goes, so — so what?" (Move 52). The next time through he concentrates on the "agitation" of the meter, as indicated by the triple-stresses, and is finally able to link form and meaning: "the meter is like reinforcing the agitation, a sense of agitation . . . so we've got this highly agitated second stanza" (Move 53). The first half of third stanza is "distanced and conventional" (Move 54), showing little agitation, but in the second half "suddenly we turn when we start talking about the mind again, we return to these stressful lines" (Move 54). And these lead right into the strong Envoi. Finally, the entire "movement of the meter" (Move 56) is evident. The first stanza is calm, the second is very agitated, leading up to the climactic lines *Does a thought in thee still as a thorn's wound smart? Does the fang still fret thee of hope deferred?* — "that's what we've been leading up to all this time" (Move 56), at least in the reader's mind. Then the meter calms before "things start gearing up again" (Move 56) in the second half of the third stanza and finally reach a second climax in the Envoi.

Having found a progression in the meter of the poem clearly pleases Carlos — "that makes me feel fairly on top of the poem, right now" (Move 57) — even if the details of the progression aren't very clear. When he returns the next day he notices again that in the second stanza "all the language seems to infer a quietness in the, but the meter is, everything is closing down but the meter is highly agitated" (Move 58). The agitation the meter reflects is presumably the heart's; when the heart is not mentioned, as in the opening of the third stanza, the agitation vanishes, and when specific references to the causes of its unrest are made — the thought like a *thorn's wound*, the *fang of hope deferred*, *true love's truth* or *light love's art* — the language climaxes. But this is not spelled out very clearly.

Various aspects of form (meter, syntactic constructions, phonetic effects) are thus incorporated into his readings in three ways: they may reinforce the meaning of the poem (as the triple-stresses in the second stanza), they may contrast with it and thus contribute to a pleasing tension (as the internal structure of the triple-stress groups leading to verbs contrasts with the lack of action in the poem), or they may form progressions of their own (as the triple-stress groups do). And these progressions may either complement or oppose the overt (progressions of) meanings in the poem.

But even when he cannot relate formal qualities to progressions or theme, Carlos is sensitive to them. The first aspect of the poem he reacts to is the meter—"these feminine endings and the rhyme . . . I don't like offhand" (Move 1). Alone among the readers he immediately links the poem to the medieval ballade (Moves 13 and 14), and even though he thinks that it builds upon "a slight conceit," he admits that the language is "pretty" and catalogues precisely how several times (Moves 14, 42, 44). During his reading he considers not only the meter and form, but the distribution of the masculine and feminine rhymes (Move 21), the relation between syntactic form and metrical line (Move 21), the repetition of rhetorical questions in the first two stanzas (Move 29), alliteration and assonance (Move 44), some onomatopoeia (Move 44), and the scansion (Moves 46 and 52). Some of these formal features are later fitted into progressions—the distribution of rhymes and questions within the stanzas reflects their bipartite thematic nature—but others are not.

Since it is impossible to predict what formal aspects of a poem will be important—in "A Ballad of Dreamland" it is stress; in "Carrion Comfort" it is tense and sentence type—Carlos seems to have a kind of formal or technical checklist he follows to guarantee that everything possibly relevant will be examined. He considers rhyme scheme and stanza construction, enjambment and sentence types, meter, alliteration, and assonance. Phonetic devices affect him strongly: the feminine rhymes immediately strike him in the Swinburne poem, and in "Carrion Comfort" he early on (Move 4) defers discussions of the "internal rhyme" and then returns to rhyme, assonance, and alliteration each time he begins afresh (Moves 25, 40). Believing as he does that form and meaning are closely linked, he must sometimes expand the concept of meaning to include effect on the reader, as in discussing assonance and alliteration: "again it holds together in a way because of that, because of the sound; the sound seems to have the effect of unity, well unity of effect, how else can I talk about it?" (Move 41). For example, *sheer* and *clear* express two different qualities that are somehow united by the assonance, just as *hand* and *heart* are by alliteration (Move 41). The explanation may be neither precise nor convincing, but the fact that he insists on offering it is symptomatic of its importance for him.

With the rhyme scheme he is more successful. At first he doesn't notice it and excuses his oversight with "it's always said that the greatest rhyme is one that you don't notice" (Move 23). But once he does discover it, he immediately links it to the alternation between statement and question he had earlier discussed (Moves 14–15). In the octave the rhyme scheme distinguishes the affirmation from the question, but in the sestet, the alternating rhymes bind the two together, "so all these lines are bound together; the question is bound in a way more intimately with the affirmation" (Move 23). Curiously, he never recognized this as a sonnet, even though he decided that it contained two stanzas, one of eight lines, the other of six, each broken in the middle into two sub-stanzas, that there was a well-defined rhyme scheme, and that the enjambment occurred only within the sub-stanzas (Moves 22, 42). Perhaps he was prevented by his rush to link form and content: when he discovered the rhyme scheme, he read the rhyme-words instead of spelling out the scheme, immediately related the form to the earlier divisions he had found, and thus went on to discuss the content of each of the formal divisions. Had he been less eager to make this connection (and had the lines been shorter), he might have noticed the sonnet form more quickly.

All of his discussion on his last day of taping is devoted to the form of the poem, and particularly to the assonance and alliteration, the first things he noticed. Unfortunately, he ran out of tape before he finished, so it is not clear whether he would have gone further; but as he ended he was trying to develop another of his progressions, this one from short units defined by alliteration in the octave to the long syntactic unit ending the poem. It is not clear how far he would have gotten, but the attempt itself is quite typical.

The same concern for form and its relation to content is present but less striking in his reading of sonnet 94. Again his first observation about the poem concerns form. "The poem certainly does seem to be cut in half by the line *The summer's flower is to the summer sweet*" (Move 2), and again he decides to scan the poem, "just because, for Shakespeare it is always a good idea" (Move 10). He has forgotten some of his technical vocabulary—he can't remember 'spondee' and he confuses trochee and dactyl—but he does notice that the first line is metrically strange. (As I have explained, the strangeness was due to a typographical error which inadvertantly provided an interesting opportunity to observe how readers would react.) He spends some time on this line, trying various distributions of stress, and finally arrives at Théy that have pówer to dó húrt and will dó nóne: dactyl, dactyl, spondee, iamb, spondee—a very strange line indeed (Move 11). The rest of the poem scans more easily, only lines three (which he reads with an opening spondee), five, and seven (both of which are read with initial trochee) calling for further comment. Lines five and seven are similar both in their metrical patterns and in their feminine endings, and this is perceived as a pattern (the first step toward a progression): "These feminine lines seem to have reversed the iambic pattern to a dactylic [read trochaic] pattern" (Move 12). But the initial scanning, whether or not it is always a good idea with Shakespeare, reveals nothing new this time, and he abandons his reading complaining of feeling "fairly uninspired" (Move 12).

More inspired when he returns, he is able to link the meter to the meaning in the first quatrain. The tone of the quatrain bothers him — he thinks it is ironic, or sarcastic, or sardonic (Move 16; he seems to confuse this with his earlier reaction that the second quatrain sounded "tremendously ironic, it's sardonic perhaps," Move 6). And this feeling is supported by the tension between the active meter (three of the accents in the second line fall on *do* in his reading and so stress the idea of action) and the passive content of the statement, *And do not do the thing they most do show*. In "A Ballad of Dreamland" and "Carrion Comfort" the meter reinforced the meaning by emphasizing triple-stress groups that were thematically important and by unifying alliterative groups; here the disparity between the meter and the content contributes to the unclear tone (Move 16).

The third time he turns to the meter, it is specifically to find something new after he has arrived at a generally satisfactory reading of the poem. He selects the trochaic openings of lines one, three, five, seven, eight, and fourteen, but can do nothing with them except note the metrical similarity between the openings of the first and last lines (Move 34). After scanning the octave again, he does perceive a justification for the trochaic openings: they emphasize the *they* in the poem; when the topic shifts to the flower in the sestet the trochaic openings vanish (Move 36). He hints at this as a progression — "but in the third quatrain with the *summer's flower*, suddenly you're out of the world of identifiable individuals and into qualities as it were" (Move 36). Though he continues to find 'irregular' feet and concludes that "there's a lot of irregularity, I mean, it's not the straight poem" he expected (Move 37), he is frustrated to find no pattern, nothing that can be made into a progression, and he stops taping again.

When he returns to the poem, he is finally able to justify as a progression the contrast he discovered between the octave and the sestet, and to relate this formal contrast to the thematic movement he has already found in the poem. The change from the plurals in the octave — emphasized by the trochaic openings — to the singular in the sestet is associated with the "movement from the real to the abstract — I mean, from the real metaphor for the real world to metaphor for the abstract" (Move 43). As we would expect, once at least some formal aspects of the poem are related to content and shown to belong to a progression, Carlos is satisfied, and he does not return to consider form again.

Throughout his readings, then, there is a strong emphasis on the formal aspects of poetry and an expectation that the form relates to the meaning either by reinforcing it or contrasting with it. At the very least, form is relevant because of the effect it has on the reader. And it should come as no surprise that a reader believing this is in fact quite successful at relating form, content, and effect.

Like the other readers, Carlos perceives the poems against a literary background, but literary references serve three quite different functions in his reading. On the one hand, there are words or phrases that fleetingly remind him of something else, often for no reason other than verbal similarity: *all that toil, that coil* in "Carrion Comfort" reminds him of both the lilies of the field (a favorite allusion of his) because "they toil not" and Hamlet's reference to "This mortal coil" (Move 10); the *grain* recalls the biblical separation of grain and chaff (Move 9); the *rod* calls up Aaron's rod, but since he can't remember anything about Aaron's rod, it doesn't help him much ("*rod* — what could we talk about, could we say Aaron's rod? Actually, Aaron's rod, I've forgotten offhand what Aaron's rod is," Move 19); and *lay a lionlimb* "seems like the lion laying down with the lamb turned to a different purpose" (Move 3). These minor allusions are simply noticed; they are not incorporated into the reading or reconsidered. Sometimes they seem to be a show of erudition, but sometimes they provide what might be real insight into the structure and accessibility of parts of the mental lexicon: who having read and pondered Hamlet's soliloquy is not reminded of it fleetingly whenever *coil* is mentioned?

Similar to these are references that seem to be used the way Elaine uses hers: to bolster a particular reading by showing that other poets, or the same poet on other occasions, have had similar ideas. Carlos's excursus at the end of his Shakespeare protocol about *Richard II* serves this function: if the queen and the gardeners in that play discuss nature's riches in gardening imagery — "and that's exactly the terms in which the gardeners are talking about it" (Move 46) — then it makes good sense to suppose that Shakespeare treated the same topic in the same way in the sonnet. Similarly, Hopkins reminds him of Blake ("it's very similar to Blake, it reminds me a lot of Blake . . . a certain cynical use of angels and God and Christ to represent things in Blake's cosomology very different from what they meant otherwise," Move 17), but this has little effect on his reading; instead it serves to reinforce his suspicion that it is possible and permissible to speak of God this way.

Where Carlos differs from the other readers is in placing the poems very strongly within the traditions he is familiar with as a medievalist. By this I don't mean merely his use of the Shakespearean background to suggest a lover in the sonnet — "I suppose there's some suggestion of a cruel lover, at least that's the thing I, just because it's a Shakespeare sonnet, but it's not there specifically" (Move 4) — since this is similar to what the other readers do. Instead, he tends to locate a poem in a tradition especially if he is having trouble interpreting it, and then to allow that tradition to guide his reading.

This happens most clearly with "A Ballad of Dreamland." After his first detailed pass through the poem, he recognizes it as one of the numerous offspring of *The Romance of the Rose*: "Ok, well *The Romance of the Rose* is clearly the thing that comes to mind, so I should probably go to external things to try to pull this together" (Move 7). This identification is at first an elaboration of the earlier suggestion that the rose and snow symbolize passion and purity: "That horrible rhyme links the two things and you have red versus white, possibly passion versus purity" (Move 3), since in the *Romance*, "The rose symbolized the, . . . was the flower of the beloved, the love the beloved, however anatomically you want to interpret it" (Move 8). But other features of Swinburne's poem contribute as well: in the second stanza, "the narrator's heart is affected by love, unrequited love, similar to the position of the lover in the *Romance of the Rose*" (Move 11). And the poem is in a medieval form that he links often with Eustache Deschamps (Moves 13, 14, 31, 36), even calling it on one ocassion "The Deschamps form" (Move 31), and less frequently with Chaucer and Marie de France (Moves 14, 36). What begins as elaboration, however, soon becomes predictive: knowledge of this form makes him expect the Envoi to address the intended recipient of the poem directly, and he twice considers this Envoi, justifying it as an explanation addressed to the reader (Moves 13, 36) rather than what one would expect from the medieval model.

But the main effect of identifying the form as self-consciously medieval — "the language sets . . . up the idea of a ballad, a ballade actually, again like Deschamps or Marie de France, or those people, in that tradition, which — Swinburne being pre-Raphaelite oriented — that, I mean that all makes sense" (Move 14) — is to bring into play the whole tradition of Neoplatonic love poetry. The red and white of the rose and the snow are initially and repeatedly related to the tradition — "The still unsolved question for me is why roses, cause the soft white snow is, clearly, you know, cold, passionless, pure, all those things that [it] represent[s] conventionally in all Neoplatonic love poetry, for instance, purity and virginity, and roses of course representing in that same tradition

passion, love, and so forth" (Move 29); "so, i.e.: the heart is hiding in a
nest of roses. It's as if couched in the very material of love imagery"
(Move 32); "the nest of roses opposed to the soft white snow: again the
reference to Neoplatonic love poetry in those two kinds of images"
(Move 33).

The landscape of dreamland becomes a garden, just as in the *Romance*:
"Ok, we're dealing with a dreamland that's a garden inhabited by a lot
of birds . . . but there's some disruption in this perfect paradise" (Move
9), and this identification is alluded to throughout the protocol. This
garden is then associated with a pastoral escape to the world of the imag-
ination: "The garden is traditionally the delineation of the poetic imagi-
nation; that's what the pastoral can be seen as, some sort of a realm to
which the imagination can retreat . . . and certainly Swinburne is trying
to revivify that conventional idea" (Move 15). This identification be-
comes progressively stronger, so that later in his reading Carlos refers to
"The universe that's being defined by dreamland, or the world of the
imagination or this garden" (Move 36). Within this pastoral garden, the
nest of roses becomes a "bower": the heart is "as if couched in the very
material of love imagery, a bower" (Move 32; cf. Moves 34 and 38), and
the secret bird is also contained in this bower — the song of a secret bird
is "something that is part of those birds in that landscape so natural to
the dreamland that we're talking about, something welling up within the
bower, within that self-contained bower" (Move 38). The interpretation
is summarized in one of his general explanations of the poem: "The
heart's ensconcement in a sort of a magical realm, a bower of roses, that
that represents a sort of perfected garden, pastoral garden, of the imagi-
nation" (Move 39).

Typically medieval (if not specifically Neoplatonic) is the inclusion of
the God of Love and his minions. Picking up *keen sun's dart*, Carlos
tentatively suggests: "We can, if we give credence to a pun on *sun*, or
even without, we can think of the God of Love or Cupid the son of
Venus, with his darts certainly appropriate in this context" (Move 17), a
thought that later becomes a reference: "with the reference to the God
of Love, or Cupid or something with the keen sun's dart, at least that's
what occurs to me. It seems like a *Romance of the Rose* type of image,
Guillaume de Lorris' half of the *Romance of the Rose* actually" (Move 41).
If the *keen sun* is the God of Love, then perhaps the bird images
throughout the poem are actually cherubs: "surrounding [the heart] are
these little birds, cherubs, as if taking the idea of personifying forces as
some sort of cherubs or gods, taking it the next step and turning them
into birds" (Move 33).

By the end of his reading, Carlos has made Swinburne's poem at least partially into a medieval dream vision. The narrator, like the typical dreamer, is asleep, while his persona—in this case the heart—is actively taking part in adventures, ensconced in a bower of roses within a pastoral garden inhabited by the God of Love and his attendants. Details that do not fit this general picture precisely—for instance, the absurdity of the heart hiding from love in the very material of love—can be explained as paradoxes "of the sort inherent to dreams"—an explanation Carlos does not find very convincing (Move 30)—or as results of Swinburne's toying with a medieval form, which "actually makes [Carlos] mistrust any deeper meanings that [he] might want to try to mine out of the poem that may not be [there]" (Move 14). But whether the picture is completely satisfying or not, it is clear that the poem supplies only part of it, the rest coming from Carlos's medieval background. Other readers felt frustrated by the poem, partially because they had no background to relate it to. Carlos was more successful than the other simply because he could supply some schema against which to project the poem, and so was able to avoid the frustrating questions (what is the secret bird? and what is its song about?) that bedeviled the others.

To a certain extent, relying on an outside frame of reference and finding a satisfyingly inclusive progression within a poem are alternative strategies. When a poem has an obviously close texture, as the sonnets do, Carlos tends to emphasize close reading and explication; only when the poem itself doesn't seem to cohere does he go to externals (see "Dreamland," Move 7). So in dealing with the sonnets, the effect of the literary frame is less obvious. But it is, I think, still there: he immediately places "Carrion Comfort" within a biblical tradition—as we have already seen, the *lionlimb* reminds him of the lion laying down with the lamb (Move 3), and *toil* calls up one of his favorite allusions, the lilies of the field (Move 10). More important is the question whether the poem is about Satan or God—and he understands these in Old Testament terms: Satan is "the heroic Satan, the Miltonic Satan maybe" (Move 11); "a God of vengeance are we talking about here, or are we talking about Satan? Of course if we are talking about the God of vengeance, he's connected with Satan certainly, is certainly shown by his connection to Job" (Move 15). Even after he decides the poem is about God, he returns to the dichotomy in a slightly different form—the initial uncertainty of identification reflects "a sense of very ambiguous nature of God, or man's ambiguous perception of God" (Move 16). This redefinition allows him to call in Blake (Move 17) and to retain the Old Testament flavor: "the thing is that he's putting it in very Old Testamenty terms by talking about his fight with God, fighting with God almost as if he were another Satan, because that's what those ideas of *hero* bring out to me, particularly because of the use of the word *hero whose heaven-handling flung me, foot trod Me*: that tends to sound like a reference to Satan being cast out of heaven to me, but it doesn't necessarily have to be I suppose" (Move 37). Finally, most of his information about despair is literary, from Spenser (Move 26).

Similarly, Shakespeare's sonnet 94 is dense in texture and confusing in structure; in itself it presents enough puzzles to engage the reader's full attention. But even here, he flounders around talking about aristocrats and power until he remembers the various kinds of hierarchies in the Renaissance: "of course then you have that Renaissance world view, your Tillyardesque idea of the hierarchy, which is — to a certain extent this is some sort of discussion of the hierarchy" (Move 18). Then the aristocrats can be located within a schema, and the whole poem related to the *de casibus* tradition. He refers only to *Richard II* — a splendid exemplar — but the description he gives ("The higher you are the harder you fall," Move 21) is a fair characterization of the whole tradition. Once these identifications have been made, the poem quickly falls into place, and the lilies of the final line are seen to be doubly apposite — "we have the aristocratic connotations of lily, not only the fleur-de-lis of France, but we also have the lilies of the field in the Bible . . . the lilies carry the symbolism of the poem beautifully because it refers to a temporal authority . . . and to also the most classic piece of biblical quotation about husbanding a perfect grace" (Move 23).

The influence of various traditions on Carlos's readings is thus great. His favorite is Neoplatonism — in the group discussion of sonnet 94 one of the other readers invited him to "do the Platonic business then" — probably because it is so widely applicable and because it leads so easily to hierarchies and progressions. Similar to the progressions, the traditions both provide a guide for the process of reading and a measure for success — an interpretation that discerns progressions is good, but one that both discerns progressions and places them within a well-known tradition is even better.

In comparing the actual procedures Carlos uses on the three poems, it is possible to observe a relatively well-defined script for confronting a poem. The three characteristics of his reading discussed so far — his expectations of unity, ideally expressed as a progression, of a strong relation between formal elements and thematic movement, and his belief that the poem can often be located within a well-known literary tradition — characterize the second phase of his reading. But there is a stereotypic quality to his initial contact with a poem as well, reminiscent of standard book openings in chess. Typically he reads through the poem quickly two or three times before treating it in detail. Then he makes one or two careful passes through it, concentrating on the images and their connections with the outside world and each other, and generalizing themes. The first phase of the reading ends with a detailed discussion of the form of the poem.

This procedure is clearest with "A Ballad of Dreamland," since that poem contains little syntactic complexity and so allows Carlos to move immediately to what he prefers. After reading the poem twice and objecting to the feminine rhymes, he begins his first detailed pass through the poem by reading the first four lines and offering a preliminary generalization: "Ok, it seems pretty certain that it's a poem of a lover hiding his heart" (Move 3). He then goes through line by line, noting especially the images ("we start with an image, a strong fantastical image: hiding one's heart in a nest of roses"), how these poetic images translate into real-world occurrences ("Immediately I think of it sticking on a bunch of thorns"), the connections between them ("that horrible rhyme links the two things, and you have red versus white"), and their traditional implications ("possibly passion versus purity," all Move 3). The second half of the first stanza is read, and again Carlos emphasizes general deductions ("in other words, something has awakened the heart"), the images ("we've got two bird images"), and their implausibility (the rose tree "complicates the image of the roses a little further" because roses grow on bushes, not trees), and the connections between them ("And we have the connection between sleep fluttering his wings and the secret bird," all Move 4).

He continues through the rest of the poem, noting similar features (if in less detail) before deciding to resort to external exemplars — in particular, *The Romance of the Rose* — because the "symbolism" (including the imagery) seems neither consistent nor coherent (Move 7). The second close reading of the poem emphasizes again the basic images of the poem, what they symbolize, especially in the tradition of the *Romance*, and how they relate to each other. There is very little paraphrase, the one example of it aborted almost before it begins ("in other words, the win-," Move 10); instead Carlos is constructing the general picture of the poem he gives in the eleventh through thirteenth moves, a picture strongly reminiscent of the general situation in the *Romance*: a garden inhabited by personified forces (here birds rather than people), including a rose bush or tree and a secret force — the secret bird.

The fourteenth move constitutes a brief formal intermezzo emphasizing ornamentation and repetition before he returns for his third progression through the poem, a long one during which he stops at phrases that strike him as important and explores their significance in relation to the other elements of the poem and to the general view of the movement of the poem as a kind of dream vision he is constructing. He considers the rose tree and the song of a secret bird, recalling the traditional symbolism of the garden and relating it to the opening of the poem, perceives the recession of the heart (Move 15), and returns to his earlier generalization that the powers in the poem are personified as birds (Move 16). He then moves on to the second stanza, relating the keen sun's dart to the God of Love (Move 17) and the thorn's wound to the song of the secret bird (Move 18). The first four lines of the third stanza are paraphrased (Move 19), the recurrence of bird imagery in the second four lines noted again, and the Envoi is read and paraphrased (Move 20).

In the twenty-first move he turns his attention to the form of the poem, a shift that marks the end of his typical opening. Here he checks the rhyme scheme and the meter, looks for enjambment and the distribution of feminine rhymes, and examines the sentence types, noting what he calls the apostrophe in the first stanza as opposed to the dialogue in the second. By the end of the opening in the twenty-third move he has read the poem twice quickly and three times in more detail, concentrating on the images and what they symbolize, introduced the literary tradition to explicate the symbolism, and considered at least some aspects of the poem's structure.

The opening of the reading of "Carrion Comfort" is similar except that more paraphrasing is necessary because the poem is so elliptical. Again Carlos reads the poem several times before beginning to consider it closely, and again his initial reactions concern general theme and imagery: "well, clearly a religious theme . . . it seems like there are some inversions of biblical things" (Move 3). The first progress through the poem (Moves 3–12) emphasizes the images and the way they translate into real-world scenes, so *carrion comfort* is "almost as if you're feeding on the most mundane — I mean feeding on a body, feeding on earth as it were — feeding on the most mundane of realizations" (Move 4); *wring-world right foot rock* is explicated "in other words why would you stamp probably on me, or some sort of victor's, almost like a victor putting his foot on the neck of his defeated" (Move 7); and *lapped strength* is "like a cat lapping milk" (Move 10). Equally important is the tradition the images recall, here largely biblical: "*lay a lionlimb against me . . .* calling forth the idea of the lion laying down with the lamb" (Move 8); "the old separation of the grain and the chaff . . . biblical metaphor there" (Move 9); and *toil* recalls the lilies of the field (Move 10). He attempts to connect different images, ideas, or lines: "*Despair* is *carrion comfort*" (Move 4); *thou rude* is "another appositive," like *carrion comfort, despair* (Move 7), and *the hero whose heaven-handling flung me, foot trod me* "sounds like again despair, in terms of the heroic Satan, the Miltonic Satan maybe" (Move 11). Quick generalization of major themes is also apparent: the fourth line elicits "in other words here we're talking about suicide perhaps . . . so there's still a certain ability involved, you still have choice, there still is some sort of free will" (Move 6).

What is different about this poem is its elliptical expression, which encourages more attention to syntax and paraphrase. Carlos worries whether *despair* is appositive to *carrion comfort* (Move 4), identifies *rude* as appositive to *thou* (Move 7), paraphrases the sixth line as "But why would you rock your world-wringing right foot" before translating it ("in other words, why would you stamp probably on me," Move 7), and glosses *lapped strength* as "like licked up perhaps, took strength" (Move 10). But this effort toward paraphrase supplements his typical attention to images, themes, and their connections rather than displacing it, as is indicated by the fact that each of these examples of paraphrase leads into a discussion of the value of the phrase as an image. The only exception is *rude* and Carlos's comment ("*rude* is very interesting; that's a very interesting use of rude," Move 7) immediately relates the poetic use to its normal use, much as he converts images into real-world scenes to comment on their implications.

The thirteenth move begins to consider form (compare the similar interlude in Move 14 of "A Ballad of Dreamland"). He identifies the two "stanzas" of unequal length and begins to break the octave into quatrains before the God with a wring-world right foot recalls him to the earlier question whether a God of vengeance or Satan is being discussed, and this leads back to the biblical background of Job and the lion laying down with the lamb (Move 15). This becomes a second detailed consideration of the poem or, in Carlos's typical fashion, a consideration of the words and phrases that strike him. The suggestion of wind in *fan* is related to the *pneuma* (Move 16), and the rod recalls Aaron's rod (Move 19); the discussion of God in lower case "really gives you a sense of very ambiguous nature of God, or man's ambiguous perception of God" (Move 16) and recalls Blake's "cynical use of angels and God and Christ to represent things in Blake's cosmology very different from what they meant otherwise" (Move 17). The general explanation provided in Move 21 summarizes the results of this second pass through the poem.

Again the opening ends with a self-conscious turn to form: "Tha- so, ok, well let me (cough) in terms of s-, structurally this is a very interesting looking poem" (Move 22). The formal analysis here deals with enjambment, alliteration, assonance, the vocatives (which he calls 'interjections' and 'ejaculations'), the second-person pronouns, and the relation between the rhymes and the sentence types in the quatrains and tercets.

The opening encounter with Shakespeare's sonnet 94 is much briefer than the other two — Carlos complains at the end that he feels "fairly uninspired right now" (Move 12) — but it exhibits the same characteristics, some in more striking form. Generalizations about the poem are especially apparent: "ok, first quatrain, we're talking about attitude and action I guess" (Move 3); "It seems to be a poem about power" (Move 4); "ok, we're talking about a certain kind of purity then all the way through" (Move 7). Various traditions influence his reading — the lilies are immediately linked to the lilies of the field (Move 5), and he supposes "there's some suggestion of a cruel lover, just because it's a Shakespeare sonnet, but it's not there specifically" (Move 4) — and he connects the images or characters in the poem to their real-world counterparts ("but then lilies do not have the power to do hurt," Move 5) and to each other, as the idea of aristocracy in the octave is related to "all that aristocracy in the *lilies that fester smell far worse than weeds*" (Move 9). The connection between the second line and the rest of the poem is unclear: "that line is the one in that first quatrain that bothers me; otherwise the first quatrain falls together with the last, with the third quatrain" (Move 8), and it also seems to conflict with the final line (Move 9).

The turn to form occurs very early, but in a typically self-conscious manner: "Well, this time I'm going to scan the poem right away, or fairly soon, just because, for Shakespeare it is always a good idea" (Move 10). And here he does limit his discussion to scansion, devoting a good deal of time to the errant first line ("God, that's an interesting line," Move 11) and suggesting a similarity between lines 5 and 7 based on their metrical structure. But even in formal analysis he is uninspired — he never looks for his favored enjambment — and so he quickly abandons his reading for the day.

This opening script is of obvious utility in Carlos's reading. It provides a set way to approach a poem, and by concentrating attention on the images, their relation, and the general meanings of the lines and of the larger units, it identifies the raw material for the progressions he seeks later in his reading. The consideration of form at the end of the script reflects his general interest in structural matters at the same time that it provides additional material for progressions or for their corroboration.

It is thus possible to predict with some confidence how Carlos would approach another short poem. He will read through it two or three times, commenting on it very briefly between these readings. He will then go through it in detail, identifying the images, commenting on their relation to the outside world and to each other, and trying to identify general unifying themes for the various sections of the poem. The images will be related to a literary tradition, biblical or Neoplatonic if possible, and probably more specifically to particular influential authors. He will probably progress through the poem in this fashion twice before considering the form of the poem in detail. This formal study will identify rhyme scheme (unless it is obvious, as it is in a Shakespearean sonnet), phonetic effects, syntactic features, including sentence types, and will seek examples of enjambment. How complete it is will depend on Carlos's "inspiration" at the time and whether some aspect of the structure is either intrinsically interesting (as the meter of the first line of sonnet 94) or relates to the themes and images already found (as did the alternation between statement and question in "Carrion Comfort").

After this opening phase of the reading he will return to the poem, perhaps at another time, seeking progressions in the images and formal features he has identified during the opening. This section is less determinate than the opening (like the middle game in chess), since the progressions can be of any kind and can be constructed from any aspect of the poem. After having identified some progressions, though, he will reconsider the form of the poem (see Moves 40–57 in "A Ballad of Dreamland," 40–43 in "Carrion Comfort," and 34–37 in sonnet 94) to see whether he "can find any structural things that open it [the poem] up any more" (Move 40, "A Ballad of Dreamland"). Structural progressions may well be discovered during this phase of the reading, and even if they are not, Carlos will try to relate various aspects of the form to the thematic progressions he has by now defined. He will conclude his reading either when he has discovered a comfortable match between thematic and formal progressions or when he can find no further formal features to discuss.

6 Readers and Strategies

Wolfgang Iser nicely describes the problem this book has confronted:

> Reading is an activity that is guided by the text; this must be processed by the reader, who is then, in turn, affected by what he has processed. It is difficult to describe this interaction, not least because the literary critic has very little to go on in the way of guidelines, and, of course, the two partners are far easier to analyze than is the event that takes place between them.[1]

As I argued in the first chapter, most of those interested in literary response, perhaps in reaction to the very difficulty of analyzing the event of reading, have shifted attention in one way or another to the reader, concentrating on what he says or writes some time after the act of reading or on what competences he must bring to the act to negotiate it successfully. Iser himself illustrates the opposite tack, and much of both *The Act of Reading* and *The Implied Reader* is a discussion of textual features that either provide specific perspectives on the narrative or require concretization by an implied reader, with little attention to how actual readers utilize these features in their reading.[2]

It seems a fair question whether the kind of protocol analysis this study utilizes also deflects attention from the normal processes of preaesthetic reading. Writing about the use of protocol analysis in studies of composing letters, John D. Gould has recently suggested some limitations of the method:

> Initial protocol results make writing appear more complex than do analyses of actual performance results obtained, i.e. the written record or videotapes of composition. . . . Do protocols make automatic processes appear less so? In protocols, are decision points mentioned by participants that, if they did not have to think aloud, would hardly be conscious decisions at all? In the process of providing a verbal protocol, do participants think more analytically than usual, and does this affect the actual composition in unknown ways?[3]

These questions apply equally to the study I have presented here, and deserve to be considered. Protocols do make automatic processes appear less so, but this is an advantage of the method rather than the disadvantage Gould implies, especially if one is interested in observing the activities of readers (or, as in his study, writers), simply because these processes, automatic or not, are constituents of the reading (or writing) process, and thus important aspects of the object of study. Videotapes of readers reading would be frustratingly unrevealing about what the reader is thinking during those longish periods spent staring into space or at the text. Even the protocols suffer from this disadvantage, for during silences there is no information about mental activities. And, as I have argued, the outcome of the reading (or writing) process as presented in published analyses, or class papers, or simple conversation (or letters) reveals nothing about the process by which it was arrived at.

Similar considerations apply to Gould's second question. The whole experimental situation, which required the readers to talk aloud to a tape recorder (with nobody else present in the room) induced a slight but general self-consciousness about their activities, reflected in the protocols by their excusing themselves after sneezing or referring to the later transcription of the tapes. And the slight payment they received encouraged them to be more complete in their activities than they might otherwise have been. These two factors undoubtedly contributed to a greater than usual awareness of "decision points." But again this is a salutory outcome, since these decision points occur in any reading; the difference here is that they are presented for scrutiny rather than being automatic and covert.

Gould's third question gets to the heart of the matter: does the situation of verbalizing one's thoughts interfere with the normal (i.e., unverbalized) course of these thoughts? Does verbalization not only present conscious decisions that are normally unconscious, but also encourage new decisions that would not otherwise have been made at all? More generally, does the verbalization present, not the processes a reader normally uses, but different, more analytical, ones, paralleling the analytical problem-solving routines readers use to unravel syntax when their normal procedures have failed? Undoubtedly there is some small effect along these lines. But four considerations suggest how slight it must be. First, the kind of preaesthetic reading studied here is inherently analytical, and given its goal of producing knowledge about a text, it is hard to conceive of any experimental situation making it significantly more analytical. Second, it is highly unlikely that readers could adopt an entirely novel method of confronting a text specifically for this study. At worst, the kinds of reading they produced must be parts of a repertoire they control already. The third and fourth points corroborate this: none of the readers was at a loss for something to do when presented with the poems. None exhibited the kind of hesitation or surprise they would have if I had given them, say, a second-order differential equation to solve or a matrix to diagonalize instead of a poem to interpret. This suggests that they had well-developed ways — what I have called scripts — for dealing with the situation of reading a poem. None of them complained that his overall reading process was strange or atypical, though several did explain what was odd about portions of it: Philip began his second day of taping with an explanation of what had been abnormal about his procedures on the first day, and Elaine characterized as strange the fact that she saw the subtler meanings of sonnet 94 before the more obvious ones. These readers were generally forthright enough, both on their individual tapes and in the group discussions (as evidenced by their vocal dislike for Swinburne) to have commented on the oddness of the situation and its deleterious effect on their own readings. But they never suggested this effect, and since many ended their tapes proclaiming their satisfaction with what they had accomplished, I think it fair to conclude that what they had done did not strike them as particularly unnatural.

What initially seems to be a drawback of protocol analysis is thus actually one of its strongest advantages: by increasing self-consciousness slightly it foregrounds processes that are normally all but automatic. In their normal reading — and it must be emphasized that we are talking about a statistically abnormal kind of reading, the preaesthetic or professional reading one undertakes to prepare for formal discussion of a poem — readers may remain unaware of the decisions they are continually making, but that does not mean that these decisions are not being made. It simply means that they are not noticed. The aim of protocol analysis is precisely to reveal these natural but unnoticed activities, to provide a record of the temporal flow of mental activity that would be impossible for the reader to construct for himself because the self-monitoring required would interfere drastically with that normal mental activity. Verbalization also interferes (and is probably all but useless in dealing with the particularity of nonverbal images), but since so much of understanding a poem, especially for these readers, involves verbal manipulation, that interference is not likely to be great.

What do these protocols tell us about this specialized kind of reading? The first thing is that Newell and Simon's characterization of problem solving, discussed in the second chapter, does seem to describe to a large extent the behavior of these readers. The typographical error on the distributed version of the poem provided a fortuitous opportunity to observe the distinction between the external task environment and the problem space: Joel, George, and Carlos internalized a poem with an extra *do* in the first line, and the latter two considered its scansion with some ingenuity. Philip and Ann immediately 'corrected' the environment, and Elaine somewhat more warily adopted the standard version, but to the end of her reading entertained the possibility that the distributed version was from a different manuscript and so was equally valid. Philip consciously transformed the task environment into his typical problem space for Shakespeare sonnets by using a standard edition of the poem (complete with glosses), and this allowed him to consider other sonnets close in the sequence (something none of the other readers did) and the introductions by Douglas Bush and Hardin Craig.

The slight discrepancy between the text distributed and the poem internalized is a clear illustration of the difference between the task environment and the problem space. But a more important difference is evident in the way the readers approached the poem. The instructions I distributed — a component of the task environment — asked the readers to come to a complete enough understanding of the poem to participate in a group discussion of it but did not stipulate what that understanding should consist of. Each reader had to make these general instructions more specific in terms of his own problem space. Since these spaces are largely the result of literary education, it is not surprising that these readers, all of whom have received similar training, should work within such similar spaces. Indeed, their actions may seem so natural that one must remember how many simple operations are not exemplified in any of these spaces: none of the readers bothered to count the number of words in the poem, for instance, or checked to see whether any lines began with the same letter or syllable.

Within these problem spaces, each of these readers seems to operate in accordance with a script, a predetermined, stereotyped collection of actions. These scripts are most apparent when a reader confronts different poems in very much the same (stereotyped) manner, as Carlos did. But it is possible to observe scriptlike behavior in the reading of the others as well, and many of them, conscious of their own typical practice, comment overtly on it. Philip's prediction at the beginning of his reading ("So what I'm going to try and do is just what I usually wind up doing with Shakespeare sonnets it seems, is spend a lot of time just trying to paraphrase it," Move 3) is a fair description of what he does with all three poems, and thus seems to outline his basic script. Joel calls his postulation of an external exemplar "a hermeneutical device" that will help him "get a clear idea of precisely the sort of character that Shakespeare is talking about" (Move 5). George explains to the other readers during the group discussion that he usually tries to "come up with a little story that explicates the poem," wondering "what circumstances would have occasioned me to write a poem like this." Ann refers to her habit of relating poems "to my own preoccupations or [to] something I can hook on to, something that appeals to me or intrigues me." These passing references attest to the existence of scripts without, unfortunately, providing much information about their composition.

But at least some components of the scripts can be derived from the protocols. Formal considerations clearly play an extremely important role in Carlos's script, and this appears to be equally true of Ann, who considers the rhyme scheme and syntactic divisions of the poem before anything else (Move 3), and who later comments on the form of the poem at the beginning of her second session of taping (Move 25). Joel's practice of comparing the poem line by line with an external example or concept, evident in his reading first in terms of Iago and then of Angelo, and in his progression through the octave seeking an antecedent for *deeds* (Move 30), is stereotyped behavior that recurs in his reading of the other poems, as is Philip's careful progress through the poem seeking what he calls paraphrase. These characteristics seem to be important parts of the readers' scripts, but only detailed comparison of these readers' transactions of other poems would allow more precise description — to the extent, at least, that the description of Carlos's script is precise — of what is only suggested in the reading of any one poem.

Working within their problem spaces in accordance with their personal scripts, the readers are at the same time very similar to each other and quite idiosyncratic. The mechanism of this apparent contradiction is clarified by Herbert A. Simon's characterization of problem solving in semantically rich domains: he posits a "human problem solver, whose basic tool for solving problems is a small repertory of information processes. . . . When the processor is solving puzzle-like problems, the memory plays a limited role. . . . When it is solving problems in semantically rich domains, a large part of the problem-solving search takes place in long-term memory and is guided by information discovered in that memory."[4] The readers' similarity, then, stems from the fact that they use the same basic repertory of elementary operations or information processes. No matter how different their final interpretations, they arrive at them by READing sections of the poem, SELECTing smaller chunks to process, and then manipulating them by one or more of the other elementary operations. And it is reasonable to suppose that any reader will use these operations or some subset of them, simply because they are the inescapable form of understanding rather than its content.

The readers differ primarily in two areas: in the emphasis they place on different operations, and in the information, stored in their long-term memories, used during reading. Even though all the readers in this study are similar in their general approach to a poem, being 'close readers' in a basic New Critical mode, the different types of operations each preferred produced distinctive interpretations of the poem. Ann's frequent CONNECT:WORLDs led to a conception of the poem that related it to contemporary life, while Philip preferred CONNECT:LITERATURE and CONNECT:POEM and so arrived at a paraphrase but not at an interpretation of the poem. In a similar way, Carlos's close attention to the form of the poem is manifested by a heavy reliance on the operations of FORM, PHONOLOGY, and so forth, while Elaine spent little time considering this. However — and this is the important point — she had the competence, in the technical sense, to do so; that is, she used the operations required, proving that she did in fact control them, but she used them infrequently.

And this can be generalized: a reader resolutely autobiographical, by choice or training, will not be inventing a new kind of operation but will simply be emphasizing a particular kind of CONNECT:WORLD, while a Neoaugustinian, ordinarily glossing whatever he finds, will rely on one restricted type of CONNECT:LITERATURE. It may well be the case that these operations need more specification, and some could be further analyzed — what I have here called CONNECT:LITERATURE could obviously be subdivided into connections to literature proper, to history, to the author's biography, to religion, etc. — but that should not be allowed to obscure the point that readers are similar in using a very small set of operations in their reading. And it seems a fair extension of this point to suppose that readers with less academic training, or those reading in other circumstances, will use these same operations, though probably not all of them, and probably not as persistently as my readers. So a reader whose interaction with a poem consists mainly of identifying lines and images he likes will not be doing something different in kind from Ann, who reads what she thinks are the "great lines" in sonnet 94 (Move 4), but only in extent.

Where readers differ is in the contents and organization of their memories, and this is what allows similar or identical operations to have such different results. In the third chapter I distinguished between a public tradition and a private one, the former a result of education, the repository of institutionalized knowledge passed down from teacher to student. This includes, in the present case, facts about Shakespeare's life, the Elizabethan sonnet tradition, the Elizabethan World Picture, and so forth. Added to this literary-historical knowledge are generally received conceptions about the world. Though it is obviously more difficult to distinguish between shared and idiosyncratic knowledge in this case, included here would be noncontroversial information about plants, farms, lilies, weeds, etc. As is clear from the protocols, not everybody has equal access to this public or shared knowledge, since parts of it may not have been learned in the first place, recollections of what has been learned may be fuzzy (see Ann's comments on Shakespeare's complicated love life, Move 11, or Carlos's uncertainty about Hopkins's Catholicism, Move 36) or mistaken (as is Elaine's feeling that weeds live forever). But this public kind of knowledge provides the backbone of many of the readings I gathered, especially with so institutional an author as Shakespeare, with whom everybody can be expected to have some familiarity. Thus we find large parts of Elaine's and Philip's readings validated (for them) by what they know about Elizabethan sonnet conventions, and Ann's reliance on a current situation stems in part from the fact that the poem frustrates the expectations she has about the structure of Elizabethan sonnets: it lacks both an obvious occasion and the proper logical structure. This public or shared knowledge is what one checks his conclusions against before presenting them publicly, and what one uses to buttress his arguments: it is immediately negotiable, the currency of the academic world.

Private knowledge is quite different: idiosyncratic and based on chance connections, it is much more difficult to glimpse. This individual knowledge cannot be validated by reference to anything outside the person involved; it is the realm of what are usually called "private reactions." So Elaine was reminded of Spenser, Keats, and Stevens for reasons that someone else would be unable to duplicate; Ann thinks of Jane Austen because the reference to flowers in the sestet recalls beauty, which fades, like the bloom of young ladies of past ages; and Carlos related "toil and coil" in the Hopkins poem to the lilies of the field because they toil not, and to Hamlet because of his reference to "this mortal coil." Some of these connections seem to be the result of chance: in different circumstances Ann might not be reminded of Austen, or Elaine of Stevens. But others are quite permanent: we have seen that the parable of the lilies of the field is one of Carlos's favorite biblical passages and can expect any allusion to it, no matter how veiled, to recall it. A few minutes' introspection (whatever its limitations in other applications) will convince the reader of the existence and stability of at least some aspects of this private knowledge: as I write I am aware that "mortal coil" leads me to "shuffle off this mortal coil," which leads (embarrassingly but irresistibly) to "shuffle off to Buffalo." Connections to private knowledge, it need hardly be said, are usually not publicized unless they can be related to shared information.[5]

Variation among readers is due partly to the quite different private knowledge they have and to the probability that they do not have equal access to what is shared: it is a perplexing question why readers do not use *more* of their shared knowledge (which could be elicited in other circumstances). But an even more important cause of variation is the semantic richness of the domains we are dealing with: the memory is the repository of a vast inventory of information, just as the poem consists of a large number of different elements, and it is impossible to predict which poetic element a reader will select for processing or which bit of information in memory he will relate it to. In fact, the sheer size of human memory, the number of facts possibly relevant to any given fact, would be quite enough to guarantee different readings of a poem even if we could somehow ensure that all the readers had access to exactly the same memory. In practice, of course, this is impossible: readers have different memories, they activate those memories to different degrees, they select different elements of the poem for concentrated attention, and these differences lead to their different readings.

The idiosyncrasy of these connections is most obvious when they are made between elements that are themselves the result of interpretation. Many of Elaine's references to literature are of this kind: the word *retentive*, which reminds her of Wallace Stevens's poem, appears nowhere in sonnet 94; it is the result of her conception of the octave. Similarly, it is not only the word *summer* that recalls sonnet 73 and "To Autumn" but the realization that a season can represent a period of human life. And the reference to Spenser stems from her conclusion that *they* in the sonnet are hoarding themselves unnaturally. Here we have examples of a system of connections doubly impossible to predict: first because each is based on an interpretation of part of the poem rather than on some poetic element, and second because each connection is to an element of private knowledge.

Even in cases where readers deal directly with elements of the poem, however, it is difficult to predict what they will do with them. This is most easily observed in the case of allusions. Of the readers, only George and Carlos identified the lilies of the final line with the lilies of the field in Christ's parable, and they made quite different uses of this same CONNECT:LITERATURE. Early in his reading, George recognized the allusion and linked it explicitly with ambition: "I can't help thinking of the parable about the lilies in the fields, who neither sow nor reap,

who aren't bothered by ambition or infected by ambition, but live their
own natural — that is, true to their own nature — lives" (Move 4). After
some difficulty in reconciling the flower of lines 9 and 10 with both a
nobleman and the parable, he decided that "if the flower lives in some
kind of natural dignity it's better off. That would work both as an ex-
tension of the lilies of the field parable and the reading I'm giving the
poem" (Move 19). Toward the end of his perception, he provided a third
version: "Then the lesson in the sestet concerning the sweetness of the
natural flower, which I do think is allied with Christ's lilies of the field
parable, the beauty of the natural flower that lives only for one season
and has no concerns other than that one season; in other words, it isn't
concerned with titles and family and inheritances the way the titled
classes are" (Move 28). In the course of his reading the lilies carried
three different significances: first as a warning against ambition, then as
an example of natural living rather than class conceit, and finally, in a
modified version of the second, as something that lives naturally for, and
is concerned with, one season only rather than being part of (and influ-
enced by) a continuing line. It is important to recognize that these three
versions are cumulative; the later ones do not so much replace the earlier
one as modify it, so the conception of the lily as a being that lives a life
sufficient unto itself contains the suggestion that it avoids the kind of
ambition characteristic of those too concerned with class distinctions and
genealogy.

Carlos also noticed the allusion early in his reading, but was unable to
relate it to his interpretation because his early conception of the poem
concentrated on power: "But then there's the image of the lilies at the
end and you of course recall lilies of the field — but then lilies do not
have the power to do hurt. The issue seems to be not lilies of the field,
who labor not, but something beyond that where there's power, poten-
tially malignant power" (Move 5). As his reading progressed, he iden-
tified the lilies with aristocrats (Moves 9 and 17) and then with the
fleur-de-lis: "And of course we have the aristocratic connotations of lily,
not only the fleur-de-lis of France, but we also have the lilies of the field
in the Bible . . . so the lilies carry the symbolism of the poem beautifully
because it refers to a temporal authority, inimicable actually to the En-
glish at this point, the French, and to also the most classic piece of
biblical quotation about husbanding a perfect grace" (Move 23). The
symbolism of the poem carried so beautifully is a double concern with
aristocracy and with moral purity, which was clarified toward the end of
his reading: "It seems as if the poem is an indictment of the whole world
of action, which actually is what the lilies of the field passage in the

Bible is more or less about" (Move 38): the festering of the lilies repre-
sents the spiritual consequences of power (Move 41). The aptness of this
conclusion is appreciated fully only if one remembers Carlos's initial re-
action to the lilies: they labor not. Only when the lily abandons its bibli-
cal function and acts does it ally itself with power and thus fester.

I think it is fair to say that this biblical allusion is an aspect of shared
knowledge, something that can be checked in reference sources. But
neither reader does this, and both determine its significance according to
their momentary interests, just as they interpret the other elements of
the poem. That is, neither the elements of the poem nor the contents of
memory are primes from the point of view of interpretation: both require
further explication. This is most obvious when the element of memory
seems somehow to invite further interpretation, as a parable or another
poem, so it does not seem strange to find Carlos and George interpreting
the parable for their own use, or Elaine supplying an understanding of
sonnet 129 when *expense* reminds her of it. What is more surprising, at
least initially, is that practically every element in the poem can be linked
to elements in memory that are subject to the same kind of unlimited
further interpretation.[6] Thus even for readers who do not recognize the
biblical allusion, the lilies are more than a particular kind of flower.

For Elaine, they initially represent "purity, beauty" (Move 8), but she
soon links them with the other flowers and the sweetest things that die
no matter what they do (Move 14, cf. 24 and 50). In sharp contrast are
the weeds that "proliferate and grow" (Move 14), and even though there
are varieties of the lily, like the tiger lily, that grow wild (Move 21), this
fecundity suggests that perhaps the weed is somehow more natural than
the lily (Move 58). The lily's "falling from grace" is greater because of
its original sweetness (Move 40), something emphasized by the ex-
tremely strong image of the lily festering—"the smelling and the fester-
ing of the lily, a souring" (Move 42), "that awful image of rotting lilies at
the end" (Move 56). This wide range of association to the lily nicely
illustrates the operation and interrelation of public and private knowl-
edge. Some of her connections seem clearly traditional—the lily is pure,
fragile, beautiful—and some are shared conceptions of the world—lilies
are a kind of sweet flower; they die no matter what they do. But others
are more idiosyncratic: Elaine is the only reader to distinguish between
tiger lilies and cultivated lilies, to relate the sweetness of flowers
suggested by the poem with the sourness of festering, and to consider
the lilies somehow less natural than the weeds because of their need for
cultivation.

Joel's initial response to the lily is to see it naturalistically: in an inter-
esting echo of Elaine's comments on sweetness, he wonders whether the

lily contains sugars that cause it to smell worse than weeds in decomposing (Move 13). But he soon relates the festering to a moral quality, something that "stinks morally" (Move 18). Philip's reaction is almost entirely literary. He never mentions the lily as a flower, instead relating it to the *de casibus* tradition (Move 10), and when he returns to the line, it is only to discover that it also appears in *Edward the Third* (Move 23) and then to observe that it seems too powerful a conclusion for a sonnet (Move 34). From the beginning, Ann loves the line (Move 4), but more for its quality as a graphic illustration of "how the mighty have fallen" (Moves 19, 33) and for the way it summarizes the third quatrain and relates to the thirteenth line (Move 10) than for anything else. This group of readers suggests how an element can recall a literary tradition even when it is not seen as an allusion, and how it can be interpreted by relating it, not to information in memory before the encounter with the poem, but to information that becomes available only during the reading of the poem, that is, information about the poem itself. And they also illustrate the difficulty of predicting what information in memory a poetic element will be related to: why didn't they recall more of what they know about lilies?

The same kind of variation among readers is apparent in their understandings of many of the important terms in the poem: *hurt, rightly, heaven's graces*, and so on. These words may seem to invite specification, since there are many different kinds of hurt, grace, and excellence; but the same variation is apparent, if less striking, with words that seem more determinate: *stone, summer's flowers, live and die*. To say that these words (or the concepts they refer to) have connotations that are activated (or that the reader activates) in the process of reading is partially true, but it suggests that each word has a more or less determinate set of connotations matching the set of denotations recorded in a comprehensive dictionary. What the activities of readers suggest instead is that the operative set of connotations available for any element — the other elements or concepts to which it can be related — is virtually unlimited. And while some of these connections are considered only momentarily (see Elaine's quick dismissal of sexual overtones in *die*, Move 48), others are retained and made public.

Another factor contributing to the variation among readers is apparent from the discussions above. Like the studies of visual perception that reveal subjects fixating over and over on locations of especial salience,[7] the protocols illustrate how frequently readers return to words or lines or ideas that either cause them difficulty or seem to be particularly relevant. Often these reconsiderations repeat much of what had already been said, but since there is usually something new added as well, the overall effect is of a spiral. Final interpretations typically reflect only the final turn of the spiral, and thus overlook or discard not only earlier hypotheses that have been discarded but also the filiations any idea has developed during its evolution. It is true that some insights are entertained only in passing, or are fully developed in their initial formulation, and these seem to lose little if anything from passing mention: George thought "others but stewards of their excellence" a play on the title for a nobleman, "Their Excellencies," which related nicely to his concern with the nobility as a class, but he did little more with this idea during his perception than present it (Move 9). In the group discussion he suggested it, but didn't insist on it when Philip pointed out that " 'Excellency' isn't a title that would be used for any British nobleman; 'Excellency' is a republic's title for lofty people like ambassadors." Thus Empson's parenthetical presentation of the same insight "(with a suggestion of 'Their Excellencies')"[8] would seem a reasonable expression of George's experience.

But most of the ideas important for a final interpretation are given extended, and repeated, attention, and the expression of these ideas in final interpretations almost always subdues the resonance of the conception. Compare Hallett Smith's reference to the lilies of the field to either George's or Carlos's development of it: "The self-sufficiency of the flower was of course established or fortified by a sacred text, 'consider the lilies of the field, how they grow; they toil not, neither do they spin,' and it may have been the recollection of this verse which brought into Shakespeare's mind the line."[9] Now it may be that Smith is saying something rather different from George, but compare the richness of the allusion for George, with its relations to ambition, transience, and being true to one's own nature. And it must be remembered that "ambition," "transience," and "being true to one's own nature" are merely shorthand references to concepts that are fully meaningful only in the particular use George makes of them in his perception. I assume that the allusion had similar associations for Smith, but the conventions of published interpretations provide little opportunity to express or explore them in full detail.

As a final example, we might recall the difficulty the readers had with the penultimate line of the poem: "For sweetest things grow sourest by their deeds." The mention of "deeds" after apparent inactivity of the octave caused the readers endless trouble, especially Ann, who kept returning to the line in annoyance because it did not connect logically to the octave, and Joel, who read through the octave seeking something that could be called "deeds." Booth refers to this difficulty: "Shakespeare presents the reader with *their deeds;* 'they' in the octave who are capable of deeds do none; it is *sweetest things* that are likely to act."[10] Despite his insistence that "throughout the poem, the reader has to cope with conflicting reactions, impressions, and systems of coherence,"[11] Booth's interpretation (*any* interpretation) must substitute for that experience merely a reference to it, a reference that will be effective only if the reader has (or has had) the experience. That is, a reader *experiences* what an interpretation only names, something Empson hints at in introducing his interpretation of sonnet 94: "There is no reason why the subtlety of the irony in so complex a material must be capable of being pegged out into verbal explanations. The vague and generalized language of the descriptions, which might be talking about so many sorts of people as well as feeling so many things about them, somehow makes a unity like a crossroads, which analysis does not deal with by exploring down the roads. . . . One can't expect, in writing about such a process, to say anything very tidy and complete."[12]

But readers do explore down the sideroads, and that is why Culler's analyses of published interpretations, for all their insight into the constituents and structure of those presentations, are so unrevealing about the processes whereby readers reach interpretations of poems. By concentrating on what has already been published, he hopes to stress "everything that is public and explicable in the reading process."[13] But, as I argued in the first chapter, this approach emphasizes rhetorical efficacy rather than psychological realism: the interpretations are public because they have been made public — publicized — by readers satisfied with their results, and these results are so ordered as to be most compelling to future readers rather than most reflective of their origins. When autobiographical information about origins is provided — as in the introduction and headnotes to the articles collected in Stanley E. Fish's *Is There a Text in this Class?* — it is also for a rhetorical purpose, to convince a reader to accept a view he finds initially strange by chronicling the complicated process by which the author himself came to accept it. The actual experience of a poem, as the protocols illustrate, is much more various and confused, and especially repetitious, than what appears in the final published interpretation of it. The conventions Culler discusses, then, are as likely to concern the process by which a rather untidy perception is arranged for presentation as the process which is the perception in the first place.

The reason for this is that the conventions Culler proposes are teleological, dealing with the aims or results of reading, rather than operational, dealing with the experience; and the same is true of many of

Stanley Fish's interpretive strategies. To see how in greater detail, let us compare them with the operations they are modelled on, the rules of transformational grammar and the perceptual strategies of the psycholinguists. Each rule of a transformational grammar consists of two parts, a condition and an operation, the one specifying the structures the rule applies to, the other, the changes it makes in that structure. The condition appears to the left of an arrow (single for phrase-structure rules, double for transformations), while the operation or change is on the right:

$$S \rightarrow NP + Pred\ P$$
$$NP_1 + Aux + V + NP_2 \rightarrow NP_2 + Aux + be + en + V + by + NP_1{}^{14}$$

The first of these, a phrase-structure rule, says, roughly, "replace the symbol S (for Sentence) with the symbols NP + Pred P (for Noun Phrase plus Predicate Phrase). The second, a transformation, says that any string that can be analyzed as having the structure on the left can be changed to a string having the structure on the right: the noun phrases are switched, *by* is added before the last one, and *be* + *en* is added after the auxiliary. Both of these rules are operational or formal, specifying explicitly what structures the rule applies to and what changes it effects.

Perceptual strategies depend more heavily on semantic information but are still largely formal in this sense:

> Strategy A: Segment together any sequence X . . . Y, in which the members could be related by primary internal structural relations, 'Actor, action, object, . . . modifier'.[15]
> Strategy B: The first N . . . V . . . (N) . . . clause (isolated by Strategy A) is the main clause, unless the verb is marked as subordinate.[16]

Both strategies identify a structure, the first one utilizing semantic information, the second apparently not, and then specify the operation to be performed: label the sequence a unit; label the unit a main clause.

By contrast, consider two of Culler's conventions: the convention of unity, expressed either on the model of the synecdochic series, "where a list of particulars are interpreted as instances of a general class to which they all belong," or on the "pattern of *aletheic reversal:* first a false or inadequate vision, then its true or adequate counterpart";[17] and "the convention that parallelism of expression creates parallelism of thought."[18] Although these conventions seem to provide fairly precise descriptions of the structures they apply to, they in fact do not: upon encountering a number of parallel constructions (assuming these can be

defined), should one consider them a list and seek a more general class
to which all the members belong, consider them an aletheic reversal and
see the later members as progressive refinements of an originally in-
adequate vision, or emphasize the parallelism of structure and explore
semantic similarities among the members? And the operations are even
more general: what kind of general class or parallelism of structure
should one seek, and how? In their present form Culler's conventions
are not much help to somebody who does not already know how to use
them: they lack the explicitness that is a prime requisite of linguistic
theories. The fact that they are initial formulations may account for this;
further research may lead to an aletheic reversal. But this seems un-
likely, since much of their utility in characterizing interpretations de-
pends upon their generality, and it is difficult to see how they could be
made much more explicit without multiplying alarmingly.

Many of Stanley E. Fish's "interpretive strategies" are similarly tele-
ological, even though they are clearly modelled on the perceptual strat-
egies of the psycholinguists. As I argued in the first chapter, his strate-
gies tend to concern either the linguistic level (in the terminology
suggested there, the perceptual level) or the level of significance. Con-
sider an example of the former: commenting on a passage from
"Lycidas,"

> The willow and the hazel copses green
> Shall now no more be seen
> Fanning their joyous leaves to thy soft lays,

Fish claims that the reader effects closure after the second line. That is,
applying something like perceptual strategy A, he decides the construc-
tion contains the requisite object and action (being passive it requires no
agent), and so is complete. Fish continues:

> In this case, the demarcation my interpretation calls into being is placed
> at the end of line 42; but of course, the end of that (or any other) line is
> worth noticing or pointing out only because my model *demands* (the word
> is not too strong) perceptual closures and therefore locations at which
> they occur; in that model this point will be one of those locations, al-
> though (1) it need not have been (not every line ending occasions a clo-
> sure) and (2) in another model, one that does not give value to the activ-
> ities of readers, the possibility of its being one would not have arisen.[19]

When this example is examined closely, it turns out to be very like a
self-consuming artifact. First, the claim that his model "*demands* . . .
perceptual closures" is a bit of bombast: all models require closure, since
without it there would be no way of distinguishing one perception from

another and consequently no perception at all, except possibly the infant's buzzing blooming world. More specifically, any language demands closure, and any speaker has learned this long before encountering Milton. So Fish's claim must be that in his model line endings encourage closure when it is perceptually possible. This seems inoffensive enough, since perceptual strategy A would actually require more frequent closure. To make his claim novel, Fish must modify it radically, arguing that his model *forbids* closure in some (or all) cases where normal language processing requires it or seeks it. And the fact that a different model does not explicitly recognize closure is irrelevant, since closure is an operation all readers already utilize by virtue of being speakers and readers in the first place.

Although the example seems to me muddled, I think that this kind of strategy could be made formal and operational so long as there were not too much insistence on the reader's creating all features of the text. A reformulated strategy would require two steps: identifying line endings (on the basis of some formal definition), and trying to apply perceptual strategy A to the units so identified. But insisting that line endings are themselves the result of interpretive strategies (as a literal, though uncharitable, reading of Fish would suggest) begins an infinite regress that will never allow operational rules and will be comforting only to those seeking to lose themselves in Browne's "O Altitudo!"

Even more obviously, the interpretive strategies relating to significance are teleological in nature. Consider what Fish calls Augustine's "dazzlingly simple" rule of interpretation: "everything in Scriptures points to (bears the meaning of) God's love for us and our answering responsibility to love our fellow creatures for His sake. If only you should come upon something which does not at first seem to bear this meaning, that 'does not literally pertain to virtuous behavior or to the truth of faith', you are then to take it 'to be figurative' and proceed to scrutinize it 'until an interpretation contributing to the reign of charity is produced.'"[20] Fish characterizes this as "both a stipulation of what meaning there is and a set of directions for finding it, which is of course a set of directions — of interpretive strategies — for making it."[21] But the directions — take it to be figurative and proceed to scrutinize it until the proper goal is reached — are not very specific; what is missing is any notion of what form the scrutiny should take. What operations should the reader perform? Originally, of course, the form was implicit in Augustine's rhetorical tradition, but Fish's adaptation of the injunction today, when that rhetorical tradition can no longer be assumed, reveals unwittingly the extent to which his interpretive strategies emphasize goals rather than the operations that lead to these goals.

In short, both Culler's conventions and Fish's interpretive strategies are teleological and prescriptive, characterizing the goals of interpretation without providing much information about how to attain them. Similar conventions and strategies for playing chess would be: checkmate the opposing king; protect your own king; control the center; exploit forking positions. Now these prescriptions are all useful, and probably characterize the goals of anybody competent at chess, but they do not tell the neophyte what to do, how to control the center or to recognize forking positions. In contrast, linguistic rules and perceptual strategies specify quite explicitly what to do in particular situations, but they furnish no explanation of why it is being done or of what goal is intended. And the same seems to be true of the elementary operations I have discussed.

Elementary operations and interpretive strategies (or conventions) are thus usefully complementary: the latter specify the (kinds of) answer a reader will accept to the problem posed by the poem, while the former characterize the procedures a reader uses to arrive at that answer. Interpretive strategies tell you when you can stop reading; elementary operations tell you what to do until you stop. To return to the discussion in the second chapter of whether reading poetry (in the preaesthetic way this study concerns) is a kind of problem solving, we can see again that it is, since the interpretive strategies or conventions a reader adopts supply the element of Newell and Simon's characterization of a problem that seemed most problematical in the reading situation: the answer. I argued there that each reader projects his own answer to the problem posed by the poem, and it is now apparent that Culler's conventions of thematic unity, metaphorical coherence, significance, and the various forms or models these assume,[22] are constituents of successful interpretations, of the answer the reader seeks. The protocols illustrate precisely this search: in each of the poems Carlos works toward the same preferred model of thematic unity (a progression), and Ann's annoyance with sonnet 94 stems largely from the fact that she cannot find a logical unity stemming from metaphorical coherence. Philip and George seek their unifying principles in something that could actually have happened to Shakespeare; Joel finds his in another character; and Elaine relies on a metaphorical coherence bolstered by knowledge of the rest of Shakespeare.

From this perspective, interpretive communities undoubtedly exist, but they consist of those who agree on the constituents of a final interpretation of the text rather than on those who use the same operations in their reading. Fish's characterization of these communities requires only slight modification: "interpretive communities are made up of those who share interpretive strategies not for reading (in the conventional sense) but for writing texts, for constituting their properties and assigning their intentions. In other words, these strategies exist prior to the act of reading and therefore determine the shape of what is read rather than, as is usually assumed, the other way around."[23] The reader constitutes not the properties of texts but the properties of the final conceptions he has of texts; and strategies "determine the shape of what is read" in the sense that a reader will not be satisfied with his understanding of what he reads unless it assumes a particular shape. How it comes to assume that shape has been the topic of this book.

Appendix: The Protocols

The protocols presented here were produced verbatim from the tapes the readers made. To save space, readings of several lines of the poem have been reported rather than transcribed. Punctuation, obviously, is editorial, intended to reflect as much as possible the information contained in intonation. Quotation marks surround sections that seem to be read from the text. Ellipsis marks indicate pauses of more than three seconds.

JOEL: SONNET 94

1

It is Wednesday, October tenth 9:15 in the morning and I have opened the poem that Mr. Kintgen has distributed. There are no, are no instructions on how to respond, record our responses to this poem — I suppose it'll be the same directions as before. Uh, Sonnet 94, Shakespeare's. Well I foresee one of these intricate sonnets of Shakespeare's in which there is um use of technical jargon from some, technical language from some profession uh probably, and lot of intricate working of images in terminology, uh, let's see though what is involved.

2

//read ll. 1 – 3 with "do hurt" in l. 1// Immediately I get this image of Iago, um. "Unmov'd, cold, and to temptation slow; / They rightly do inherit heaven's graces." That strikes me as being ironic, I don't know why. Um, //read ll. 6 – 14 with: "uh uh uh" after l. 7; repeating l. 9; and with l. 12: The barest weed outbraves his dignity.// Hum. Well I was wrong about uh um a body of technical terminology that appears throughout the, the sonnet.

3

"They that have pow'r to do hurt and will do none, / That do not do the thing they most do show." "Do not do the thing they most do show." Again, I, I, immediately to my mind jumps the character of Iago. Uh, I suppose it's fresh in my mind because of having seen the uh opening night of the Metropolitan Opera oh about two weeks ago in which uh, uh, Verdi's *Otello* was featured, and being so uh, I was so uh, g-, am always bowled over by that opera, I forget between the times I see it how towering it is, towering a masterpiece it is, and then when I start seeing it again I'm just sucked into it uh by its, by its uh greatness, um, so I'm seeing Iago right now.

4

"Who, moving others" — again I see uh Iago uh i-, having his uh henchmen uh, unwitting henchmen, uh help him do his dirty deeds. "Who, moving others, are themselves as stone" — emotionally "as stone," but um Shakespeare is uh I believe is speaking about uh someone who, to the public, that is, is the uh is the true oh lord and owner of his face uh is uh, can completely control the um, i-, uh outward uh expression t-, uh, what he reveals to the public, and of course in the, it doesn't quite, uh that would be uh I would be able to see uh Iago in this role only uh with all the soliloquies that he has cut out, because of course he reveals himself to the, to the audience.

5

Uh, "mov'd, cold and to temptation slow," "Unmov'd, cold, and to temptation slow." That sounds more to me like a uh, some sort of uh mistress at this point that he's speaking about, "Unmov'd," uh because a character like Iago is certainly a mover and 'ims-, himself is not moved perhaps by the uh normal uh uh human uh emotions uh but he is moved by certain rather unusual emotions, although he uh i-, there are kinds of emotions that would leave a person "cold," let's say, "to temptation slow." I'm uh um continuing with this uh casting Iago in the role of the uh person that's described in the sonnet simply because I have an, (cough) I, I, I have a feeling, a hunch that it may help me to visualize the poem as I go through it and when I get to words and phrases that do not jive with uh my understanding of Iago uh then I can make corrections at that point and go back through the poem and try to get a clear idea of precisely the sort of character that Shakespeare is talking about, uh in the poem, so it's sort of a uh uh a lucky guess uh as to uh what the character may be that's being portrayed and, but I don't put much stock in this guess, I'm also uh using it sort of as a uh, um, a device for uh interpreting what is uh meant, I guess sort of hermeneutical device, um.

6

"To temptation slow," "to temptation slow." Now again see that, my, the immediate uh meaning that pops into my mind is uh uh, a mistress who is slow to uh respond to uh sexual temptation with the uh, with the suitor, but let's see. Again, it's, it's a little more uh complicated for me to see Iago in this light, "to temptation slow" because he certainly is tempted, oh, well I suppose he takes his, he t-, he grabs opportunity, he doesn't uh force opportunity, he grabs opportunity by the forelock numbers of times. But certainly there is uh strong temptation which he gives in to, to uh degrade Othello um, and to pull down several other people with him. So I have to sort of shelf this adjective, adjectival phrase "to temptation slow," for a second. "Show," "stone," "slow" Um.

7

"They rightly do inherit heaven's graces / And husband nature's riches from expense," "They rightly do inherit heaven's graces." Well now if he's not being ironic then I have really uh cast the wrong person from the beginning of this poem, if "They that have pow'r to do hurt and will do none" is actually um, a compliment then it's very interesting that I would have uh been misreading it as a, ah, fearful criticism from the beginning. Let's see.

8

"And husband nature's riches from expense," "nature's riches from expense." "From expense" gives me a little problem, that uh locution "And husband nature's riches from expense." "Husband" them, "husband" them "from expense," or "riches from expense"? And goodness, I'll have to uh come back to that.

9

"They are the lords and owners of their faces, / Others but stewards of their excellence." So there's this un image of a castle-keep or a hu hu medieval or Renaissance courtly life with lords of the castle and, and "stewards," "stewards," keepers, "owners" of the lord's "excellence." Huh. So the "lords" are "owners" of their outward appearance, simply the façade, while the stewards are the owners of their riches or their virtue, their power.

10

"The summer's flow'r is to the summer sweet, / Though to itself it only live and die." Let's see, the flower in itself may simply live and die, it may lose its individual existence but it is sweet, pleasing and sweet to a larger phenomenon, summer, for the use that it has for summer, for the season.

11

"But if that flow'r with base infection meet, / The bas-t-est weed outbraves his dignity." Uh a flower infected will uh wilt, look um mangy, and "The basest weed" will um will outshine him uh as far as um being larger and looking healthier, uh, his dignity." Uh, so the higher nature or spirit, the flower, is useful to summer and sweet to summer because of that, but if it is infected, "The basest weed," uh summer will not do anything to help the individual flower and "The basest weed" will in comparison look dignified.

12

"For sweetest things turn sourest by their deeds," "For sweetest things turn sourest by their deeds," "their" — does that refer to "sweetest things"? Or does it refer to the "They that have pow'r to do hurt," the "lords and owners of their faces," the summer — is that who "their" refers to? "Their deeds." Let's see, "their deeds," uh, "their deeds." "Deeds," hum. My goodness. "For sweetest things turn sourest by their deeds." Sweet to sour, healthy flower to sick flower.

13

Hum. "Lilies that fester smell far worse than weeds." Hum. "Weeds," "smell far worse than weeds." I suppose that must be a um natural f-, f-, fact of nature which I can't comment upon, um, rather than simply some kind of uh borrowing from emblem literature or, uh, herbal folklore I suppose, although it could be that. But it could be that the sugars uh and different elements in a flower may indeed uh smell more sour than a uh, when they decompose, than a, a weed that decomposes. I don't know whether that is a um natural fact or not.

14

Ok, now my problem at this point is trying to relate the little allegory of the flower and summer and the weed, those three actors, together with the concluding couplet which uh draws upon the imagery in that uh, the last quatrain, the third quatrain — trying to relate that to the characters, the human characters, in the first two quatrains. Hum. And then a big problem is to establish what Shakespeare's tone is to this, to all three characters involved. Um. Right now I'm going to go catch a bus in to class and come back to the poem uh later today.

15

It is now eight o'clock on Thursday evening October eleventh, and I'm coming back to the Shakespeare sonnet. //read ll. 1 – 8 with "do hurt" in l. 1// Hum. Again the big problem I'm having is uh, at the moment is whether or not to take Shakespeare at his word or to attribute to him um a, an irony that may be in reality more characteristic of later centuries, um, or at least of other poets. That is, uh, the irony I'm speaking of is whether or not he is being ironic or facetious when he says that these people who don't show their real emotions do rightly "inherit heaven's graces / And husband nature's riches from expense."

16

I shut off the uh tape recorder for about three minutes while my very noisy furnace uh did its thing, uh I'm afraid I would be almost inaudible on this tape with the furnace going, uh so I might be stopping and starting uh a number of times this, this evening.

17

Uh, let's see now if I can resolve my problem, go on to the third quatrain. //read ll. 9 – 12// "But if," a certain condition, "though," "But," "then," though but then. Hum. "Summer's flow'r is to the summer sweet." Personifying summer.

18

//read ll. 10 – 14// Hum, is it that "Lilies," or things that *seem* virtuous, when they fall from virtue stink morally even worse than less virtuous beings when they fall? "For sweetest things turn sourest by their deeds," can "turn sourest by their deeds" I suppose, can may be implied.

19

Let's see if, what that helps, if it helps at all. "They that have pow'r to do hurt and will do none," "pow'r to hurt," "and will do none," no hurt, "That do not do the thing they most do show." Hum, it seems very, hum, "They that have" the "pow'r to," "to do hurt and will do none." They have the power and they won't do it, do any hurt. They don't "do the thing they most do show," Well they show, huh, do they show no outward attempts to hurt and therefore they actually do, um by other means, that they hurt others by other means?

20

"Who, moving others," that is through others? Or does that mean "Who, moving others," some sort of, um, someone indifferent to love? Again, I, I, I come back to this uh feeling that it's, uh, uh, addressed to a, addressed to some kind of love object at this point,

21

"Who, moving others, are themselves as stone" — s-, "as stone" in their passions or "as stone" in their uh determination? Uh, uh, in their determination possibly not to have passions like Iago.

22

"Unmov'd, cold and to temptation slow; / They rightly do inherit heaven's graces / And husband," husbands "nature's riches." Slow to temptation, but not necessarily immune to temptation. Well now that's, it's slow to temptation but they're "Unmov'd," "themselves as stone, / Unmov'd, cold and to temptation slow," "Who, moving others, are themselves as stone." Huh. "Who, moving others, are themselves as stone, / Unmov'd, cold, and to temptation slow." "They rightly," they by right "inherit heaven's graces," "heaven's," "heaven's graces / And husband nature's riches from expense." "Husband nature's," is that possibly a pun? "Husband nature's ri-," n-, as in husbandry but also as in to mate, as opposed to their uh aloofness from mating in the first quatrain? Tsk, hum. Uh I'm going to turn off for a second and check uh my supper on the stove.

23

That took uh just a minute. Uh, "husband nature's riches." "They are the lords and owners," well my problem here is that if there is a beloved implied, or addressed, then "lords and owners," which has a kind of masculine gender, obviously, um, at least "lords" does, doesn't agree with the female beloved.

24

"They are the lords and owners of their faces, / Others but stewards of their excellence." Goodness. I think I will get my OED and check all of the possible meanings for "expense," and my other dictionary, my Collegiate Dictionary, for "husband" to see all of the meanings f-, meanings of "husband." Wait just a second, I'll be back.

I'm back again about a minute later. I'm looking at my Webster's New World Dictionary under the verb "husband," if there is one listed. "Verb, to marry a woman, to become or act as the husband of" — ok. "To manage economically, conserve," to "husband nature's riches." Well there's a possibility there of still a pun, um. "Archaic, to provide with a husband. Obsolete, to cultivate soil or plants." Well obsolete doesn't mean Shakespeare couldn't have used it obviously, or that it wasn't current in his day. Now I'm looking up "expense." . . . And I see, let's see, of course quite a lot of entries. "Expense, Latin, expendere, expendere," hanging from, but it doesn't say that, "the action of expending, the state of being expended. Disbursement, spending, laying out of money." um "The expending or using up of material resources, the state of being expended or used up. Consumption of produce or provisions." Let's see.

SIDE 2

I'm still looking under definitions of "expense." "Loss of a possession," huh, "as in the Shakespeare sonnet" as an example — "'Then can I expend none,' 'Then can I moan the expense of many a vanished sight,'" the expense, the loss. "Husband nature's riches from" loss. Well, that doesn't sound too likely, let me go back and see in, if in fact they cite Shakespeare as um an example of some of these other usages. Um, "expending or using up of material resources or immaterial resources," hum. *Love's Labours Lost*, 'I implore so much expense of thy royal sweet breath as will utter a brace of words'" — hum. See what else. "Money expended." "Burden of expenditure, the pecuniary charge, cost, or sacrifice involved in any course of action," mm. "To lie at expense, at the expense of, at the expense of, so great expense, to be at expense. To put a person to expense, to be at the expense." Nothing about "from expense." Well, I'm not sure I've settled anything by checking the OED. Think I'll shut it and look again at the poem.

25

These people in the first quatrain by right "inherit heaven's graces" and these people also "husband nature's riches from expense." "Husband . . . from expense," "husband nature's riches." Tsk, hum. It's difficult for me, I guess the most difficult line for me. I'm going to check my supper once more.

Five minutes later, I'm back, still conscious that the sixth line is the most difficult f-, for me to understand, and I think I'll put off understanding it for a few seconds, trying to understand it.

26

These people are "the lords and owners of their faces,   /   Others but stewards of their excellence," so it seems there an image, imagery of kind of feudal relationship. See in the third quatrain imagery of "flow'r," summer season, weeds, disease. And the couplet, "weeds," flowers, disease. First quatrain, "stone," movement. Second quatrain, um, husbanding ri-, husbanding riches, whether that mean cultivating riches? mating riches? There goes my furnace again.

27

Three miniutes later. Um, inheritance, husba'ding, husbanding riches. "Riches," "riches," inheriting "riches," husba-ding ri-, husbanding "riches from expense."

28

Well, I'm not getting very far at the moment, so I'm going to try some shots in the dark, just looking at rhymes and punctuation — that's usually the last things I ever look at, if I can help it. Let's see, "none," "show," "stone," "slow," "graces," "expense," "faces," "excellence," "sweet," "die," "meet," "-nity," "deeds," "weeds," "-fection meet," "summer sweet," "excellence," "expense," "faces," "graces," inheriting "graces," owning "faces," "temptation slow," "they most do show," "themselves as stone," "will do none," um. Well right offhand the rhyme scheme doesn't help, as emphasize connections, any that I can see, connections between, or doesn't forge connections between particular words and concepts, at least I don't see it at the moment,

29

uh. Let's see, I looked at the punctuation, the first comma, at the end of the first line is a comma. "Who," da-da [ten times, imitating rhythm] "They rightly" da-da [seven times]. "They are the lords and owners of their faces,   /   Others but . . . -s of their excellence." Ok. So that's really one sentence for the first two quatrains. Well that's mostly what I knew already because although the uh imagery changes radically in the third quatrain. Let's see, "Though to itself . . . die,   /   But if" uh d-d-d-d-d "basest weed," "his dignity," colon, "For sweetest things." Well the punctuation seems to s-, uh, reinforce the kinds of patterns and subdivisions of the poem that I've already deciphered, on my uh, using other means.

30

Um. "Sweetest things turn sourest by their deeds." Well, let's see what kinds of deeds are involved in the poem. Refraining from hurting, doing "the thing they most do sh-," do, not doing, refraining from "the thing they," "they most do show." "Moving others," is a deed. Let's see, "sweetest things turn sourest by their deeds," "sweetest things turn sourest by" refraining from hurting? No. By refraining from doing what "they most . . . show"? No. "For sweetest things turn sourest by" "moving others"? No. "They" richly "do in-" "sweetest things turn sourest by" inheriting? By owning "their faces"? Hum. Well none of the "deeds" in the first part of the poem really make sense to me in this little apothegm in the couplet of the poem.

31

"Lilies that fester smell far worse than" roses, "than weeds," (laugh) than roses. Well, I guess they would smell far worse than roses. "Smell far worse than weeds." "Weeds" and f-, "Lilies," weed and flower, "stewards" and "lords," uh "others" and "Unmov'd" movers. Well let's see if that parallel follows. "Lilies that fester smell far worse than weeds." Flowers with "base infection" look "far worse than weeds" because their former beauty is apparent, mixed with the, their lamentable present state. Ok well that matches.

32

Um, "lords" and "stewards." "They are the lords . . . of their faces, / Others but stewards of their excellence." Oh ok now, I said before, "stewards of their excellence," I was saying that "their" referred to "lords and owners," as if "stewards" were in the employ of the "lords and owners." But it could be that st-, "their" refers to "stewards," that is of "their" own "excellence," other people are "but stewards of their" own "excellence." Loo-, let me look up "steward" again and uh, "steward" in the New World Collegiate Dictionary. "Steward." "Steward — a person put in charge of the affairs of a large household or estate who does duties including supervision of the kitchen and the servants, management of the household, accounts, et cetera." Well management versus ownership. That's what I originally thought. Let's see, "one who acts as a supervisor or administrator, as of finances and property for, for another or others." Hum. "Person who buys the provisions, supervises the kitchen et cetera in a club or institution. A person, usually one of a group, in charge of arrangements for a ball, race, meeting et cetera. One of the staff of servants on a passenger ship, an officer on a ship." My. Well, those kinds of definitions seem to reinforce what I thought already. Let's see. Other people are not "owners" of their own "excellence" but only "stewards." They manage their own virtue, their own "excellence." But the people in the first part of the poem are "lords and owners of their faces." The appearance, this reminds me of the appearance of poor sick flower in the third quatrain. They're "owners of their faces" so they have more of an obligation to um conserve their, preserve their "excellence," "their faces," "faces" maybe in the uh sense of reputation, uh, to save face. Ok. "Lords," "stewards."

33

Now "They that," the "others" who are moved and the "Unmov'd" movers. The "Unmov'd" movers. The "others" who are moved do not have as much power and therefore are not as responsible for abusing the power they have?

Let's see, the "Unmov'd" movers who have the "pow'r to do hurt" — now all of a sudden the character that comes to mind is um, I believe his name is Antonio in uh, uh, *Measure for Measure*, a character who is placed into charge of the kingdom of, let's see, is it Bohemia or, I think it's Bohemia, by the Duke, and he has power over the characters in that play. He has the power, Antonio has the "pow'r to do hurt" and should "do none," let's see if he is, is an example of a character who, one of these flowers who meets "base infection," one of these "Lilies" that smells "worse than weeds."

34

"They that have pow'r to do hurt and will do none" — that is, what Antonio should have done, should have been. "That do not do the" things "they most do show" — that is, um a kind of Machiavellian virtue of not showing your hand. Uh, in uh, in *Measure for Measure* that m-, seems to be, Shakespeare seems to imply that that is a good uh quality of the administrator, the ruler, uh — 'cause, because the Duke certainly does not show his hand, he's, always has a, ace up his sleeve, he's got things uh going in the background, um. And also I think in other plays, I think of uh Richard the Second, uh, in some of the opening scenes where I, I believe his um restraint from showing favoritism to uh Malbury is an indication possibly of, of many things but possibly also of eh a virtue which is very good for a ruler to have, of, of publicly, publicly not showing favoritism or not always showing what you think or what you intend to do. Let's see, "They . . . That do," "They . . . That do not do the thing they most do show, / Who, moving others, are themselves as stone," that is "Unmov'd," an "unmov'd" mover like the Duke in uh *Measure for Measure*. "Unmov'd, cold" — well there is something a little bit "cold" about the Duke — "and to temptation slow" — well that's uh, that's um consistent with the Duke's character also, "to temptation slow." So I'm getting now the, the picture of a um, sort of an ideal ruler, the virtuous ruler.

35

"They," these virtuous rulers "rightly do inherit heaven's graces / And husband nature's riches from expense," "husband riches," that is — ok now I'm, I'm thinking of an uh uh of the agricultural metaphor now. I'm thinking of "expense" being a field uh, an uncultivated field with uh wasted "riches" in it so to speak, and to "husband" that w-, field of wasted "riches," you are able to um bring about "nature's riches," particular kinds of "riches" that can be used. Uh, let's see, and "husband nature's riches from expense." "Expense." Well, I'm not sure that quite works, somehow I thought it, it worked, "expense." They that "husband nature's riches." "They," that is, that is, they are, these successful ones who husband ri-, "nature's riches from expense" — oh my. "From expense." They till and cultivate and produce "riches from expense," "from" out of "expense"? "Husband . . . riches from expense." Hum. "Husband nature's riches from expense." Um (whistle) that's the tough line for me.

36

"They are the lords and owners of their face-" I think I've got this poem uh figured out as far as my own interests are concerned. These successful ones are the r-, "lords and owners of their faces," they're in complete command in other words of their semblance, what they show and what they don't show, the hands they show and the hands that they don't show their opponents, or their subjects.

Other people are "but stewards of their excellence." "Stewards of their excellence," they manage their "excellence" but they don't own it.

37

Let's see, I can make more sense to myself of that. "Are but stewards," they manage their "excellence," they're not in complete control, other, there's someone else who owns their reputation. Other people own their reputation. Let's see, other people own, how could another person own your reputation? How could you simply manage your reputation? Uh, let's see, the Duke in *Measure for Measure* is definitely an, a lord and owner of his face. Oh wow, um, well in that play I mean all of the other characters are "but stewards of their excellence" to a certain degree in that the Duke is so omnipotent in that world of Bohemia, h-, he's really the "Unmov'd" mover that in a way uh is in power, has power over their "excellence" because he can put them in situations which will cause them to make decisions about uh staying firm or giving in. Other people "but stewards of their excellence."

38

Ok. "The summer's flow'r is to the summer sweet," "The summer's flow'r is to the summer sweet," now is that mean as in the lord's face, the steward's "excellence," that is reputation, uh, outward semblance and reputation, outward reputation? The sun's flower, "summer's flow'r is to the summer sweet / Though to itself," "Though to itself" the flower "only live and die"? That's how I had been interpreting it. "Though to itself it only live and die" — that is it has no uh larger existence of its own. "But if that flow'r with base infection meet" — if you are not firm in your semblance, in your reputation, in your face, your "excellence," meet with some kind of sullying influence — "The basest weed outbraves his dignity" — "The basest" reputation looks better than the fallen dignity, than fallen virtue. "For sweetest things turn sourest by their deeds" — the s-, the most virtuous things, the most exalted things, can look in comparison even lower if they are demeaned or degraded or lost, can look even lower that is than something that is in itself not as exalted. "Lilies that fester smell far worse than weeds." Well now I've come to the opinion that this has to do with face, "excellence," a kind of public excellence which is connected with a private excellence, that is a private virtue, an inner virtue, but not uh congruent with that because hypocrisy is not necessarily a bad thing, it can be a very useful thing, powerful thing.

39

//read ll. 1–10 with "do hurt" in l. 1// Now. //read ll. 11–14 with l. 14: Lilies that fester smell, smell far worse than weeds.// Now the only two lines that still give me trouble are that sixth line and also the uh, let's see, seven eight nine, tenth line with this new interpretation I, with this new uh, yeah, interpretation I have come to, I have a little problem with that. "Though to itself it only live and die," because I'm reading "flow'r" as being uh kind of a public virtue, public reputation. "The summer's flow'r is to the summer sweet, / Though to itself it only live and die." Eh. "Though to itself it only live and die." Let's see — but if it meets with "base infection" it does more than "only live and die"? Hum. "Though to itself it only live and die." Reputation. "Only live and die." Um. I think I'll take a break at this point and finish my supper and come back if I have, come back and try to hassle the little leftover meanings.

PHILIP: SONNET 94

1

"They that have pow'r" . . . misprint, I think. "They that have pow'r to hurt and will do none." "They that have pow'r to do hurt and will do none," wouldn't scan. Either I've been misreading the line all these years ah or that's a misprint. Time out to check. Ok, uh, I checked it and it is "They that have pow'r to hurt" So I'm going to change that . . . and go on.

2

//read ll. 1 – 7// — that line rings some sort of bell, as the title of a book maybe? Ah, not sure.   //read ll. 7 – 14//

3

This is a, a sonnet that I've read often but have never really sat down with and it's a, I can remember that it struck me before as a, as a puzzling one, uh, as one with perhaps more, more problems uh, just of deciphering than a lot of the Shakespeare sonnets seem to contain. So what I'm going to try and do is just uh what I usually wind up doing with a, with Shakespeare sonnets it seems, is spend a lot of time just trying to paraphrase it, uh, and in the process sort of unravelling the, the wordplays.

4

"They that have pow'r to hurt and will do none" — no guesses yet as to who "They" are. "That do not do the thing they most do show." "They that have pow'r to hurt and will do none," uh . . . the two lines, there's, are in apposition but they don't seem right away to say the same thing. If you "have pow'r to hurt" but "will do none," you're showing some kind of restraint, but "do not do the thing they most do show," uh, suggests not restraint but a misleading if not false appearance. Uh but "do the thing" is perhaps hur- uh, "do not do the thing," "will do none," "do not," "hurt," "most do show," perhaps show that they have the "pow'r to hurt" — need to come back to that,

5

"Who, moving" — or these may be, this may be a list, the two, the two lines may be a, may not mean the same thing, it may be "They that" one, "have pow'r to hurt and will do none," two, separate characteristic, "do not do the thing they most do show," then third characteristic, uh "Who, moving others, are themselves as stone," Unmoved mover — probably not capitalized unmoved mover, if only because it's plural, "Unmoved, cold," "stone," "and to temptation slow" — reminds you of the "pow'r to hurt." Ok they have "pow'r to hurt" but don't hurt. They, their appearance is deceptive perhaps because their power is clear — I'm s-, begi-, I'm wondering if maybe these are, maybe some, maybe the nobility or certain nobles — I'm resisting the temptation to start thumbing through uh notes in my edition of the sonnets. Uh, but possibly the nobility, uh, and possibly not.

6

"Unmoved, cold, and to temptation slow." Uh, ah I'm just going to go on. "They rightly do inherit heaven's graces" — the people who show all these characteristics — "And husband nature's riches from expense" — I take it "husband" uh their own resources and do not expend them, "from expense," they don't use them up, uh, they, they keep them, say if they nurture them, they "husband" them.

7

"They are the lords and owners of their faces, / Others but stewards of their excellence." Uh, "owners of their faces" sug- . . . that's tough — seems to, seems not to jive completely with "do not do the thing they most do show," uh that is if at line two their appearance is somehow deceptive, uh, how are they "owners of their faces"? Perhaps in the sense that they've got perfect control of their faces, perfect control of the appearance they present uh, even though it may not be, it may be in some sense a false appearance or a deceptive one. "Others but stewards of their excellence." Don't know who the "Others" are. So, first time 'round, not much luck with the octave, uh.

8

Pause for structure. Uh, there are stops at the, at line, there is a stop at line four, uh, so that there are three quatrains and a closing couplet, but as so often there's, the strongest stop is after the eighth line so that in a sense there's an octave and a sestet too. "The summer's flow'r is to the summer sweet, / Though to itself it only live and die" — and the problem is obviously going to be once we figure out what the octave is talking about uh, to see what the connection is bridging that period at the end of line eight.

9

"The summer's flow'r is to the summer sweet, / Though to itself it only live and die" — uh, that is perhaps it makes, the flower makes a contribution to the total effect of summer, though in its own restricted terms uh, its own personal terms, its life may be very short.

10

Uh, "But if that flow'r with base infection meet, / The basest weed outbraves his dignity" — and that will lead into the, to line fourteen or to the, to the uh couplet as, as a whole. "For sweetest things turn sourest by their deeds; / Lilies that fester smell far worse than weeds." A great, a great man brought low descends into worse villainies than a man of lesser stature uh, something that, I guess it would be safe to say, a theme that runs through the tragedies and perhaps uh some of the histories as well, certainly, maybe not *Hamlet* but certainly uh, among title characters at least Macbeth, Othello, Lear, perhaps Richard the Third and you could probably add others to the list, and of course you could add a lot, a lot of characters from other Elizabethan literature, especially drama. Faustus might be the archetypal character of "sweetest things turn sourest by their deeds."

11

Ok so back to the beginning. Uh, somehow we've got to make a connection between the "They," the first word, uh, and these flowers, uh, with their tremendous potential, uh, for both good and ill in effect uh, for both uh beauty and corruption.

12

//read ll. 1–4// One of the problems I've always had with, with the sonnets is that the meter and the rhyme and often I think probably subtler features of the, of the word choice and the uh sound patterns of the lines themselves, uh, tend to carry you from line one to line fourteen at a pace that almost prevents you from stopping to understand the individual lines or, or clauses, sentences, whatever, themselves. There's a tendency I think with Sh-, with, maybe especially with the sonnets uh, to just let the flow of the verse carry you without understanding and just let these wonderful words of this compelling uh, form sort of pull you along uh and you get to the end of it and you think 'isn't that wonderful' but you have very little idea what it means.

13

"They that have pow'r to hurt and will do none, / That do not do the thing they most do show." Well what they "do not do" is "hurt" and what they "most do show" is perhaps that they have the "pow'r."

14

"Who, moving others" — influencing others maybe — "are themselves as stone, / Unmoved, cold, and to temptation slow" — temptation sounds like "the pow'r to hurt and will do none," sound, that sounds like a temptation refused, uh, but "moving others" — moving them to do what? Uh maybe simply influencing them in a general way by their own stature?

15

"They rightly do inherit heaven's graces" — that makes it sound like the nobility uh. "Inherit heaven's graces,"//read ll. 6–8//Perhaps the people moved uh "moving others . . . Others but stewards of their excellence," so that by "their excellence" they move others and the others, there's the, there's the metaphor, going nowhere, there's the metaphor though of "husband nature's riches from expense," uh, carried down to "stewards" as if the whole operation were seen as the operation of a manor, uh, in which the lord perhaps "Unmoved" in the manor house uh husbands the riches of the estate but actually does, as any good Marxist would point out, none of the work, uh, "Others" whom they move, whom they influence, when they command uh, serve as uh stewards and execute the, the orders, bring their uh, turn the lord's "excellence" into some sort of profitable action. Uh, lot of interruptions, I'm going to stop now uh, maybe a good thing, uh maybe a fresh view would be, tomorrow will be better.

16

Ok that first sessions was uh Wednesday evening about six and this one is Thursday morning, about 10:30. Uh, in the interim, couple of things — I realized that I, I didn't spend a lot of time thinking about the sonnet but I did realize this morning that I was doing a couple of things that were unnatural in a sense in this process. One just in method uh, that working from the typed text in front of me, that really if I knew that what I was using was a sonnet uh, that the poem was a, was a Shakespeare sonnet, uh which I think I'd know even without the, the title 'cause, I, while it's not one I've read a lot it's one that I've known for a long time, uh. I realized that I would very early in the process check uh, with an edition of the sonnets not so much for interpretation but for uh just glosses on

lines, so that the next time I go through it I've got my handy Pelican Shake-
speare here which does nothing but gloss the lines uh, and I will, I'll use that for
the next reading. The other unnatural thing I realized that I was doing was, and
I guess it was, I guess that the original thing that got me off on this tack, which
I'm now pretty sure is a wrong tack uh, was the, the "They" of the first line and
the repeated plurals throughout the poem, got me thinking that this was a poem
abou-, to an indeterminate audience about some general class of people, possibly
social class uh, possibly not but anyway a, definitely a, a group of people and
that the poem was addressed to no particular audience, i-, what it, what it had to
say about this group was being said to uh, to no one that you could really put
your finger on. I realized that that, if that were true it would be extremely
unusual for uh Shakespeare sonnets or I guess any Elizabethan sonnet, that the
poem must be, or is probably much more personal than that, uh, written to, or at
least ostensibly to a particular person, and probably with a relatively personal
message. So that I think what I ought to do now is just start over again at the
beginning — I don't remember much of what I said last night anyway and that's
probably good uh, 'cause even while I was saying it, it seemed pretty, I seemed
to be floundering a lot, uh, just start over again from the beginning and start
looking for the sorts of things that it would be reasonable to expect in a sonnet.
The one thing that I haven't done uh, and I may do a little later, is figure out
where, get my bearings in, in the sonnets for sonnet ninety-four. Uh, I can't
remember offhand how may of the sonnets are explicitly addressed to, uh, the
anonymous, or probably anonymous, young man, uh, and how many are ad-
dressed to the Dark Lady. My recollection is that the Dark Lady sonnets are th-,
at the end and there aren't many of them, uh and I know that, or I think I know
that one-ten is the "Two loves I have, of comfort and despair" uh so that
ninety-four may still be addressed to the young man or, or it may not be, and I'm
not quite sure, I may check it later but at the moment I'm going to go through,
go through it one more time without that.

17

Ok. "They that have pow'r to hurt and will do none" — oh that's right, I'm going
to, supposed to look at the glosses. "They that have pow'r to hurt and will do
none" — glossed — " 'and will do none' i.e. without actively trying to hurt."
"They that have pow'r to hurt," without, "and will do none." In other words
and, oh I see, "They that have," have the "pow'r to hurt" and the will to do
none hurt — what's that line, 'I do none,' something 'I do none harm.' Uh, ok
that really doesn't change the meaning much from what I think a normal modern
reader would see there.

18

"They that have pow'r to hurt and will do none, / That do not do the thing
they most do show" — " 'show,' i.e. seem to do or seem capable of doing." No
news there.

19

//read ll. 3 – 5// — " 'rightly,' as a right, veritably" — surprise, uh,

20

"And husband nature's riches from expense; / They are the lords and owners
of their faces" — " 'owners of their faces,' permanent possessors of the qualities
that show in them."

21

"Others but stewards of their excellence" — " 'stewards,' dispensers" — may want to come back to that. I would have thought, and I think I, the last time through I was thinking along these lines too, "stewards" less as uh, well 'dispensers' — I remember saying something about executing the lord's orders, following out the imagery of that uh, of the second quatrain, uh, maybe that uh "Others but stewards of their excellence," maybe uh, might turn out, the steward might turn out to be a figure for the poet, possibility.

22

//read ll. 9– 12//   Twel-, line twelve, " 'outbraves his' equals outglories its"

23

"For sweetest things turn sourest by their deeds; /   Lilies that fester smell far worse than weeds," "Lilies that fester" s-, fel-, (whistle) "Lilies that fester smell far worse than weeds." "This line also appears in the anonymous play *Edward the Third*, 1596, two, one, four-fifty-one, in one of the scenes frequently attributed to Shakespeare." Never read *Edward the Third* . . . ok, really, really not much help there, which is fairly common.

24

I'm going to check and see what — well no, I won't go that far. I was going to say I'm going to, going to check and see where they, uh, where they said the poems to uh the young man uh end, but I won't, let me just look at a couple of the nearby ones and see what they suggest. Sonnet ninety — //read ll. 1– 4 of sonnet 90 with 1. 4: And do not drop me in, And do not drop in for an after loss// — glad I don't have to do this one. "Ah, do not, when my heart hath scap'd this sorrow, /   Come in the rearward of a conquer'd woe" — well it's certainly personal, anway.

25

Ninety-one.   //read ll. 1– 4 of sonnet 91//   — I don't think I've ever read this one —   //read ll. 5– 8 of sonnet 91//   — "Thy love" — a-ha — //read ll. 9– 14 of sonnet 91//Also personal, though as usual, it's almost impossible to tell whether this is a poem to the young man or a poem to a woman except that all the uh, all the "birth," "skill," "wealth," "body's force," "garments," "hawks and hounds," and "horse" all suggest the nobility which really suggests the young man. So we'll say that ninety-one is the young man.

26

Ninety-three.   //read ll. 1– 10 of sonnet 93//   — this is, this interesting, uh, deceptive appearance, "owners of" they, uh, "owners of their faces." //read ll. 10– 14 of sonnet 93//Somewhere in the back of my mind there's something in, my uh career with the sonnets has been so broken up I don't know that I've ever read through the whole cycle or collection, uh, more than once, and even then I have a feeling there are sonnets that I never read, uh. Ninety-one just did not sound familiar at all. Uh, flipping ahead there are more than I realized, there are a hundred and fifty-four, I thought there were a hundred and thirty something. If there are a hundred and fifty-four then ninety-four probably still is solidly in the young man's territory, and somewhere in the back of my mind there's a sort of half-memory of an introduction or maybe a lecture that I, that I heard talking about uh, a possible, a suggestion that the young man falls in love and steals the affections of.

SIDE 2

Uh, the last words were, 'a young woman that Shakespeare was also interested in,' in case they didn't get recorded. Uh, and I don't remember much of the particulars but that seems to be suggested by ninety-three here, "like a deceived husband," uh, "So shall I live, supposing thou art true, / Like a deceived husband." Course this could be to the woman. I think I've, I think I've opened a can of worms here, uh, and I think what I'll do is try and close it by going back to ninety-four and if it doesn't close then I'm going to turn off the tape, read the Pelican introduction, uh, and then report back what I found and whether or not it seems applicable to ninety-four, uh. I saw 'Sonnet ninety-four, Shakespeare' at the top of the page, I thought, a-ha, this is going to be a breeze, I've read so many sonnets, this one can't be tough.

27

Anyway, sonnet ninety-four, Shakespeare. "They that have pow'r to hurt and will do none" — whichever way you take the uh syntax, suggestion for the new perspective is that "They" is still a class of people but a class in which he is perhaps, a class of people with a very specific application to the person, whoever it is, uh, that, that the poet is addressing. So, and "pow'r to hurt" uh, especially with uh ninety-three there, suggestion of uh, to hurt in love or in personal relationships of some t-, of some sort, uh, because still it's, I'm still trying to leave it open uh whether this is the friendship for the young nobleman or the uh romantic relationship.

28

"They that have pow'r to hurt and will do none, / That do not do the thing they most do show" — that line is still a problem, uh. "Do not do the thing they most do show, / Who, moving others, are themselves as stone, / Unmoved, cold"? — underline "cold" — "and to temptation slow." [clicking with tongue] That's interesting, uh, ok. "They that have pow'r to hurt" — uh, I wonder if "hurt" is really there uh . . . not so much, oh, ok, it's maybe it is not uh, "They that have pow'r to hurt" someone in a personal relationship, that is uh, play with their affections, deceive them, betray them, whatever, uh, so much as "hurt" with some sort of suggestion of uh the old courtly poetic convention of love itself as a wound, uh. "They that have pow'r to hurt and will do none," uh, they that arouse love without intending to, "do not do the" — and this would solve the second line — "do not do the thing they most do show," uh, that is they don't fall in love even though they look as if that's what they're made for, uh. "Who" — and therefore, and — "Who, moving others," to love, "are themselves as stone, / Unmoved, cold," — unpassionate or un-, uninvolved — "and to temptation slow." The temptation then isn't the temptation to hurt from the first line but the tem-, but temptation as sexual temptation perhaps, uh.

29

Ok, "Unmoved, cold, and to temptation slow; / They rightly do inherit heaven's graces" — ok so if the poet approves of them, which seems clear enough, uh, it's funny because then he's got to approve of "stone, / Unmoved, cold," uh as well as "to temptation slow," which seems sort of, the picture you get of this, of this type in the uh, in the first quatrain is a mixed one so that "They rightly do inherit heaven's graces," that firm judgment uh comes as maybe something of a surprise. "They rightly do inherit heaven's graces" —

30

and now we get the uh, the manorial metaphor, uh, but really as a metaphor for, for a very personal sort of thing, I mean it's not a — forget that, uh. "They rightly do inherit heaven's graces / And husband nature's riches from expense," uh perhaps their beauty, perhaps their capacity for love, affection, whatever. "They are the lords and owners of their faces," uh, not only uh are their faces accurate reflections of themselves uh, so much as they are in control uh, what was the gloss on this? " 'Owners of their faces,' permanent possessors of the qualities that show in them." eh. Uh. . . . That's ok for "owners of their faces" but it sort of leaves out "lords," uh, they've got to be "lords . . . of their faces" too which suggests not only possession but control, uh, complete mastery. Uh, "They are the lords and owners of their faces, / Others but stewards of their excellence," and the gloss said " 'stewards,' dispensers." That could be, that could be a, a suggestion of the poet's role uh, specially if this is the young man about whom he's been writing over ninety-four sonnets now, uh, he has certainly dispensed a lot of the young man's "excellence" in the course of, of that work, uh. But also of course he's — he also, I've, I always think of stewards as less 'dispenser' as caretaker, uh, and in that, in that sense it's true too, and of course it's the point that he constantly reiterates, the uh, beauty is preserved by the poet in verse, uh (cough) so "Others but stewards of their excellence," the "Others" suggest in part at least the poet, and of course the "Others" of line eight have presumably got to be the same "Others" as the "others" of line three, who were moved by these people though the people themselves are "Unmoved."

31

(cough) Ok, so the octave then suggests, suggests real approval for, uh, for people like this, uh, with the suggestion that, not explicitly in the poem but the suggestion in context that, that this i-, well I think for the whole poem uh that all these "Theys" and "thems" are really being held up as an example to a particular person uh, who belongs in some sense or may belong or may want to avoid belonging, uh, in the class, in this class. So the octave is on the whole positive, uh. In the first quatrain there are these people who are moved, possibly some suggestion of people who are hurt, uh, but it's not by the will of the "They," uh, and the "They" themselves are "Unmoved, cold," which sounds negative, but "to temptation slow" which sounds positive, and then the second quatrain they're entirely in control of themselves on the model of a lord's control of a manor, uh, they "inherit heaven's graces," as the nobility does, they "husband nature's riches," uh, they are "lords and owners," and uh "Others" are "stewards," preserving or dispensing, depending on which way you, which implication you like for "stewards," uh, the resources of the estate, in this case the, standing for the personal resources uh of people of this sort. Period, end of octave.

32

"The summer's flow'r is to the summer sweet, / Though to itself it only live and die." It's an interesting switch there, uh, having talked consistently about

"They" and 'them' un through the first eight lines and in the s-, in lines five to eight having given you a, a metaphor that sort of conjures up the idea of vast, vast lands held by the lord and governed by "stewards" uh, "nature's riches," they "do inherit heaven's graces" and uh, then line nine immediately brings you down to a single "flow'r" which might, if this isn't too fanciful, in effect it's sort of closing in the focus, the single flower could be a single flower in one of these fields, uh — that is perhaps too fanciful, but I think there is a sense that uh the scope of the poem changes if only because "The summer's flow'r" is singular and everything else about, that the poet has been talking about, has been "They," "themselves," uh "They rightly do inherit," "They are," i-, "the lord an-," "lords and owners," "of their excellence," and then down to the single "summer's flow'r is to the summer sweet,   /   Though to itself it only live and die," uh, as I said before contributes to the total effect and a long-lasting effect though its lifespan is brief uh and in itself it's perhaps — this goes a little beyond the line but perhaps unaware of its contribution to a greater whole uh. It's a little hard to see how that, those two lines uh really fit into the poem — I'm, may have to come back to that — because uh . . . mm, he's got to establish "The summer's flow'r" because what he's going to go on to do with the whole sestet is, having played up these people who are "lords and owners of their faces" he's now going to, in the sestet, show the dangers uh inherent in this sort of stature, uh and he's going, he's got to introduce the flower because it's the, it's the metaphor for people of this sort throughout the sestet.

33

Uh but his real point comes in lines eleven through fourteen — "But if that flow'r with base infection meet" — all he really has to do to s-, establish that line or to establish that idea is to uh, get a flower in there so he can say "if that flow'r with base infection meet,   /   The basest weed outbraves his dignity" — uh, obvious enough if, if the flower becomes corrupted in some sense uh, then it's, it's worse than, uh, this valueless plant next to it. Uh, "if that flow'r with base infection meet,   /   The basest weed outbraves his dignity: /   For sweetest things turn sourest by their deeds" — the moral, uh, as often in Shakespeare sonnets, the moral in the couplet — "For sweetest things turn sourest by their deeds;   /   Lilies that fester smell far worse than weeds." I don't have a copy of *Edward the Third*, I wonder, I'll bet though that that line is uh, uh closes a rhymed couplet in *Edward the Third* too, uh, either at the end of a big speech or the end possibly of a scene or an act uh. . . . You can imagine the sort of great dramatic pause after a line like that in fact, uh, it seems almost, and this may simply be influence from knowing now that it also appears in a play, but I think I really did feel this the first time I read it though I didn't know quite what I, uh, couldn't have put it into words — it seems almost too much of a final punctuation for a poem as short as a sonnet, uh, almost as if it's out of proportion somehow, that's really, I wouldn't want to go to court on that, uh.

34

Ok, back to where all this started uh, lines nine and ten uh, the "flow'r," "The summer's flow'r is to the summer sweet,   /   Though to itself it only live and die" — I'm still not sure, that seems like almost a gratuitous sentiment tossed in there uh, to establish the flower and fill lines nine and ten, uh, because the, the short life of the flower really doesn't seem relevant to what the poet is, is doing with it, uh. . . .

35

But we've got at least the, the basic outline now uh. Here are these people, uh, and ideally they work like this, the octave, uh, they may have the "pow'r to hurt" but they don't intend to hurt, uh, they don't have the will to hurt. They do not, though they appear maybe made for love or they appear, uh, made to engage some sort of passionate admiration, uh, they don't let themselves solicit that sort of thing or get involved in it in an unfavorable way

36

— it's pretty vague, at least it seems to be that it's pretty vague what uh, really what he's getting at, there's a, there would be a lot of room uh — a critic who wanted for instance to argue for Shakespeare's homosexuality, uh, if this sonnet is in fact addressed to the young man, there's enough vagueness in those opening lines so you could certainly read them that way. Uh — "do not do the thing they most do show," uh, could be interpreted very specifically as someone made to encourage homosexual affection but does not himself indulge in anything of the sort — uh, but obviously the line is much too vague to be able to pin down to that. "Who, moving others, are themselves as stone, / Unmoved, cold, and to temptation slow" — they arouse feelings of whatever uh, again you know it could be anything from — and of course this can s-, this could still I think be about a woman though "sweetest things turn sourest by their deeds; / Lilies that fester smell far worse than weeds." That sentiment seems to be one that Shak-, that elsewhere at least Shakespeare applies mainly to men, uh, as I said before, Othello, Lear, Richard the Third, Macbeth et al. uh. But there's no reason I don't think why it couldn't be, it couldn't be applied to a woman, and in a sense I suppose the flower would argue, the flower image would argue, he might be talking about a woman.

37

Uh, ok, they move others but they're unmoved themselves, "cold, and to temptation slow," and lest you think that this is undesirable, uh, we go right on to "They rightly do inherit heaven's graces" — they preserve their resources, they don't, again in paraphrasing you want to keep trying to substitute something more specific for the, for Shakespeare's metaphor and it's very hard to know what to substitute. "Husband nature's riches from expense" could be anything from an explicitly sexual metaphor uh, they're chaste, to — gosh that could be couldn't it? "They that have pow'r to" . . . "do not do the thing they most do show, / Who, moving others, are themselves as stone, / Unmoved, cold, and to temptation s-," tem-, again "temptation slow." It would be possible if you had nothing but this, of all the sonnets if this one existed alone in isolation you could get a whole school growing up uh, thinking that Shakespeare is talking about uh, some tremendously attractive priest uh (laugh) or monk or something uh, and it's possible that he really does mean that line six to be sexual but of course it could also be, uh, the resources of personality, of personal strength or courage or almost anything uh, gene-, a general sort of noble character.

38

"Husband nature's riches from expense; / They are the lords and owners of their faces" — and that of course suggests something more general and more uh abstract. Uh, they're in perfect control, they're in complete possession of their faculties, uh, and others are simply their, the people who, who execute their orders or who in some sense or other work for them,

39

So that the octave as a whole is, there are these, there are these people, uh who arouse admiration in others uh, but who are themselves in, well arouse admiration and possibly uh love, all sorts of things including things that might be hurtful, uh but they are themselves in complete control and remain untempted I guess to exploit the sort of power that they have, uh.

40

Then to the sestet, with an implied 'but' as usual, uh, but if these people go wrong they go very wrong uh, that is they've got so much power, or they have the potential of exercising so much power over others that if they choose to exercise it, they can turn into uh monsters and I guess — again like a lo-, like a lot of the sonnets you have the feeling of a story behind it that you can never uncover, uh, that what the poet is saying and what perhaps the person addressed, if there, if there was in fact a single person, uh, what the poet understands, or what the poet intends and what the person addressed understands is something very concrete, uh, but to, to everyone else it's, it remains uh, simply elusive and mysterious and more in the realm of suggestion than any sort of real narration. Uh, but in any case the sestet is obviously saying that these people described favorably in the octave or maybe better still a, you've got a class of people described favorably in the octave and then you bring it down to a single individual, it's possible for some one member of this class, "The summer's flow'r," uh, and the singular "that flow'r with base infection meet," uh — that the people with this potential or one member of the class of people with this potential, uh, can go very wrong if they.

SIDE 3

. . . saying. Oh that mess about the whole class versus the individual member, uh. Take it from the top uh. So the sestet is saying that an individual member of this class of people that have this tremendous, these tremendous resources and this tremendous potential uh can go very wrong if they fall into whatever the temptation of the fourth line is really supposed to be, uh, and can rapidly go from being figures of tremendous dignity to figures of no dignity whatsoever. And then the, and then regeneralized uh, the couplet takes the specific instance of the third quatrain, and regeneralizes a moral from it, "sweetest things," the "sweetest things" of the octave, "turn sourest by their deeds" — the deeds of the quatrain, the third quatrain, whatever thes-, those deeds are — "Lilies that fester smell far worse than weeds."

41

I think the real problem with this poem is that in isolation at least, uh, and I'm not sure that, it may be that you can never work it out, but certainly in isolation, you simply don't have enough evidence to know what the poet is talking about, uh. You can work out, and I think I have pretty well, uh worked out what he's saying about it, about this situation, but without knowing what the situation is, what occasion gives rise to the poem, and it's obviously an occasional poem, uh, it's almost impossible to pin down its meaning uh so that even now I wouldn't want to make a large bet on whether this was written to a man or a woman, though if I had to I'd bet on the man uh, but like so many of uh the poems that are definitely written to the young man, uh, they make almost as much sense if you imagine them addressed to a woman.

42

So what I'm going to do now is flip to, and I think this is really the — well there are two things I could do now. I could, I could go through and read all hundred and fifty-four sonnets as a way of putting ninety-four into context and try and develop my own theory of the sort of shadowy narrative behind the whole cycle, uh, or maybe narratives, uh, or I can just flip to the introduction here and hope that they'll give me some clue about where in the cycle ninety-four really comes. Um, well the introduction may not do this. This is incidentally, for the record, the introduction to uh the Pelican Shakespeare edition of the sonnets, uh, by Douglas Bush. Ok. "In contrast," uh, "dramatic 'plot' . . . has seemed to many" char-, "critics to carry special marks of actuality," "Mr. W. H.," "leading candidates," . . . "one fact is that we know nothing," . . . Browning's famous statement, uh, "Italian sonnet," "English" sonnet, this and that, "argument normally proceeds by quatrains" — I'm not sure we're going to get anything here (laugh) — "son-" — looking at the n-, at the numbers of the sonnets, uh, cited, so far nothing on ninety-four, oh one-forty-four is the "Two loves I have, of comfort and despair," one-ten must be uh "My mistress' eyes are nothing like the sun" then. No, that's one-thirty — I don't know what one-ten is, maybe it isn't anything, oh, no, "Alas, 'tis true I have gone here and there / And made my" — oh, "And made myself a motley to the view" — I don't know why I got that number in there, it wasn't what I meant. "The expense of spirit in a waste of shame" — there's, now there's a use of "expense," just popped off the line at me, in sonnet, a reference to sonnet one-twenty-nine in the introduction here.

43

"The expense of spirit in a waste of shame" is love in action. Uh, there is a suggestion of that, I've got to admit, in "husband nature's riches from expense." And that, if you really wanted to build a narrative on that basis, would argue, uh, could be taken to argue for Shakespeare perhaps addressing the young man and saying uh 'don't get involved with this woman'? Women in general? It's hard to say, uh, and I don't think this introduction which doesn't go in much for talking about the plot, uh, is going to help me — I'm going to check, I'm going to turn the tape off and check a couple of other things. If I can't find anything else I'm just going to stop here.

Ok final note from uh the old edition by Hardin Craig, his complete Shakespeare uh he has a nice section on "The Story of the Sonnets" uh, number so-and-so and so-and-so tell about such and such, uh, and what he says about ninety-four to ninety-six I think makes a good note to close on. "Numbers ninety-four to ninety-six dwell obscurely on some fault committed by the friend" period — I think that's probably, probably should stand as the last word on the subject. I think that it's probably not possible uh, from the evidence of the poem and if Hardin Craig is right, uh, I realize that people have had a lot of years since then to come up with other, other readings, but if Hardin Craig is right in a sort of generali-, general scheme for the sonnets uh, there's the uh, I've, something I've forgotten about, the sonnets shortly before this dealing with the, the possible rival poet, uh, and then these are really apparently isolated, uh, and there's very little, at least Craig seems to think that there's no real context for them, uh. Certainly I think ninety-four alone, which after all is what the experiment provides, ninety-four alone uh, can be paraphrased but it can't really be interpreted, uh, that is it's del-, uh, it's deliberately esoteric, concealing essential information you need to uh, to be able to understand it in concrete terms, uh, so that about all you can come up with finally is it's a warning that there is a class of people who are exemplary uh and, in the normal course of events, paragons of virtue but who if corrupted can become, can fall to the opposite end of the spectrum, uh — I don't think you can fall to the end of the spectrum, uh, go to the other extreme, uh, or fall from the highest point to the lowest point, uh, and with its moral close, I think you can say that the poem is really a warning to someone to avoid doing something, uh, and that, it's really not possible to be more specific than that on the evidence that the text itself gives you.

ANN: SONNET 94

1

Ok I'm going to start now. It's Friday morning quite early and I've devoted a stretch of time to see if I can do this all at once. (sigh) First I should read the poem.

2

//read poem with 1. 4: Unmoved, cold, and do tem-, and to temptation slow; and 1.5: Their rightly do inherit n-, heaven's graces; and 1.6: And husbands nature's riches from expense.//   First of all I should say that I'm not using the copy on the paper that we got because I had lost it. I'm using the uh Norton Anthology uh of English Literature, Volume One, and the first line is different in this, um. I think on the paper it's "They that have power to do hurt and will do none," so uh I assume that the paper has a misprint.

3

//read poem//   Ok it's a sonnet, that much is obvious. Uh the syntactic division is uh into um an octave, or an eight-line unit, and a, a, a sestet, and um beyond that, major uh units of punctuation occur at the end of line four, um, line six, ok the period at line eight, uh, nine ten eleven, and then uh line twelve and thirteen. Hum, ok, the rhyme scheme, might as well get into this stuff — A-B-A-B-C-D-C-D-E-F-E — "die" and "dignity," I guess — F uh G-G. Ok and that would go along with the syntactic boundary um, so that the thing would be divided up according to the rhyme scheme into an octave, um I can never figure out whether octave or oct-, octet is the correct word to use there, and a sestet uh the last two lines of which form a kind of couplet um,

4

it's a strange poem. It seems inaccessible, it seems to have a very personalized kind of meaning that uh, I mean it's the kind of poem one would show to someone having written it in a fit of pique. It seems very personal. It really is hard to figure out. Has some great lines. //read ll. 7– 10// And I love that "Lilies that fester smell far worse than weeds." But on the whole the thing doesn't seem to hang together particularly well.

5

Um, how to go at it. //read ll. 1 – 8 with 1. 6: And husbands nature's riches from expense.// All right um, those people who have power to hurt others, uh, and this is unclear and it's either — umm, I guess "They th-" um, they that have power to uh to hurt others but disdain to do so presumably, that do not act uh in the way they would seem to act um, who move others, to passion or to rage, to hurt, whatever, but themselves uh remain impassive, remain distanced um, "cold," uh and refuse to become tempted to do anything, refuse to be tempted, uh,

6

"They rightly do inherit heaven's graces." Ok um, "And husband nature's riches from expense." Ok I guess they "inherit heaven's graces." This is unclear whether it means a certain uh, something to do with appearance, fortune, uh uh disposition um, personal qualities, I have no idea. But presumably um they inherit these things because they don't squander nature's ri-, "nature's riches," um they don't spend themselves on anyone else or for anything else. Uh, they're cons-, they uh, they work on conserving kind of uh, of what they have, because of that they merit more.

7

Ok "They are the lords and owners of their faces," um, "Others but stewards of their excellence." They control themselves, they uh, I guess in that sense they own their faces. "Others but stewards of their excellence." Ok other people are put in the position presumably of uh responding to them all the time? Uh, of trying to generate some response from them, in short by paying attention, by being compelled to pay attention or, or to react to these people in whatever way, um, they are stewards of the people's excellence, um — it's very hard to figure out the tone of that line, well as it is to figure out the tone of the whole thing.

8

Ok, after this uh series of statements, uh this series of reflections on um a type in human nature or a person or whatever, um we get into kind of an illustration. //read ll. 9 – 14 with 1. 11: But if that flow'r with infection meet.// Ok, "The summer's flow'r is to the summer sweet," um. "The summer's flow'r" is beautiful, it's an emblem of something, it's attractive uh it means, to those who observe it or to those who observe the seasons, that something happens, it presages uh the coming of another season or the arrival of a season or whatever, um, "But to itself," um, it lives and then it's gone. That's it. Has a short life.

9

"But if that flow'r with base infection meet." Ok presumably if it rots, whatever, gets some kind of blight or whatever it is that flowers get, "The basest weed outbraves his dignity." All right in adverse situations the flower is anything but sturdy, um, is anything but able to preserve and protect itself, and certainly is anything but able to conceal the particular kind of uh disease or misfortune that has befallen it. Um, if you mutilate a, if you mutilate a tulip or if you mutilate a jonquil or whatever, it's very clear that some, that it has been mutilated, um, there's no way to disguise that, where I suppose a weed just grows back in about a day.

10

"For sweetest things turn sourest by their deeds / Lilies that fester smell far
worse than weeds." Ok the "Lilies that fester smell far worse than weeds," those
uh, well with the um, it's a perfect, someone's out in the hall, I'm listening to
them. I don't know, lot of crazy people here. Um, ok, this last line, "Lilies that
fester smell far worse than weeds," goes uh, i-, and it's, it's a perfect aphoristic,
very concise illustration of what's um being talked about in the first four lines of
the sestet, uh. I guess that's all there is to say about it, um. The next to last line,
though, "For sweetest things turn sourest by their deeds," all right, that links
the octave to the sestet, in an odd kind of way. It's clear that something very
different is being talked about, um. I mean on the one hand . . . in the sestet
you're talking about flowers and uh, since they are so beautiful, when they meet
with some kind of misfortune, um "base infection," uh, it's very obvious the
thing is ruined for good, the particular qualities that make it attractive or that
make it um worth paying attention to uh are, are destroyed, are no longer part of
it. But this "For sweetest things turn sourest by their deeds." Ok, a "base infec-
tion" is certainly not a deed, not necessarily unless flowers get gonorrhea, some-
thing that is bro-, uh they bring on themselves. However um, this does link the
sestet with the first part of the poem. Hum, "Lilies that fester smell far worse
than weeds," the implication being that uh something that one brings on oneself
to do with base behavior uh is going to cause uh that person to um to "fester," to
lose whatever predominant uh i-, you know charms or attractiveness he or she
has.

11

I think I can remember, . . .as I said before uh, I either did this poem for the,
the Stylistics seminar or looked at it some other time and I would tend to think
that I looked at it um for the Stylistics seminar though I probably never partici-
pated in any discussion. And I can remember reading a paraphrase of it um,
some kind of contextual information I guess, and a paraphrase either in this, the
edition of Shakespeare sonnets that we used for that class or in something else
that um I looked at to prepare for whatever it was that we were supposed to do
with the poem, and uh the context was that, and this was, it came, I guess, from
someone who was reading the whole series of sonnets as uh commentary, I'm
not, a running commentary I guess on uh, on Shakespeare's kind of complicated
love life. Apparently um what this person said, claimed had just happened, was
that um, Shakespeare was re-, reacting to the falseness and deception of uh the
young male um in whom he was interested or for whom he had feelings because
the male was making it with Shakespeare's uh mistress, which seems like a very
odd thing, and this was a um kind of sustained, the sonnet was a kind of sus-
tained expression of, of pique at this person um. I don't know enough about the
sonnets to know whether that makes any sense at all, and I simply don't know
enough about uh Shakespeare's uh proclivities or love life or anything else to
know whether um it makes an-, that makes any sense at all. Um, and the para-
phrase as I remember wasn't very good. It uh basically consisted of, of unravel-
ling certain syntatical um cruses, cruxes, whatever, in the sonnet, and it didn't
really uh help me then, which I suppose is why I didn't remember it very well.

12

The thing that interests me most about it is um the tone, the audience. I mean
it's unclear I think to the reader now who exactly is being addressed, um, what

exactly was done. Yet the psychologi-, well, the tone of the thing really is intriguing um. I had a discussion recently with a, a very disturbed person who was very upset about something, and the tone of the discussion or of the things that the person said to me were very much like this uh, the sonnet, very bitter, kind of ironic, um expressing intense frustration with the way things were, yet at the same time um hoping that something terrible would happen to the person that had upset her and at the same time trying to um indicate that this of course, this terrible thing, would happen to the person who had upset her. This thing works the same way. //read poem dramatically with 1. 6: And husbands nature, husband nature's riches from expense.//

13

Ok I guess the thrust of the octet is that uh, those who don't, "They," and presumably this "They," I mean that's a, that's an interesting part of it, this particular, the sonnet seems to have a very clear focus and seems to be directed sort of toward some particular act, some particular incident of behavior that uh has uh upset the author very, very much and has uh particularly colored his regard to a certain person. Yet I, I love this "They that have power" (laugh) it's a wonderful. Um. "They that have power to hurt and will do none," Ok the thrust of the whole octet seems to be that, octave, seems to be that uh, a railing against people who um don't deign to respond to others who either care for them or care about them, even to the extent of hurting those people. They can't be tempted to do anything, they can't be inveigled to react or respond at all. They're "Unmoved," they're "cold," yet at the same time they move others. The potential for them to hurt others is always there even if that's not realized, even if they don't deign, or they don't condescend, to participate in hurting the person that they've so disappointed. Um. They're "stone," they're "cold," they're "Unmoved."

14

Ok "They rightly do inherit heaven's graces / And husband nature's riches from expense." That "rightly" is kind of confusing, although I think that uh the tone of this is, it is, it, it's still railing against these people um. They don't squander nature's gifts but presumably they should, or at least allow others, those who care about them, or care for them, to uh, or who react strongly to them, to participate in nature's gifts. And because they don't squander the stuff, they "husband" it, they get more, ok,

15

"They are the lords and owners of their faces, / Others but stewards of their excellence." I talked about those two lines before but again it seems that by refusing to react to other people um they maintain complete control over themselves, over their own emotions and over what they think, and uh the reaction that other people, the action, th-, what other people do to them, and what other people do in relation to them, pretty much is generated uh by the other people, uh, there's not going to be a response of any kind. Um, and in that sense the other people become "stewards of their excellence," cultivate them through all the attention paid.

16

And really (laugh) ok that's a funny uh eight lines. The people, I mean the, in a way it's very odd, the persons who refuse to hurt, umm "will do none, / That

do not do the" things "they most do show," these people are deceitful, in others
words they seem as though they will do a certain thing, either respond to passion
or uh commit themselves, whatever it is that they seem as though they're about
to do, they won't do it um, so that they've just uh, they're also
"stone, / Unmoved, cold," slow to temptation. Ok the stone, unmoved, cold
um, as stone I guess, unmoved, cold are important, um, the people are frozen,
and in a way sort of uh uh dead. The person being described here, the person
being talked about or addressed directly by the writer is sort of put in uh, you
know becomes an artifact rather than a human being.

17

Ok, "and to temptation slow," //read ll. 5–8 with l. 7: They are the lords and
owners of their grace, faces.// Ok this business of inheriting "heaven's graces,"
husbanding the "riches from expense," being "lords and owners," "Others but
stewards," um. That language is very interesting because um it sets up some
kind of a social tension, or at least the social tension is a metaphor for something
else for uh, and that is that these people um who are like this are likened to uh,
I don't know um how even society worked particularly in that time but um,
become aristocratic, become property owners, become those in control. They
"inherit heaven's graces." They husband their "riches from expense." Ok so
they're frugal about these riches that they have inherited um, they not only don't
squander them but presumably they don't give them out to people uh uh where
they sh-, when they should um, or when the gifts are deserved. "They are the
lords and owners of their faces." Um again they're "lords," they're "owners,"
they're uh, and all that that implies, um, haughty, uh in a position to dispense
crumbs or not dispense crumbs or not dispense anything, um. More crazies in
the hall, um. Ok they're in a position to uh, to be haughty, and to dispense, you
know deign uh, to dispense disdainfully or not to dispense at all, um "Others
but stewards," ok, others but caretakers, protectors, cultivators, guardians of uh,
of the excellence of these people, at their beck and call. That's really, huh,
that's interesting — the construct here, the position that the people who have
power, "They," the, the "They," um, is put in.

18

All right, and after that finishes off //read ll. 9–12// Maybe this is where the
confusion begins to come in because um these four lines are talking about some-
thing else, you know the focus is uh, the focus is shift, is shifted, uh. Certainly
it's implied, I guess or certainly these four lines are supposed to imply that
something uh could or may happen to the, the "They," "They that have pow'r
to hurt and will do none," um, and certainly when they meet with some kind of
adversity, meet with a situation that they can't control whatever that is um, I
guess the extension from this uh [rhythmic t-t-t] from lines nine through twelve
is that they'll um come out of it uh far more poorly than other people would, and
that certainly whatever it is about them that's so compelling uh will be destroyed
forever, be quite obvious that something bad has happened. All right um. All
right.

19

"Things," "sweetest things turn sourest by their deeds," all right but, that's very
different um. Presumably the flower isn't, as I said, bringing any kind of "base
infection" on itself or bringing any kind of misfortune on itself, um. "For

sweetest things turn sourest by their deeds." Again that can't, that doesn't deal with the flowers at all, that jumps right back to that uh first eight lines, and that implies that um through this deception, through this coldness, through this refusing to react to other people um, these people will uh, oh I don't know what it is, turn sour, have something happen, um lose the qualities that make them so compelling to others um, or lose whatever it is that makes others attracted, but that they'll lose this as a result of the way they act. "Lilies that fester smell far worse than weeds." Ok and that presumably s-, sums up the whole of the poem. It certainly illustrates graphically what will happen to the flowers, and it also uh is supposed to illustrate what will happen to these people. It's real clear though, "by their deeds." The point in the first eight lines though is that the people don't do anything, the "They" doesn't do anything, has "power to hurt and *will do none*," "That *do not do* the thing they most do show," and the, "they most," it seems to um they "are themselves as stone," "to temptation slow," they "inherit," that's a passive thing, someone gives you a bunch of clap and that's it, um. They "husband," all right "husband," again presumably main-, maintain, uh involves not doing anything. They "husband" uh "nature's" uh "riches" by not um exerting themselves I guess in any way shape or form towards other people. Does that mean when they finally do something, they turn sour? And this is very i-, this is really very confusing. The line definitely doesn't say that's, anything is going to happen to these people as a result of the way they are. "Lilies that fester smell far worse than weeds."

20

I mean instead of any kind of reasoned meditation or reasoned series of accusations, the whole thing comes out as much more uh, as an instance of, as pique, the kind of thing that one would uh, would write to a lover who had really pissed one off, or the kind of thing that uh, that someone would come out with in the heat of an argument, or in the heat of uh some kind of intense emotional reaction, to someone who isn't responding. And beyond that it just doesn't seem very accessible.

21

The "They" first of all I guess doesn't really describe the type, all that is a reaction to one particular person, and presumably either to one incident um, some kind of uh sexual disappointment, or else to a series of uh inadequate responses I suppose. Ok so that'd be a series of incidents, a series of inadequate responses. But it seems like a reaction to that and uh, this "They that have power to hurt" is almost comical, it's like um the discussion that I had with the person, it kind of seems to uh (laugh) contain certain echoes of the sonnet. Uh the person kept going um, people who do this um shouldn't have X-thing happen to them, or people who will stoop to doing that shouldn't get whatever it is that they're going to get, or certain people, and it was very much the same as this "They."

22

"They are the" or "lords and owners of their faces, / Others but stewards of their excellence." All right it seems that in that line a certain kind of resentment um, of a particular person at being, at uh I guess feeling himself to be a "steward" of someone else's "excellence" uh is coming out, so that again it's not "Others," it's "They" and "O-," well "They" and "Others" but it's really uh 'thee' and 'me.' (laugh)

23

That sestet is so strange. I mean 'this is what's going to happen to you, you're going to actually get worse than everybody else.' It's wishful thinking. It's an odd kind of illustration. I guess beauty is often compared to uh, to flowers, that's certainly a classic uh comparison, you know it's been used throughout literature because certain kinds of physical beauty are transient. And if this is written to um a young male, I mean certainly that kind of uh appeal is transient, um. I mean the, Shakespeare is older and everything, uh and, and women's, you know, one has one's bloom and then it goes very quickly, uh, or least to uh, I don't know, I guess in the twentieth century nobody blooms but I'm thinking of Jane Austen, *Persuasion*, the women have blooms and pass their first blooms, pass the blush of their beauty and so on and so forth, um. Ok so that comparison is interesting, but it doesn't really work, simply becuase what happens to a flower is by and large in the course of things, it's going to rot, you know it's going to wither, if you pick it out the ground it's going to do that a lot more quickly than it would left in its natural environment, but it's going to do it eventually and that's in the nature of things, whereas what Shakespeare is implying is that um, or what the author is implying, is that uh, what's going to happen to "They that have power to hurt and" and uh, "will do none," is uh, what's going to happen to them is that um, they'll lose their uh, their "riches," their "excellence," as a result of particular things that they do, as a result of the way that they conduct themselves. Maybe it gets back to that thing I think that In-, Ingmar Bergman said um, at forty we have the faces that we deser-, or we, each one of us, will have the face that he or she deserves. That kind of a thing? I don't know, um. This is getting inp-, unproductive. Also a side of the tape is up, so what I'll do is stop now, take a break, come back to it very shortly.

24

SIDE 2

Ok I'm back to doing this after a break of about 45 minutes, um. During the break I ran into Elaine who told me that she figured out what bothered her about the poem, so I suppose I should say this so that anything I may say on the tape that seems to come from this point of view will at least have its origin explained, um. She thought that the problem with it was that it seems to be a poem of praise but it really isn't a poem of praise, um, and that that's not obvious until the sestet um. And she didn't really deal with the issue, but uh she did see that to be the crux and she also saw a problem between um the idea of plants meeting base infections and then the "sweetest things" grow sour, uh, "turn sourest by their deeds," how that analogy doesn't work, but I'd already talked about that anyway, um. But that was all the uh, the only thing I did that really would impinge in some kind of a direct way on what I have to say about the poem or on my understanding of the poem.

25

//read poem with 1. 13: For sweet (cough), For sweetest things turn sourest by their deeds.// [rhythmic t-t-t] Um, ok, in a way I guess I was doing a little bit of thinking while I was on my break about um, one reason that it's difficult to uh, that the poem doesn't really lend itself to all the pondering that the Swinburne thing did was be-, i-, 'cause the form is fairly straightforward and uses to which this form can be put are, are almost a commonplace, they're something that um it would seem dumb to talk about at great length. For example it would seem dumb to spend a great deal of time talking about things like the rhyme scheme, the fact that it's set up in uh you know units of uh eight and six lines, that it ends with a couplet, th-, to scan the poem, things like that would seem to be even too routine to even spend a lot of time with, whereas um the ballade was, was the kind of thing that it was just, well it was just so strange first of all, but i-, th-, the form is, is um, i-, it's not that it's, I guess it is a little bit um more different, um. It's the kind of thing that lends itself to um, to more running off at the mouth on tape.

26

The other thing that I th-, was thinking about, and I guess this probably had to do with my little uh t-, uh uh uh what Elaine said to me, is that um the tone of the poem is really a questionable sort of thing. If you take the poem as a poem of s-, praise, take the stuff as very, very straightforward, the first eight lines, um, and then read that setset, read the business about the flowers and read especially the last two lines, then you have got a crux there, because it seems um as though someone is being praised, but really this uh awful comment is being made, um. And I have really, I don't real-, I don't t-, read it that way, um. The first eight lines seem to me to be very ironic uh, although I can't show definitively why that's the way they should be read. Part of this seems to be that the person, the "They," uh becomes um an unnatural thing, an artifact, "as stone, / Unmoved, cold," not something that acts, um, and that the "They" also come, becomes in um an odd way uh a sort of a false object of respect or object of restee-, of esteem um, much like the uh, the despised aristocrat or the um, the hated property owner or the uh, the landlord whom you respect because you have, seem to respect because you have to but is a real piece of shit, um, any inherit, the husbanding riches, "the lords and owners," "Others but stewards" — those words would make me read the poem in th-, in that light and make me read those lines in that light, um. It seems to me that the octave is really constructing a rather devastating series of comments on a particular person, um, namely that the person uh, is inhuman, and is husbanding uh his or her uh gifts, charms, attributes by refusing to be human um, refusing to participate in the natural cycle of things, by becoming "stone, / Unmoved, cold," an artifice, um, and that this person uh isn't, even though this person refuses to hurt, the person is a constant source of pain to anyone who is attracted to him or to her uh because um he or she refuses to respond, in any way uh, even, as I said, refuses I suppose to condescend to respond. And in refusing to do that yet at the same time being an uh, an object of desire or an object uh of attraction, uh, the person puts those who would admire, uh or feel strongly toward him or toward her, in a demeaning position, as a steward is to the lord, but, an un-, albeit uh uh an unwilling steward. Seems to me that those are how uh the lines can be read.

27

Also the person is um presumably deceitful, "That do not do the thing they most do show" — either, oh that line can be read several ways. Either it can refer to overt deceit um, it can refer to uh seeming, the kind of misleading promises or misleading behavior — it will seem as though he or she will respond to me but he or she really won't respond to me. Um he or she is a tease, promises to respond yet doesn't respond. It's, he or she creates a potential for believing that some response will take place but that really won't take place, um so that those lines can be read that way.

28

"Who, moving others, are themselves as stone." It's also devastating comment on wasted -oten-, on uh, well not wasted but on uh mistused potential, misused potential, because um "moving others," the person or the "They" obviously has the um capacity to move others, the capability uh for moving others or to move others, um, in fact can't help it would seem but move others, yet at the same time uh, they "are themsel-," "are themselves" uh "as stone," you know refuse to respond. It's like yeah, yeah, all right, you know, do it to me but don't expect to get anything back, um.

29

"Unmoved," cannot be moved; "cold" — all right again we get to that like a stone, uh, unnatural, "and to temptation slow" — can't even be um provoked into doing something nasty or crummy, I mean can't even be provoked into telling uh someone to fuck off in a direct way. And it seems that all these things are very devastating.

30

These next four lines really do seem to be heavily i-, um ironic. //read ll. 5 – 8 with 1. 8: Others but, Others but stewards of their excellence.//

31

And I guess in that light um, the next six lines are almost a uh, they're calmer, I don't know that they're necessarily straightforward but I get a feeling that this is a much more um, it's an explication of what's going to happen and um I suppose the using of the plant uh the s-, especially the um "summer's flow'r" that is i-, ultimately going to fe-, well not necessarily fester, but at least will wither, dry up, wilt, um after its i-, it, its time, its season, um, gets across the idea that in the course of things, these people who've sort of perverted the natural order of human emotions, of um of human activity and have refused to participate as humans in um becoming involved with other members of the human race uh in any kind of a mutual way, are ultimately subject to the natural order of things. You know, they're the ones that'll have (laugh) to-, horrible faces at forty, I suppose um.

32

And I think the problem with the poem is that um, presumably that's the connection that one's supposed to make and it's, d-, I guess, that one can make — except that the analogy isn't really right. Shakespeare's not saying at the end um you, they are uh, are going to get it eventually, or they are going to lose their charm eventually, um they are going to lose the capability that they have to uh elicit certain kinds of responses from people eventually, um, and it seems that the problem is specifically in the, in the next to last line, "For sweetest things turn sourest by their deeds." First of all the complaint about th-, the "They" is that they don't act, they don't do anything, um. Yet when they do finally do something or be-, because of the way they conduct themselves, um they will turn sourest, they will become most repellent, most unappealing, um. It's just not clear how exactly that happens. I mean does that have to do with their "heaven's graces" that they "inherit" or their "nature's riches" that go down the toilet, I mean what does it have to do with um, and what specifically are the deeds that are going to bring that thing about? "For sweetest things turn sourest by their deeds." That's a, -t's a very odd idiosyncratic uh kind of line. I mean it's a compelling line, but I don't know that it's uh, a true line or a legitimate line in the ways that "Lilies that fester smell far worse than weeds" is, um, simply 'cause it doesn't, although it does kind of get you thinking back to the, the first eight lines, doesn't make any kind of a clear, explicated or legitimate connection, and it certainly doesn't connect in a, any kind of legitimate or clear way with the "base infection." I mean it's a whole different thing that's happening to the flowers and that's happening to the uh, that will happen to the people. I guess one, some, well, to try to explain the thing seems to be the problem, um.

33

If it is an expression of pique and has the same kind of psychological ex-, uh escalation um that expressions of that kind, if you try to sustain them, i-, in some kind of uh, protracted utterance um, tend to have, then it could be read a-, the first um four lines could be read as a kind of a um describing in a, in a detached way what it is that has the author piqued or pissed off, the next four lines could be read as uh, kind of an ironic extension of this, um what seems to be the attitude of world, the world and fortune and so on and so forth towards these people or towar-, uh i-, i-, who piss the author off or pique him, um and it seems, and this next, these four lines also um contain I think a very important element of what piques the author and that is that uh "They that have pow'r to hurt and will do none" force others who care for them into a very demeaning position in the relationship. I mean if you posit a relationship and conduct yourself as though there's a relationship and the other person refuses to nod or turn his or her head, you know, that's ver-, pretty demeaning, um, you do become the steward of, of someone else's excellence (laugh) in that case. Um, the irony in those four lines it seems, or potential irony, whatever, is much more biting, so that the escal-, the psychological escalation uh kind of culminates in "They are the lords and owners of their faces, / Others but stewards of their excellence." Then that part of the poem is over. The next uh — one two three four — four lines it would seem, has, have to do with some kind of an attempt to construct an analogy, not really a clear analogy on the other uh, the, the person who piques or pisses off the author's, um, behavior but uh what's going to happen to that person, why the person shouldn't be so fucking complaisant about things. The reason the person shouldn't be so complaisant is 'look what's going to happen,' 'look what's going to upset people.' I mean no-, not, huh woo, think you're back to my weird conversation um. Look what's going to up-, you know, look what's going to upset sort of [rhythmic t-t-t] the order of uh human activity and of behavior that these uh e-, equalities of th-, the, "heaven's graces" and "nature's riches" have sort of predicated in the first place, um. You're not always going to be like this, things aren't always going to be like this. "The basest weed outbraves his dignity." All right persons who have s-, uh, you know, do not have compelling attributes um are going to fare better in a more enduring way than uh the "They" talked about, railed against in the first eight lines. Um, and then the, the next to last line is a very kind of uh (laugh) huh direct jab, "For sweetest things turn sourest by their deeds." Whatever it is that piqued the author or that pissed off the author, is ultimately going to lead in some kind of direct way to the destruction of the "They," (cough) excuse me, "Lilies that fester smell far worse than weeds." And I guess that's a, kind of a graphic illustration of what all is going to happen, you know, how the mighty have fallen. If you're high, you know, you fall a greater distance than most people, you know I mean it's, the consequences are going to be worse for you, that kind of a thing.

34

And it seems that you can read it that way, um. It does seem to be a, be a very uh, and in that way there's no problem really with the thirteenth line, you know it's getting back to the psycholo-, the escalation of uh, of pique, and of frustration, of being pissed off that it seems to me is operative in the first eight lines, um, you've got to connect that analogy, or that business with the flower, back to what really is upsetting you at some point, and that connection is made in an odd way in the thirteenth line, so that would account for the thirteenth line.

35

Um . . . but the poem really is inaccessible at any other level. I don't think I've every had very great luck with his sonnets but this sonnet in particular seems uh to be um a weird one partly because um well it would seem that some kind of rejection, spurning of affections, is at the root of this, one just can't be sure. Also one just can't be sure whether it's uh specific behavior or whether it's um you know that, that's pissed the po-, uh, the poet off or something that was done to him or to her or just a pattern of lack of response, and that's a real problem. I mean if something is written on the death of the lover, then the motivation for it is very straightforward. Something is written on the departure of the lover, the marriage of the lover to another um, the direct cessation of, of affections that the lover has for the other lover, you know, those kinds of things make for I think a much more accessible sonnet than, than this does, um.

36

I guess another way that the whole thing could be read is that the, th-, you know, the first four lines do describe what is pissing the poet off and the next uh four lines contain kind of a, a much more bitter, ironic extension of this, and then the business of the um, the analogy and finally the thirteenth line contains maybe more than the poet had wanted to say about uh, or uh to bring up about what is really upsetting him or is ex-, upsetting her, 'cause it seems that it's a quality of behavior in those first eight lines but then in the, the thirteenth line it seems as though something is, has been done that really is upsetting — and that that's ultimately the motivation of the sonnet and what's beyond the, uh, behind uh the f-, the sense of frustration.

37

I can't think of any other kinds of coherent readings for the thing. One thing that I found to be a problem was that um, or no, not a problem, kind of a point of issue, well I guess and this gets back to the problem of line thirteen, is that the poem seems to be a lot about passivity, will do no hurt, "do not do the thing" that they seem to be going to do, they "are themselves as stone," "Unmoved," slow to temptation, they "do inherit" — that's a passive thing — they "husband" — generally you "husband," by not doing anything, I mean that doesn't really mean protect, well it means protect but it's not the kind of protect that you go off and fight off anything that's going to uh attack uh "nature's riches," I mean you just kind of you husband uh, husbanding w-, would involve protecting by refusing to do anything that would involve spending or squandering or losing or whatever, um, it's about passivity in that sense um, yet "For sweetest things turn sourest by their deeds." I mean it'd seem that the whole problem in the first eight lines is that "They" who, "that have power to hurt and will do none" are passive, you know too passive, or passive when they shouldn't be. They're adopting a willful um haughty kind of, kind of pis-, passivity that is destructive to other people, um, so it, uh, the deeds that that'll cause them to st-, "turn sourest" um is the deed, remaining passive, so that the deeds would be this repeative, pa-, -peated passivity, refusing to do anything, um. It's odd, kind of what's known in the Catholic Church as 'sins of omission,' um — or what? You know, I really don't understand that. It seems as though it's about passivity, but clearly something has been done that peet-, piqued the poet very much, um. "The summer's flow'r," and the plant thing, I mean the plants are totally passive, you know, they don't do anything to bring "base infection" upon themselves. Stuff happens to plants, people do things to plants, animals do things to plants, ultimately other plants even do things to plants, I mean weeds can fuck up I suppose certain kinds of flowering plants simply by crowding them out of, or uh, their area, you know taking up the nutrients and taking up the sunlight and taking up the space and so on and so forth, um. So that it's about passivity but it isn't about passivity. It's about not acting uh as a human but eliciting very human responses from people. And it's about, it seems to me, some kind of rejection, although again that's uh in that morass of, of stuff, whatever the im-, uh the, the source for this sonnet is, that uh makes it inaccessible, you can't really figure out.

38

Um . . . I don't know what else to say about it. In a way I feel kind of guilty 'cause I haven't even really talked an hour on the thing, but I just don't know what else to say about it. I've explained what I thought the problems are and I've explained ways that I think the thing can be put together and can be read. Oh I should also explain before I end that as last time I didn't listen to any portions of the tape um, except that I listened to about thirty seconds of th-, the first side after I was done with it to make sure it recorded and that it was audible. But I didn't listen to anything that I had done, and although I first um looked at the sonnet on Tuesday ni-, T-, uh yes Tuesday night, prepared to do it at that time, discovered that I had done this sonnet before, had looked at it before um, and then didn't record, you know, until I had checked about that, um, I didn't look at it again until now, and I didn't record until now partly because I didn't really have large unbrok-, you know several hours in time at a stretch where I felt that I would be energetic (laugh) um, so that I did look at it a couple of days ago, although I don't think I really thought about it, I mean I can't remember thinking about it, (laugh) I ce-, certainly didn't have any great ideas when I came to the thing this morning. Um . . . I think I'll stop now 'cause it just really doesn't, I can't think of anything else to say. There's a chance that I'll go back and record again before the uh, we have our discussion, but I just don't know.

GEORGE: SONNET 94

1

About 10:15, and before I look at the poem I ha-, I probably should say that uh one of the people in the uh project did mention to me more or less inadvertently that uh the poem was a sonnet so I, I know that before I look at the poem, that. So, here we go.

2

Sonnet 94, Shakespeare, hum.   //read poem with l. 6: And husbands, And husband nature's riches from expense.//   Huh. I missed that almost completely the first time through um, but that's usual for me on a poem.   //read ll. 9–14//   I'll have to go back to the b-, uh beginning of the, of the poem.

3

//read ll. 1–6//   I guess I should um stop here. This part seems uh mm ironic, to me here uh. "They that have" the "pow'r to do hurt and will do none, / That do not do the thing they most do show." What does he mean by "show"? Well at any rate picking up at the line "Who, moving others, are themselves as stone." I guess I, I guess he's not being inon, iron, ironic but uh "Who, moving others, are themselves as stone," I uh, I was interpreting as uh manipulative um people, who move others but uh, to emotion w-, um, while they themselves counterfeit it, but I think that's wrong already. "Unmoved, cold, and to temptation slow; / They rightly do inherit" — I thought this was, this part was ironic, "inherit heaven's graces / And husband nature's riches from expense; / They are the lords and owners of their faces, / Others but stewards of their" — which, faces? Their own faces' excellence?

4

//read ll. 9–14//   Um ni-, it sounds like to, to thine own self be true. Uh the uh, the sestet, uh.   //read ll. 9–12//   Is this poem against uh the nobility, the flowers, the flowers as uh nobility? um, which is corrupted because of, of the base in-, "base infection" with which, with which the flower meets, uh then "the basest weed" uh, that is they uh, commonest of commoners uh outbraves his, the noble's, the flower's, dignity. "For sweetest things turn sourest by their deeds; / Lilies that fester smell far worse than weeds." Yeah let's see if he's um, um, it seems as if he's talking about uh great men, men with, with power who, who go bad, uh go against their natures . . . I say go against their natures because it, it seems that um he's, he's saying that uh the "summer's flow'r" or the, or the n-, the natural flower "is to the summer sweet, / Though to itself it only live and die." That seems as if he's bringing up the idea that uh, uh, well I can't help thinking of the uh uh the para-, parable about the uh, the lilies in the fields who, who neither sow nor reap um, who aren't uh, bothered um by ambition uh or infected by, with, ambition um but live their own um natural, that is uh true to their own nature uh lives even if it seems i-, uh I'm trying to paraphrase the uh, the sestet. "The summer's flow'r is to the summer sweet, / Though to itself it only live and die." Even if the lily doesn't understand that it's better off um simply being a lily and billying, being uh sweet to the natural world uh without any sort of um ambition, even if it doesn't achieve anything, even though "it only live and die," it's better off that way than uh being infected with, with ambition because then it's really rotten, it's, so that, that the poem doesn't seem to be against uh the nobility such, uh a-, as such but um, powerful men who, who go bad, in, in some sense, and I think he explains that sense, that's wha-, -ts, what he's doing at the beginning of the poem.

5

Let me see, I'm not, I'm not sure of his tone here. Of course he, he would have to be um, if, if these poems were circulated, and um I have to admit my ignorance again, I, I just don't know whether, whether these, these sonnets were, were circulated or not, let's see, uh. Lord, the plays were put together after his death but, well assuming that, that uh someone saw the poems uh, that they were circulated in private if, if not, I mean a-, as was usual in, in a n-, in those days, then um he would have to be, he would have to be very careful about uh a poem that, that seemed to be attacking the nobility because they would tend to be the men with the most power.

6

"They that have pow'r to do hurt and will do none,   /   That do not do" — now that seems um positive, on the face of it, but I'm suspicious, I can't say why yet. "That do not do the thing they most do show." Is he saying uh it's un-, this kind of restraint is unnatural? A corruption of, of man's nature? "Who, moving others, are themselves as stone," Well n-, the tone there is, is negative, um, and then the next line is, is very sliding uh both ways uh. "Unmoved, cold," which is negative, both, both of them um, I mean if they have sufficient reason to be uh moved and move others but hold themselves back and simply manipulate um, are simply "cold," that's not good, then the pause in the line, "and to tempta-tion slow." Well in a strict Christian sense that's good, but uh, I think with what, with what goes before . . . he means that uh these people have the same quote-unquote virtue um as Christians but with them it's, it's, it's been twisted from its, from its natural purpose or its original purpose, um, i-, it comes now not from a, that, that, that being uh slow to temptation, comes not from uh, any kind of, of natural goodness or, or willingness to follow uh the tenets of the, of the reli-gion but uh from uh, an unnatural kind of self control uh a willingness to ma-nipulate that I, I, I talked about uh above, I gue-, I guess since the tape will be transcribed uh. Which, which definition of, of the first four lines, that is that he's, that he's discussing um slyly uh and making a judgment about uh powerful men who manipulate and that, that those men are unnatural um twisting even the uh simple Christian or, or, or twisting even the uh the most important uh Christian virtue um to a kind, kind of unnaturalness um.

7

Then in the fifth line he starts it off again uh very vaguely with um an indefinite referent. "They rightly do inherit heaven's graces   /   And husband nature's riches from expense." . . . Oh boy, I think I probably need the OED um for expense but I'm I'm going to go look uh, I'm going to go look it up in the, in the dictionary that I have, which i-, which is a modern dictionary um. One moment. No it has nothing um, simply a uh, the usual definitions of expense as, as cost, uh something paid out, but um I was looking for a more ob-, obscure definition uh to see if he was, if he was slipping, slipping something in here that uh, that I wasn't going to catch.

8

Let me start again with the fifth line. "They rightly do inherit heaven's graces." Now, a question — who are they? Are, are they, they seem to be those ma-nipulative uh powerful men, probably noblemen, but um, but let's see. "They rightly do inherit heaven's graces   /   And husband nature's riches from ex-pense." Oh I see, he's not, no, he's not, he's not being um, not using any meaning of the word that seems a, that isn't obvious uh. Anyone who husbands "nature's riches from expense" but not from their own labor, who get uh, who manage to manipulate others into uh doing the work and making, therefore making, making them rich, um, there, there does seem to be a — I left that sentence hanging, um, sorry. Those people who, who do not work to, in order to husband, who don't in a more natural sense "husband" uh "nature's riches" the way say um the farmer would gather a harvest um b-, um but instead the men who, who "husband . . . riches from expense," these must be the same, the same unnatural men uh he was, of whom he was speaking before um, seems to be a play in "expense" because uh they pay money uh to have uh husband, well to have "nature's riches" husbanded for them but uh it's at a cost to themselves as well because they're, they're losing something essential in, in their own nature by um paying for having nature's reshe-, "nature's riches" husbanded for them, for uh twisting, twisting the natural, the natural order again. Um maybe he is talking more directly about the nobility, I'm going back and forth on that um.

9

"They are the lords" sound like nobilities, nobility but uh, "and owners of their faces / Others but stewards of their excellence." The only way I can read, the only way I can read that is that the uh nobles, manipulative nobles, powerful men at any rate, um who are self-possessed, who have this ability to uh, to remain unmoved um and remain as stone while they're moving others would naturally be um in, in such, ha-, control of themselves that they'd have uh absolute control over their, their facial expression so they're the lo-, "the lords and owners of their faces, / Others but stewards of their excellence." Um, let's see. Other people are "but stewards of their excellence," which you would address a powerful man, a noble, as — no in the plural, it would have to be their excellences. "Others but stewards of their excellence." The reason I'm puzzled here is, is because I thought I had a, a reading of the line, I, I thought I'd already arrived at a reading of the line which was that uh others, other people, um are subject to their emotions, of uh, and show the emotion, that emotion on their f-, on their faces therefore uh, so that uh others are "but stewards of their," their faces', and "excellence" is a, is an odd word, a word that, that, that stands out and um is really intriguing um. It's a, a judgment given the, the reading I just, I just gave, it's a, it's a judgment that uh people who show the emotion on their faces uh, and are, and are stewards of, of their faces' excellence, "excellence" stands in the, in the line as, as a judgment saying that they are uh, that that's better, that's a better condition, that the faces that show emotion are excellent, the faces therefore that don't show emotion because of, because of an unnatural kind of, of self-control um aren't excellent even though they may uh, I don't think the two readings are contradictory. If these, if these powerful men are indeed lords, then they own far more than their faces and other people are in fact "stewards of their excellence" um, other people are their servants and their excellence is a title that, that uh, by which these uh powerful men are known, but uh I, I think Shakespeare is, is um loving, sneaked in a uh, uh, another reading here um so that other, other people um si-, doesn't, do-, doesn't, the secondary reading doesn't change the referent um, are but servants not, not of the lords but of their faces' excellence. I think he's, he's hidden one reading in with, with the other.

10

And then the uh, the endstop which I remember from my qualifying exam as being a volta, um, has nothing to do with uh the poem uh. He makes the lesson a little clearer in, in a kind of parable that uh, he makes I guess not the lesson,

what follows in the sestet is, is the lesson but he's, he's making what he's dis-
cussed uh in the, in the octet, above, uh . . . more clear in a, in a kind of, of
parable. //read ll. 9–14// I think that that, wha-, what I've suggested uh as
the reading is, is what is going on in the poem, uh I can't help, I can't help um,
(laugh) even though my new critical tendency is, is, is to uh say shame on you,
don't think this uh, poem has no existence except on a page, but uh, I keep
thinking of, of Shakespeare um smarting from, from some rebuff, Shakespeare
the commoner, being hurt.

SIDE 2

Ok, nothing, nothing lost on the, on the tape change um except enough time to
change the tape, I mean on, on turning the tape over. Uh Shakespeare smarting
from uh some put-down from a nobleman, his, assu-, assuming that nobleman to
be his, his patron, someone from whom he had not expected to meet that dis,
traditional distinction in races, uh in, excuse me, races um, in classes, and uh
evidently, evidently did. I, a-, at least I keep thinking uh why would, why
would Shakespeare write this poem, why write the poem, and that, that seems to
be the only occasion um for, for a poem like this, it seems to be the one that to
me i-, is the most plausible for, for a poem against uh the nobility, and, and uh,
because the uh, the couplet there um gets m-, more barbed um, the insult or the
uh, the insult to the patron or uh the rebuke to the patron and, and the, the
writer's own pain uh becomes more obvious in the couplet. And as he says "For
sweetest things turn sourest by their deeds." And this, this of course makes me,
uh makes me think of, of oh the young noble who was uh not only his patron but
uh with whom Shakespeare was supposed to be in love um. I accept that theory
and, and read the poem from, from that viewpoint um. "For sweetest things turn
sourest by their deeds" — I, I assume, I, a real um personal relevance to Shake-
speare in those, in those lines. And then he, he sums it up again, "Lilies that
fester smell far worse than weeds." And that is a definite shot at um, at the
nobility but it um, maybe because of, of what I've just said which is, which is
why I said it, but it um, to let you know how I arrive at this but i-, it seems to
me to have a um, a personal touch to it. Um he leaves it in the plural, Shake-
speare leaves it in the plural, lil-, "Lilies that fester smell far worse than weeds,"
but um, I don't know the, the emotion in it seems personal and, and therefore
singular in spite of the fact that he's, that he's written more than one lily into the
flower, into the, into the poem.

11

Let me go back and, and read the uh, the entire poem again and see how well
my reading works. "They that have pow'r to do hurt and will do none, That do
not do the thing they most do show." I wonder if I can go out on a limb here. It
occurs to me, if this is directed against Shakespeare's patron-lover, um this sec-
ond line takes on, on a significance. "That do not do the thing they most do
show." A show of love, or at least of, of affection, whi-, which is not real. And
then "Who, moving others," that is, in this case, the poet himself, Shakespeare,
um, who does love, who does feel a great deal of affection um, "are themselves
as stone." I, I think it's a very personal poem, these people who "are themselves
as stone," are also "Unmoved, cold, and to temptation slow."

12

Am I reading that right, with, with, pronouncing the E-D? "Unmoved,"
"Unmóvèd, cóld, and tó temptátion slów." Yeah, right, ok. If, I'm not sure if the

recorder caught all that. I was muttering about, I, I was counting out the uh, the metrics in the line t-, uh to make sure that I was getting five, five feet without uh, uh, making sure that I was right in, in pronouncing "unmov'd" "unmovèd" for the s-, for the sake of the metrics.

13

"They rightly do inherit heaven's graces." Oh, has, that has to be ironic, "They rightly" — even the stress comes down um almost as a, as a pointer, pay attention to this word. "Rightly" — do they "rightly . . . inherit heaven's graces / And husband nature's riches from expense"? Well they own all the land um. They pay to have . . . uh, the original reading I did on, on these lines is, is breaking down, which is why I paused. "They," that is the, the men, the men of power, um, mm, and as, as, as I'm reading it uh, Shakespeare's patron who's, who's hurt him, "They rightly do inherit heaven's graces." Well Shakespeare knows as well as anyone that that's uh a simple accident of, of birth. So that "rightly" is, is ironic in the extreme.

14

"And husband nature's riches from expense." Um I really wish that the punctuation at the end of that line, "And husband nature's riches from expense," had, had come out more clearly on the mimeograph. It seems to be a semicolon. Well it shouldn't be a full stop. Right, there's a, there's a semicolon above at the end of "Unmoved," "Unmoved, cold, and to temptation slow," and it's typed a little clearer but uh shows the same pattern. All right it's, it i-, it is a semicolon,

15

um. "They rightly do inherit heaven's graces / And husband nature's riches from expense." Is he saying that they hoard "nature's riches," they "husband nature's ri-," "riches" from being spent? I'm going to have to go look up um "husband," which I, I should have done, I suppose, when I looked up "expense." A moment. Ok I found the definition that I expected um, to uh conserve, uh, to husband one's resources frugally. In other words he's, he's saying that uh . . . these lords, the nobility, and I think, I think it is directed um against the nobility now uh, given uh my, my reading of, of the personal nature of the hurt and from whom that, that hurt came, a nobleman. Who "husband nature's riches from expense," who hoard "nature's riches," I mean um, "They rightly do inherit heaven's graces," uh they have all the uh, they g-, not only get uh, inh-, inherit all the, all the beauty . . . um and intelligence that, that heaven can bestow but they uh, they hoard earthly treasures as well, rather than heavenly treasures. So all right, they're uh, they're talented, mm, beautiful, rich uh semicolon,

16

"They are the lords and owners of their faces, / Others but stewards of their excellence." Um. I wouldn't say now that I feel that uh that reading that I gave earlier of the others' faces being "stewards of their excellence" is, is invalid but it doesn-, it doesn't seem in line with the, with the reading that I'm giving now, um. He's simply, simply saying very directly o-, others are their go-fors, Shakespeare as the commoner rebuffed writes in bitterness, "They are the lords and owners of their faces," yeah of their, of their faces as well. They own everything else, all the land, they also own, and they lord it over their, their faces because of, of this self-control.

17

"Others but stewards of their excellence. / The summer's flow'r is to the summer sweet." Now I've got uh, now I've got to make the uh, make, see whether, whether or not the uh, the sestet will fit with the reading that I've started to give the poem. //read ll. 9–11// What would the "base infection" be in this case, I, with, with the second reading that I'm giving the poem? Um not ambition now but, a coldness? An ability to remain "Unmoved" while moving others? Lets try that on and see how that works. "The summer's flow'r is to the summer sweet." Summer. Now I'm, now I'm running into trouble trying to, trying to fit this uh, this sestet into uh into my reading, um. It worked fine as, as the sestet, that is as a restatement of the lilies of the field, and uh a statement, as a statement against ambition but I don't believe that's what, that's what Shakespeare's referring to. And yet I have the, I have the, the hunch that it, that it works because the las-, because of uh the last line before the couplet, "The basest weed outbraves," and outbraves uh resonates um, "outbraves his dignity." Uh I think the nobles, the young nobles were known as, as bravos uh, at least I know that, that definition, the young fops or swells up on the latest fashions. And yet "The basest weed," that is the lowest commoner, "outbraves his dignity," which might be another, another play on uh his dignity be-, might be another play on uh his hereditary dignity or his, his title, I don't know if you would refer to a, a noble as His Dignity. The couplet still makes sense and that's what started me off on this reading, which turned the poem around for me but um what I'm having trouble with is the first two lines of the sestet. "The summer's flow'r is to the summer sweet, / Though to itself it only live and die." The meaning there is escaping me for the moment and so I'm going to have to come back and, and try to figure it out uh. I'm going to continue recording, I mean to come back to the lines.

18

"The summer's flow'r is to the summer sweet, / Though to itself it only live and die." . . . Why "The *summer's* flow'r"? Why bring in the summer? . . . Um, is that a possible change on the uh, the cliché the, the flower of the nobility? Is, is he referring to the nobility as uh the summer? It would fit in with uh, the poetic tradition and the uh, the, the habit of, of putting um, different things in, in hierarchies, um based on, on the, on the chain of being, summer would be the, the highest, the highest season in the hierarchy of, of seasons. It does seem like that would be a natural comparison to social classes, the nobility. Course the sun itself would have to be uh . . . royalty, but the summer — I can't tell whether I'm explaining or trying to convince myself — the summer would be a good metaphor for the nobility. "The summer's," now let's see how that works. "The summer's flow'r," all right this young nobleman, this flower of the nobility, is "sweet" to the nobility.

19

"Though to itself it only live and die." Now that line puzzles me. If he's not using something like the lilies of the field, what is he using? . . . "Though to itself," "to itself it only live and die," meaning that the nobleman is wrapped up in his own existence to the exclusion of all else? That he's that egocentric? "Though to itself it only live and die." Could be. //read ll. 9–14; 9–10// He might, it might, those two lines might still work as a kind of, of lilies of the field, an adaptation of th-, of that parable. "The summer's flow'r is to the summer sweet, / Though to itself it only live and die." Uh once I, once I take the lines apart, um I have to read them again more quickly uh in order to get the sense of the entire line, well then that may be more than one line, that is the unit I'm trying to put back together may be more than one line. "The summer's flow'r is to the summer sweet, / Though to itself it only live and die." . . . No I can't, I thought I could make it work, those two lines work with uh, as a variation of the parable but, a-, and in terms of the, of the reading I'm giving the poem but I, I can't see, can't see it now. It all depends, it all depends on, comes down to the one line, "Though to itself it only live and die." Well both, both lines are important but that seems to be the key. "The summer's flow'r is to the summer sweet, / Though to itself it only live and die." Well I'm, I'm confused at this point. Does he mean if the flower lives in some kind of, of natural dignity it's better off? . . . That would work both as an extension of the lilies of the field parable and the reading I'm giving the poem, that it's better to rely on natural beauty, the lily would be better off if it relied uh on its own natural beauty, "Though to itself it only live and die; / But if that flow'r with base infection meet." But then if the, if the flower, if the no-, nobleman gets infected with uh a kind of class conceit, then "The basest weed outbraves his dignity."

SIDE 3

Um, on that tape change, then "The basest weed outbraves his dignity," it did interrupt my train of thought um. I was starting another sentence and I've completely forgotten what it was. Um it did interrupt my train of thought. So we go back to um "The summer's flow'r is to the summer sweet, / Though to itself it only live and die." Right now I'd, I would say he's, he's, he's recommending some kind of natural dignity rather than the assumed conceit of the upper class, because then the warning follows, "But if that flow'r with base infection meet, / The basest weed outbraves his dignity," and I've already um expicate-, explicated or at least tried to explicate um "outbraves."

20

But let's see, am I really happy with that? Um, "The summer's flow'r is to the summer sweet, / Though to itself it," "it only live and die." Um the reading I just gave to the, to the lines, that it is better, even if you are a lily um that is a nobleman, to live and, and die in, in your own natural dignity, seems to me much, a reading to which the lines lend themselves much more readily than, than trying to see um, than, than dragging in the great chain of being and um summer may be uh a metaphor for the nobility but it could simply be just a, a, well a, a traditional, poetically traditional uh description, I mean if, if the young man is, is beautiful enough, the young nobleman is beautiful enough to be a flower, a, a lily, then, well naturally the, the growing season of that, that flower, the lifetime then of the man, would be in the summer. It could just be a uh, a statement of when he lives. No, I change my mind while looking a-, at the line, uh. I think summer probably is, it's probably both, I, why should I, why should I uh cripple Shakespeare and make an either-or situation, uh the summer is the natural lifetime, uh growing season, the, of the flower and there-, therefore of the, of the nobleman, but I think that reading that I was giving, trying to give before, uh "Though to itself it only live and die," uh that being some kind of uh, uh that it, that it only lives and dies *to*, or, well it would actually have to be *for*, itself uh in order to be uh that, that the nobleman is, is that selfish. I think that reading is wrong now. Um it seems to work with, the line seems to work better with the poem if, if I put the, take the two together and read it as, as saying that it's better to live um, it'd be better for the flower to live in its own natural sweetness, the sweetness of the nobleman's own personality without, that is, adding any uh defects of the noble class which is, which is a kind of uh, condescension, uppityness um, and uh a tendency to uh hurt commoners, in particular this commoner.

21

Now that I've gotten that uh, to my own satisfaction at this point straightened out, let me, let me go through the entire poem and see if I'm, if I'm happy with, with what I've accomplished. "They that have pow'r to do hurt and will do none." I pause because that seems almost contradictory, that first line seems almost contradictory to the reading I've been giving. If they will do no hurt then, then what's Shakespeare talking about? Let me go on with the poem. "They that have pow'r to do hurt and will do none, / That do not do the thing they most do show, / Who, moving others," I think I've arrived at an understanding, huh (laugh) um. Could it have been . . . a fight, say, even a lover's quarrel between Shakespeare and the nobleman? But rather than becoming angry as he would have done, disregarding class, and on a p-, on a purely personal level, he would have made some kind of retort to, say, something Shakespeare said in anger to him. He holds back because of, of a class dignity, he retreats into his class dignity and because of that, looking ahead to the lines "Who, moving others, are themselves as stone, / Unmoved, cold, and to temptation slow." They're slow to temptation — at least I was right about it being a, a, t-, a twisting of, of the uh Christian virtue. He's, he's slow to temp-, temptation, that is to, to retort or to reply angrily and on a personal level to the poet, to Shakespeare, because he's, he's retreate-, retreated into his uh, his class's uh nobility. He's not reacting on a personal level as one human to another, but he retreats, avoids the confrontation and puts the uh, the encounter or conflict back on a, on a class footing and becomes aloof, dignified, cold, um as would be fitting for a nobleman arguing with a commoner. That's even contradictory, a nobleman wouldn't stoop to argue with a commoner. That seems to be Shakespeare's complaint here, that he didn't, he reacted as a nobleman and not as a person.

22

See how that goes now, huh (laugh) now that I've made up my own little story of, of what really happened behind the poem. //read poem with l. 6: "And husbands nature's riches from expense."// If I'm right then this is, this poem is, is based on a, on a personal argument, my God, if, if the nobleman ever saw that last line, what a, what an incredible shock that would be. He's not only been called a festering lily, he's been told that he smells "far worse than weeds." My imagination is getting away from me today, um. The thought just crossed my mind, could he have, could he possibly have insulted Shakespeare for being a commoner, for, uh, specifically for, for smelling? I'll never know.

23

Let me read the poem once more. //read poem// Ok. What I, what I seem to have arrived at is um that the poem is, is the uh, the response of the poet to a uh quarrel between himself and his lover, a young nobleman, um who rather than responding to Shakespeare on a human level retreats into the, the traditional roles uh that uh the class distinctions between upper and, and, and I suppose

Shakespeare was middle class but, retreats into the uh given class roles and refuses to argue, refuses to settle the quarrel or even to engage in it. Um, he complains about the nobleman's having done that in an earlier quarrel, and then in the next, the second four lines of the octet very ironically says uh, well yes that, that class, those class differences do exist and they are natural, I mean that's the way it is after all, um he was only doing what could have been expected of him. That is the young, the young nobleman, the young lover was only doing what was expected of him by retreating into his title, as it were. And then in the sestet, Shakespeare says it would be better, it would have been better, for the young nobleman to have stood on his own natural dignity because i-, in not doing so . . . he fell in effect below Shakespeare's level as, as a, both as a, as a commoner but, but more importantly as a person. And then in the couplet the uh, the warning with as I, as I said before more of a, more of a barb to it um, that the young nobleman was wrong and by retreating into his title and avoiding the confrontation um came off much worse than he would have by going ahead and reacting to Shakespeare as one person to another. And having said that I think this is the end of this session.

24

Ok it's about uh 12 o'clock, high noon, on Wednesday now, um and I, I was just going back uh playing this half of uh the tape I'm on from the beginning uh, puzzling, listening to myself puzzle out uh those two lines "The summer's flow'r is to the summer sweet, / Though to itself it only live and die." And I um, I saw myself hitting all around uh what seems now to be the, the essence of the line. My, my reading still stands but I um, I knew then, when I was, when I was making the tape to begin with uh that I wasn't quite explaining it uh to my own satisfaction, uh or I wasn't, I wasn't quite explicating it uh a-, correctly, I hadn't hit on the, on the meaning of the, of the lines. Um, well now that's not exactly true because I, I think that the, the meaning that I pulled out of the lines was right in spite of, of my inability to pin down precisely what the lines were about, but I, I think I know now that it's, it's another one of those things that's um, now seems, seems obvious and I feel a little silly for having, having missed it, so far, I, th-, that, having missed it for so long. "The summer's flow'r is to the summer sweet, / Though to itself it only live and die." He could very well mean um the n-, the nobility and, be referring to the young gentleman as, as the uh, the young nobleman as the flower of the summer, th-, uh, the summer as the nobility um, but that's I think secondary — if I were writing the line I w-, I would leave that secondary meaning in there, I mean uh put as much meaning as I possibly could in the line but uh, i-, I, it's really secondary to the actual meaning of the line which is, which is that uh the flower lives for one season and one season only. It, it lives for a summer and is sweet during the summer even though "to itself it only live and die," even though its, its existence is only uh personal or subjective, though it, it, it begins and ends there during that one un-, that one season, that one summer. But the essence of, of nobility and of, of the upper class is, is in well i-, I almost said of the titled class and, and that's it, it is a titled class, the, the family line inherits the title. It's important, in other words, for the line to continue from one summer to another summer. So what Shakespeare is saying is um it would be better if that concern with the title, or as I put it before that retreat into the title, didn't exist for, for the young gentleman, for the young nobleman um. It would be better for him if he lived as flowers live, from one season, for-, for just one season, forget about um, the essence of his class a-, uh, or in other words forget about his, his class as, as nobleman whose duty it is to pass on his title, because i-, if he doesn't he's very likely to meet with uh, well here the reading simply continues uh what I said before, uh, because if he, if he doesn't give up that, that class uh, those class concerns, as he didn't in the quarrel, then uh he stands the chance of, of meeting with, with a "base infection," um, which I think I, I rightly said was, was a real tendency uh to ignore and to condescend and to hurt commoners, and uh that's what I just hit upon and since that's all I thought of um, now I *am* through.

25

Ok it's uh Friday morning October 12th about 8:30 in the morning and I just realized a few minutes ago that uh I simply took it as a, as an article of faith that uh this was a sonnet and never really did anything with the formal structure, it seemed uh, well he actually rhymes, so I think I'll go through that. "They that have pow'r to do hurt and will do none," "They that have pow'r to do hurt and will do none, / That do not do the thing they most do show." Ok, it's a, it's a, a five-beat uh roughly iambic line, though that uh, that first line is, the stresses fall on, let's see, "They that have," first syllable of "pow'r," "to do húrt and will do nóne." Um "They," first syllable of "pow'r," "hurt," "do," and "none." "They that have," "They that have pow'r to do hurt and will do none." Right, it's a little odd. Uh the rhyme scheme should be A-B-A-B-, ok, uh, C-D-C-D, right, E-F-E-F, right, G-G, ok. What does he rhyme? "None" and "stone," "show," "slow," "graces," "faces," "expense," "excellence," "sweet," "meet," "die," "dignity," and "deeds," "weeds." That doesn't do anything for me.

26

Let me read the poem. Right now I'm, I'm pleased enough with the reading that I've already given and don't want to repeat it but let me see if I, if I come up with something new. "They that have pow'r to do hurt and will do none." The stresses could come on "and wíll do nóne," so that they come on uh, they come on "will" and "none" rather than "do" and "none." Be that as it may. // read ll. 1 – 6//

SIDE 4

Ok well, to pick up where I uh ran out, ran out of tape um.   //read ll. 5 – 8 with l. 6: "And husbands nature's riches from expense."//   I was saying um, after I had run out of tape that uh since Shakespeare does um a half-rhyme uh at the beginning uh, "none" and, and "stone," uh, although he does other full rhymes, that the rhyme on, on "graces" and "faces" the first time I read it through uh, you didn't hear the second half uh, you didn't hear me read the "faces" line because I had run out of tape. But I was commenting that that seemed to uh stand out more this time, or at least that time when I read it, um. Since you've heard me on this side of the tape read it, I read it once since and it didn't seem to stick out then, um and I can't, at any rate I can't do anything with the uh, with the rhyme being a little stronger thematically, let's see. "They rightly do inherit heaven's graces." Ok. "They are the lords and owners of their faces." Well the accent comes down on the first syllable of, of "graces," the first syllable of "faces." Does that help any? //   read ll. 5 – 7 //   I wonder if he's uh, it does seem to stick out a little uh, that rhyme seems a little more obvious than some of the others, I wonder if he is trying to uh relate the nobleman's, the nobleman's face as, as one of "heaven's graces." It would be a, a fairly typical uh compliment, but it's, it's no real help, to my reading of the poem.

27

I had better start over again.   //read poem//   No, nothing, nothing to uh, to really add from the last taping . . . except that I've uh, I've forgotten the definition of "expense" that I found so I'm going to have to go look it up again to make sure that w-, see if I, I'm still satisfied that uh my reading of the line was good enough for me. Oh the definition I'd forgotten was the definition of "husband," to uh conserve, or uh keep track of, of frugally, um. "They rightly do inherit heaven's graces   /   And husband nature's riches from expense." Yeah I, well, I still think that's an ironic statement of uh, of the current social order, um Shakespeare the commoner being, being just uh extremely sarcastic. //read ll. 9–14//   Uh I was, I was, I went back to try to look, uh uh I was looking again at uh "And husband nature's riches from expense," trying to see if there was any sense, any way I could uh read the line so that uh a paraphrase of it would be um "And husband nature's" branche-, n-, uh, well hoard "nature's riches" um "from expense" not meaning in the sense of simply being, being spent, but uh at a cost to themselves, at the expen-, me-, meaning "expense" as in the phrase 'at the expense of' themselves, but it doesn't read that way uh, at least it doesn't seem to, to me. It seems, it seems straightforward here uh, no plays on any of the words.

28

"They rightly do inherit heaven's graces." The stress coming down on, on "rightly" really I think is the key to um seeing any kind of sarcasm. Course I suppose the key to my entire reading is the uh, the biographical details, but I still see this as uh Shakespeare's rebuttal after a quarrel with uh his patron, or a youn-, a young, a young nobleman at least who, who is a lover and I think the current theory is that uh the young nobleman who was his patron was also, at least possibly, his lover, uh with the whole controversy between uh the sonnets being written for that nobleman and then the Dark Lady appearing and so on and so on. Um, Shakespeare rebukes the young nobleman for retreating, I'm repeating the uh reading that I had before — be interesting to see if there are any differences between what I, what I think I said last time and oh think I, what I think I arrived at w-, and w-, what I say now. Uh this is after a quarrel um during which rather than, rather than responding um as he would have done naturally the nobleman um refused to argue with the commoner Shakespeare and uh withdrew um into um a typical class role of uh a kind of disdain and haughtiness uh which uh precipitates Shakespeare's scorn in the second half of the uh octave, uh, "They rightly do inherit heaven's graces," and so on, "They are the lords and owners," "They are the lords and owners of their faces, /   Others but stewards of their excellence." Then the lesson in the, in the sestet um concerning the uh, the sweetness of, of the natural flower which uh, which I do think is, is uh allied to uh, or with, uh Christ's lilies of the field parable, the, the beauty of the natural flower that lives only for one season and has no concerns other than that one season uh, in other words it isn't concerned with uh titles and family and inheritances the way the uh the titled classes are uh — which is, which is a behavior that uh, that because it's typical of, of the titled classes just as the uh, the haughtiness is, it uh, that kind of, I suppo-, what I'm stumbling around trying to say is that uh, Shakespeare lays the blame uh for the concern with the uh inheritance a-, and family name finally um, the concern with the title to uh, he blames that behavior as, as being the, the root of uh the haughtiness, um, that, that troubles him so much in this, in this poem, and he, he calls that uh, that kind of behavior the, the concern with, with uh titles and haughtiness, presumably, uh a "base infection" which brings the uh, the lowest commoner, that is the "basest weed," uh to a higher level than uh the infected flower uh, and I, I've already explained the play on, on, that I see in "out-braves" and uh 'bravos,' and 'outbravos' really I think is what he's after uh, it's a veiled, another veiled insult, uh saying that the, that the young nobleman is only after all a young fop, a young um swell, uh for all his title and inherited dignity. It might be something, that might be something that he's drawing a distinction between. Well no, let's see, inherited dignity and, and natural dignity. Why not? I think he does. The natural dignity of the flower is much better than, than the supposed inherid-, inherited dignity of the titled classes. Lord, is that all I was trying to say and stumbling around for so long? Hah, and then he repeats it uh, as usual he, he makes the point beautifully in, in the closing couplet uh, the "sweetest things turn sourest by their deeds; / Lilies that fester smell far worse than weeds," and then my open-ended speculation that uh . . . the nobleman may have insulted Shakespeare, or at least, at least referred to him, I mean not, not simply have said 'well you smell bad' but uh, but he may have uh . . . refused to quarrel with Shakespeare because of Shakespeare's status as a, as a commoner. Oh and, and I, and I suppose commoners um, I'm sure were, were thought of by the nobility as, as being an, an ill-smelling rabble, um, which is what Shakespeare plays on, I mean there's no, there's no real reason, um I think I've just satisfied my own speculation which I said earlier, I would never know whether the nobleman ever told, whether the quarrel actually happened but uh, not only that but whether or not uh the nobleman had actually told Shakespeare that, that he smelled bad um, I don't think so, because um the be-, opening of the poem leads one to believe, leads me to believe, let me not hide behind the, the indefinite pronoun um, that Shakespeare's complaint is that he refused to argue, I me-, he, he didn't actually insult Shakespeare but that uh the insult there that Shakespeare smells bad is, is inherent in the reason that the nobleman didn't quarrel with Shakespare, that is because Shakespeare is a commoner and so on, I've already explained that.

29

Um, I don't really see anything more than uh, or at least I don't think I've seen anything more than I, than I saw at uh, at the first reading and, and taping. I suppose I, I should say uh, the part of um, although it, although took me uh quite a while to figure out "The summer's flow'r is to the summer sweet, / Though to itself it only live and die," um, those two lines took me a while to figure out, but I seem to remember, um, I'm sure I must have read this poem myself before, but I, I seem to remember someone, uh a professor, well I'll just give you what my impression is. I, I think at one time I was, I was sitting with um a couple of professors in California uh who were talking about uh which of Shakespeare's sonnets they liked best and one of them mentioned uh number 94 to the other uh. The other one couldn't think of which one that one was but uh, so the, the one who ha-, had mentioned it uh referred to it uh, by using and explicating to, to some extent, uh those two lines, or at least I think, and after I-d, after I'd done all that work on, on what I thought was my own, I think I have heard that those two lines um given a, a very brief treatment by someone, either, either in that context or it may have come up in a class somewhere, I don't know. Um it's, it's been too long. But uh, I hate to, I hate to steal my own thunder but uh there it is. That's all I can come up with.

CARLOS: SONNET 94

1

Ok, the poem, first time. Sonnet 94, Shakespeare, ah. //read poem with l. 6: "And husband's nat-, husband nature's riches from expense."//

2

Uh, that's a, oh, another reading here, at least. //read poem// Ok that's a, the poem certainly does seem to be cut in half by uh, at the, the line "The summer's flow'r is to the summer sweet, / Though to itself"—so I, it's mostly, I mean there's a, there's a um, some sort of parallelism.

3

//read ll. 1–4 with l. 2: "They do not do the thing they most do show." and l. 4: "Unmoved, cold, and to tempsation slow."// Ok, first quatrain we're talking about uh um (sigh) attitude and action I guess. "They that have pow'r to do hurt and will do none." "To do hurt," nice uh emphasis there. "And will do none, / That do not do the things they most do show." "That do not do the thing they most do show." It sounds—"Who, moving others, are themselves as stone"—unmoved, coldly—"Unmoved, cold, and to temptation slow"—oh man.

4

//read ll. 5–8// It does seem, I mean it seems to be a poem about power, and it does seem to suggest something uh, uh lordly about the execution, power to the extent that you don't need to um actually act. Your very presence is so strong that if, it acts upon others and forces them to do the um uh, whatever work is to be done. I suppose it, there's some suggestion of a uh, of a cruel lover, at least that's the thing I, just because it's a Shakespeare sonnet but uh it's not there specifically.

5

But then there's the image of the lilies at the end and you, of course recall lilies of the, lilies of the field, so there, themselves—but then lilies do not have the power to do hurt. That's the uh, the issue seems to be not, not lilies of the field, um who don't, who labor not, um, but uh something beyond that where's there's power, malignant, potentially malignant power that isn't used as, is not an active, uh it doesn't act itself but it only causes others to react.

6

"They rightly do inherit heaven's graces / And husband nature's riches from expense." Second quatrain, that sounds tremendously ironic, it's sar-, sardonic perhaps. //read ll. 6–8//

7

. . . Hum. I see. Well then you have //read ll. 9–12, repeat 11–12// Ok, we're talking about a certain kind of purity then all the way through, um in other words the effect you have on the, on the uh outer world, one thing can have on the uh outer world, something defined by its presence in the world, um because of the, for instance "summer's flow'r is to the summer sweet," its quality is, is based on its relationship to the rest of the world, "Though to itself it only live and die," in other words it's uh um, it's a passive agent.

8

//read ll. 11 – 14 with 1. 12: "The bravest weed, the basest weed outbraves his dignity."//   But are we saying that the, it doesn't seem to me that the, what's being talked about are sweet, sweetness, it's the line, that, "That do not do the thing they most do show," in other words it's, it's not simply they, they have the, that they're not acting upon their power to harm but that they're showing somehow the power to harm. That doesn't seem, I mean that line is the one in that first quatrain that bothers me, otherwise the first quatrain falls together uh with the, with the last, with the third quatrain.

9

"Who, moving others, are themselves as stone, / Unmoved, cold, and to temptation slow," and then uh um "They are the lords and owners of their faces, / Others but stewards of their excellence." So somehow they're the uh, they're the aristocracy of the earth somehow and of course there always, there is all that idea of aristocracy uh in the \"Lilies that fester smell far worse than weeds," in the sense of uh um a ruler gone seriously wrong, uh, or a, an aristocrat who'd gone seriously wrong is a far worse thing than a, than a weed, just by the simply purity. Of course that's reversing the idea, those "that have pow'r to do hurt and will do none," um w-, in other words they are the ones who uh, when they s-, take it in their hands to move //read ll. 4 – 6 with 1. 6: "And husband's nature, And husband nature's riches from expense." repeat l. 6// is another problem line for me. "Husband nature's riches from expense; / They are the lords and owners of their faces."

10

Well this time I'm going to s-, going to scan the poem right away, or fairly soon, just because, for Shakespeare it is always a good idea. Find something to uh balance this on. Ok. "Théy that háve pów'r to dó húrt," //read and scan poem with l. 4: Únmóv'd, cold, unmóvèd, heh, I'm not sure, Unmóv'd, cold, and to temptation slow; and l. 5: "They rightly do inherit heaven's graces" Feminine.//

11

Ok, "Théy that have pów'r to do," "Théy that have pów'r to dó húrt and wíll do nóne." God, that's an interesting line. "They thát have pów'r to dó húrt," "They that have pów'r to dó húrt," "Théy that have pów'r," all right. This first line, I was trying to break it up into actual feet. I'm not sure where the first foot is, that's the problem. It seems like "Théy that have." Ok, it's "Théy that have pów'r to do," "pów'r to dó húrt and wíll do nóne." Two, four, five, ok that's a pentameter verse so it's trochee trochee um, two stress, what is a two stress, can't re-, well double stress, "dó húrt," iamb and then a double stress, "do none."

12

And then a perfect iambic pentameter line, "That dó not dó the thíngs they móst do shów." Then, again an interesting, "Whó, móving óthers, aŕe themsélves as stóne." Ok, one, two, ok so double stress. "Who, móving óthers, are themsélves as stóne, / Unmov'd, cold," "Unmóvèd, cóld, and tó, temptátion slów." Ok, so, I think we're going to have to say "Unmovèd," there, gives you five pure feet. //read ll. 5–7// "They are the," "the lords and," oh well, "Théy are the lórds and ówners óf their fáces." . . . Ok well that's interesting, 'cause that's like "Théy ríghtly do inhérit heaven's gráces." These feminine lines seem to have reversed the iambic pattern, to a uh um dactylic pattern. "Théy rightly dó inhérit héaven's gráces." But anyway. Um, I don't know, for some reason I feel fairly uninspired right now so I think I'm going to uh shut off and come back to it later.

13

Ok Thursday, 5:30 P.M. Read the poem again here. //read poem with l. 12: "That basest weed outbraves his dignity."// Ok, now that's one thing um. We've got, they're all natural images in this. Uh you move from stone, uh "Unmoved, cold, and to temptation slow," to uh someone who rightly husbands, "And husbands nature's riches from expense." Ok. And then uh, and then in the last quatrain, ok that first quatrain stone, second quatrain, uh there are the husbanders of nature. In the third quatrain uh we talk about the uh um "summer's flow'r," so we get, go from stone to husbandman to, to uh //read ll. 9–14, with "ok" after l. 12//

14

Ok now what occurs to me is that maybe they uh um, um, there's a gardener image. Ok um, garden and gardener, uh all, and they "husband nature's riches," "They rightly do inherit heaven's grace / And husband nature's riches," "nature's riches from expense." Ok from loss. In other words they conserve nature's riches and uh that metaphor is followed through in uh "The summer's flow'r is to the summer sweet,"

15

um and, "But if" to that, "if that flow'r with base infection meet, / The basest weed outbraves his dignity." In others words uh um, um, if that flower is not well tended, the "basest weed" who is uh, uh, uh, in other words a flower is more, is more subject to infection in some ways than a base weed, it's more likely to uh um, to be given up to disease or, or problem, uh and a, the "basest weed" just in its own uh purity uh, outbraves the dignity of a, of a, of a blown, not a blown but a uh, a diseased flower. Ok so we're talking uh, I think this all is larger, it's all a larger metaphor for reflection upon human nature of course, um.

16

But it's a, it's a strange movement because it's, there's something, it seems very ironic or sarcastic or something about the opening quatrain. //read ll. 1–4// Ok, it's uh, it's kind of interesting 'cause that first quatrain um, there's a lot of movement, "That do not do the thing they most do show," for instance. It, in the, on the one hand it's making a statement that uh, of, of not doing, of being passive, but the meter itself is fairly, is a fairly active in uh just the wording, "dó not dó the thing they most dó show," uh, is uh, is surprising, um, that is surprisingly a-, uh um active, I don't know what other word uh, you know frantic maybe. Uh, and then "Who, moving others, are themselves as stone, / Unmoved, cold, and to temptation slow." Ok that seems to uh um, I don't know, it sort of slows it down I guess. But uh, so we have a very static and not, the tone is not clear at all.

17

They have no power, "They that have pow'r to do hurt and will do none," we're talking about a certain kind of aristocracy clearly because uh "moving others are themselves as stone, / Unmoved, cold, and to temptation slow." Ok we have a um, a questionable, a, a somehow a, a, uh unclear tone, and then we move into uh "They rightly do inherit heaven's graces," and husband's nature, "And husband nature's riches from expense." Ok. "They rightly do inherit heaven's graces." Uh "They rightly do," um uh, they're invested with a certain beauty I think, you know the, uh, like a lily, in other words. In other words uh we're given some sort of outward manifestation of their inner, inner quality of, of, of aristocracy, uh. "And husband nature's riches from expense." Ok uh, they by virtue of their, of their nature um hoard the riches of nature, in other words certain uh inner qualities um, of which the power to do hurt in um, and uh, and will do none seems to be one. In other words uh um, power of action, a power to do hurt though, that's a, I mean there's the uh, uh for all the positiveness of this quality it's, we're talking about the power to do hurt as the basic, as the basic premise. We're not talking about love or, or uh friendship or anything else, it's the power to do hurt, it's, so of course that is aristocratic, in the sense that uh power is the ultimate privilege of the aristocracy, the ultimate uh uh, a weapon too of the aristocracy, uh, the only privilege of the aristocracy, (sigh) I don't know, that's again marxist,

18

uh, at least in Shakesp-, uh uh, of course then you have that Renaissance, you, uh the Renaissance world view, your Tillyard-esque uh idea of the hierarchy which is, to a certain extent this is some sort of uh, uh, uh discussion of the hierarchy though you start with the (laugh) I, it's the, the irony, I mean, he's comparing it to a stone, uh and a stone is the lowest of inanimate, a-, animate objects on that sort of a uh, on the scale, um.

19

And uh, ok, so we have, but anyway we have, so we have aristocratic notion in //read ll. 6–8// Ok again, uh the aristocratic idea, uh "Others but stewards of their excellence." In other words their excellence is such that it radiates off them and others are more or less uh um, are in some sense uh um, uh the keepers of it. They aren't themselves the keepers, the keepers of it, as is um um shown in the line "The summer's flow'r is to the summer sweet, / Though" it "to itself it only live and die." Which actually is a beautiful way that those two quatrains, the second and third quatrains, um um uh uh interplay with each other.

20

"The summer's flow'r" but again we have "The summer's flow'r is to the summer sweet, / Though to itself it only live and die." Ok, "But if that flow'r," and then suddenly we've moved away, we're moving into a question of a, of a, which has not come up before uh anywhere of the question of, of some sort of infection, and we've moved several steps away from the question of aristocracy, and moved it to some much more um universal image in the summer's flower uh, "Though to itself it only live and die." Um, again that's, there's that, the thing of uh um, not knowing yourself but, or not being the beneficiary yourself of "heaven's graces" but uh um, giving, your benefit is for the world, to its, to yourself you're only un um, uh you know, one more creature, uh.

21

"But" uh "if that flow'r with base infection meet," And then suddenly we're back into the terms, aris-, aristocratic terms when before we're talking about flower as some sort of a uh, I mean a flower is a flower. "But if that flow'r with base infection meet," the brav-, "The basest weed outbraves his dignity." Ok, so suddenly we have a, a real class consciousness arrive out of this, this otherwise perfectly natural image and, and suddenly uh nature is, is set up hierarchically, um, but set up with an interesting difference in that uh "The basest weed" in, in some sense is pure to itself, um uh, more pure than, than a flower, than the, the, an aristocrat who falls falls further and harder, I suppose. The higher you are the harder you fall I guess, you know Richard the Second type of uh, of uh um, attitude perhaps. But the, but it's, so there's a, a sense of a moral hierarchy, a n-, a moral aristocracy is I think, actually that probably is it, it's a moral aristocracy that we're talking about. He's using the language of a, of a, of a um, of aristocrat, of, of power, natural power, but it suddenly is turned into a moral question.

22

And um I was going to say that uh it seems to me that the comparison of the summer's flower, showing its sweetness to the summer, what does that have to do with those that, "They that have pow'r to hurt and will do none," 'cause that's a very worldly uh, a worldly um, um description somewhat, a real, a very realistic factor and it's, it uh, um, uh it is not like the metaphor of a "summer's flow'r is to the summer sweet, / Though to itself it only live and die." Uh ok. "But if that flow'r with base infection meet, / The basest weed outbraves his dignity." And "For sweetest," and so, so suddenly we have a moral question and then the quatrain of course really, really pulls all those things together. "For sweetest things turn sourest by their deeds," ok, "Lilies that fester smell far worse than weeds." In other words "Lilies that fester" uh festering is in itself a deed, ok, moral turpitude is in itself an act, ok, or that's the question uh, I mean that's the, that's the answer in some ways that uh, a descent into moral turpitude is in itself an act, it's, it's the power to do hurt, it's an, it's some sort of um, uh manifestation of the power to do hurt.

23

So uh, "For sweetest things turn sourest by their deeds," uh, "Lilies that fester smell far worse than weeds." And or course we have the aristocratic connotations of lily, not only the um uh, uh the fleur-de-lis of France but we also have uh uh the lilies of the field in the Bible, and if I had a Bible with me I would look up that passage, but um, uh, i-, so it has the, the double, the lilies carries actually uh, carries the symbolism of the, of the poem beautifully because uh it refers to a temporal authority, uh inimicable actually to the English at this point, the French, and uh um, to also the most classic uh um, piece of uh biblical quotation about husbanding a perfect grace, uh, in uh, look at the lilies of the field who toil not uh nor do they, what, actually it's, toil not nor do they . . . (sigh) I can't remember. Heh. God, that's shameful. But uh, so anyway that's, that's really very nice.

24

So that's, the structure um, you start out with this um, um, with a very odd tone towards "They that have the pow'r to do hurt and will do none." Because it seems to me uh, well maybe it's just for me but uh um, uh I suppose everyone has the power to, to hurt but uh it's, there's some, there is some s-, sense of the aristocrat involved, some sense of uh, of the uh, you get some idea of noblesse oblige being ironically uh brought in here, or sarcastically brought in, I don't know, I, it's, I'm pretty sure that there's, the tone is unclear anyway for the first quatrain because uh, you have "Who, moving others, are themselves as stone," Unmov'd, eh, "Unmoved, cold, and to temptation slow." That's not a very positive way to talk about, about anything, and it's certainly is uh, stands in stark contrast to the summer f-, "summer's flow'r" who's "to the summer sweet." The summer flower is not "unmoved, cold, and to temptation slow." I mean there is, those are not the qualities that you would necessarily associate with it.

25

But uh um, um, nonetheless they, they, they hook up, ok because um "Unmoved, cold, and to temptation slow," It's like the walls of the garden I think uh they "are themselves as stone" uh keeping up the garden image, they are the, they are, they are external um face

26

even though he says "That do not do the thing they most do show," which to me is a problem line and I'm not sure exactly how to um.

SIDE 2

I was saying "They do not do" the things, um, well, maybe it's recording now. Ok, what I was saying uh, "That do not do the thing they most do show," it seems to me is a problem line because uh, it really seems to work if you talk about, first if you talk about the stone wall of the garden uh, again that's a progression into the poem, in a way. You start with the metaphor of they "that do not," "that have pow'r to hurt and will do none, / That do not," "That do not do the thing they most do show." Ok what is it that, that they most do show? Uh probably power, potential power. But it still, it doesn't, it uh, I still have problems with this, uh, uh.

27

"Who, moving others, are themselves as stone, / Unmoved, cold, and to temptation slow." Ok, uh what I'm saying is that the uh um, is that they themselves is, their, their exter-, is their external um, uh features, their face, their façade, is of, is as of stone, i.e.: the stone walls of a garden. We move inside the stone wall and uh, and we look upon a garden, ok. "They rightly do inherit heaven's graces / And husband nature's riches from expense." Inside this uh forbidding wall uh suggesting the power of I suppose an old medieval castle or something, all the associations you have with walls and the, and the person who built them, that being a sign of power perhaps, a wall being a sign of possession or power. "They rightly do inherit heaven's graces / And husbands nature's riches from expense," Ok. And inside, they're, they're in the process of, their, their inner spirit, they're husbanding uh nature's riches from expense or from loss um, from uh useless expenditure.

28

Uh, what is it, that sonnet, uh um, waste of spirit, the one about sex basically, is ah, about the tremendous uh waste of spirit that lust, i-, i-, is um, that's what this one reminds me of, um. God these things, I've just been away from them for so long, I can't none of the quotes will come back to me, but um, oh, well, no way, ok, um.

29

"Husband nature's riches from expense; / They are the lords and owners of their faces." Ok, they are the lords of this whole situation. "Others but stewards of their excellence." Ok and that tends to reflect or that tends to set up the idea, uh, k-, picks up the idea, "Who, moving others, are themselves as stone," is expanded to "They are the lords and owners of their faces, / Others but stewards of their excellence." So it's no longer um a question of their, what, what it is they're moving, it's not an amoral turn, amoral idea, moving others, we're now moving to "stewards of their excellence," so we've moved inside um, moved uh beyond just the amoral question of power to some sort uh of spiritual question. So "They are the lords and owners of their faces, / Others but stewards of their excellence." So there's some moral quality, ok, some moral purity that seems to be suggested, and uh um, this new comparison of uh, of a moral, a moral excellence or some sort of excellence is communicated to others but um, uh, it's not necessarily theirs uh within their own person, i.e. he's not, um,

30

well actually that doesn't come, that, that particular suggestion doesn't come until the third quatrain when it says "The summer's flow'r is to the summer sweet, / Though to itself it only live and die." That actually makes the idea a little more complex in that, that we don't really have the sense that they are, that to, "to itself it only live and die," um, except for the idea they "are themselves as stone, / Unmoved, cold, and to temptation slow." In other words somehow there's um, uh, it's some s-, and I guess it's paradoxically that their perceptions are, or that their excellence is such that uh um, they don't s-, they don't understand their own, their own greatness or their, their own uh perfection. It's not something that they're necessarily aware of, and certainly, you know, in accord with ideas of humility I suppose.

31

But uh uh, but then finally at the end of the, in the final um two lines in the third quatrain, "But if that flow'r with base infection meet, / The basest weed outbraves his dignity." Ok so we've moved from stone to the, to the gardener to the element of the garden itself, which is now I think, we're not talking about the whole person but we're talking about the spirit, um, the spirit inside this, this wall of stone and so forth. "If that flow'r with base infection meet," if that spirit is diseased, ok, "The basest weed outbraves" the dignity of an, of an aristocratic spirit or some excellent spirit that has fallen into disease.

32

"For sweetest things turn sourest by their deeds." "Sweetest," sweet and sour, that's uh um, that picks up the uh, if sun-, "summer's flow'r is to the summer sweet," "sweetest things turn sourest by their deeds; / Lilies that fester smell far worse than weeds." Ok so we connect um, uh a moral process with a very physical uh, an idea of physical decay, ok, moral and physical decay, and the idea of "Lilies that fester smell far worse than weeds," is uh um, is beautiful in that way. "Fester smell far worse," "fester," "fester" is a great word.

33

Ah, ok, uh, and that to a certain extent, I mean I'm not sure what else I can, what else I can come up with. Let met just read through the poem again and, and see if uh um, anything else occurs to me, if not I think I'll probably uh turn off once more and maybe give it another try. But uh I can't believe it's, it seems more accessible now to me than it probably should. Ok.   //read poem//

34

Ok let's see if uh um the meter gives me anything new. I scanned it before, of course. Um, you have some strong uh . . . ok you have "They that," line one. "They rightly," uh again strong stress, um . . . ok, opening, the stress on the opening line happens in line one, three, (sigh) maybe four, but I think, but one, three, five, seven, and then eight. "Others but stewards of their excellence." And then uh it doesn't happen at all uh in the third quatrain and it doesn't happen again actually until the, the final line of the couplet. "Lilies that fester," that uh, which is the same as "They that have power," "Lilies that fester," "to do hurt," "They that have pow'r to do hurt," "They that have pow'r to do hurt and will do none."

35

Ok that's uh, the, the meter I think is the most interesting in the opening lines. "They that have pow'r to dó húrt," double accent, "and will do none," "and wíll dó none," "and will dó none" —could be that way either, also. "That dó not dó the thíng they móst do shów," again that's a sort of an off accent on "do none," "do show," um, at the end of that line. "Moving others,"   //read and scan ll. 3–8//

36

Ok now that makes some sense, that the strong accents on "They" coming up three times in the first two quatrains because uh you're talking about them as it were, uh, and you're still sort of within the human world in the first two quatrains but in the third quatrain with the "summer's flow'r," suddenly you're out of the, the um, world of identifiable individuals and into um uh qualities as it were, 'cause the "summer's flow'r" it seems to me is, you're talking much more about a quality than, the flower is, is necessarily a metaphor for a specific human existence. So we'll see how that, I'm not exactly sure how that works but we'll, but we'll see, um.

37

"Though to itself it only live and die; / But if that flow'r with base," You know, that's a, there's "pow'r to do," "flow'r . . . to," there's a lot of uh trochaic uh, uh, feet in this poem really. There's a lot of irregularity. I mean it's not a, it's not the straight, it's not the straight poem, but I'm not, I don't see a pattern. They that are, "They are the lords and owners of their faces, / Others but stewards," "are themselves as stone." //read ll. 4–7// "Others but stewards," "Théy are the lords," "Óthers but stewards," "The summer's flow'r is to the summer sweet." "Tó the," "tó the," "tó do," a lot more uh of those kind of feet for sure. "But if that flow'r with base infection meet." Um, I don't see any really — "Unmoved, cold, and to temptation slow; / They rightly do inherit heaven's graces." Ok and of course "heaven's graces" go well in a garden, um all in all. //read ll. 6 – 8, 11 – 14 with "uh" after l. 13// No I don't think, I'm going to turn off for a while. I don't seem to be getting any further.

38

Uh Friday 12 noon around. One more, one more look at the poem I think here. //read poem// Actually there's one thing that I see this time that didn't, that didn't really occur to me. It seems as if it's an indictment of the whole world of action, uh which actually is what that uh, uh lilies of the field passage in the Bible is more or less about. Somehow action in itself uh seems to be corrupt in this vision of the world, which may be why um the opening quatrain is so, is so sarcastic, or so uh um, not sarcastic, sardonic, again. I still, I, the tone, the opening tone still escapes, I don't have a proper way to describe it but um, we're talking about the exercise of power in the opening um, opening quatrain.

39

The thing is that uh um, "base infection," a flower meeting with "base infection" is not specifically the c-, a case of "sweetest things turn sourest by their deeds." It's uh um, it seems like it's more um, uh it's outside the flower's, the flower's power as it were. But uh um, again we're talking about the flower, if we see the flower as a spirit reference and not the whole being reference, then the, the whole idea of uh, um, of uh uh power, the use of power corrupting, corrupting the spirit um, still stays more or less intact, and uh um, uh the wielding of power is in itself the corruption of the spirit, I think is what I would, is what I would finally come down to,

40

and uh again the lilies, the lilies representing both the uh the lilies of the field and the fleur-de-lis of, of uh um, of uh the Plantagenets I guess, uh France. Uh let's see. And that would go along with "That do not do the thing they most do show."

41

Ok the opening of the poem is a very clear discussion of power um and it's, and actually the three quatrains are uh, we move from power to the relationship between power and spirit uh "They rightly do inherit heaven's graces," in the second quatrain and then the discussion of the spirit itself in the third quatrain. And then uh um, the issue of power and spirit um are summarized in "For sweetest things turn sourest by their deeds." Ok, power, lily that s-, "smell far worse," "Lilies that fester smell far worse than weeds," the spiritual conse- quences. Ok that, I, I think that that, that's, that makes good sense to me as a reading really.

42

//read ll. 6 – 8// There's that sense of multiplicity. We go "They," "They," "They," in the first two quatrains, and then the singular in the third, third qua- train. That's an interesting point that I hadn't noticed before. And you of course don't have any of the strong opening line accents like "They that have pow'r" and "Who, moving," "They rightly do inherit," "They are the lords," and so forth, "Others," uh, all those opening um, uh, what's the reverse of iamb. God I've lost so much of this uh, my technical vocabulary. Um so that's a, we move from a plural to a singular um, uh the first two quatrains to the singular,

43

and that's interesting 'cause there is sort of a movement from the uh, from the real to the abstra-, I mean real, from the real metaphor for the real word, world, to metaphor for the uh, for the abstract, in other words a metaphor for the real world uh, well we have the real world. "They that have the pow'r to do hurt and will do none," "do none." Then in the second quatrain we move to a um, um, a metaphor for the uh, a large, a larger metaphor for this uh um, uh, real world, i.e. They husband heaven's graces. They suddenly become gardeners of their, of their virtues. And then in the third quatrain it suddenly, we have the spirit and it's almost as if it's a single immutable um thing, it's almost a metaphor for a metaphor, the s-, I mean "The summer's flow'r," um, a metaphor for the um, for what the soul need here which is um, in itself a-, an abstract. So there is a real movement through these three quatrains, and the discussion, it evolves from the um uh purely uh uh mundane discussion of power, mundane really in the sense of "are themselves as stone," to um, moving to the garden idea uh, and a more, and a, and a mi-, middle-level abstraction, the, the, the garden actually it's sort of half way to pastoral, isn't it. And uh, and then we get all the way to a pastoral image or to a uh elysian, uh or Platonic image, ok. It's sort of like you go from uh um real world to pastoral to Platonic in the three quatrains um, if that's uh, although it's not really Platonic because we're talking about the summer flower, "summer's flow'r is to the summer sweet," it's still uh um response to the husbanding image somehow.

44

They all interconnect very nicely, and again the idea of the stone or the garden, un they're not explicitly connected to make up the components of a garden 'cause we just have a reference to a stone, you have a respite, a reference to nature, to "husband nature's riches" and uh a reference to the summer flower, these things don't actually add up to a garden but they interconnect by an upper-level association I mean a, in a more abstract level association of uh, of uh ideas.

45

And the, the chain of um, of uh the progress of the poem tends to reinforce that I think with "They that have" the "pow'r to do hurt," and then "They rightly do inherit heaven's graces," and then "The summer's flow'r is to the summer sweet." Those three opening lines of the first, of the quatrains um, all uh um, really delineate the schema, I mean the uh the schema of, of the kinds of images that get used and they, it changes very significantly from one quatrain to the next I think and, and progresses in a way that I've been talking. . . .

46

But there's still that vegetative sense, it's still all done in, in the early Shake-spearean style of uh well Richard the Second or the, or One Henry the Four, uh Henry the Fourth and things where garden imagery, the, the garden, the, the rank, the base garden, it reminds me of uh, of that passage in the um, yeah it's Richard the Second where uh, uh the Queen and, and one of her attendants comes out in the garden, as they're talking and uh, and uh uh, uh he uses the uh, it's clear that Richard is not husbanding "nature's riches from expense" and that's exactly the terms in which the gardeners are talking about it, um, and it relates to a number of other things of that nature. John of Gaunt, John of Gaunt. Ok well I think that's it, I mean as far as I'm concerned for the time being.

CARLOS: "A BALLAD OF DREAMLAND"

1

Ok first reading of the poem, ah, 9:15 Monday night. //read poem with: chuckle after 1. 3; 1. 4: Under the rose I hid my — Under the roses I hid my heart; 1. 8: Only the songs of a secret bird; 1. 9: Lie still, I said, for the wing's wind — wind's wing closes; 1. 15: What bids the lid of thy sleep depart?; 1. 24: Only the song of a secret vird — bird; 1. 27: Of true love's truth and or of love — light love's art.// Ok. These feminine rhyme, these feminine endings with, and the rhyme "is," "dozes," "snow's is," "dozes," "grows is," "roses," "closes," and "closes" really — heh — I don't like offhand. Um, let's try it once more though.

2

//read poem with: 1. 9: Lie still, I said, for the wing-wind's wing closes; 1. 10: And mild leaves muffle the keens sun's dart; 1. 14: Does the f- st- fang still fret thee of hope deferred?; 1. 15: What bids the lids of thy sn- sleep depart?; 1. 22: And sleep's are all, sleep's are the tunes in its tree-tops heard; 1. 23: No hound no, No hound's note wakens the wildwood hart.// Ok. Um.

3

//read ll. 1 – 4// Ok, um. It seems like, it seems pretty certain that it's the poem of a lover, um, hiding his heart, ok we start with a, uh, um, an image of um a strong fantastical image: hiding one's heart in a nest of roses, "Out of the sun's way, hidden apart." Um (chuckle) immediately I think of it sticking on a bunch of thorns but uh, um, we'll accept it as, as, as potentially ambiguous but a nest of roses, of rose petals maybe. "In a softer bed than . . . soft white snow's is." Ok that's "roses" and "snow's is" are, uh, that horrible rhyme links the two things and you have red versus white, possibly passion versus purity. Um, "Under the roses I hid my heart," with a cover of passion, with a cover of, of roses rather than a cover of uh soft white snow perhaps.

4

//read ll. 5 – 8// Um, ok, in other words, um, something has awakened the heart. And we have the connection between sleep fluttering his wings and the secret bird, we've got two bird images. And uh why "never a leaf of the rose-tree stirred?" Um, a rose tree. All right, it would s-, it complicates the image of the, of the roses a little further with the, uh, a rose tree is not strictly speaking, you could have an arbor, but uh maybe this is a, the exigencies uh of the meter, I'm not sure, let me go on anyway.

5

"Lie uh Lie still, I said, for the wind's wing closes,   /   And mild leaves muffle the keen sun's dart." //repeat ll. 9–10// Ok one more of the uh personifica-tion, uh bird-like personifications for the wind. And "mild leaves," ok we're back to the leaves, "muffle the keen sun's dart." Uh (cough) relatively self-explanatory though I have a, uh, um, excuse me I have to kill a mosquito. "Lie still . . . for the" ok uh "And mild leaves muffle the keen sun's dart." I don't know, there's something about this that, that irritates me 'cause I mean, um — roses are always on the outskirts, on the, on the outside on a bush — um, not uh, the leaves don't hide the uh, the blossoms though I mean it's a more uh the image, it makes it more of a ac-, a cryptic, more hidden um quality to the uh, to the heart.

6

"For the wind on the warm sea dozes." Ok, the wind is off on the warm sea. "And the wind is unquieter yet than thou art.   —   Does a thought in thee still as a thorn's wound smart?" Ok, roses, "Does the fang still fret thee of hope deferred?" Uh, the fang of hope deferred. "What bids the lid of thy sleep depart?   —   Only the song of a secret bird." Well. "The green land's name that a charm encloses,   —   It never was writ in the traveller's chart." Ok, it's what is it? Ok, the land that encloses the charm was never, ok, the green land, ok, the soil in which something is, is planted, what, ah, clearly some sort of reference to uh, uh to a lover or something, I'm not sure. Was never "writ in the traveller's chart,   /   And sweet on its trees as the fruit that grows is,   /   It never was sold in the merchant's mart." Ok. "The swallows of dreams through its dim fields dart." Um, more bird imagery. //read ll. 22–28// Ok, uh.

7

Ok, well the, *The Romance of the Rose* is clearly the thing that, that, that comes to mind, so I'll, I'm, I should probably go to external things to try to pull this together, together because the, uh, uh, the symbolism doesn't seem to be, um, well I don't know.

8

Uh, ok. "I hid my heart in a nest of roses." Ok, now what is "a nest of roses"? The rose uh, symbolized the vir-, in, in *The Romance of the Rose*, of course, was the, the uh, the flower of the loved, of the beloved, the uh, uh, the love of the beloved, however anatomically you want to uh, um, interpret it, um.

9

"In a softer bed than the soft white snow's is,   /   Under the roses I hid my heart." Ok, um, we're dealing with a, a dreamland that's a, a garden inhabited by a lot of birds, uh with a, um, uh the forces all tend to be personified as birds. "Only the song of a" and uh, but there's something, there's some disruption in this, in this perfect, this perfect uh uh paradise. Uh, a secret bird. Ok, some secret force, in other words, because everything else, every other natural force seems to be personified as a bird, then this secret bird is also some sort of uh, uh, uh, a natural force. Ok, uh, you know, could be anything like uh, um, love, something of that ilk.

10

(cough) Ok. "Lie still, I said, for the wind's wing closes," in other words the win- //read ll. 10—16// Ok uh, second stanza, um . . . second stanza is clearly the uh, lets you in that it's uh um, a lover's heart that's being hidden away and it's being hidden away in, for some sort of, uh uh, healing purposes it seems um, uh, which is o-, odd, the whole business of, of the heart being a, of, laid on a nest of roses, um, in a nest of roses, under roses, hiding it among roses, is a curious piece of sym-, uh, symbolism perhaps suggesting that uh, um, uh, I don't know (chuckle), what is the heart slumbering or uh I mean I could say that uh it would be difference between uh, uh, some sort of light passion and true love but that's um, uh, that idea's proscribed by the uh, the Envoi, so um.

//read ll. 16—20//   Ok so we move from, all right, move, start with, start with the uh, uh description of the h-, of the position of the heart and where it uh, um and the fact that it seems to be uh, um, having a little trouble of it can't sta-, it can't stay asleep, um, something is bothering it, the song of a secret bird. The second half it's clear that it's a, I mean the se- second stanza it's clear that the, the heart is a um, is affected, the poet's, the narrator's heart is affected by uh, um, by love, uh, uh unrequited love, similar ok to the, to the position of the lover in uh, in uh *Romance of the Rose*, um, and uh um . . . b-, but uh, uh, uh it's, the thing is th-, th-, that's sort of somewhat denied by the, the way the refrain is only the song of a secret bird, is set up, 'cause you say "Only the song of a," "What bids the lids of thy sleep . . .   /   Only the song of a secret bird," as if the problem, uh, of the heart or whatever it is that's waking up the heart uh is com-, uh purely contained in the song, uh i-, in the song of a secret bird.

12

//read ll. 17—20//   Um.   //read ll. 21—24 with: 1. 23: No hound's note wakens the, how, wildwood hart; 1. 24: Only the songs of a secret bird.   //   Ok, so we move away from that question back into the, the garden, uh, much more, um, uh, specifically um, uh, well, defined there, we, you get the green land and the trees, um, all ah somehow separated, clearly separated from reality and uh, um. "The swallows of dreams through its dim fields dart,   /   And sleep's are the tunes in its tree-tops heard." Ok sleep's again are, uh sleep is again personified as a, as a bird, uh in the same way as uh, the sleep flutter, "What made sleep flutter his wings and part." "No hound's note wakens the wildwood hart,   /   Only the" uh, ok, heart and hart, wildwood, um, hart, "Only the song of a secret bird."

13

Ok, and the Envoi, instead, uh, seems to be addressing itself instead of the traditional, to the lovers, uh, in the, more in the Eustache Deschamps line of thinking this seems to be addressing itself to the reader, uh, for the sake of uh explanation, um. //read ll. 25—28// Ok. //read ll. 25—28// Um, ok so, uh, the question is what kind of success is this dreamer having in this world, um.

14

I don't know. Um, it does, it seems to me off ha-, I mean, a slight conceit, uh, very uh, uh, highly ornamented, um, and I'm not sure, uh, I guess, what the ornamentation is, why the ornamentation is there, what exactly its purpose is, aside from being highly poetical, um, and pretty, uh, which it is — pretty, the uh, the language is very uh, is very affecting, uh. "In a softer bed than the soft white snow's is." Repetition gets used a lot. "I hid my heart in a nest of roses, / Out of the sun's way." "Hid my heart," "hidden apart," "softer bed than the soft white snow, snow's is, / Under the roses I hid my heart." Uh ...ok... We have a lot of wings... But I still, "For the wind on the warm sea dozes, / And the wind is unquieter yet than thou art." Ok, "Does the st-" // read ll. 13–16 // Um there's something that, uh, it seems almost too facile to me uh, "bids the lids of thy sleep depart." Um, meditation on um, uh, uh a fantastical, and certainly I, I mean, the language sets that up, um sets up the idea of a ballad, uh, a ballade actually, ah, again like Deschamps or uh Marie de France, or uh those people, uh, in that tradition, um, which, as, Swinburne being the uh, uh, being pre-Raphaelite oriented, that's, that's, that, uh, I mean that all makes sense, and uh, and that actually tends to make me mistrust the uh, any deeper meanings that the poet may uh, that, I might want to try to mine out of the poem that may not be here, there's more uh, uh decorative than, than uh, uh, a specifically evocative uh um imagery.

15

But uh — ok, so, um, but we've still got "roses / Out of the sun's way," um ... //read ll. 4–6 stopping at "rose-tree"// Rose-tree, what is it, rose-tree, is that a, um, conscious or an unconscious uh, of use of that? "O-, Only th- song of a secret bird." Ok, there's a conscious, a conscious um, ambiguity I think in the use of "Only the song of a secret bird," in other words uh um, you have a very uh um, beautiful image of a, of a um, "the song of a secret bird" somehow hidden in this mass of rose, roses, and rosebu-, rosebushes, that are, um, seems to be singing to the, to the heart, singing to the heart of this uh of S-, of uh Swinburne, and uh, or of the poet, and there, there is something to be said for uh the garden is traditionally, um, um, the uh uh, the delineation of the ima- of the, of the poetic imagination, that's what the pastoral can be seen as, is some sort of a, a realm for the imagi-, to which the imagination can retreat and, and enjoy its pastoral um pleasures and certainly, uh, Swinburne is, is, is, is trying to revivify that conventional idea, um, uh, with the uh um, um idea of "I hid my heart in a nest of roses" ok "Out of the sun's way" uh in other words his heart that the ef- effective uh uh, sentiment, uh, sentimental or or, um, yeah I guess it's simply sentiment, um, organ of sentiment, um, is being hidden by the imagination uh in a pastoral setting, "Out of the sun's way," um, "In a softer bed than the soft white snow," "Under the roses I hid my heart," um, so we start with "*in* a nest of roses," and then we have "*Under* the roses," and then we have go f- further go under the leaves, um ... which seems, which actually if, if any, anybody who knows anything about *roses* knows that the leaves are always, are usually down below uh the blossoms. So um, uh, it seems to be sort of a retreat of, of the heart, it seems to recede further and further into the uh, um, uh foliage so to speak, uh.

16

And uh, um, oh the powers again being referred to as, as as birds, uh, for instance the wind, uh, closing its wings, sleep, fluttering his wings, um, uh, and wind uh um, sitting on the, sitting on the ocean which is uh um, uh, and "The swallows of dreams through its uh, uh, dim fields dart," uh, uh, can't think of, I was trying to think of a parallel, I can't really think of anything that this uh reminds me of, except that it seems to um, the personification of all these things as birds, uh, again seems uh, um, uh, uh anachronizing in some way, uh.

17

We have the sun, "mild leaves," "mild leaves muffle the keen sun's dart," um, in other words the sun's dart, we can, uh, if we give the, give uh credence to a pun on "sun" or even, even without we can think of uh, um, the God of Love, or Cupid the son of Venus um, with his darts certainly appropriate in uh, in this context, um, shooting arrows at the, at the uh um, at th-, at the heart. Hidden underneath the roses, underneath the, underneath "mild leaves."

18

And then "Does a thought in thee still as a thorn's wound smart?" Oh — in other words the song of a secret bird somehow is trying to reanimate, um, the sleeping heart, uh, it won't leave the uh, the imag-, the heart in this, in this uh beautiful old garden uh completely alone, uh.

19

//read ll. 17–20// Ok, now is that all uh one large periphrasis, is this a statement that we're in dreamland, that we're uh in a, an exotic um, um realm? I think, I think so. Uh an exotic dream like that, you know separate from, from ordinary reality in every way, uh, and people buy nothing, um uh except, uh, um, birds, uh "The swallows of dreams," "sleep's," uh the songs of sleep, the tunes in the, in it's tree-tops and uh the s-, um the song of a secret bird.

20

Ok. //read ll. 25–28// Ok only the inner, the inner uh workings of the, of the spirit, because clearly that bird is lodged in there with the heart in the uh, in the depth of all that foliage and uh, and vegetation of one kind or another, the uh, external symbols of, of passion and love um, actually hiding, hiding his heart. Uh, what exactly those, the roses refer to, um I really am not sure,

21

so I'm going to leave that for the moment, uh, take a look at it structurally and see if that gives me any, any help. Um . . . An A-B-A-B-C-D-C-D uh, whoops, A-B-A-B uh B-C-B-C, right? Um, I forget, I know what that, that kind of stanza's called, with the sh-, with the tetrameter line at the end. //read ll. 1–6, whispering line 4 and with l. 5: Why would it sleep not? why should it st- Why would it sl- Why would it sleep not? why should it start.// Um, a lot of trochees, um, and dactyls, or dactyls. "Why would it" uh, uh trochee. //read ll. 5–8, emphasizing rhythm and with l. 7: Whát made sleep flútter his wings an-, What made sleép, What made sleep flutter his wings and part?// Uh, ok there's no enjambings in any of these lines, um, except in the Env-, in the Envoi, uh Envoi [French pronunciation], there's that one enjambing between line two and three uh, um. And again we have the, the feminine endings of uh, of uh the feminine rhyme, masculine rhyme, feminine rhyme, uh in the first half, well the feminine rhyme, masculine rhyme in the first half of the uh, of the stanza, in the second half they're both masculine, and uh of course that pattern runs all the way through, um. Uh, "a softer," it certainly does, having the first line with a, with a feminine, with a, a final feminine syllable certainly softens the, the rhythm uh, uh, of the poem.

22

//read ll. 2–4 omitting "hidden apart," l. 2//   Um . . . let's see. Ok uh, uh, again a- another interesting thing is that the, the poet holds a dialogue, uh with his heart, in the, in the second, in the second stanza, um. Whereas in the first, in the first stanza he just apostrophizes it, or uh just apostrophizes. //read ll. 5–7// Uh and then, the, the refrain um, and in the second stanza um he speaks to it directly, holds, holds a dialogue with the "Lie still, I said," "Lie still . . . for the wind," um, "wind's wing closes, / . . . Lie still, for the wind on the warm sea dozes," um, "And the wind is, is unquieter yet than thou art."

23

Um, ok. (chuckle) And I really don't like "What bids the lids of thy sleep de-part." What uh is the point, what is the "lids of thy sleep"? Is that a um, synec-doche for uh um, is "lids" a synecdoche for, for uh opening of the eyes or something, uh uh or the whole process of the opening of the eyes? Um, it's, it's, it's not, it doesn't strike me as beautiful.

24

Uh . . . ok, but now, but in the third stanza we expand um, to start considering this, this whole thing within the, within the context of some sort of uh, um, uh , well within the world, uh certainly because there's "never was writ in the travel-ler's chart," never, it uh, it was never "sold in the uh, uh merchant's mart." Uh, so you get the, the you start talking about uh um, the larger ques-, I mean you start setting the landscape, um, setting up the landscape, um, in terms of the world somehow, uh defining it in terms of the world, um, and we get more description um, description entirely actually separate um from the heart, there's no discussion of the heart in this stanza. It's just uh, um, uh, two, two phrases, "The green land," uh, two uh uh double lines, "The green land's name that a charm encloses, / It never was writ," and then "in the traveller's chart, / And sweet on its trees as the fruit that grows is, / It never was sold in the merchant's mart." Um, um, it impli-, uses a negative both times to uh um, uh imply uh the subtlety, it's, its non, its non-realistic quality, um, it's like something, I, I, well I was reading this thing about Griselda today, about the Clerk's Tale, uh or Griselda, uh uh and this seemed right to me, Griselda gets described in al-, always in terms of she was not, of what she was not, and what she could not do, um, and what she would not do, and that tended to uh, to glorify somehow um, her in a, in a special, in a speical sort of way um it's a, um, didn't delimit the qualities of, of her capacity. In other words um it, it, it leaves a certain kind of ambiguity that intentionally glorifies the subject, um, by not, by not discussing it, by only closing off the potential negative sides, um, and also gives you a s-, a real sense of the separation between the real world, or the real character of people in, in what Griselda is, in other words it tends to separate Griselda entirely from the worldly, and this tends to also, um by using the negative tends to fairly effectively uh and uh economically separate this land uh from, from its uh, uh worldly uh um, potential worldly uh, uh referent point, reference points. Um, ok, and we, and we have "traveller" and "merchant" to uh, um, uh uh representatives of people who uh have the most concerns with· exotica, I suppose.

25

And now, and also we have uh trans-, trans-, uh uh, -figuration, I don't know, a change, in the way the, of the, the use of, of the word "dart," the "swallows" are darting now through its dim fields, no longer is, are we talking about the sun's dart, we're talking "swallows through . . . dim fields dart," "dart," and uh, uh actually this seems to me uh to start moving into uh more of a sleepy uh quality, "The swallows of dreams through its dim fields dart," ok, so we have "dim fields," we aren't talking about the keen sun anymore or uh um, or the wind, we're talking about "swallows" and "sleep's are the tunes in its tree-tops heard," in other words the chirping of birds which is um, reminiscent of, of evening, particularly when you're talking about "sleep's are the tunes in its tree-tops," uh and "No hound's note wakens the wildwood hart," ok, we have a lot of sleeping, uh, even though we, we're not sure that there's a, even a "hound" or a "wildwood hart" in this particular um, uh world. Everything is uh, um, is closed down. But then we have "Only the song of a secret bird," the refrain, saying that th-, "Only the song of a secret bird," uh "wakens the wildwood hart,"

26

and of course there's the, the reason, or a good reason for having the, the pun on "hart," hart H-A-R-T, heart H-E-A-R-T, um, um because that's, ok we come, we come uh full circle to uh um, to a natur-, from a natural creature back to a, to a final personification really of uh, of uh um, the heart, uh of the po-, poet, of the speaker, uh, personified in the uh, the "wildwood hart," um, now, by now an entirely separate entity completely uh um, uh independent in nature some-how uh, um and in quality, uh which is also awakened by the "song of a secret bird," uh.

27

Ok. "In the world of dreams I have chosen my part, / To sleep for a season and hear no word," et cetera. Uh "part" comma (chuckle) that would, you mean his part, his heart, uh, um, "my part" can refer to number one, uh, uh his role? uh or number two it can really refer to uh his anatomical part, heart, "To sleep for a season and hear no word," um. It's a little curious because it uh, um it's sort of reuniting uh the poet and the, and uh the organ that he had before relegated to uh its place under the rose bush, um. So, I don't know. Ok, and it's clear that what he's hiding from is anything having to do with, with um, love, either true love or light love. Uh but again he's hiding in the, in the bed of roses, um which is paradoxical, uh, in that sense.

28

"Nest of roses" may uh um, I can see now that might have um, he might have used nest is because of the suggestion, one more bird suggestion, the fact that the secret uh bird seems to be living in that nest of roses as if the, it's a, a integral part of it. I'm not sure. Uh, well.

29

//read ll. 3 – 5// "When never . . ."um. Ok, lines five six seven in the first stanza, lines five six seven in the second stanza are all uh these uh rhetorical uh questions, uh why why when what, does does what, um, and then the uh, uh the questions, again they don't come back in the third stanza, um.

30

We're dealing with uh, but why uh, um, it's interesting that the setting is not done until the final stanza, uh, but the setting is, all the uh, the first stanza we are immediately concerned with the problem of uh, of, of the poet's heart and where it is specifically, and uh um, um, it's compared to "soft white snow" which um, again is uh uh, a-, antithetical to uh to what roses symbolize. The — still the unsolved question for me is why roses, 'cause th-, the soft white snow is, um, clearly you know cold, um, passionless, pure, all those things that represent uh um, uh conventionally in uh um, uh, well all Neoplatonic love poetry for instance uh, uh purity and virginity and roses of course rep-, representing in that same, uh, tradition uh passion, love, um, and so forth. So the paradox is that if the, the dreamer is saying that he's hiding his heart um away from "true love's truth" or uh "light love's art" in a bed of the very things that uh represent, uh that, and perhaps that's why it's "A Ballad of Dreamland," it's a paradox, uh, of the sort inherent to dreams, that uh um, a heart to be couched in a, in a bed of roses and in the very act of, of immersing itself in that sort of uh, uh environment um, hides itself at the same time. Heh, I don't know, that still doesn't sound too uh, convincing to me, so I, I think I'm going to close off here for a little while and come back to it later.

31

Ok, Thursday 4:30 AM, uh well Thursday the uh, 27th? I think? No matter. Uh, 4:30 PM, returning to the poem, "A Ballad of Dreamland." Ok. Ballade. Ok, it is in the, the uh ballade form, right, the uh, the Deschamps form, uh, a reading of it, I think, though here.

32

//read poem with: l. 10: And mild leaves muffle the keen sun dart — keen sun's dart; l. 14: Does the fang still fret thee of hope dis- deferred?// Ok um — uh I'm going to stop for a second and close the door. Ok, now what, what strikes me this time is that uh, the overall uh interpretation is that he's talking about, uh love, uh some pure internal stirrings of love, as if uh um he's entirely retreating into the mind, i-, mind or the imagination as a resource for um, uh, um, some uh wellspring, some spiritual wellspring, something that makes him think, uh the poet thinks that uh um, he's hearing a pure, unadorned uh expression, natural expression of some, of, of some feeling that has to do with love I think. So uh i.e.: the heart is hiding in a nest of roses. It's as if uh um couched in the very uh um material of love imagery, um, a bower, uh though (chuckle) uh it's kind of a ridiculous bower because there's, again th-, the anatomic specificity of taking your heart out and putting it in a nest of roses still bothers me. I can't get uh, uh, uh get over that, maybe that's, uh a sign of, of my times or something.

SIDE 2

33

Ok, uh the anatomical specificity still bothers me, but uh um, uh, ok uh, the thing is that, I'm seeing the same things I saw before I think, uh, that the nest of roses, um opposed to the soft white snow, uh again the, the uh reference to Neoplatonic uh uh love poetry in those two kinds of images, uh, und-, and then of course it's the uh "in a nest of roses," "Under the roses," then under the uh, uh under the leaves, as if the heart is receding back in the process of the poem. Um, and then uh um, only surrounding it are these little uh, uh, birds, cherubs, as, as if uh taking the idea of personifying forces as some sort of cherubs or gods, going, taking it the next step and turning them into birds like the wind, um sleep, fluttering his wings. Uh of course I'm just assuming that they're birds, uh, they could very well be cherubs with wings or some sort of uh um, winged gods.

But uh uh, the image of "the wind's wing closes" uh, for some reason suggests to me um, suggests to me that.

34

So we have the, so we have a garden, but it's, it's a much more restricted and s-, and s-, uh particularized garden, um, in that we've just got a, the only things that we see in the whole first stanza is the roses, for the first four lines and then the second four lines are the discussion of the uh, uh, the feelings of the heart, um, and the uh um, the uh, the little uh repeated line the refrain, "Only the song of a secret bird." Uh, and again in the second stanza that happens, it's, although it's uh um, apostrophe, "Lie still, I said, for the wind's wing closes, / And mild leaves muffle the keen sun's dart." We have external, talking about external action, um. "Lie still, for the wind on the warm sea dozes, / And the wind is unquieter yet than thou art." Ok, uh, all four lines emphasizing external things and then we have uh um, uh. "Does a thought in thee still as a thorn's wound smart? Does the fang still fret thee of hope deferred?" Um. "What bids the lids of thy sleep depart?" And then the, the refrain, the answer, "Only the song of a secret bird." So uh um, there's some sort of a, a, a, a division in the narrator between his consciousness and his, and his heart clearly. He thinks uh or he's has some rational approach that it's a uh, an old love wound that's bothering the heart but it's not, it's uh something, um, it's, "it's the song of a secret bird," it's, it's something uh um, in that bower, in the very quality of the bower that's, that's doing it to him, um, the secret bird that's supposedly, you assume is ensconced somewhere with the uh, with the heart.

35

And then, ok again we get the uh um, we go, we move to the external world again, and we finally i-, in this paragraph uh, move out further to, to the garden per se. "The green land's name that a charm encloses, / It never was writ in the traveller's chart." Ok that's a very conventional uh um, sort of statement. Uh, "that a charm encloses," though, we still, still have the emphasis on the enclosed um, uh, enclosed heart, I think is, is what the charm is referring to. Uh "And sweet a-, on its trees as the fruit that grows is, / It never was sold in the merchant's mart." Again uh um, or another conventional utterance uh, about the separateness of this garden is that, you know the pastoral quality, uh, the separateness of this pastoral quality, it's not something that you go back and forth to, uh within the world, it's, it's highly, it's other-worldly. And uh um, actually the use of something like uh uh the "merchant's mart," "sold in the merchant's mart," um, uh, tends by negative example to show how other-worldly the uh um, the garden is. In other words it doesn't avoid the issue of its, of its relationship to uh, uh, something like commerce, it uh, it brings it up, uses it, as a foil. Um and "The swallows of dreams through its dim fields dart," ok, we really, that really gives you an idea of uh, of the mental landscape specifically a uh, an imagination landscape, dreams flitting through uh, flitting across the sky, flitting across the visible horizon of uh, uh, the imagination. Uh, and "No hound's note wakens the wildwood hart," ok, there's that um, the hart uh heart pun again. "Only the song of a secret bird." Ok, once more.

36

And so uh, the Envoi uh, strangely enough is not an envoi at all, it doesn't, it doesn't address it to anyone which in Deschamps, Chaucer, all those people, the use of an envoi was uh, um, to address it to, to return to uh um, to address the world in some way. This does address the world, it actually, it um, opens up the poem to the extent of saying "In the world of dreams I have chosen my part," in other words, um, it's telling you outright, uh what's going on, "To sleep for a season and hear no word / Of true love's truth and of or of light love's art." Ok, so um, we're not talking about true love's truth, which the song of a secret bird you might be able to say uh um, uh well it's "hear no word / Of true love's truth" I suppose, so you still could consider "the song of a secret bird" some sort of "true love's truth" O-, but we're, it's not a matter of, of, of uh words, of verbiage, it's a matter, it's the s-, it's a song. Ok, thought is not, uh rational thought or, or some sort of formulated thought, is not a part of the universe, ah that's being defined by uh dreamland, or the, the world of the imagination or this garden.

37

So uh um, ok. The interesting thing I guess is that it starts with a, the nest of roses, moves out to the wind and the sun and the sea in the uh um, uh second stanza. Third stanza we get the, we get the uh garden delimited uh specifically for us and then uh, in the fourth stanza we connect to the, to the uh uh, uh real world, I mean it, there, its relationship to the real world is defined specifically for us. So there is sort of a progression there.

38

And uh um, in the second half of uh um, um, of each one of these stanzas, uh, addressing the uh um, the issues of uh, of the heart itself we start from uh um, the question of why would it, why wouldn't it sleep, why wouldn't um, to the, stanza two when it's, specifically says, uh, we're told that it's the song of a secret bird, line two, I mean stanza two, the second half we discover that it's not um, uh a lo-, a question of old love, of a "thorn's wound smart," um, it's uh something, completely, completely uh uh different or it's um, something separate from that whether it has anything to do with that, the sense is that it's not that, it's "the song of a secret bird" something, um, that is part of those birds in that landscape so natural to uh the dreamland that we're talking about, something welling up um within the bower, within that self-contained bower, and uh um, we hear that there are other, the other uh birds, there are other birds, sleep is a bird, um singing, swallows, dreams are s-, are swallows, um. So we consolidate dreams an-, dreams and sleep are the two things that um, are the qualities that somehow uh shelter, surround the heart. Ok, uh, in other words, "What made sleep flutter his wings and part?" which means to say that uh, in the first stanza that is uh, uh that is to say that sleep was there in the first place. Sleep was one of the things that was ensconced in the bower but sleep is no longer there uh, uh, for the rest of the uh um, rest of the poem in fact sleep is in the t-, in the treetops at this point so the heart is clearly awake and perceiving even though it's receded way down into the uh, into the rose bush, into the bower, down, down into the leaves, God knows where the thorns are, um, though that's not explicitly said, um. And uh uh, the only song is, is sleep's, "No hound's note wakens the wildwood hart, / Only the song of a secret bird," again suggesting that the heart is awake and perceiving and somehow functional, um, within its, within its uh imaginative context which I suppose is a re-, a redemptive feature of dreamland, um.

39

So. But then again um. "In the world of dreams I have chosen my part,   /   To sleep for a season and hear no word." So *I* am, am asleep, the "I" is asleep, the person is asleep, but the heart is not asleep. Ok, that seems like a, a contradiction but I think that what it's saying i-, b-, by the fact that the opening line is "I hid my heart in a nest of roses," uh, the personality and the, and the heart, the heart of, heart of the narrator are separating, somehow he's uh, you think of it in terms of persona and uh, an inner spirit. And so I, the persona, the social persona, is probably sleeping and it's this inner, inner spirit this heart that's being hidden within the nest of roses that is uh um, um, how you say, present, functional. But only, uh, this can only, only seems to be possible, uh, within a garden, within the shelter of, uh, of this dreamland that's described in uh um, uh stanza three. And that's, uh the movement is towards that, is towards understanding that it's a uh, um, that the heart is alive and, aware in this uh garden, separate from the world per se, and the persona, the "I" of the poem is asleep, whereas the first three a-, as it says in the Envoi, whereas in the first three stanzas, the "I" is always, I mean um, sleep is referred to as being separate from the heart. Ok, so we're definitely sure of that, I'm repeating myself I know but uh um, uh that seems to be the, the deeper level of the poem that I can work with is that uh um, is that that's going on, is that, that it's about the separation of the heart and the, and the persona, the external persona, um, and it's and the heart's uh ensconcement in a um, sort of a magical realm, uh, uh, a bower of roses, that that represents a, a sort of perfected garden of the, pastoral garden of the imagination. Um, ok, now let's see, I mean, that's as much as I, as I think that I can get out of this poem, not that I like it very much really

40

but uh, uh let me see if I can find any structural things that, that open it up any more. Of course as I say, uh, the eight line stanza is uh, in the ballade, is uh, is separated, uh, perfectly each time in that in the first two stanzas uh by moving from statement to question. And in the third stanza by, from statement, from uh, negative statement about the landscape to positive statement about the landscape in other words "The green land's name" . . . was never "writ in the traveller's chart," the fruit was never sold "in the merchant's mart," ok that's the first half, second half is uh, "swallows of dreams" and "sleep's are the tunes in its tree-tops uh heard;   /   No hound's note wakens the wildnote hart" —

41

ok we're back to uh, um, uh dream, sleep, and uh um, the wildwood hart. Ok, all the references uh um, uh, to the qualities surrounding um the bower, ok to the bower specifically, to that small, contained uh area in which the heart is sheltered, um, which is not really the same as uh um, in the second stanza where it opens up a little mu-, bit, where we're talking about the wind, the keen sun and the warm sea, which gives you an idea of a, of a larger landscape, gives you a horizon uh from which to contemplate, you know natural forces somehow, um, and gives you an idea of agencies like the keen sun, th-, with the reference to the God of Love or, or uh, or Cupid or something somehow with the "keen sun's dart," at least that's, that's what occurs to me. It seems like a uh, I mean a *Romance of the Rose* type of uh, uh, uh type of image, uh, uh, uh Guillaume de Lorris, uh half of the *Romance of the Rose* a-, actually uh,

42

and the wind's wing uh closes, that is a um, again uh uh, it's a very spiritual picture because something like the wind having wings is uh, is quite a nice sensual image, you have the uh um, the wing coming across a-, as the, seeing the wind as a, as a wing, um, rubbing across the uh, across the landscape is uh uh, is nice, seeing the elements as a, uh personifying the elements in those terms is, is, seems like it's, it's, a good idea. Um, but uh, and "the wind is unquieter yet than thou art," uh, suggests the uh the bliss that the uh, the heart, even though it's hearing the song of a secret bird, is enjoying, um.

43

But that actually is, it seems contradictory to me 'cause then the poet uh goes and says "Does a thought in thee still as a thorn's wound smart?" after the poet has assured the heart that "the wind is unquieter yet." Either the narrator is dumb or it's uh, um we're trying to refine even further the, the problem of the heart, uh in, in that case the uh the thing about "the wind is unquieter yet than thou art" seems somehow inappropriate to me. Uh, I don't know. There's uh, I'm so tempted to be judgmental with this poem. I don't know,

44

uh . . . The *language* is very pretty, I mean, uh, overall. "I hid my heart" ok, uh, "hidden apart," "softer bed than the soft white snow's is, / Under the roses I hid my heart." Uh, "Why would it sleep not? why should it start." Uh, "the song of a secret bird," a lot of alliteration, uh, a lot of uh um, uh, um, uh vowels linking up together, actually I can't think of the (laugh) can't think of the term, it's been so long since I've used it, um, for vowels working together, in other words uh, "snow's is" and "roses," uh that's a rhyme of course but then there's uh, "When never a leaf of the rose-tree stirred," a leaf of the tree. Uh "flutter his wings and part." But then uh "bids the lids of thy sleep depart." I really can't stand that. Uh, "Does the fang still fret thee," uh is pretty good onomatapoetic, uh, effect. Um, "thorn's wound smart," there's a lot of uh, be still as a thorn's wound smart's um, uh, separating those words really, uh it's choppy and uh um, uh, percussive there and, with the "fang still fret thee," "fret thee" a-again, uh, the separation there makes it more percussive, uh, more effective. "The green land's name that a charm encloses."

45

(Pause) Ok the uh, uh sentences tend to uh, go in segments of uh um, express themselves in lines of two, there's uh, uh, no enjambing to speak of,

46

uh, uh, there are a lot of extra syllables, it, it tends to follow the Coleridge, uh, you know Coleridge's lead in uh um, in using syllables a little more freely. "Out of the sun's way, hidden apart; / In a softer bed than the soft white snow's is." Um, uh you can call it, I mean you could scan it probably for trochees and uh um, and dactyls, as I was talking about before, but uh um. Well I could scan it really. Let me get out the pen here . . . If I've got it . . . Ok, scanning it.   //read ll. 1–3 stressing accents//   I hate that feminine ending, God. "Under the, under the roses I hid my heart." Um, now the alliteration falls pretty well on the uh um, on the accent patterns.   //read ll. 5–9 with: l. 6: When uh never a leaf of the rose-tree stirred? and l. 8: Only, Only the song of a secret bird.// Uh three stresses in a row there. "And mild leaves muffle" — yes that's, that's not bad — "the keen sun's dart." Actually uh, they all, that's interesting where the stress, that's all . . . "Lie still, for the wind on the warm sea dozes." Again that seems like a three-stress on the "warm sea dozes," //read ll. 12 – 28 with l. 12: And the wind is, the wind is unquieter yet than thou art; l. 16: Only the song of a secret bird. Um, ok; l. 18: It never was writ, writ in the traveller's chart; l. 27: Of true love's truth and or of light love's art.//

47

Um . . . ok. There are a couple other uh, triple-stress, actually that's, that's interesting, the one thing in this is that there are some triple-stress lines, um, I mean triple-stress groupings, what I would have to, you'd really have to call triple-stress groupings, like "When never a leaf of the róse-trée stírred." Uh I, I think that that, they would all scan as stresses, "róse-trèe stírred." I think doesn't, doesn't work. Um, one in, b-, in uh, in stanza one, in stanza two we have "wind's wing closes," ok, that's a triple stress I think, "keen sun's dart," "warm sea dozes," three, "thorn's wound smart," four, four lines. The first three of that uh second stanza, and then um, line five, and then the uh um . . . "dim fields dart" I think in li-, in, is definitely, you have that stress, and "wildwood hart" maybe, "wildwood hart," uh is, is more dubious. And then in the Envoi, you could say "hear no word," "hear no word" might be a triple-stress, and "light love's ar-," trúe lóve's trúth or of líght lóve's árt" also use these, sort of a triple-stress pattern,

48

and that's actually, all right, I mean I'll, I'll grant it that, um, it seems to come at effective uh um, uh um, entities, uh you have, it's always some uh, it's a, it's a verb, almost always a verb and a, and a uh um, um, noun, adjective — noun — verb. "Wind's," "rose-tree stirred," "wind's wing closes," "warm sea dozes," "thorn's wound smart," um, "dim fields dart," "tree tops heard," um, "true love's truth," "light love's art," that's, that's uh um, uh ok, that's kind of inter-esting 'cause it starts out using almost entirely um, these three s-, triple-stresses for uh um, with that sort of effect, leading up to a uh um, um a verb, uh, when you see that there's so little, so little action. There is more uh, I mean the poem doesn't seem to express much in the way of action whatsoever, but uh um, the emphasis does tend to lead up to these verbs.

49

Um, "rose-tree stirred," uh, "closes," "dart," "dozes," "smart," um — ok. And the verbs do um, uh, often get left 'til the very end of the line, ok. "Flutter his wings and part," "closes," ok "muffle"'s in the middle of the line, "Lie still," "dozes," "wind is," d-, "thought in thee still as a thorn's wound smart," ok there is a lot of uh um, um, um, oh God, uh almost Latinate but certainly highly wrought um placement of the verb at the end of the line um. "What bids the lids of thy sleep depart?" Um, um, "And sweet on its tree as the fruit that grows is" probably is as good an example of a, of the uh um, a sort of Latinate leaving the verb to the end, um, ok. So that's, the language is, is purposely um, uh, formal, wrought, highly wrought,

50

and it uses these triple-stresses that builds up to the point in the, the final, the final lines "true love's truth or . . . light love's art" are probably the uh um, uh, that's where the uh, the one enjambing in the poem comes too. "Hear no word," "To sleep for a season and hear no word / Of true love's truth or of light love's art." That's uh, the longest line and it, "To sleep for a season and hear no word," "hear no word," a triple stress, "Of true love's truth," a possible triple-stress, "Of true love's truth or of light love's art." Ok it, it does build to a real climax, a language climax there in the final uh um, in the Envoi, uh, in terms of the way the stresses sit,

51

so and, it goes one – four – one, um, in terms of the number of triple-stress lines in the ballad, or one – four – two maybe, and then in the uh the Envoi there's that very strong uh, uh, build-up to uh um, "true love's truth or of light love's art," um, and the way that, the way it's constructed, which is, which is fairly interesting, it doesn't, um, I don't know how much it, else it tells me about the meaning offhand, except that uh um, it seems to be a real rejection of uh, of that, for the sake of the "Only the song of a secret bird," for the mysterious single utterance uh, that uh, that forms the refrain, so uh um. So what?

52

All right, so it, the meter tends to uh um, um, fall into uh um, uh, uh, well iambs, uh um, some dactyls, uh, here and there that, a, a, just tend to be like "in a nest" or "Out of the sun's way," um, most of the dactylic things or trochees, tend to fall on, on meaningless words, "in a," "Out," "of the," "in a," "than the," um, "Why would it," "why should it," um, "of the," usually that sort of thing, uh on th- these prepositional things is where the dactyls come. Otherwise it's fairly, so in those, you can elide over those in the reading of the poem pretty easily, so uh it's mostly a fairly even rhythm except for some climactic points when they have like uh, a triple um, the triple-stress I'm talking about, usually "the rose-tree stirred," uh, so you get a real uh um, uh you get a noun with an adjective attached to it that you can't ignore, so, like "rose-tree," "wind's wing," "keen sun's," "warm sea," uh "thorn's wound," uh, usually combined uh with a, uh with a verb. Um, so a-, a-, and, usually, al-, always as a matter of fact, at the end of the line this comes, so it builds up to a uh, to a strong, and as I say there's no enjambing in the first three uh uh, stanzas so, um, and they're often uh, complete sentences, single complete sentences each line, so tend to go in pairs, uh as far as the meaning goes, um, so uh um – so what?

53

So uh, again it's uh um, the strongest language comes in the second, in the second uh stanza with "Lie still . . . Lie still," uh "Does a thought in thee still," uh "still," "still," all these stills uh "as a thorn's wound smart?" //read ll. 14 – 16 with "uh" at end of 1. 15 and 1. 16// Ok, so the most, all the agitation, uh really comes, or uh most of the agitation comes in the uh uh, in the stanza two where it's "Lie still" – um again you've got double stress to open the line, uh, "I said for the wind's wing closes," ok, so that's a very strong line, uh I mean there's, there's a lot, the meter is suddenly much choppier, much stronger, than in the first, in the first uh, uh and it tends to be a contradiction to uh, uh, the narrator saying "Lie still . . . Lie still," uh, but uh, obviously it's uh, the meter is like reinforcing the agitation, a sense of agitation. And "Mild leaves" uh "muffle," ok, triple-stress there, that that one is internal. "Mild leaves muffle the keen sun's dart" ok, almost entirely, "and" and "the" are the only um, uh, words in that line that don't require a specific stress. Then again "Lie still, for the wind on the warm sea dozes," uh, um, uh almost identical to the first line. "And the wind is unquieter yet than thou art." Ok. "Does a thought in thee still," "still" repeated, from the um "as a thorn's wound smart? / Does a fang still fret." Ok that's sort of a triple-stress there. "Does the fang still fret thee of hope deferred?" Ok, so we've got "still," "still," "still," "still," um. "What bids the lids of thy sleep depart? / Only the song of a secret bird." So we've got this uh, highly agitated uh, second stanza.

54

Then moving into the third stanza where there, it's not very agitated, uh, we move suddenly from this uh, discussion of the uh, uh the surrounding environment and the, and the talk of, of uh "thorn's wound smart," "hopes deferred" to uh, a much more uh distanced and conventional uh, uh picture in //read ll. 17–20// Uh, very lyrical and very uh uh uninteresting really, uh, and then, uh, with the movement into the final, the final four lines of the third stanza, um we have "The swallows of dreams through its dim fields dart." So then we have a uh, a triple-stress, "And sleep's are the tunes in its trée-tóps heárd." Another one. "No hound's note wakens the wíldwood hárt." Another possible one, uh, so the last three, and then "Only the song of a secret bird." Suddenly we, we turn when we start talking about the mind again, we return to these, to these stress, uh, stressful lines,

55

and uh um, and it sort of leads you into uh um, to that final, to the Envoi, which ha-, which really uh um, uh as I say has a, a strong effect, that "To sleep for a season and heár nó wórd / Of trúe lóve's trúth or of líght lóve's árt." Uh very strong uh um, uh use of the meter there actually.

56

Um. So there is uh um, so we come up, so, ok so that actually is, the movement of the meter tends to be uh um, uh um, in the first stanza it's fairly calm, uh, the stresses all sit right and the, and the um, unstressed syllables tend to run over um, things like "than the," "of the," "to the," so forth, um with only one, one triple-stress in "rose-tree stirred" of that type, ok starting up that pattern; then in the second stanza we have a, a great deal of agitation, almost a climax, and "Does a thought in thee still as a thorn's wound smart?" I think is uh, um, uh sort of a mirror reflection of the, uh um, agitation that "Lie still, I said, for the wind's wing closes," "Lie still, for the wind on the warm sea dozes," uh, "keen sun's dart," all those things tend to uh um, uh suggest uh, agitation, um. And then we come to the cli-, to the clim-, climactic line uh mid-way through the poem of "Does a thought in thee still as a thorn's wound smart?" Ok, that's wh-, what we've been leading up to all this time is, uh, the question that probably in the reader's mind is this uh 'what are we talking about here? Is it a uh—do we got a, a screwed up lover or what?' Um, which, I mean, using all the conventional love language, certainly that's the question that's going to uh, um going to occur, to the reader. And so "Does the fang still fret thee of hope deferred?" So he keeps up the climax for a while, and then slows it down to

"What bids the lids of thy sleep depart. / Only the song of a secret bird." Ok so it's, here's the anti-climactic, uh um, drop-off of the way the meter, after the highly agitated first uh six lines, seventh line is milder, the eighth line is refrain which is about as mild in terms of rhythm as you can be in the song and it has of course the qualities of the repetition which also makes it uh sort of soothing uh uh ballade-like effect. Ok, and then we move as I say to that uh, um, to that highly conventional first four lines of th-, of the third stanza, and then uh uh, things start gearing up again in the last half of the third stanza with the description of the landscape and then, uh, uh and then we move in the Envoi for the second climax of "To sleep for the season and hear no word / Of true love's truth or of light love's art." Ok. Agitation re-enters very strongly in two lines, two enjambed lines, and uh, and then of course we have the uh um, the uh "Only the song of a secret bird."

57

Ok actually that's, now uh, that makes me feel about as on, makes me feel fairly on top of the poem, right now. So uh um, I'm not going to go through the process of articulating it once more, uh, 'cause I just keep doing it over and over again but uh, I might turn it off now and maybe I'll come back to it, maybe I won't, I don't know, we'll see.

58

Ok, one PM Friday. One last look at the poem here, um. //read poem with l. 24: Only the, the song of a secret bird.// Uh ok, I don't uh . . . uh really nothing new seems to be occurring to me . . . except again that middle stanza, second stanza, all the language seems to infer a quietness in the uh, but the meter is uh, everything is closing down but the meter is highly agitated, uh, uh, no I won't, I won't say anything else, ok?

CARLOS: "CARRION COMFORT"

1

Gerald Manley Hopkins, "Carrion Comfort." //read poem with l.1: (No), I'll not, carrion comfort, Despair, not feast on thee; l. 5: But ah . . . O thou terrible, why wouldst thou rude on me; l. 7: With darksome devo-, devouring eyes my bruised bones? and fan; l. 8: O in turns of tempest, me heaped here, heaped there, heap'd there; me frantic to avoid thee and flee; l. 13: me? or . . . that, me that fought him? O which one? is it each one? That night, that year.// Oh man, this looks very dense,

2

but let's do another reading here (yawn). //read poem with l. 5: But ah . . . O, But ah, but O thou terrible, why wouldst thou rude on me.// Ah. Ok (yawn). One more time.

3

//read poem with l. 1: Not, I'll not, carrion comfort, Despair, not feed on thee; l. 3: In, uh — (return to l. 2 and continue reading); l. 7: With darksome devouring eyes my bruised, bruised bones? and fan.// Ok, well clearly uh, a religious theme (yawn) uh, uh, very interesting, it seems like there are some inversions of, of uh, uh, of biblical things, well, "lay a lionlimb against me? scan / With darksome devouring eyes my bruised bones," uh, is a, it seems like uh the lion laying down with the lamb uh turned to a different purpose.

4

Well let me just go through this. "(No), I'll not, carrion comfort, Despair, not feast on thee." Ok, "comfort," Ok, so that's, that's interesting. "Comfort" uh uh, you can see d-, the way "despair," I thought of it at first as a, as an appositive to "carrion comfort," um, uh well, yeah, actually now I think that's right. "Despair" is "carrion comfort," um, some sort of uh um, uh it's, it's almost as if you're feeding on uh the most mundane, I mean feeding on a body, feeding on earth as it were, feeding on uh uh the most mundane uh of realizations, "despair," and calling it "carrion" of course is a, gives it a certain rapacity and uh um uh well negative qualities, um, but I'm not sure.

5

"Not untwist—slack they may be—these last strands of man / In me or, most weary, cry I can no more. I can." Ok that seems to me pretty straightforward, um, "these last"—(yawn) oh God—"these last strands of man / In me or, most weary, cry I can no more." Uh all this internal rhyme incidentally, which I'll get back to later.

6

"I can; / Can something, hope, wish day come, not choose not to be," in other words here we're talking about suicide perhaps. "Can something," "can" do "something," "can . . . hope," "can . . . wish day come," "can . . . not choose not to be." All right, so there's still the, still a certain ability involved, you still have, still have choice, there still is some short of free will.

7

"But ah . . . O thou," "but O thou," "but ah, but O thou terrible, why wouldst thou rude on me," "rude" is very interesting, that's a very interesting use of "rude." "Thy wring-world right foot rock?" "why wouldst thou rude," "thou rude," ok there's another appositive, uh um, "rude on me," uh, "rock," in other words "rock" "thy wring-world right foot" (laugh) all right, why are you putting your, "wring-world" is a, a beautiful uh, beautiful (laugh) um uh I suppose it's a neologism, uh uh clearly are we talking about th-, "thou" is, is lower case um, and uh I kind of think of it as, as a devil, or "despair," either way. But why would you uh "rock" your "wring-world right foot," in other words why would you st-, stamp probably on me, or some sort of victor's uh um, almost like a victor putting his foot on, on the uh, the neck of his defeated (yawn)

8

and then "lay a lionlimb against me," "lionlimb" again fused together uh, a, calling forth the idea of the lion laying down with the lamb but uh um it's, that's thrown out with "scan / With darksome devouring eyes my bruised bone," "bones," ok. But would "thou," does "a lionlimb" lay "against me," ok "scan," does the lion "scan / With darksome devouring eyes my bruised bones? and fan, / O in turns of tempest, me heaped there; me frantic to avoid thee and" "fan." I don't know what "fan" means. "O in turns of tempest, me heaped there," "me heap'd" here, "there; me frantic to avoid thee and flee? / Why?" Ok why, why is he being subjected to this?

9

The answer, "That my chaff might fly; my grain lie, sheer and clear." Ok biblical para-, I mean that's obviously a, a biblical, the old uh s-, separation of the "grain" and the "chaff," "grain" from the "chaff," uh biblical metaphor there.

10

Uh, "nay in all that toil, that coil," uh, echo from Hamlet I think, "since" s-, uh also that uh um, (cough) lilies of the field, "since (seems)" in, in uh parenth-, uh parenthetical, "since (seems) I kissed the rod, / Hand rather, my heart lo! lapped strength, stole joy, would laugh, cheer." Ok. "Nay in all that toil, that," co-, "coil, since . . . I kissed the," "since" it so-, "(seems) I kissed the rod, / Hand rather, my heart . . . lapped strength" — "lapped," i.e., uh licked up perhaps, took "strength" — "stole joy, would laugh, cheer," ok. In other words, since that experience uh, the experience in terms of uh uh, of being trodden upon by "despair," for some reason uh trodden upon with the use that, that the "grain lie, sheer and clear," uh, and as a result "my heart lo! lapped strength," "lapped" up "strength" like a cat lapping milk, "stole joy, would laugh, cheer."

11

And then the question "cheer whom though? the hero whose heaven-handling flung me, foot trod / Me?" Ok "the hero whose heaven-handling flung me, foot trod / Me," um sounds like uh "the he-," uh uh again "despair" in terms of, of the heroic Satan, i-, the Miltonic Satan maybe, just that sort of thing.

12

"Or me that fought him?" Cheer myself? "O which one? is it each one? That night, that year / Of now done darkness I wretch lay wrestling with (my God!) my God." And so now suddenly, I mean it seems like we're talking about Satan all along but at the end we come up with "(my God!) my God," with the parenthetical remark "(my God!)" before "my God." So uh it's not clear what's going on. Hum. But, "(no), I'll not, carrion comfort, Despair, not feast on thee." Ok now the, the, somehow we've moved from "despair" to "God," the identification of "despair" to the identification of "God," that's the, seems to me right now fairly crucial.

13

There are two stanzas as it were, with, one, two, four, six, eight lines in one, two four six lines in the other, um, ok.

14

In other, in the first half it seems to me that the whole question of why, why is this, uh why his "despair," there's the first statement uh um, the first four lines actually are a statement of confidence in, in uh uh the ability to overcome "despair."

15

The second four lines, "But ah, but O thou terrible, why wouldst thou rude on
me," perhaps we're talking about uh uh God here, "Thy wring-world right foot
rock," in other words God is, is God possessed of "Thy wring-world," a
"wring-world," a world-wringing "right foot," a God of vengence are we talking
about here or are we talking about Satan? Of course if we are talking about the, a
God of vengence, he's connected with Satan certainly, the str-, (laugh) the uh, is
certainly uh shown by his connection to Job or h-, you know by the story of Job
where God and Satan strike a deal. But anyway "Thy wring-world right foot
rock," "lay a lionlimb against me." Ok, again uh, a strange use of the biblical,
biblical, the apocalyptic uh um idea of the lion laying down with the lamb is here
turned into a uh, a very uh um uh, very dangerous uh um, um, oh God these
words don't come to me, (sigh) dangerous, basically, suddenly uh you have a
sense of, uh, a sense of danger instead of a sense of, of uh ultimate uh uh,
ultimate peace among the creatures of the world. Ok so "With darksome devour-
ing eyes my bruised," "scan / With" devou-, "darksome devouring eyes my
bruised bones? and fan, / O in turns of tempest, me heaped there; me frantic
to avoid thee and flee?" Ok, "and fan," that last, "scan," th-, suddenly the lion
uh is taken up the role of fanning uh "me heaped there; me frantic to avoid thee
and flee,"

16

and "Why?" Ok why is he being fanned, why is this, these winds, which calls
forth of course the idea of pneuma, the holy spirit, the holy breath, um, pneuma
uh, blowing through him so "That my chaff might fly; my grain lie, sheer and
clear." Ok. "Nay in all that toil, that coil, since (seems) I kissed the
rod, / Hand rather, my heart," ok: he kissed the rod, hand rather that's very
interesting because in other words you're not talking about an extension of, of
the, the agency of power, i.e., "the rod," but the "hand" itself, "since . . . I
kissed the . . . Hand rather, my heart lo! lapped strength, stole joy," why "*stole*
joy"? Why, I don't, that's something I don't, I don't understand. "would laugh,
cheer." //read ll. 12–14//   That's wonderful, that, so it really, I think we are
talking about God here, all in lower case which is, which is very interesting,
when you're not given (yawn) of course that, I mean that really gives you a sense
of very ambiguous nature of God or the ambiguous, man's ambiguous perception
of God.

17

I don't know Hopkins well enough to know if this fits into his view of anything
so, um, but I have a sense here of a, of a almost visionary uh uh notion of God,
it's very similar to Blake, it reminds me a lot of Blake anyway of this, the whole
uh um "I lay down," I, the uh, the s-, of the, the s-, a certain cynical uh use of
angels and God and uh and Christ to represent things in Blake's cosmology uh
um very different from what they, from what they meant otherwise. I don't
think Hopkins is doing quite that but he is, he's creating a certain visionary
perspective where the power and terror of God um uh is a much deeper and
much more fundamental element of man's, man's uh understanding of him than
uh, than the uh, the New Testament uh benevolence of God,

18

and that's uh um, of course we have "Nay in all that toil, that coil," um again lilies of the field, "they toil not, neither do they sow," is that it? a-, actually I now have a Bible with me so it will be possible . . . Uh one problem with this is that I can't find it so I think I will turn off until I do find it, I don't want to just have you listen to my flipping through the, flipping through the Bible.

Well I didn't find it so, I always start getting lost in the Bible with other things to read so I'm just going to let it go.

19

So anyway "that toil, that coil, since (seems) I kissed the rod," um, there you are, so we're back in the "rod," what could we talk about, could we say Aaron's rod? (laugh) Actually, Aaron's rod. I've forgotten offhand what Aaron's rod is. Gosh. where is it . . . root . . . Well fuck it, I'll worry about that later, um.

20

"Hand rather, my heart lo! lapped strength, stole joy, would . . . cheer," "would laugh, cheer. / Cheer whom though? the hero whose heaven-handling flung me, foot trod / Me? or me that fought him? O which one? is it each one?" Ok all these seem, the, "the hero whose heaven-handling flung me, foot trod / Me" could be either an angel of God or it could be Satan but th-, I think the ambiguity again is there. "Or me that fought him? O which one?" Ok who's the, who is the uh, who is "the hero" there, who's, who's, who are they being cheered in this, in this combat, or is it both?

21

"That night, that year / Of now done darkness I wretch lay wrestling with (my God!)," exclamation, "my God." Uh, so it's, it's a, somebody coming out of a long period of, of wrestling with, with God, with the whole question of, of his relation with, ra-, relationship to God, to the, and the world, and is the, uh, is the process of "that my chaff might fly; my" "my grain lie, sheer and clear." But then there's the question of uh, of why and where the credit goes as it were, uh, and the, where, the credit go-, where does the credit go for the exaltation, the "strength," the "joy," the "cheer(s)" um, and uh he seems to come up with the idea that it's, that both uh, both uh adversaries as it were uh deserve some sort of "cheer," or is it, "is it each one? That night, that year / Of now done" darknee-, "darkness I wretch lay wrestling with (my God!) my God." Another appositive there, "I," "my," "I wretch," um.

22

Tha-, so ok, well let me (cough) in terms of s-, structurally this is a very interesting looking poem. There's all this enjambing and uh um, well in terms of formal analysis the uh, the language is very, is uh (sigh) sounds, sounds quite a bit, "(no), I'll not, carrion comfort, Despair," nor "feast on thee," there's an awful lot of action going on, an awful lot of groupings of, of uh, of alliteration. Two, two alliterations, "(no), I'll not, carrion comfort, Despair," nor "feast on thee," this whole realm of sounds in this first uh um, uh "Despair, feast on thee," that um uh uh whatchamafizzit in the end there um. Nor, "Not untwist — slack they may be — these last strands of," "of man," "last strands of man / In me or, most weary, cry I can no more. I can; / Can something, hope, wish day come, not choose not to be. / But ah, but O thou terrible." Really uh um uh a lot of interjections, ejaculatory, this is a very ejaculatory (laugh) uh, I suppose you could call it, poem. "Why wouldst thou rude on me / Thy wring-world right foot rock," "wouldst *thou*," that uh use of the formal "thou," thee, thou, um "rude on me / Thy wring-world right foot rock? lay a lion-limb against me?" "With darksome devouring," "scan / With darksome," again there's that enjambing, there's some interesting enjambing, um, actually, second line to the third line, uh fifth line to the sixth line, "why . . . thou," "wouldst . . . rude on me / Thy wring-world," um, then sixth to seventh, seven to eight — all those are enjambed, with uh, "scan, / With darksome . . . eyes my bruised bones? and fan,"

23

um. Oh actually the rhyme scheme is quite formal, it's something that's lovely, that's the, it's a, ou-, it's always said that the, the greatest rhyme is one that you don't notice (laugh) I didn't even notice, "thee," "man," "can," "be," "me," "scan," "fan," "flee," "clear," "rod," "cheer," "trod," "year," "God." Um. Ok well that's proper because uh in the first, the first stanza the grouping as I said before, the first four lines group together and the, and the rhyme scheme does that for you in terms of the uh, the statement, the affirmation, there's a, the, the poem opens with an affirmation of the conquering of k-, of "despair," "carrion comfort," um, and uh, and then uh the second half is uh, uh is sort of a return to, to the questioning of why, why he'd been put to that kind of a test in the first place. Then again in the first half of the second question um, uh first three lines that, instead of the first four um, you have the question repeated or the affirmation repeated, "Why? That my chaff might fly," and then uh um, uh the, the "hand," the "coil," uh, "nay in all that toil, that coil, since (seems) I kissed the rod . . . rather," "hand," "hand rather, my heart lo! lapped strength," "joy," "lapped strength, stole joy, would laugh, cheer." Ok, so we have uh um, uh another affirmation in that uh, um number one, the separation of the "grain" from the "chaff" ok, um, and number two there's some sort of great "strength" uh uh gained out of it and then, but then we return back to the question, in, in this st-, stanza interestingly enough because the rhyme scheme is uh, is done in couplets, i.e., "clear," "rod," "cheer," "trod," "year," "God," so all these lines are, are bound together, the question is bound in a way more intimately with um, with the affirmation. "Cheer whom though? the hero whose heaven-handling flung me, foot trod / Me? or . . . that," "or me that fought him? O which one? is it each one? That night, that year / Of now done darkness I . . . lay wrestling," ok that last, these last two lines um uh, there are all these uh um, you have this sudden uh uh burst of questions. "Cheer whom though?" — last three lines —

24

"Cheer whom though? the hero whose" heavelin-, "heaven-handling flung me, foot trod / Me? or me that fought him? O which one? is it each one? That night, that year / Of now done darkness I wretch lay wrestling with (my God!) my God." That's, that last line is, is a long, after all those sent-, excuse me short sentences, there's this long, prolonged almost as if it were a description of the anguish through which the poet had gone or the speaker had gone um, dou-, "now done darkness I wretch lay wrestling with" and then one more delay of the final, of the final assertion of who it is, "(my God!)," the interjection "(my

God!),'' and then "my God." Very very interesting. Well I think I'm going to, to, well, I think I'll stop for the moment and take this up later.

25

Ok Thursday around four, four P.M. Back to the poem here. "Carrion Comfort." //read poem, with l. 1: (No), I'll not, carrion comfort, Despair, not feast on thee; l. 4: Can something, hope, wish day come, not choose . . . to be; l. 8: O in turns of tempest, me heaped here, me frantic to avoid thee and flee?// Hum. Ok, again it's a, the thing that is, always strikes me when I first read this is the int-, interior rhyme, internal rhyme, um, the "not feast on thee," "slack they may be," "strands of man / In me," "man," and then k-, and then of course uh uh the two lines, "done" let's see uh, . . . uh (sneeze)

26

ok, now the the the thing about "carrion comfort" here a bit, the idea of "carrion comfort," uh, "Despair." Now when I think of "despair" I always think of Spenser and the character of Despair and that's actually where I get most of my knowledge about the ideas of "despair" and uh.

SIDE 2

Ok where I get most of my ideas about "de-," uh, about "despair" is from Spenser, uh, but this idea of "carrion comfort," again the uh um, a line of the poem, I mean the title of the poem, the fact that it's the the the title of the poem suggests that uh there's more involved in it than uh, than it seems. It seems like um the speaker gets beyond the idea of "comfort" in, within the first, first lines, uh, in some way, so, because he says "I can no more. I can," "cry I can no more," "in me or, most weary, cry I can no more. I can; / Can something, hope, wish day come, not choose not to be." Ok and that last line, "not choose not to be," in other words um uh "not choose" to commit suicide, basically. And "not untwist — slack they may be — these last strands of man / In me," um, that's again uh a reference to suicide. So "carrion comfort" ac-, that, uh, what it seems to me is, is um, uh well "despair," "despair" feeds off the idea of death, of the peace of death I think, um, peacefulness of death, the pleasantness of death and that's why uh um, um in Spenser the, the character is trying to con-vince uh uh Red Cross, Despair is trying to convince Red Cross to commit suicide, and so there's a, an immediate understandable idea of "carrion comfort," um, idea, the "comfort" to be, to be bought by you being "carrion," by you being turned into "carrion" instead of a um a thinking uh, a thinking being, but uh uh, there's also that idea because it says uh, there's more to it because he says "I'll not" uh "carrion comfort, Despair, not feast on thee," in other words it's i-, as if um, "carrion comfort" is, has some quality that, that he can um uh (laugh) chew on, whatever, uh right th-, right then and there, or by the perhaps by the act of commiting suicide, um chew on. Ok, um and so it k-, wha-, what I was saying before I think uh the last time I was t-, uh, talking to the tape machine, uh, is that the, the quality of "despair," is, is a kind of "carrion," there's a kind of r-, a r-, ravin for um, for man reduced uh to a certain state, to a certain kind of bestiality as a result of his struggles, but uh um, this seems uh, what he's talking about seems to me a very basic existential struggle with God

27

um, "O thou," which comes up in the second four lines of course, "But ah . . . O thou terrible, why wouldst thou," "thou rude," "rude" "thou," appositive,

"Thy wring-world right foot rock," "on me," ok "on me   /   Thy wring-world right foot rock," "wring-world," ok so, "lay," and then uh um again so we have, though we are talking about God here, God is, is God, the God of vengence, and then the idea of the lion laying down with the lamb is brought up again but a-, again brought up with the, with the, the uh, the sense of destruction and vengeance, "lay a lionlimb against me? scan   /   With darksome devouring eyes my bruised bones? and fan,   /   O in turns of tempest, me heaped," h-, "heaped there; me frantic to avoid thee and flee?" Uh, I'm not sure what the se-, uh, if there's any specific biblical ref-, reference. I'm not really sure what "fan . . . in turns of tempest, me heaped," h-, "there," except that, um, you know the winds of conflict, or something blow um, and then that uh um, ok, and that becomes the image that, that gets i-, when you go into the second strophe, uh second stanza rather um, it gets taken up in the opening line.

28

"Why? That my chaff might fly; my grain lie, sheer and clear.   /   Nay in all that," roi-, "toil, that coil, since (seems) I kissed the rod,   /   Hand rather, my heart lo! lapped strength, stole joy, would laugh, cheer." And then uh uh again uh we go back to the questioning "cheer whom though? the hero whose heaven-handling flung me, foot trod   /   Me? or me that fought him? O which one? is it each one?" Ok it doesn't exactly, "heaven-handling flung me" doesn't uh refer specifically to anything um in the first stanza, though uh "foot trod   /   Me" does of course, the "wring-world right foot rock," uh. "Or me that fought him" doesn't uh um uh refer to anything unless it's "me frantic to avoid thee and flee." "Why? That my chaff might fly; my grain lie, sheer and clear." Um, ok, and then we, so. Again it's connected um,

29

there's the, there's, there are two three line uh segments to that, ok so when we return to the se-, the uh, the questioning we uh go from "cheer," "would laugh, cheer.   /   Cheer whom though?" And so the question is whether, who's he cheering, who is he for, uh um "the hero," i.e., God, "whose heaven-handling flung me, foot trod   /   Me? or me that fought him? O which one? is it each one?" Ok, is it both? "That night, that year   /   Of now done darkness I wretch lay wrestling with (my God!) my God." Ok, "now done darkness," so we do reach a uh um some sort of conclusion at the end of the, of the poem, it's, but the conclusion is that the fighting is over, the questioning is not, or the, the understanding of it is not um uh, sort of uh oh captured actually, that question there, the, the uncertainty is, is uh um captured in that "(my God!)" uh in parentheses followed by ah, is the, um ejaculatory "(my God!)" and then "my God," specific reference to uh "my God."

30

So um, again this, what this seems to me to be like is a, is a discussion of man's state, uh man's perennial state in relationship to God. You can go through uh um, uh "despair" uh, we have to return to the beginning of the poem because now I ha-, there's an understanding of "despair." This isn't, "despair" was not engendered during the struggle with God, the struggle with God was something separate, um. "Despair" seems to be engendered afterwards, ok, something that ha-, tha-, something that comes to him after he's gone through all this process of uh um, of fighting with God, and lays uh with his uh "chaff" flown and his "grain" lying "sheer and clear," um, even though his "heart lo! lapped strength, stole joy, would laugh" and "cheer," um, still the questioning goes on, who is the uh, uh, I'm not exactly, what, what the question is when he says "cheer whom though?" except that it has something to do with the relationship of himself to God in, in that uh um, uh somehow "despair" enters into that and it probably seems simpler, uh that seems much simpler than tha-, than a, than the question of uh, of, uh, continuing to struggle on these, on the, you know, the mortal "coil."

31

Let's see. And it seems like uh um, "can something, hope, wish day come, not choose not to be," all seem to center around the idea of suicide um. In other words there's a power of action, uh, but a power of action that is specifically not, suicide is the one, is um, of course is the one power of action that we all have to discuss with ourselves, according to Camus, it's the uh, the one philosophical question and it's the uh, and so that's, actually that's what Hopkins is, is dealing with.

32

And no sooner does he uh um, it seems to me like there's, he's got an endless circle set up here because uh um, uh the only present tense that's, that's used, um — the present tense is used in the opening stanza, the past tense is used in the second stanza, and uh you start with the present tense, "(no), I'll not, carrion comfort . . . not feast on thee" with a future, like, um, with a future meaning, I will not "feast on thee," I will "not untwist . . . these last strands of man / In me or, most weary, cry I can no more." So the opening lines are what look into the future, uh. And then you go, and then you return and discuss the past and the fas-, last line actually s-, seals the past for you "of now done darkness I wretch lay wrestling with (my God!) my God." Um, so the poem concludes, closes the past in a sense or, or concludes what had happened in the past that you have to return to the present again and so you return to this uh, so there's a sense of return to the first stanza when I, whenever I read this poem through I have to, you have to recall um "Carrion Comfort," the title of the poem which is in the opening line and uh uh return to the notion that uh um, ok what next? And we, the what next is that you uh have to make a basic decision about the power of action and uh um whether y-, or not you want to commit suicide, um, based on the way you're living, and then th-, and then uh um, and then in the second half of that first stanza uh we have sort of a uh, uh um, a subjunctive mood I think, "why (would) thou," um, well op-, is it an optative? I don't, to tell you the truth I don't know enough about English grammar to uh know whether you can talk about optatives in English or not, but why would the, "why wouldst thou rude on me / Thy wring-world right foot rock?"

33

Ok so in other words um in this, and in the first stanza we're talking about sort of p-, a perennial situation um. He's questioning it basically, in other words uh even though the second stanza tells us that he's already gone through it, now he's done and he's received his, his improvement, his ch-, his "grain," his "chaff" and "grain" have been separated and he's "lapped strength" and "cheer" from it, um he's still in the first stanza clearly in the process of questioning, even though the second stanza tells us that he's gotten past it to some, some extent, and he still is thinking of the possibilities of an on-going battle with God, so um, "darksome devouring eyes my bruised bones? and fan, / O in turns of tempest, me heaped there; me frantic to avoid thee and flee?"

34

Uh, so, well I'm having trouble articulating this but what it seems to me is that, is that the way he set it up with the present, with the, starts w-, with the future, goes to the present, um, and then some sort of a subjunctive um o-, or optative or whatever and then to the past in the, in the second stanza, uh, that does not return to the present, uh, means you return to the present uh um, means you recall the first stanza by the time that the uh um second stanza is over because uh there is no return in the sense of uh uh, of uh recalling you to the present of the voice, and so that there is sort of a circular motion in the sense that a-, again to recall the uh opening of the poem, you have to recall the opening line and the title and so forth uh, at the end of the poem, so you're sort of set into some sort of a cycle, "(no), I'll not, carrion comfort, Despair, not feast on thee," uh, because that's uh, you need that sort of after the last two lines of uh "Me? or me that fought him? O which one? is it each one? That night, that year / Of now done darkness I wretch lay wrestling with (my God) my God."

35

That's uh um, 'cause in the other, um, the first, the first stanza the, the pattern that gets set up is that the second half of it is questioning, and you need another stanza, the first part of another stanza to, to uh answer it. Now in the second stanza uh you have a, the second part of it is questioning in, but you do not move to another stanza to answer. The only answer that you get in this is uh um, in the structure of the poem as it stands is tha-, that last line uh, "of" my "now done darkness I wretch lay wrestling with (my God!) my God," which is a kind of a statement but it's not an answer to the questioning. The answer to the questioning is uh in going back to the opening line, "(no), I'll not, carrion comfort, Despair, not feast on thee."   //read ll. 2 – 4//   So um it seems to me that that, the, that there's some sort of setup that draws you into a, into a circle, into an eternal circle of conflict, reso-, um, partial resolution, and the um facing up to the question of "despair" and suicide a-, as if that's a permanent cycle of man's life in the world, uh, and uh um (laugh) the only way out of it is "carri-," is "carrion comfort," uh "carrion comfort" in the sense of death, uh, not in the sense of um "despair" specifically

36

and uh. Oh, now there's a point, um. You'd have to separate the difference between "carrion comfort," uh if you killed yourself, uh, s-, it's a mortal sin, right? And you wouldn't go to heaven, so you would not be eternally um, you would not have eternal life, um, and so your "comfort" is definitely much mo-, is "carrion comfort" and not heavenly "comfort." Ok so your "comfort" is definitely a "comfort" of the flesh, your flesh is being comforted but your soul is not being comforted. So um, maybe I, so I think that that's, i-, the sense is that there is a uh um, a difference being drawn here between what "comfort" can be drawn, uh, spiritual "comfort," some sort of uh, um, oh I don't know. The thing is that I uh, I know, I don't know enough about Hopkins' Catholicism either to uh, to make any, any good guesses as to what exactly he, he's, he's saying, but I do know that he was Catholic or had a strong Catholic bias so uh, or training or whatever so uh clearly there's a difference between "carrion comfort," the "comfort" of, of death, the very mundane fleshly "comfort" that suicide would bring and the "comfort" of eternal life uh if he manages to win this battle uh t-, win his struggle,

37

and uh the thing is that he's putting it in very Old Testament-y terms by, by talking about his fight with God, fighting with God almost as if he were a, a, another Satan, um, because that's what those, that i-, those ideas of "hero" bring out to me particularly because uh um, of the use of the word "hero whose" heavelin-, "whose heaven-handling flung me, foot trod / Me," that tends to sound like a reference to uh um Satan being cast out of, cast out of uh um heaven to me, but uh it doesn't necessarily have to be I suppose.

38

Uh, let's see. So um in other words what I'm saying is that the, the way the poem is set up it seems to give a sense of the eternity of the struggle uh between man and his relationship with God, uh, in other words it's, it's a constant feature of life, there's something cyclical and endless about, about it, uh, s-, something that defies uh any kind of uh resolution outside of the death either uh a death reconciled to God or a death um despairing of God, and that's uh, very interesting because uh um, again as I say it seems to be very centered in the idea of power of action, uh, "I can no more. I can," uh. It seems like the idea of your relationship to God is uh um specifically uh linked to the idea of your, the way you act within the world, y-, your power within the world. When you fight God um will you deal with, will y-, you deal with the blows that God deals you um or will you not, and that's uh um, the idea of "I can no more. I can," uh, that idea is, is um, the idea of being able to take it is, is, is uh embodied in that line, but then it's brought to the next uh step from mere passive suffering to an active choosing not, an active choosing not to die, in other words just "(c)an . . . hope, wish day come, not choose not to be," all relate to the idea of, of taking, taking the roo-, the route of uh suicide out so um, the struggle, it moves from uh um, uh the passivity of being willing to accept the struggle of God to a certain active um, uh statement that you're going to what, that you're going to actively engage God. I'm not sure.

39

I'm going to uh um, uh turn off here for a minute, for a few minutes I think and, and uh try to look up uh uh something else biblical that just struck me. Chances are it won't be there but I promise I won't think about the poem while I'm looking it up so I'll just go to the Bible now and come back later.

Well another unsuccessful search so I'm going to uh stop here I think, come back later for one last look maybe.

40

Um Friday 11:15, I'm back for one more look at the poem here. "Carrion Comfort." //read poem with 1. 1: (no), I'll not, carrion comfort, Despair, not feast on thee; 1. 9: Why? That my chaff might fly; my grain lie, sheer and clear, clear, clear (laugh) yeah.// (sigh) Well let me, th-, this uh, I don't know how much I've talked about the, the, it's, one thing that interests me, I don't know how important it is offhand but uh um again there's the i-, I talked about it briefly before, is the um alliteration, there's "(no), I'll not," "carrion comfort," um, "me or, most weary," "cry I can no more, I can / Can something," uh, tho-, "O thou terrible," "wring-world right foot rock," "lay a lionlimb," "darksome devouring eyes my bruised bones," "turns of tempest," "frantic to avoid thee and flee," um, "since (seems)," "hand rather, my heart lo," uh "hero whose

heaven-handling flung me, foot trod   /   Me," "done darkness," "wretch . . .
wrestling with," "wretch," wrethli-, "wrestling with," all these uh uh, well ac-
tually the whole poem, uh th-, with the alliteration and the um uh assonance of
uh "feast on thee" or um uh "last strands of man" uh or um "wouldst thou rude
on me," uh, oh what else uh, "avoid thee and flee," "chaff might fly . . . grain
lie, sheer and clear," "toil . . . coil," "hand rather," let's see, there's uh, th-,
those are the best examples of assonance I guess um.

41

Aside from, oh I think that I, I feel fairly much on top of the meaning still, that
whole circular thing that I was talking about yesterday, um, but it's very interest-
ing to me the way uh um, the sound, it's very very complex in terms of sound,
reminds me of that Gibson, Gibson — was that his name? — Gibson poem um
that I did first here um. It's a very interwoven uh sound um. The internal rhyme
is very, is very interwoven um, there's all this enjambing throughout the poem,
i-, a-, there's all this uh um um alliteration and assonance, and the thing is that
they, what these tend to do is uh um they tend to group words, uh, group
concepts often or uh like "carrion comfort," ok, or "feast on thee," there's
something about it uh um, ok, and then there's "slack they may be," there's all
this interconnecting, uh "these last strands of man   /   In me," ok, or uh "O
thou terrible, why wouldst thou rude," and then "rude on me   /   Thy wring-
world right foot rock," ok, there's that whole, uh, there's something, it's almost
like it hooks it, there's this, all this incredible um, "rude on" thee, "rude on
me   /   Thy wring-world right foot rock," is uh um a very energetic phrase
suggesting all sorts of conflict in the "wring-world right foot rock," but they're
all hooked, they're all appended in a way to one thing because it's all, because of
the alliteration, it holds it together, it doesn't turn into, into, it isn't a-, as
choppy, it's somehow self-contained because of that kind of alliteration, the
same with "lay a lionlimb against me." Ok, there's a proximity uh suggested by
that, "lay a lionlimb," and particularly because "lionlimb" is, is uh (laugh) is a
single word, sort of a neologism of a, of Hopkins, um. Again "bruised bones,"
"darksome devouring eyes," there's something uh um uh, the power of it is, is
more uh unified, of all these, "turns of tempest," again uh, it holds together in a
way because of that, because of the sound, the sound seems to um have the
effect of, of uh uh unity, well unity of effect, how else can I talk about it? Ok,
"my grain lie, sheer and clear," ok, "sheer and clear," "sheer" in almost a um,
clean, sharp, "sheer," "clear," uh the, the sound itself is like that and again um
you're talking about two qualities, "sheer and clear" but they're somehow united
by that assonance, and then "in all that toil, that coil," um, "since (seems) I
kissed the rod," um, "hand rather . . . heart." "hand . . . heart," um there's
some connection even though it's the, the, the "hand" of God really, and "my
heart lo! lapped strength, stole joy, would laugh, cheer," that "lapped strength,"
that's interesting, that's almost doglike in a way, but uh, uh, let that go. Ok so
that, and all the internal rhyme, and all the assonance means that this is a very
highly woven, woven poem, in other words there are all these uh, it's made up
clearly of, of units of, of sound and sense, um, it really does seem to raise it
poetically up a-, up another level like "carrion comfort," uh uh, that alliteration
uh uh really, really holds the concept together uh even though the idea of "car-
rion comfort" is a, is a fairly complex one uh the two words do bond together
very beautifully that way, and then the whole uh expression of "wring-world
right foot rock," again that's uh, even though that's uh (laugh) it's only, it's one
long noun and, and adjectives with a, with a curious uh verb, "rock," um uh, it

does, it all s-, it all holds together even though there's all that uh tension uh set up by the, the internal, the vowels of "wring-world right foot," it's all al-, actually that's a little sing-song-y, "wring-world right foot rock,"

42

uh. Tremendous that but I'm not sure, I mean what else, I don't see anything (sigh) clearly the enjambing uh like between "these last strands of man / In me or," the enjambing comes between lines two and three, uh, six and seven, in the first, in, in, in other words they're in the same place in uh um the first stanza, two and three, six and seven, in the center, and then the rest of them are straight um, and uh um, the only place it happens, the enjambing happens uh um, well it happens between two and three and uh uh, well five and six, and well two and three, five six and seven, then they're, the fact that they're only short units. Uh well that, actually that's true, there's sort of a progression from these word units, these alliterative units, there's very little u-, uh, alliteration in the last, in the, in the second stanza. The second stanza, in the second.

Notes

CHAPTER 1: READER RESPONSE AND LITERARY PERCEPTION

1. Susan R. Suleiman, "Introduction: Varieties of Audience-Oriented Criticism," in *The Reader in the Text*, ed. Susan R. Suleiman and Inge Crosman (Princeton: Princeton University Press, 1980), p. 3. The other collection is *Reader-Response Criticism, From Formalism to Post-Structuralism*, ed. Jane P. Tompkins (Baltimore: The Johns Hopkins University Press, 1980).

2. Alan C. Purves with Victoria Rippere, *Elements of Writing about a Literary Work: A Study of Response to Literature* (Urbana: NCTE, 1968), p. 2.

3. Ibid., pp. 6 – 8.

4. Lee Odell and Charles R. Cooper, "Describing Responses to Works of Fiction," *RTE* 10 (1976): 203 – 25.

5. Ibid., p. 221.

6. Ibid., p. 224.

7. Purves, pp. 3 – 4.

8. Ibid., p. 4.

9. Alan C. Purves, *How Porcupines Make Love: Notes on a Response-Centered Curriculum* (Lexington, Mass.: Xerox, 1972), p. 27.

10. Odell and Cooper, p. 203.

11. Ibid., p. 211.

12. Jonathan Culler, *Structuralist Poetics* (Ithaca: Cornell University Press, 1975), pp. 123 – 24. Hereafter, *SP*.

13. Jonathan Culler, "Prolegomena to a Theory of Reading," in Suleiman and Crosman, pp. 48 – 49. Hereafter, "Pro." This essay appears, extensively revised, as "Semiotics as a Theory of Reading" in his *The Pursuit of Signs: Semiotics, Literature, Deconstruction* (Ithaca: Cornell University Press, 1981), pp. 47 – 79. Some of the quotations I cite are absent from this later version, but since they express views implicit or explicit in Culler's project since *Structuralist Poetics*, I assume they have been excised "to give the book focus and continuity" rather than "to eliminate what now seem to me mistakes" (xi).

14. Culler, *SP*, pp. 122 – 23.

15. Culler, "Pro.," pp. 48 – 49.

16. Ibid., pp. 49 – 50.

17. See, for example, Chomsky, *Language and Responsibility* (New York: Pantheon, 1979), pp. 58 – 59, 107 – 108.

18. Culler, "Pro.," p. 48.

19. Charles J. Fillmore, "On Fluency," in *Individual Differences in Language Ability and Language Behavior*, ed. Charles J. Fillmore, Daniel Kemper, and William S.-Y. Yang (New York: Academic Press, 1979), p. 90.

20. Culler, "Pro.," p. 52.

21. Noam Chomsky, *Aspects of the Theory of Syntax* (Cambridge, Mass.: MIT Press, 1965), p. 3.

22. For a good introduction to the history of psycholinguistics, see Jerry A. Foder, Thomas G. Bever, and M. F. Garrett, *The Psychology of Language* (New

York: McGraw Hill, 1974), especially chapters 5 and 6. See also Thomas G. Bever, Jerrold J. Katz, and D. Terence Langendoen, *An Integrated Theory of Linguistic Ability* (New York: Thomas Y. Cromwell, 1976); Fillmore et al. (see note 19); and Morris Halle, George A. Miller, and Joan Bresnan, *Linguistic Theory and Psychological Reality* (Cambridge, Mass.: MIT Press, 1978), especially Joan Bresnan's "A Realistic Transformational Grammar," pp. 1–59.

23. Culler, "Pro.," pp. 51–52; compare *SP*, pp. 122–23.

24. See *Sociolinguistic Patterns* (Philadelphia: University of Pennsylvania Press, 1972), and especially "Contraction, Deletion, and Inherent Variability of the English Copula," in *Language in the Inner City* (Philadelphia: University of Pennsylvania Press, 1972), pp. 65–129.

25. Culler, "Pro.," p. 53; compare *SP*, p. 124.

26. Culler, *SP*, p. 124.

27. Chomsky, *Aspects*, p. 21.

28. Ibid., p. 11.

29. Culler, *SP*, p. 124.

30. Ibid., p. 117.

31. Culler, "Pro.," pp. 56–57.

32. For discussion, see Bruce L. Derwing, *Transformational Grammar as a Theory of Language Acquisition* (London: Cambridge University Press, 1973), especially pp. 236–51; B. L. Derwing and W. J. Baker, "On the Re-integration of Linguistics and Psychology," in *Recent Advances in the Psychology of Language*, ed. Robin N. Campbell and Philip T. Smith (New York: Plenum Press, 1978), pp. 193–218; W. J. M. Levelt, *Formal Grammars in Linguistics and Psycholinguistics*, III: *Psycholinguistic Applications* (The Hague: Mouton, 1974), especially "Grammars and Linguistic Intuitions," pp. 14–65; and R. P. Botha, *The Justification of Linguistic Hypotheses* (The Hague: Mouton, 1975).

33. See chapter 6 in Foder et al., *The Psychology of Language*; W. C. Watt, "Mentalism in Linguistics II," *Glossa* 8 (1974): 3–40; and S. J. Miller, "Syntax and Semantics for the Psycholinguist," in *Recent Advances in the Psychology of Language*, pp. 243–62, especially 244–48.

34. Culler, *SP*, p. 123.

35. Culler, "Pro.," p. 56.

36. Noam Chomsky, "Form and Meaning in Natural Languages," in *Language and Mind*, enlarged edition (New York: Harcourt Brace Jovanovich, 1972), p. 102. For related criticisms, see Gerald Prince's review of *Structuralist Poetics* in *PTL* 1(1976): 197–202, and Barbara Herrnstein Smith's discussion in "Surfacing from the Deep," in *On The Margins of Discourse* (Chicago: University of Chicago Press, 1978), especially pp. 178–83.

37. See chapters 5 and 6 in Foder et al., *The Psychology of Language*. The study using multidimensional scaling is Charles Clifton, Jr., and Penelope Odom, "Similarity Relations among Certain English Sentence Constructions," *Psychological Monographs General and Applied* 80 (1966).

38. See the references in 22, especially *Linguistic Theory and Psychological Reality*.

39. Stanley Fish, *Is There A Text in This Class?* (Cambridge, Mass.: Harvard University Press, 1980), pp. 26–27. Since this is the most accessible collection of Fish's papers, all references will be to this volume.

40. Ibid., p. 166.

41. Ibid., p. 171.

42. See the essays from "Interpreting the *Variorum*" on.

43. Fish, p. 49.

44. Ibid., pp. 66–67.

45. Ibid., p. 269.

46. Eric Donald Hirsch, Jr., *The Aims of Interpretation* (Chicago: University of Chicago Press, 1976), p. 15.

47. See Fish, pp. 149−52, 23−25, 153−54, 155−57, and 164−65.

48. Ibid., pp. 159−60, 93, and especially note 33, pp. 379−80.

49. Ibid., pp. 168−69, 170.

50. Hirsch, p. 15.

51. (Bloomington, Ind.: Indiana University Press, 1979).

52. See Dillon's "Introduction: Style and Processing," pp. xv-xxxi.

53. Dillon, p. xix.

54. Ibid., p. xx.

55. Fish, p. 168.

56. Ibid., p. 52.

57. Ibid., p. 169.

58. Ibid., p. 168.

59. Ibid., p. 297.

60. Ibid., p. 355.

61. Ibid., pp. 338−55.

62. Norman N. Holland, *5 Readers Reading* (New Haven: Yale University Press, 1975), p. 44.

63. Ibid., p. 56.

64. Ibid., p. 209. The italics are original.

65. Norman N. Holland, "A Transactive Account of Transactive Criticism," *Poetics* 7 (1978): 183.

66. Ibid., pp. 183−84.

67. Holland, *5 Readers*, p. 45.

68. Ibid., p. 44.

69. Ibid., p. 45.

70. David Bleich, *Subjective Criticism* (Baltimore: The Johns Hopkins University Press, 1978), p. 214.

71. Ibid., p. 147.

72. Ibid.

73. See chapter 5: "The Pedagogical Development of Knowledge," and chapter 8: "The Construction of Literary Meaning."

74. Ibid., p. 148.

75. Ibid., pp. 166−67.

76. Ibid., p. 149.

77. Ibid., p. 150.

78. Ibid., pp. 219−22.

79. Ibid., chapter 6: "Relative Negotiability of Response."

80. Ibid., pp. 181−82.

81. Ibid., p. 167.

82. Ibid., note 3, pp. 150−51; see also *Readings and Feelings* (Urbana, Ill.: NCTE, 1975), pp. 12−13.

83. Ibid., p. 148.

CHAPTER 2: THE ELEMENTS OF PERCEPTION

1. Roman Ingarden, *The Cognition of the Literary Work of Art*, trans. Ruth Ann Crowley and Kenneth Olson (Evanston, Ill.: Northwestern University Press, 1973), p. 5.

2. Ibid., p. 6.

3. Edward C. Carterette and Morton P. Friedman, *Handbook of Perception, Vol. X: Perceptual Ecology* (New York: Academic Press, 1978), xiii.

4. Allen Newell and Herbert A. Simon, *Human Problem Solving* (Englewood Cliffs, N.J.: Prentice-Hall, 1972), p. 3.

5. Ibid., p. 5.

6. Ibid.

7. Ibid., p. 59.

8. Ibid., pp. 274–81.

9. Ibid., pp. 197–209.

10. Ibid., p. 72.

11. Ibid., p. 73.

12. Ingarden, pp. 233–300, especially pp. 240, 252–53, and 262–78. Ingarden unduly stresses the phonetic stratum of the poem; we may substitute for that a concern with its linguistic structure.

13. Roger C. Schank and Robert P. Abelson, *Scripts, Plans, Goals, and Understanding* (Hillsdale, N.J.: Lawrence Erlbaum, 1977), p. 14.

14. Ibid., pp. 42–46.

15. *CE* 37 (1976): 462. See Holland's reply, "To David Bleich," *CE* 38 (1976–77): 298–99, and Bleich's response.

16. Stanley E. Fish, "Normal Circumstances and Other Special Cases," in *Is There a Text in This Class?* (Cambridge, Mass.: Harvard Univ. Press, 1980), p. 284. See also p. 308.

17. See the studies in *Readings and Feelings* (Urbana, Ill.: NCTE, 1975) and *Subjective Criticism* (Baltimore: The Johns Hopkins University Press, 1978). Additionally, it is somewhat startling to reflect how much of what we consider knowledge of mental operations derives from the processes either of people mentally ill or of students who perform various tasks as part of the requirements for passing a course they are required to take.

18. See the brief review in Stephen Booth's *An Essay on Shakespeare's Sonnets* (New Haven: Yale University Press, 1969), pp. 152–59.

19. See Martin T. Orne, "Communication by the Total Experimental Situation: Why It Is Important, How It Is Evaluated, and Its Significance for the Ecological Validity of Findings," in *Communication and Affect*, ed. Patricia Pliner, Lester Framer, and Thomas Alloway (New York: Academic Press, 1973), pp. 157–91.

20. Alan C. Purves with Victoria Rippere, *Elements of Writing about a Literary Work: A Study of Response to Literature* (Urbana, Ill.: NCTE, 1968); Lee Odell and Charles R. Cooper, "Describing Responses to Works of Fiction," *RTE* 10 (1976): 203–25.

21. For references, see the sections on The Structure of the Lexicon, The Perception of Language, The Effect of Surface Structure on Comprehension, and Transformations and Deep Structure in "The Psychological Study of Language and Literature: A Selected Annotated Bibliography," by David Bleich, Eugene R. Kintgen, Bruce Smith, and Sandor J. Vargyai, *Style* 12 (1978): 127–46.

22. See the discussion of the problem behavior graph, Newell and Simon, pp. 172–90.

CHAPTER 6: READERS AND STRATEGIES

1. Wolfgang Iser, *The Act of Reading: A Theory of Aesthetic Response* (Baltimore: The Johns Hopkins University Press, 1978), p. 163.

2. *The Implied Reader: Patterns of Community in Prose Fiction from Bunyan to Beckett* (Baltimore: The Johns Hopkins University Press, 1974).

3. John D. Gould, "Experiments on Composing Letters: Some Facts, Some Myths, and Some Observations," in *Cognitive Processes in Writing*, ed. Lee W. Gregg and Erwin R. Steinberg (Hillsdale, N.J.: Lawrence Erlbaum Associates, 1980), p. 125.

4. *The Sciences of the Artificial*, 2d ed. (Cambridge, Mass.: MIT Press, 1981), pp. 103–104.

5. This is obviously not true of the 'interpretations' encouraged by David Bleich and Norman Holland. See, in addition to the works cited in the first chapter, Holland's "Re-Covering 'The Purloined Letter': Reading as a Personal Transaction" in *The Reader in the Text*, ed. Susan Suleiman and Inge Crossman, pp. 350–70, and Holland et al., "Poem Opening: An Invitation to Transactive Criticism," *CE* 40 (1978): 2–16.

6. This idea bears a certain similarity to Umberto Eco's conception of unlimited semiosis; see "Peirce and the Semiotic Foundations of Openness: Signs as Texts and Texts as Signs," in *The Role of the Reader* (Bloomington: Indiana University Press, 1979), pp. 175–99, and, more generally, *A Theory of Semiotics* (Bloomington: Indiana University Press, 1976).

7. See David Noton and Lawrence Stark, "Eye Movements and Visual Perception," *Scientific American* 224 (1971): 34–43 and references there.

8. *Some Versions of Pastoral* (Norfolk, Conn.: New Directions Books, 1950), p. 93.

9. *Elizabethan Poetry* (Cambridge, Mass.: Harvard University Press, 1952), p. 190; quoted in Stephen Booth, *An Essay on Shakespeare's Sonnets* (New Haven: Yale University Press, 1969), p. 155.

10. Booth, p. 167.

11. Ibid.

12. Empson, p. 90

13. Culler, "Prolegomena," p. 57.

14. These are simplified for the purposes of the example. Similar rules can be found in any introduction to transformational grammar, e.g., Owen Thomas and Eugene R. Kintgen, *Transformational Grammar and the Teacher of English: Theory and Practice* (New York: Holt, Rinehart and Winston, 1974).

15. T. G. Bever, "The Interaction of Perception and Linguistic Structures: A Preliminary Investigation of Neo-Functionalism," in *Current Trends in Linguistics XII*, ed. Thomas A. Sebeok (The Hague: Mouton, 1974), p. 1169.

16. Ibid., p. 1173.

17. Culler, "Prolegomena," p. 58.

18. Ibid., p. 59.

19. "Interpreting the Variorum," in *Is There a Text in this Class?* (Cambridge, Mass.: Harvard University Press, 1980), pp. 163–64.

20. Ibid., p. 170.

21. Ibid.

22. See *Structuralist Poetics*, especially p. 116 and chapter 8: "Poetics of the Lyric."

23. Fish, p. 171.